UNIQUE

UNIQUE

KELLY HOLMES

A MEMOIR

MIRROR BOOKS

To all those who have felt different,
have not had your voices heard,
don't feel that you are living your best life,
feel undervalued or scared,
I hear you.

Just remember the other side of pain is beauty,
because it is unique and purposeful for each and
every one of us, it can teach us things that we
would not be able to see otherwise.

To Dad,

Without you my life would have
never been the same.
I love you x

To Mother Dear,

I hope you can see me now,
keep sending the butterflies.

MIRROR BOOKS

Kelly Holmes collaborated with Gemma Aldridge.

1

First published in hardback in Great Britain and Ireland in 2023 by Mirror Books, a Reach PLC business.

www.mirrorbooks.co.uk
@TheMirrorBooks

ISBN: 9781915306463
eBook ISBN: 9781915306470

Photographic acknowledgements:
Kelly Holmes personal collection, Alamy, Reach Plc.

Every effort has been made to trace copyright.
Any oversights will be rectified in future editions.

Production: Christine Costello

Printed and bound by CPI Group (UK) Ltd,
Croydon, CR0 4YY.

CONTENTS

Five Years

FIVE YEARS. WE HEAR ABOUT THAT TIME PERIOD ALL through our lives, don't we? *Where do you see yourself in five years' time? What's your five-year plan?* At school, in job interviews, even among friends and at family gatherings, people always want to know what's coming next. It's easy to answer those questions when you have a dream or a clear and achievable goal in your head, as I've found out over the years.

I knew when I was 14 without doubt that I wanted to be a soldier in the British Army and five years later I was serving the Crown and my country. I also knew I wanted to be an Olympic champion and it was five years after joining the British Army that I started competing internationally in pursuit of Olympic glory. Five years after that I was leaving the army to concentrate full-time on my career as an elite athlete.

It might have taken me another few years to become the first British woman to win two individual gold medals at the same Olympic Games but in my heart I always knew I would do it. All through my life, I've had goals and aspirations and every time,

I've fought to make them happen because I never give up, it's in my DNA.

But what happens when the thing you think could make you happiest in the world seems out of your grasp? How do you even start to fight for something that seems so far out of reach? What happens when any plans you make get turned upside down after a life event totally floors you? Five years ago, despite all my achievements in life, that was the situation I was in…

In 2017, my mum Pam, or 'Mother Dear' as I called her, died aged 65 from a rare form of blood cancer called Myeloma. Her death completely destroyed me, it turned my world upside down and I felt like a part of my heart died with her – it still feels that way sometimes today. But when she died I realised something about myself that changed everything else in my life forever.

I realised how much I was hiding away from the world and not really living; how I could never truly be happy until I was honest about who I am – a gay woman who has led a life of fear, standing behind my achievements so I would never have to face judgement or persecution for just being me and loving the people I want to love. I knew inside I had to change something otherwise one day it would be the end of my life and I never would have been truly free or truly me. So that was where my journey began. In many ways it was the toughest journey of my life – and there have been a few!

It was five hard years after that dreadful realisation that I came out publicly for the first time at the age of 52 (or 39+13 as I like to call it!). You might wonder why, in the 21st century, I've felt unable to be honest about my sexuality when society has moved on so much and being gay is so much more accepted now than it once was. That is why I'm writing this book.

The truth is that my experiences as a young woman scarred me to a point where I've been paralysed with fear of punishment for my sexuality for most of my adult life. You see, when I fulfilled my first big dream of enrolling in the army and pledging my allegiance to the Crown, I also unknowingly joined an institution that outlawed homosexuality and would make me a criminal just because I was attracted to women instead of men.

Not many people seem to know, but even though it was decriminalised for civilians in 1967, the ban on being gay in the military remained in force right up until the European Court of Human Rights ruled it illegal in 2000, long after I'd served my nine and a half years in the army.

Throughout my athletics career, being made a Dame, an Honorary Colonel and a household name as Team GB's 'Golden Girl', it might have seemed to the public like I had the world at my feet, but deep down I was terrified, just waiting for someone to 'out' me as being gay. Like so many others, I learnt early on to hide my feelings away to protect myself and I never got over that trauma. I was convinced if I was found out I would be publicly shamed, stripped of my military honours and even prosecuted for breaking the law when I was a serving soldier.

So I spent 34 years trapped in a cage of my own fear, speaking quietly, dressing conservatively, living my life in black and white instead of the bright colours I like wearing now. I said 'no' to things I would have loved to do, avoided new friendships and turned down work opportunities, just so I didn't draw attention to myself or have to have conversations about my personal life. I never let anyone get too close in case I had to lie to them about who I really was and avoided any personal subjects in media interviews.

I lived two separate lives in public and in private and by the time Mother Dear got her cancer diagnosis in 2014, it was tearing me apart. Despite all my achievements the one thing she wished for me was that one day I would just set myself free by being open about my sexuality, so I could live my life for me. It wasn't easy and it was a slow process but just short of five years after I lost her, I finally did it.

Those five years transformed my life beyond recognition. It's been a journey of grief, anxiety, stress, mental breakdown, burnout, healing, self-discovery and finally a celebration of who I am. I've gone from hiding away in the shadows to living my life in full rainbow colour and now I say 'yes' to things instead of 'no'. I've gone from living in the shade of other high achievers, to standing in the spotlight, and although it still doesn't always come naturally, I'm happier than I've ever been. I've even fallen in love with a wonderful woman who I now share my new life with, but more on that later…

When I've told my story before, I've always hidden the real Kelly, and left out a huge part of me that makes me who I am. Now it's time to celebrate it. This is the true story of Dame Kelly Holmes, who I am, and how I got here. I think Mother Dear would be proud.

1
—

Black, White, Gold and Rainbows

STANDING ON STAGE LOOKING OUT AT THE SEA OF rainbow flags and glitter-covered faces, my heart started pounding in my chest. As I stood there, wearing my own rainbow outfit – a long, multicoloured caftan with a Progress flag full length on the back, like the one Jason Donovan wore in *Joseph and The Amazing Technicolor Dreamcoat* – the roar of the crowd around me echoed, and the enormity of the occasion dawned on me. It was London Pride in 2022 and there I was; centre stage.

My mind whirred. What the hell did I think I was doing?! It was massive enough coming out in a national newspaper and making my documentary which had taken months to curate and edit so that I could tell my story as I wanted. It was another thing entirely appearing on stage in front of hundreds of thousands of people in Trafalgar Square in London city centre. Being there with what felt like the entire LGBTQIA community (a title I had now become accustomed to) and allies of our capital city staring at me, I started to wonder if I'd bitten off more than I could chew. I have no idea what they were expecting of me. If anything, I wasn't sure if I should say something profound or insightful about equality and diversity or make a big political statement, but all I did know is that I wanted to say something from my heart.

Back stage I'd scribbled on a notepaper in a tent. None other than the tent Emeli Sandé was getting ready in before her performance. The last time I saw her was at the launch party of her album. I was still a bit starstruck, after all I had been a fan for years!

I had spent decades avoiding Pride and all things related with it for my entire adult life because I was convinced if I was seen to be celebrating the gay community, then straight away they would make assumptions about me too. That was my biggest fear of all. Look; I had no doubt, of course, that a few people along the way knew for sure, and also that a huge amount of people who followed my career had assumed I was gay, but in my mind assumption was not MY freedom.

Now, whatever anyone thought – that I had lived a lie, that I was ashamed or hiding a secret – was not my concern. They were not living my life! Finally it was time for me to tell my story, in my own words and give myself the freedom to speak.

As a soldier in the British Army, I've been on parade more times than I can remember. In my career as a world-class and Olympic athlete, I've had my share of time on podiums, along with some incredible homecoming parades. Trafalgar Square had an energy I'd not witnessed since the announcement of the Olympic Games in 2005, and the atmosphere was like nothing I've ever experienced.

The crowd was deafening; singing, cheering, laughing. Faces smiling and carefree. People were standing on the statue plinths, hanging over railings, messing about in the water fountain and waving their different community flags loud and proud. The parade was still going, music echoed in the distance, this was such a massive event to be part of. Being introduced to the crowd just after they had announced an estimated one and a half million people were in attendance, filled me with a euphoria, my heart was racing, butterflies in my stomach. I got this overwhelming sense of emotion running through my body, because this was the start of a new life for me.

My name was in lights and I had the platform to say whatever I wanted. The organisers had told me I had a few minutes before I would introduce Emeli on stage so I was a nervous wreck even before I looked out at the enormous crowd.

Having been a professional speaker for many years, travelling around the world for corporate engagements and motivational speeches, these days I rarely use notes, I don't really get nervous, I just feel an adrenaline rush. But today I was a bag of nerves, I just wanted the words to be right. I pulled the folded piece of paper from the pocket of my jean shorts, took a deep breath and started to speak into the microphone…

"For those who don't know me, I am an Honorary Colonel with the Royal Armoured Corps Training Regiment, I am a Dame Commander of The British Empire, I am the first British woman in the history of the Olympic Games to win two gold medals at the same games, I am mixed-race and I am also a gay woman…"

The crowd erupted and I had a lump in my throat as I carried on, tears pricking my eyes. My voice got stronger with every word.

"For 34 years I have never been able to say those words until two weeks ago, due to the fear of judgement and retribution that was instilled in me since the age of 18, because the laws in the military and being in the public eye didn't allow me to do it. I could never speak before but I have realised no matter if you are lesbian, gay, bisexual, transgender, queer, intersex, asexual, black, white, short, tall, big, small, however you identify and even straight (as I giggled), we have the right to stand side by side with each other, we all deserve to have our voices heard.

"All I can definitely say now is I'm 52, I'm never going to live behind that curtain again. Freedom is my voice!"

The crowd roared and I felt myself embody a campaigner, asking the crowd to chant with me, "FREEDOM IS MY VOICE, FREEDOM IS MY VOICE, FREEDOM IS MY VOICE!". I felt like I was in a different world: invincible, important, influential but most of all accepted. Proud doesn't even get close to the feeling I experienced that moment.

*　*　*　*　*

As with many life-changing moments, the Pride stage nearly didn't happen. I still laugh at the thought of it. When Gok Wan messaged me to join him and the ITV team on their double-decker bus in the Pride parade the weekend after my documentary aired, I was excited at the thought of finally joining in on all the fun that I had missed for so many years. This was my first Pride EVER! But, equally, I was nervous.

It turned out my first one was in a good year. The UK's Pride march started in 1972, inspired by the Stonewall riots in New York which sent a shockwave through the gay community and triggered gay pride movements around the world. 2022 marked 50 years of celebrations and protest, and London was set to be bigger than ever before.

There were more than 600 groups and 30,000 people registered to take part in the parade, the public lined the route as floats, bands, dance troupes and lobbying groups led the procession through the city from Hyde Park Corner to Trafalgar Square. Talk about a baptism of fire.

"It'll be fine, stick with me and we're on the ITV bus," Gok reassured me when I told him how nervous I was. "Everyone will be there together."

So after a couple of drinks for Dutch courage at the ITV rooftop party, we all meandered down to the bus. Gok, Lorraine Kelly, Philip Schofield, Alison Hammond, Linda Robson, my relatively new partner Lou and I all piled onto the bus, ready to party. It was Phil's first Pride too, since he came out at the age of 60 back in February 2020, so I felt a bit of solidarity with him. We climbed the stairs to the top deck, chatting, taking selfies, dancing to Gok DJing and going live on Instagram. I realised, when the bus before us started moving and we weren't actually following, that something was wrong.

"The buses in front are going," I said, starting to wonder if we were in the right place. But just as I was saying it a bloke appeared in front of us with what looked like an oily engine part in his equally oil-stained hand. "I'm sorry guys, we've broken down," he said. "We'll be here for a while."

Suddenly panic set in. The bus was surrounded with people from this huge parade, the different communities and organisations in all their glory. Music was playing from the other buses and the bands below. There were dancers and people singing. Banners and flags flying everywhere.

"Let's get out and walk," suggested one of the ITV crew. I just looked at Phil and Gok and gulped! Alison thought it was too far, especially in the sweltering heat.

"We'll give it a while, see if they fix it," someone else suggested. But after 20 minutes it became clear we wouldn't be going anywhere on the bus.

So we began walking together. It was one of the most empowering things I've ever done in my life, as people along the way were congratulating me. It was such a positive atmosphere and for the first time I felt that my uniqueness was what made me belong, not what made me different.

Time was ticking and I wasn't going to make it to the end of the route and to the back of the huge stage on Trafalgar Square in time for my speech. So drag legend Courtney Act said she would walk with me, cutting through the streets of London. All I could think was that, out of everyone there and me trying to be slightly incognito away from the parade, I was with Courtney, all glammed up and looking spectacular in a rainbow gown, and the most fabulous coloured wig. Towering over me in her six-inch heels, we giggled with one another as she illuminated our way through the backstreets to the stage entrance.

Incredibly, in a blink of an eye, a fortnight into my journey, standing on a stage with no curtain, I had my first initiation of Pride. To make it more awesome and overwhelming at the same time Emeli, who I'd been listening to in my living room two weeks earlier, was waiting in the wings to come on stage after I announced her. Not long after, I was back on stage standing next to her with some other people I later came to know very well, singing MY song live. Yes, MY song – *Read All About It*.

I will admit I had a few tears that day, it felt like my life was being transformed. I was so emotional about what was happening that it was hard to digest the enormity of it all. What a crazy experience.

I'd made my vow in front of the world to never live behind

a curtain again and was now accountable as the thousands of voices chanted my words "freedom is my voice" back at me and I felt the weight of 34 years finally lifting from my shoulders.

The rest of the day passed in a blur with music, hype and introductions. After meeting Emeli and her partner, Jenny (Emeli's friend and PA at the time) introduced me to DIVA publisher Linda Riley – 'Head Lesbian' as I get told, trans couple and activists, Hannah and Jake Graf, as well as, Dawn Butler MP, an amazing LGBTQIA ally. Some of us went out for dinner at The Ivy with amazing, charming, strong, brilliant power women. I was just so overwhelmed. Lou and I then got rather drunk as we danced the night away at Gok's place where he was DJing again.

When I look back, 'surreal' doesn't even begin to cover it. But it was real, and here I am.

2
—

Unique

I'VE MET A LOT OF PEOPLE WHO SAY THEY KNEW even when they were kids at school that they were gay, as if they were born waving a rainbow flag or something. That was never how it was for me. For most of my early life it never even crossed my mind that I might grow up to fancy women instead of men or that this fact would affect how I lived my life for so many years. Perhaps that was because back then sexuality wasn't really spoken about as much, or maybe because there was so much going on in my life when I was a child, it was the last thing on my mind. In any case, most of my formative years were lived in a time before I had any inkling that I liked girls instead of boys.

I guess if you ask me how I felt when I was a kid, the only word to describe it is 'unique' and I still wear that title with pride now. Why would I want to be just like everyone else?

From the moment in April 1970 when I was born at Pembury hospital in Kent, I suppose I was that little bit different. I was the mixed-race baby of a white teenage mum, who'd fallen pregnant by accident after a fling with a Jamaican man her parents strongly disapproved of. Mum was 17 and hadn't long been out of school herself when she found herself with a child of her own to look after.

Looking back now, she was really only a kid herself when I came along, so it must have been terrifying for her. In the almost-entirely white, tiny, blink-and-you-miss-it village of Hildenborough in Kent, where Mum was raised in a traditional working-class suburban family, I was certainly unique. Lots of people probably used less kind words about me too and there's no question that made things hard for both Mum and me those first few years.

Mum's parents, housewife Elsie and farrier Percy Norman, had been horrified when she told them she was expecting a baby at such a young age and even more horrified that the baby was going to be 'black'. Mixed-race relationships were still frowned upon by people of my grandparents' generation back then and especially in the super-conservative community where they lived. They didn't approve of Mum's Jamaican boyfriend, so they rejected me when I came along even though I was their flesh and blood. I guess that was my first experience of being dis-criminated against, luckily I wasn't old enough to know.

Before I was born, my nan and grandad told Mum she'd have to "find a way to look after herself before she could look after me." So basically she could get rid of me or leave home and try her chances finding somewhere else to live. She was all alone in the world except for the man who got her pregnant; a man she told me later had no interest in being any kind of father to me. I still like to think that she must have loved me so much that she was willing to give up her family and her home and start a new life with someone like that just so she could keep me. But it wasn't as easy as that back then.

Over the next few months she moved into a mother and baby unit in Lee, in the London borough of Lewisham. She tried to make a go of her relationship but the cracks soon started to show. I don't know what happened or the details of how Derrick Holmes and his family treated Mum and me. Mum always found it hard to talk about those early days. Recently my brother Danny (who you will meet later) told me that May – who would have been my nan – did look after me a few times during my first couple of months when Mum went to work. But after the relationship with Derrick broke down, Mum found herself alone with a tiny baby.

Society in the 1970s wasn't a friendly place for single mothers, especially those who had a mixed-race baby before they were married. There was no support available and with no other option she returned to her family out of desperation, but that meant she had to give me up and put me into care. I hate to think of how hard it must have been for her when she was still so young. I think about the young people I work with now through my charity the Dame Kelly Holmes Trust and I see kids the same age as Mum was when she had me and it makes me sad for her and proud of how hard she tried.

Maybe it's no shock that in that world I ended up at St George's children's home on the outskirts of Tunbridge Wells when I was only six months old. Ironically, in a way, that home was the only place I actually did fit in because sadly it was full of little mixed-race and black children who had either been rejected by their families or by society because of the colour of their skin – or were with a parent like my mum. I don't know the exact details of how I ended up there because even in her later years, Mum didn't like to revisit the distant past. There are still huge gaps in my understanding of the first few years of my life, which is something I really struggle with to this day. I'm not surprised Mum didn't like talking about it given how hard she'd tried to keep me and how traumatic it must have been for her to leave me in that big Victorian house full of children and babies, for someone else to look after.

The reason I'm telling you this is that one thing I've learnt when reflecting on my life is that the trauma you go through as a child can stay with you for years and haunt you if you don't address it. One of my earliest memories is of standing up in a cot as I clung onto the wooden bars and looked out over the large room in the children's home. There's a photograph of me there, which I saw years later. The room was filled with other children and it was only in recent years I realised (when looking at photos that I had been sent by a lady who had apparently been one of my carers) that almost every other child in there was black or mixed-race.

It never occurred to me as a child that there was a connection between skin colour and the children who found themselves in a home for abandoned kids – or that my race was to do with why I was rejected by my own family. Now, sadly I realise all too well the reasons why. It took me decades to accept that racism played such a big part in my life story and especially the way I started out.

When people asked me whether I'd ever experienced racism I used to just say no without thinking, because no one had ever abused me in the street or called me racial slurs to my face. It's only now that I realise looking back at my life the insidious impact it had on me and still has on so many people around the world today.

When the murder of George Floyd by police in the US sparked the Black Lives Matter movement around the world in 2020 and people started asking me about my experiences as a mixed-race woman, I started to properly address how it has affected me. I also thought how life would have been so different if it had been influenced by the cultures of both sides of my birth parents.

Talking about our early life together often caused conflict between me and Mum, right up until about 10 years ago when I went on Piers Morgan's *Life Stories*. That hit her especially hard and we had a massive fall-out over me doing the show, but I felt I had a right to.

The ironic thing is that I fought so hard to tell the story of where I came from, yet I was still hiding my sexuality. How I kept that away from Piers Morgan was a miracle! In hindsight I can see how that must have seemed confusing to my mum and I wish we hadn't wasted precious time fighting about it. One thing about losing someone is that it's so bloody finite. There are still so many things I want to ask her and, while writing this book, I've wished she was here a thousand times so I could ask her to fill in the gaps.

I told my life story before in my autobiography *Black, White and Gold* in 2005, but I always knew there were big pieces of the puzzle missing but I was too scared to go digging up the past. This time, I wanted to find out as much as I possibly could and share it with you. Reflecting on over 50 years, especially with peri-menopausal 'brain fog' has been interesting to say the least!

* * * * *

What I do know is that Mum tried her best for me from the start and she even left a promising career in London as a diamond grader and cutter for De Beers Diamond Trading Company when I was three years old, and got herself a job at Unigate Dairies in the laboratory testing milk samples because it was close to St George's, so she could come and see me as often as she liked.

But it was so distressing every time she had to go home without me. I would ball my eyes out and so would she as it was so heart-wrenching for her, when she had to leave me in my bed with my cuddly toys. All I wanted was to be cuddled by her. Every time she left, I was terrified she wasn't going to come back for me and that I would never see her again.

The impact that's had on me in adulthood is huge, I'm sure. I have had abandonment issues and for years I still needed to have something weighted on my feet to comfort me when I was trying to sleep, a triggering reminder of what I used to have for comfort at the end of my bed in the home. It sounds crazy but I bought one of those weighted blankets a few years ago and it really helped.

There have been impacts on how I deal with the people around me too. I'm such a 'people pleaser', terrified of upsetting anyone or disappointing them. In relationships I struggle to let my guard down – all because the sense of rejection and abandonment I felt as a child still lives on inside me. I was always terrified of being left, which either made me push people away or not want too much attachment, so as not to get hurt.

It must have been psychologically scarring for Mum too, I can't imagine what that must have been like for a teenager, to be torn between her own parents and the child she loved so much. I believe Mum wanted for me to have a better life than she could offer me until she got back on her feet and that's why she put me in care. I don't think she ever intended for me to be there long term and she certainly never imagined the damage that my fear of abandonment would cause me in my later life as a result – but there's no doubt damage was done.

For years after I left St George's, I had nightmares about Mum taking me somewhere and leaving me, and me searching endlessly to find her again. And it definitely made it more difficult for me to be open about my sexuality in later life, too, because I've always been scared people would reject me for that as well. I have no doubt those early experiences shaped and affected me as an adult.

In October 2019, when I led a group of runners for the second year running, on a charity expedition 'Sport with a Purpose' to Malawi, we visited an orphanage called Open Arms, which 'believes that every child has the right to survival and development'.

Prior to going in, we were told about the children that were currently there and when I walked in I became so overwhelmed with emotions I just broke down crying and had to leave. Walking into that room, I suddenly had a bout of anxiety and flashbacks to the cot, the bed (in the home) and the pangs of pain and endless crying when my mum had to leave me there.

Years later, after my Olympic wins, I found out it could have been much worse than being in and out of a children's home. Mum kept it a secret for decades but the pressure from my grandparents to give me up had become so great that at one point she'd even agreed for the carers at St George's to find a couple to permanently adopt me.

Social services came to the home to take me away but when the other woman took me in her arms, Mum broke down and couldn't go through with it. She loved me too much. This apparently happened three times as they tried to force her to sign the papers, but she wouldn't! When she told me that story, I saw the pain she felt and how she was reliving it as she spoke. I understood then for the first time how hard it was for her to talk about. Maybe it's true that sometimes you have to hit rock bottom for things to get better. Eventually Mum got me back and that was what mattered as she ended up being the most important person in my life.

I reckon it set the precedent for the rest of my life. You don't get many mixed-race, female, gay sergeants in the army who go on to win double Olympic gold and then have a career in TV. It might have made the start of my life difficult but I feel grateful to be who I am because it's brought some wonderful experiences and amazing people into my life too.

I've carried the word 'unique' with me all through my journey as an antidote to the idea of being the odd one out, weird or different. It's meant many things to me over the years and given me strength in many situations, and allowed me to own my differences at times when I've felt alone, judged or misunderstood and that's why it's the title of this book.

3
—

Brown Girl In The Ring

I'VE ALWAYS HAD A REALLY STRONG VIEW THAT what makes someone a parent has nothing to do with DNA and everything to do with love, care and attention. I'm a great believer that the step mums and dads, grandparents, foster parents, carers, social workers and respite carers of this world who give love and support to children who aren't related to them by blood are the real heroes of our society. They love and care for children out of choice; not obligation and somehow that makes it all the more special.

Having children was something I had never really wanted myself, because I was more intent on focusing on my career, and it turned out my lifestyle has never really been right for motherhood anyway. By the way, it is ok to not want children as a woman and that stigma needs to stop too, something I recently spoke about on Loose Women. But I did consider fostering or adopting when I was in my 30s, because I think the role those people do is just so important.

The man who inspired my views on parents by putting an end to the turbulent beginning of my life and teaching me what it is to be a great one was my dad. No, not Derrick, who had, by then, disappeared without trace but Mick Norris; the man who has become more of a father to me than words can describe. An old school friend of Mum's, who was reunited with her when I was about four, he is calm, laid back, quiet and unassuming and utterly reliable. When they started dating, he fell madly in love with my mum, and by extension he loved me too, from day one, without question, as his own. I think that's pretty amazing, especially given that it was going to be very obvious he wasn't my biological father, something that didn't even occur to me until years later.

Dad, as I have called him for almost five decades, was a painter and decorator who worked with his father, Geoff, and was super close to his family. While mum's parents were slowly coming to terms at the idea of me in their world, Mick's family welcomed me with open arms from the beginning and Nan Audrey, Grandad Norris and Aunty Sheila quickly became a big part of my childhood.

After a couple of years living in the estate at a smaller house we were moved next to them, into a three-bed red-brick semi-detached council house, complete with a coal bunker in the garden and metal windows, where I regularly had to scrape the ice of from the inside of my bedroom as it was so cold! I loved the close family stability of living next to them.

I can't remember exactly when I started calling Mick 'Dad', but I can't imagine anything else now and no one deserves the title more. We didn't have much when I was a kid and money was tight but I didn't feel I went without anything and from school uniforms to holidays at various Butlin's and food on the table, Dad made sure mum and I had what we needed and that I felt loved and wanted and that was what mattered. I feel lucky that he has always been part of my life.

One of my earliest and happiest memories of him, when he was dating my mum, was when he came back from Spain with his mates after a holiday, wearing flowery shirts and singing *Viva Espana* which always made me laugh! He also loves Country & Western films; Clint Eastwood and John Wayne. So much so that, on his 60th birthday, I planned a surprise Country and Western fancy dress party, complete with a Wild West town set called 'Micksville', with bar, jail, hay bales, 'WANTED' signs, a live band and line-dancing instructor.

I bought Dad a complete sheriff's outfit and, as another surprise, I had organised for a horse to be brought down from the local stables to take him to the party, because I wanted him to arrive in style. The animal was huge and I was nearly wetting myself at the thought of how we would hoick him up onto the saddle. If you know my dad, you'll know how hard a task this was, given his personal record for Buckaroo is 0.5 seconds – but I eventually got him down to the party and the smile on his face said it all.

I guess what I'm trying to say is, he's always been there for me and still is. He's been a constant in my life, and he's around at my house every day; feeding The Boys – my five alpacas – or picking me up from the station. Being a good parent is sharing in a child's triumphs, being there to pick them up when they fall and loving every part of them, just as they are, without trying to make them change, and that is what he has done for me.

When I told him I was writing this book and asked him to

know more about my early childhood, he told me something I wish I'd known sooner. Apparently, not long after my parents met, he asked Mum if he could adopt me so I would be his own in law but she said no. I would love to know her reasons but I can't ask her now. I wonder whether she was so traumatised by her experience of social services trying to have me adopted, that she thought giving someone else legal rights over me would mean she risked losing me again if things didn't work out with Mick. I guess now I'll never know but it does feel good to know how desperate Dad was for me to be his, right from the start. He is a man of very little words, and these days I feel like his mother, especially when I keep nagging him to get his hair cut, or wash his car and I get him to bring his washing around because his clothes are always stinking of the bonfire he has each week in my garden (plus I LOVE ironing!).

I never felt a massive maternal calling and I can't say I regret not being a mother because I don't believe in regrets, I believe in making the very best of the life you have, and I'm blessed to have so many wonderful kids in mine. I have ten nieces and nephews (Honey, Archie, Lola, Rosa, Olivia, Lily, Martha, Finley, Poppy and Ada Mae) between my brothers, Kevin, Stuart and Danny, and my sisters Lisa and Penny. They're not allowed to call me the 'A-word' because it makes me feel old, but I love them all to bits and I hope I can be a positive influence in their lives. My dad doesn't read much, like me, but I'm going to make him read this, as I know it will embarrass him. Dad, I love you to bits!

* * * * *

It took me a really long time to realise and accept that even though I *didn't* feel different when I was really young, from the people around me when I was growing up, I reflect on how I may have been treated differently and probably still am now. As a mixed-race kid in 'whiter than white Kent' and in an all-white household, you might wonder how I didn't feel the odd one out from the beginning. I think it's because kids do not know the difference in others unless it's pointed out to them and I just did all the same things as my friends and then my siblings Kevin and Stuart – ate the same, enjoyed the same games (when playing out in the streets on my stilts, pogo sticks and Space Hopper was still a thing!) and had the same annoying arguments with my parents. So why would I feel different?

Shortly before my seventh birthday Mum and Mick made it official, getting hitched in the local village church. As their only child, I was of course a bridesmaid, complete with frilly 1970s dress, a bonnet and shiny new shoes. I loved playing up in front of all the guests and posing cheekily for the camera as the wedding pics were taken. It didn't occur to me that it was strange for my mum and dad to be getting married with me there, unlike my friends' parents who had been married before they were born. I don't know if it was because I blocked it out but back then I didn't really have much recollection of life before Mick, so I just accepted our family as it was.

Soon after the wedding, my first brother Kevin was born. That was when everything changed. I remember Mum and Dad bringing him home from the hospital and peeking excitedly at his face wrapped inside the blanket. I threw myself into being a good big sister, playing with him, helping Mum feed, change and bathe him (she must have thought she had her own little live-in maid!). He was my little sidekick and I loved him so much.

Most of the time he wanted to sleep with me and when he was a toddler he kept bringing this tatty blanket into my bed with him but I didn't mind, he was so cute and I was his big sis. I'm not sure if I ever had that one item that stuck to me like his blanket, probably because I was in and out of St George's but I loved having Kevin around, he was my little brother and I became the boss, which suited me fine!

At school, in the playground, my different colour was harder to ignore. "Why are you brown and your brother's white?" the other kids would ask when they met Kevin. Unlike me, Kevin was fair, with white skin and rosy cheeks, he looked nothing like me. I don't think they meant to be nasty, they were just curious.

It was one thing looking different from my classmates but they couldn't understand why I didn't even look like the family they saw collecting me at the school gates. For the first time I remember being conscious of the fact I was different. But the truth was, I didn't really understand either. I wasn't just the only dark-skinned one in my family but in the whole of Hildenborough Primary School.

In 1978 when I was eight years old, the song *Brown Girl In The Ring* by Boney M hit the charts and was played on every radio station every day. The catchy tune and lyrics soon turned it into a playground song. The other kids in my class used to stand around in a big circle with me in the middle as they sang the words: *Brown girl in the ring, tra la la la la…* I loved it. I would dance around and sing… *She looks like a sugar in a plum, plum, plum*! I actually think I liked being the centre of attention, never realising in my naivety that the reason I was always picked to go in the middle was because of my skin colour. I did start to feel uneasy sometimes, just because, by now, I had questions.

On the way back from school one day, I plucked up the courage to ask Mum why I was brown and Kevin was white and that was when she told me that my Dad Mick wasn't in fact my biological father.

"There was another man that I knew before you were born and he's your biological father," she explained. I had no idea what that meant. "He's black and that's why you have darker skin, because you're a mix between him and me."

I knew deep down that Dad loved me but hearing about that other man, I felt hurt and left out and the older I grew, the more difficult it became.

When my youngest brother Stuart came along, I loved him as much as Kev but I was outnumbered – the only girl, the only mixed-race one, the only one with another father that no one ever spoke about because Kevin and Stuart didn't know any different. Plus, the older I got in school the more obvious it became. In school photos they always placed me, the only dark-skinned girl in the middle of the pictures, almost to make a point of it.

It's a strange feeling to grow up a different colour to your family but without any knowledge or experience of your different race or culture. I grew up in a white English family where we ate meat and veg and watched soaps on the telly. The furthest we ever went on holiday was a caravan park on the Isle of Wight and the only foreign food I knew was a Chinese takeaway. Nothing could have felt more distant to me growing up in rural Kent than the island of Jamaica where my biological dad's side of the family was from.

I knew nothing about Jamaican culture and to be honest I have never had any interest in finding out either. It's not that I've ever been ashamed of my colour, it's just that I don't always know how to be or what people expect from a mixed-race British person sometimes because I've been brought up white, if there's such a thing.

When I was researching my documentary *Kelly Holmes: Being*

Me I met wonderful, political activist and LGBTQ+ campaigner Phyll Opoku-Gyimah, known as Lady Phyll. I asked her why she founded UK Black Pride and I remember her saying: "The world doesn't necessarily like black queer women like myself, so when you don't see yourself represented, you create that space and you speak up."

It made me realise how important it is that people can see someone that looks like them, feels like them, sounds like them doing good things and making a difference so they have a role model to look up to. I know everyone has a story. We have no right to 'judge a book by its cover'. I believe people should be heard first and if we just talk more to each other as human beings, there would be far less anguish in the world. I hope now that I'm living authentically, I can be that person for anyone including mixed-race gay women because if I'd seen someone like myself when I was a teenager, my life might have been different.

* * * * *

One thing I've been grateful for all my life is my close group of amazing friends who have been there for me through thick and thin. Most of my closest mates have been in my life since I was just a kid.

If I have one piece of advice to anyone going through a tough personal time, it's to lean on the people who know you best and love you anyway. If I ever felt left out at home when I was a child, when I started secondary school at Hugh Christie's in Tonbridge at the age of 11, I definitely found mine. Not because I was particularly popular or I suddenly fitted in but because I found a group of girls who, just like me, also felt a bit like the odd ones out.

Looking back, maybe all girls at that awkward age feel that way but when I met Kerrie, Lara, and Kim in particular, we felt like it was us against the world. That kind of girl power we had back then (even before the Spice Girls) has seen me through some tough times in my later life. They're the people I text when I'm having a bad day or in need of friend time, they're always there for me.

Kerrie was the first person I met at Hugh Christie's, in the new starters' assembly on my first day. She was fair skinned with frizzy ginger hair and freckles and we hit it off straight away, as I remember thinking she was the only one who had hair almost as crazy as mine.

We went to our first class together and quickly surrounded ourselves with a tight group. There was Duran Duran-mad girly-girl Debbie who towered over the rest of us. I was jealous of her long blonde hair and even longer legs. Kim Ruck was sporty like me and there was Lara, who was the rebel of the group.

The girls were a massive part of my life as a teenager, but during those years my differences and my looks started to bother me loads. Unlike my mum's long brown hair that flowed poker straight down her back, I had an afro that looked like an enormous black ball of cotton wool on top of my head.

One summer, the rest of the girls decided we were all going to grow our hair long over the holidays and come back in September with long, grown-up hairstyles like the women on TV adverts and in magazines.

"What am I going to do? It's not fair," I whined to my mum when I got home from school. "I'm going to be the only one who won't have long hair for the start of the school year."

A few weeks into the school holidays, mum said she would

take me on a train up to Lewisham, Southeast London to get my hair done. Only now do I know why we went to Lewisham. She knew it because it had been where we lived before she took me to the children's home.

"I've found a place where they know how to deal with your kind of hair," she said. "You'll have long hair like the rest of them, I promise."

I was so chuffed as we walked through Lewisham, unknowingly not far from where I spent the first months of my life as a baby. The trend of the time for black women was to apply a perm that let the afro drop into thick loose curls, so that was what I had done. I left that salon walking on air, I was so happy and back home in my bedroom I couldn't stop looking at my new waves in the mirror. But disaster was about to strike.

A couple of weeks later, when I was with Mum, Dad, Kev and Stu down at the beach of Camber Sands in East Sussex, out of nowhere, my hair started to break off in clumps. Horrified, I cried to my mum about what was happening.

"I don't understand," she said, trying not to look panicked and to calm me down as angry tears fell down my face. It turned out mum had no idea how to look after my hair after the perm and that we were meant to go back and get a treatment to stop the ends splitting, putting moisture back into the hair – it was so dry it just broke off.

Weeks later back at school, while my friends were all sporting new long hair, humiliatingly, mine was no longer than an inch all over. I was so embarrassed. I became the butt of the playground jokes, like being called 'microphone head', for months until it grew back. Of course, my mates were on my side and protected me through the bullying taunts, but it was pretty traumatic.

I was never really interested in academic work at school and it didn't come easily to me either. I'd had extra help when I was at primary school but the truth was, by the time I'd started at Hugh Christie secondary school, I just didn't care about maths and English because I wasn't good at them. In hindsight I probably should have been tested for dyslexia because I still struggle with reading lots of text and spelling, but things were different back then and if you found it hard you weren't helped but were labelled thick rather than having what we call today, a neurodiversity.

I always knew if I wanted to have nice things I would have to work for myself but it never really occurred to me that we were poor until I went with mum to clean one of the big houses up one of the long lanes in the village when I was a young teenager.

Sometimes I would go with her on her cleaning jobs to help out, and that was the first time I got a glimpse of how the other half lives. There seemed to be endless rooms in this house with TVs and posh furniture and a fridge full of food. The couple who owned it even had their own ride-on lawn mower. I remember thinking that was so cool and that one day, if I was rich, I would get one for my mansion!

The one thing I was good at in school was sport. When it came to PE, I was a different person than in the rest of my lessons. All the confidence I lacked in the classroom came out when I was out on the running track. From my very first term at Hugh Christie's, it was clear I was the sporty kid. It was evident from early on that I had a natural talent for running.

A lot of my success in sport was down to Miss Page, my PE teacher who was the only person that made me really believe in myself and who told me I could do anything I put my mind to.

She was a tall, strong woman with a warm smile and a kindness that I didn't see in the other teachers. Of course she cared about me doing well in her class but I also felt like she really cared about me as a person too. She'd always be checking in about how things were going in other subjects, how things were at home and making sure that me and the 'gang' were staying out of trouble. It was Miss Page who made me do cross-country even though I hated it, and she put me in the school team to compete against other schools. It was that first race for the team that changed everything – so I should thank her really.

With my big afro, green skirt, white shirt, socks and plimsolls, I actually ran pretty well, even leading with about 20 metres to go before a girl from another school called Stacey overtook me at the last minute and I came second. Oh, wow, that feeling of being beaten hit hard in my stomach and I hated that I lost, even though I didn't even like cross-country. I think that was the moment something clicked in my head. I realised I wanted to be good at something and this set me off on my mission to be the best. I started competing against other schools in the 1500m and won lots of races in my first year. I finally had something I was really good at and proud of.

I think it's really important to call out how special a really good teacher can be to your life, especially for children who come from underprivileged backgrounds. They can give you the confidence and self-worth you need to believe you can achieve your dreams and that's priceless. I feel so lucky not just to have had Miss Page in my camp as a kid but to have her still in my life as a friend now. Every few months she meets up with Kerrie, Lara, Kim and me and we go for walks, paddleboarding or for lunch, talking and laughing about the old days and what's going on in our lives now. I believe those reliable friendships can be the best kind of therapy.

4
—

Dreams Do
Come True

WHEN I TALK TO YOUNG PEOPLE AND THEY ASK ME about how I got to where I am today and how I managed to achieve so much success, I tell them that hard work and dedication, self-belief and courage all play a part. But first you have to have a dream, you have to know what you want. It's no secret that opportunities for young people from underprivileged backgrounds can seem out of reach and that's why as a kid from a council estate breaking records and becoming an Olympic hero might have seemed like a pipe dream; but so long as you have that pipe dream there's a chance it might come true.

When I was 12, Miss Page suggested I join the local athletics club, and that was how I found David Arnold. Dave was a retired marathon runner who had to quit because of an injury, but now he was a coach at Tonbridge AC. One day after school Mum drove me over to Tonbridge School; a posh boarding school in town, where they trained, to meet him. We did interval training, endurance training and generally improved my fitness and I loved every minute. The following year I won the 1500m in the Kent Schools Championships and I was selected to represent the county at the English Schools' Athletics Championships in Plymouth, where to my shock, in my first athletics season, I won gold.

That day as I crossed the finish line, I felt that sense of utter pride and glory for the first time. The buzz of winning and achieving something was unlike anything I'd felt before and the more I won, the more I loved it. Soon, while my friends were going out to roller-discos and meeting boys, I was out training every night after school always reaching for that next big medal.

People sometimes ask me how I didn't realise when I was at school that I was gay and I think my athletics training probably had a lot to do with it. While the other girls were busy dressing up and experimenting with make-up to impress boys or obsessing over posters of their favourite member of Duran Duran, I was out running.

My idols were athletes like Sebastian Coe and Tessa Sanderson, not pin-ups like Simon Le Bon. It's not like I was interested in girls either, I just wasn't interested in romance full stop. I assumed it would be something that would come later in my life and as the child of a teen mum, I wasn't in any hurry to grow up too quickly myself.

My first kiss, though, was with a boy called Simon in the trees near my house when I was five years old! His nan and grandad lived at number 58, next door to our first house in Riding Park. But for most of my childhood I was a tomboy.

I lived across the road from Tess and Julie, two girls about my age and although we weren't the best of friends after we grew up, when we were little we used to play doctors and nurses. I happened to always be a boy doctor kissing one of them as a female nurse – all for the storyline of the role play of course. It never occurred to me I was kissing a girl, it was just a game. The Katy Perry song, *I Kissed A Girl* came out too late, otherwise maybe I would have realised what I liked a little bit sooner.

Sex education in schools back then didn't even mention different kinds of relationships, there was no diversity at all, so my options were pretty limited. The 'classes' were just a quick chat about the importance of abstinence and how not to get pregnant as far as I can remember, then we would laugh about condoms. There was certainly no mention of women being able to have a relationship with other women, let alone any other kind of diversity.

In 1988 it became law under section 28 of the Local Government Act that intentionally teaching any kind of homosexuality or publishing any materials around homosexuality in schools was prohibited. I'd left school by then but in the years running up to that, while I was at Hugh Christie's, the silence around homosexuality was definitely already well-established.

For many people in the 1980s, 'gay' was a dirty word and it was used as an insult in the playground and the workplace. The AIDS epidemic had swept through the USA and was now claiming lives in the UK. It was long before the kinds of medical advances that mean HIV is no longer a death sentence and people were afraid of getting it.

Back then I remember the horrifying scare tactics and TV adverts from Public Health with tombstones on them that were made to make you think being gay was the worst thing in the world. Maybe that explains why there was nobody I knew or had even heard of in our community who was gay. It just wasn't something I thought existed in our quiet little corner of Kent, so I never considered it for myself.

What I do know looking back is that I never really enjoyed being with boys. I liked their company as friends but when I went out with a few on brief occasions, I never got that tingly feeling when we kissed and I never was a girly-girl dreaming of getting married. Now I know why! I did have one big teenage crush on this boy called Lee. It was nothing sexual, but he was a pretty boy, and all the girls at school liked him. I soon moved on though because I got distracted by him in an important English Schools race when I was 16 and I realised I liked winning more than I liked him.

* * * * *

Instead of boys, running became my first love. In 1984 as Team GB flew out to Los Angeles for the Olympics the summer after my 14th birthday, my big dream really started to form. I was already winning national medals in school competitions and I'd had a taste of what victory felt like.

My eyes were glued to the TV during the school summer holidays, as I watched Sebastian Coe sprint to victory in the 1500m final that summer and as I watched him collect his medal on the rostrum I could only imagine the euphoria that must have been coursing through his veins. "One day, that will be me," I said to my mum.

I even met Tessa Sanderson the summer after her Olympic heroics winning Javelin Gold against Fatima Whitbread and that had a huge impact on me. Mum and Dad took me and the boys to Butlin's and Tessa turned up in a silver sports car with a javelin along the side wearing her Great Britain white shellsuit, signing autographs. As a black British woman who'd had such huge sporting success, she was a massive inspiration to many. Hearing the national anthem being played for her, Seb and Daley Thompson, who were the three athletics Olympic champions, gave me goosebumps.

But 1984 didn't bring just one dream but two. The second came when our class had a careers day at school and a soldier from the armed forces recruitment office came in to tell us all about the different jobs you could do in the military if you signed up. They spoke about the Royal Air Force, Royal Navy and British Army with such passion and gave out leaflets with the logo 'Be The Best' on them before showing us a video about all the different roles on offer after you completed basic training.

When I heard about the job of Physical Training Instructor (PTI) in the British Army, I was immediately hooked on the idea. PTIs were based at barracks and did basic training like all soldiers but then when they qualified they got to be in charge of the physical training for all the soldiers. Working in army gyms, the job of the PTI was to make sure every soldier was fit and strong enough to do tours of duty for our country, so it was a pretty big responsibility.

Back then, you had to be 17 and 9 months old to join the Women's Royal Army Training Corps (WRAC) and I could not wait. They provided your accommodation, food and uniform and everything you could need, plus they paid you. It felt like it could be my ticket out of sleepy little Hildenborough and give me something to belong to and a sense of purpose that I never really found at home.

"It's perfect for me, I really think I can do it," I told Mum and Dad, full of excitement and enthusiasm when I got home. They were stunned at first because I'd never shown any interest in the army.

My grandad, Mick's dad, had joined the Navy in 1943 because of the war but that was never really spoken about. They were pleased I had a goal, though, and so was I. I felt like lots of doors were closed to me because I didn't have the confidence in my academic ability to go into higher education and I had never even heard the word university! The army seemed like a place where my discipline, hard work and physical skills would pay off, and it wasn't just a job, it was a career.

From that day, while I carried on training with Dave for athletics meets, I also had my heart set on joining the WRAC. Although my Olympic dream was still in the back of my mind I now had one which felt much more reachable. In just three years if I worked hard and got selected I would be able to join up to serve my country and that felt like the greatest honour. Then I could work on the Olympics after that. Once a year from then on I begged Mum to take me to the Army careers office so I could pick up their latest information and imagine my life as a recruit.

When I reflect on the two big dreams I had growing up I wonder whether I would have wanted to continue with them if I'd known the impact serving in the army would eventually have on my life as a gay woman or what being a runner would have on my physical and mental health. I am not sure if I would have felt differently or whether it would have changed anything, but it definitely makes me want to make a difference and change lives for young people growing up and going into those jobs today.

* * * * *

I truly believe that every family has its little secrets – the things no one talks about for fear of rocking the boat or being judged.

Some families have bigger secrets than others and I was pretty young when I realised my family had some whoppers!

One day when I was 16, I went with Mum to Sainsbury's in Tonbridge shopping and we were walking around the aisles when I spotted another young girl with her mum who seemed to be staring at us. Weirdly, in a town full of white families, even though her mum was white, the little girl had black hair and light brown skin just like mine. I didn't think anything of it at first but then when Mum sent me off to pick up some beans from the next aisle I had to walk past them and I heard the woman say to the girl: "That's Kelly."

I literally ran back to Mum, totally confused and told her what I'd heard and asked how the woman knew my name? We walked around and Mum went up to the woman. The girl was just staring at me. I couldn't hear what they were saying but they definitely looked like it wasn't the first time they'd spoken and when Mum came back over to me, she looked cagy. Who were they? I knew from Mum's look she wanted to just finish the shop and get out of there, so I bit my tongue and pretended it hadn't happened while she paid for the shopping, but back out in the car park I confronted her.

"That young girl is your sister, Kelly," she said matter-of-factly. "Your biological father Derrick went to live with her mum Linda after we split up and they had a daughter called Lisa, that was her." Wow! Seriously, that is how I found out about a sister I never knew I had and to make it worse, she only lived six miles away from me!

It turned out that Derrick, who we'd never spoken about for all these years, had another family and was living with them just up the road from me the whole time. And while he basically didn't give a shit about Mum and me, he was living with Linda,

Lisa and her baby brother, Danny. My mind was reeling. It was a huge shock and I felt totally betrayed. I couldn't believe my mum would keep such a huge secret from me for so long, especially when they knew how I felt about being the odd one out in our family unit.

Mum said she was worried I would get too close to him if I met that side of the family and I think she worried he would try to drive a wedge between us but she was doing that herself by not telling me. What I did know is that Linda passed her a piece of paper with her number on. My mum didn't want to talk about it at all but over the next few months I begged and begged her until she finally gave in and arranged for me to go over to their flat and meet Lisa and Danny. Linda said it would just be her and the kids which was actually a bit of a relief, because I was more intrigued about Lisa.

Turning up at the front door I felt sick because I didn't know if the man I have now nicknamed 'sperm donor' would be there! I met Lisa though and we hit it off straight away. Okay, I was jealous of her hair. She had long, defined curly locks unlike my afro. Danny was this cute mixed-raced baby, but I didn't really get to know him for years.

It was a surreal part of my formative years and a lot more went on over the next year, but as I write this, I have been questioning why at '39+14' I'm still trying to piece this together? I suppose it's releasing that childhood trauma. I accept I may now know as much as I ever will about their relationship but I am at peace with my family identity and where I came from and that's really important to me.

After the Sainsbury's episode, Mum and I started to drift apart. I don't know whether it was because of the betrayal, because she seemed to be spending more and more time out of the house or because I was just growing up and moving on but we just didn't seem as close, something that took a long time to heal.

* * * * *

School finished in a flurry of school discos and shirts being signed. I had really bad marks in all my CSEs – quite frankly because schools didn't cater for young people like me who found it hard to concentrate and learn well in a classroom setting – but luckily you didn't need any to join the army.

I'd already run my last English School Championships when I was 17 in Birmingham, winning the 1500m race and, as a result, I was selected by the Olympic Committee to take part in the first mini Youth Olympics Games in Papendal, Holland. I jumped at the chance of going on the ferry with some of the other Tonbridge AC members, it was really exciting, but definitely wasn't glamorous.

The ferry was open-sided with the rain hammering down and the sea was so rough like a rollercoaster, a lot of us were sea sick. But after we recovered, we were ready to go. Mum had made the trip over too.

The feeling of representing my country was something else and when I crossed the finish line first in the 800m race I got a little taste of what it might be like to actually win a 'real' Olympic gold – it was indescribable. I stood proudly on the rostrum in my Team GB kit, a Union Jack draped around me, and the gold medal around my neck. I felt a lump in my throat as they played *God Save The Queen*.

I was still on cloud nine when I returned to Hildenborough but I barely allowed myself to dream I would experience that again. Instead, I focused on my next missions: getting a car and joining the army. First came the white S-reg Ford Escort.

I remember passing my driving test first time, being cocky as I got back, ripping my learner plates off when I was home, telling Mum and Dad that I would treat them to a Chinese takeaway, only to break down in Tonbridge and have to get a tow truck home; how humiliating!

When I was eligible to start the recruitment process for the army, Mum took me to Tunbridge Wells Recruitment Centre, where I filled in an application and had to do an entry test. I didn't score highly because my academic journey through school was so poor. I desperately wanted to be a Physical Training Instructor but I was gutted when they told me the intake was already full and I would have to choose something else if I wanted to join in March of 1988. I didn't want to wait any longer so I looked at the three other options I had and decided to go for an HGV driver course. I liked driving cars, so how much harder could it be in a four-ton truck? Plus, I knew that once I was in, I could try and retrain in another trade if I wanted to.

What some of you may not know is I actually got a sports scholarship to go to Minnesota University. I did consider it but wanted to go into the army so bad that I didn't pursue it. I think now how life would have been SO different for me. Although looking at the weather over there – sod that!

A lot went on when I was 17. I got a job at Princess Christian Hospital working days in the Oast House at the same location where Mum was working nights as an auxiliary nurse. My job was as a nursing assistant working on a ward with men who had mental and some physical disabilities and although it was really hard work it was one of the most rewarding jobs I've done.

I loved helping the patients to do simple tasks like wash and dress and some of them were so sweet I got really attached to them. I was devastated when one of the patients passed away.

It gives me such huge respect for all the doctors and nurses who work in the NHS. During the pandemic I couldn't begin to imagine what they were going through with so many people coming through their doors and passing away.

Then one night the Christmas before I was due to start my basic training, they put on a work party so we could all have a few drinks and I drove there because I didn't drink alcohol. What happened next changed my family forever and I suppose caused a lot of my issues as an adult about trust and drink.

Mum had clearly had a few drinks at the party and when I looked up from playing pool with some of the other nursing assistants, I saw her hanging off some other bloke, kissing him and laughing. I saw red. I couldn't believe what she was doing behind Dad's back, but I also felt like I might cry so I charged out of the bar and got in my car and drove straight round to the house of a guy who I was briefly seeing, which was only a couple of minutes down the road. Suddenly Mum and the mystery guy she'd been with were hot on my heels and came screeching up to the house minutes later. Little did I know he was related to my boyfriend!

"What the hell are you doing?" I screamed, full of anger, dragging the guy out of the car and then proceeding to clamber over to try and grab my mum. She ran off and I think this is where my pent-up frustrations and anger as a teenager came out because I gave the guy a black eye! How could she do this to our family, to Dad, Kevin, Stuart and me?

I rushed home balling my eyes out and told my dad: "She's pissed and you better go and get her!"

Suddenly all the feelings of hurt and abandonment I'd been carrying around all those years came crashing down on me and I felt like the world was falling apart. The one thing I felt bad about was leaving my dad and brothers that night, but I knew I couldn't be there, so I called my best friend Kerrie.

"Come and stay here, Kel, Mum says it's fine," she said. So I drove over in the middle of the night and I never went back to live at home again.

I learnt later that Mum had been having an affair with a guy for a while and soon after she left Dad and the boys. Dad was devastated and I couldn't bear to see him like that after all he'd done for us. The boys were only nine and seven so they didn't really have a clue what was going on. It was only three months until I was due to go off to Guildford Barracks and start my new life, and I couldn't wait to escape. I stayed with Kerrie and her mum until it was time to go. I visited my brothers, dad, nan and grandad but I didn't speak a word to Mum for months. I thought I might never speak to her again.

In March 1988, a month before my 18th birthday, I got the train to Guildford where a load of other new young female recruits were also waiting to start out on the biggest journey of their lives. We piled onto a bus at Guildford station and were taken to the barracks where I would be spending the next eight weeks in basic training. As we drove through the giant gates, topped with barbed wire, I felt my dream was finally coming true and I was beyond excited. I was there at last: Private Kelly Holmes – regimental No. WO804986.

Although it was one of the most difficult times in my life for many reasons, being in the army was massively influential. I still had a really close relationship with the army right up to this month as I have been Honorary Colonel for the Royal Armoured Corps Training Regiment for five years (but I am moving on now) and I'm incredibly proud of having served my country for nearly 10 years.

The army is a place where young people can feel valued, learn trades, be a part of a community, your biggest family, and learn respect and more importantly, self-respect. My journey there was a bit of a rocky one, but it made the things I achieved when I was there all the more rewarding.

5

—

Fear

A QUESTION I'VE BEEN ASKED AGAIN AND AGAIN since I came out is: "Why now?" Not why I'm gay – I think most people these days thankfully realise that your sexuality isn't your choice, it's part of who you are, as much as your IQ or whether you can sing in tune (I can't, by the way, if you're wondering!). But people do find it hard to understand why I would keep such a big part of my identity hidden away for so long in a world where diversity, inclusion and acceptance are seemingly so prevalent. I remember having to take a deep breath as I clenched my fist and silently dug my nails into the palm of my hand one day soon after I came out when a journalist asked me: "Why do you think it is that you were so ashamed to be gay?"

I have to make one thing clear right here, once and for all: keeping my sexuality private for all those years was never, never about shame. No one ever has or could make me feel ashamed for loving the people I love or living my life authentically. I believe that's my right and even though I may have done it behind closed doors and without other people knowing publicly, I'm proud to say I've always been true to myself and I've never wished I'd been born different. When that journalist asked me that question, I told myself she just didn't understand, smiled and ended the interview as soon as I could. But in hindsight, perhaps if you've never had to live through it, you wouldn't understand.

To understand, you have to know what life was like for gay women in the army in the 1970s, '80s and '90s. While there was never shame for me, there was fear, and a hell of a lot of it. You have to remember that less than three decades ago, the army was a very different place to what it is now.

On our first day, turning up to Queen Elizabeth Barracks in Stoughton, the culture shock was real. There were platoons doing drills on the parade square as senior officers yelled at them. Elsewhere, others were doing physical training sessions with their PTIs – even more yelling. We were shown to our living block which was filled with loads of female recruits. In the Women's Royal Army Corps (WRAC), I only came into contact with other female recruits those first few weeks.

When we arrived, we were allocated beds in dorms of four, on long corridors in the barracks living quarters. All thrown together, all new on the job, we were eager to succeed and pass our training, so we formed an instant connection with one another and all tried to help one another out.

Training was gruelling. We were ordered to run or march for miles on end with our Bergens and seemed to constantly be getting yelled at, though I actually enjoyed the discipline and the routine as well as pushing myself to my physical limits – something I'd learnt to do when training with Dave.

The standards expected in our living quarters were just as

exacting and an inspection from our strict senior officers could come at any time. I quickly learnt to fold the neatest hospital corners on my single mattress and to keep my few belongings in perfect order in case of an unexpected visit.

We each had a small wardrobe next to our steel-framed beds to hang our civvies in and drawers to keep a few personal belongings from home. There wasn't room for much else but it didn't bother me – I didn't have much. Plus, the fewer things you had the easier it was to keep tidy and avoid a bollocking when the senior officers came round to inspect living quarters.

Uniforms were always in line for inspection and that took a bit of getting used to. As well as our trademark green berets, we were given regulation green shirts and combat trousers with long green socks and black combat boots.

The group of girls on my floor would each take on their own role in keeping all of the kit in good nick and we would create a sort of assembly line to make sure each one was perfectly turned out. One person would have responsibility for de-fluffing our felt caps, another would make sure our boots were in order and so on. My job was ironing the shirts. I know it sounds mad but I loved it, and still love ironing now. I would take the creased cotton shirts and starch them so heavily and stiff with two parallel pleats on the back and the crease line on the sleeve razor sharp; they would stand up almost on their own. Then I would hand them out to be hung neatly in each dorm. To this day, I'm a stickler for a well-ironed shirt.

We looked after one another in those first eight weeks of training like we were a family. I have such fond and funny memories of spending evenings sitting on the floor of the corridor outside our dorms, all shining our toe caps with spit and black boot polish until they came up like mirrors.

We would share stories, gossip, talk about home and share our dreams with one another until we could see our faces in the leather. We did fail the odd inspection, but it was fun and I started to feel at home.

My first encounter with a woman was a shock. I really wanted to be able to include her name here as it was a big deal for me starting to understand my sexual identity. After all these years, I didn't even know where she was or if she would be happy for me to mention her. But amazingly, I've managed to get back in touch through the wonders of Facebook and she is happy for me to share her first name: Lynne.

One evening, as we were getting ready for inspection, I went down to the laundry room (the ablutions as they were known) at the end of the corridor where the washing machine and dryers were whirring around and Lynne was in there, sorting her washing.

I'd seen her around of course and we'd spoken a bit in the group with the other girls but now we were alone together, I realised I felt slightly nervous and I wasn't really sure why. She had a pretty face but it didn't really occur to me that I fancied her until suddenly, she leaned over and kissed me on the lips.

I remember having this overwhelming feeling once the shock subsided, that it just seemed right. It was just a kiss but felt so good, so much better and more exciting than anything I'd felt with either of the two boys I'd been out with.

Then I questioned in my head: Am I gay? Yes I must be!

* * * * *

Standing at the far end of one of the dorms, dressed all in black and white with joke-shop goofy teeth, I couldn't stop laughing as I performed the mock wedding ceremony in our barracks.

"Do you take her to be your loyal wedded wife?" I lisped as the girls all broke down in fits of giggles.

I played the toothy vicar while two of the girls stood in front of me, one with a white sheet as a dress and makeshift veil from a net curtain and the other dressed in uniform. It was inspired by the 1988 TV series *The Verger: Tales of The Unexpected*, with Harvey as the groom, Penfold as the bride and Lynne the angel.

We'd pushed the furniture to the sides of the room and lined up chairs in rows for the congregation and everyone was playing along. The two girls kissed each other on the lips, as I announced them wife and wife and everyone was howling. It was just a few weeks into training but just like me and Lynne, another two girls were now seeing one another.

Looking back now, we were so naive to do that and we were very lucky not to get caught because I dread to think what would have happened. But to us it was just fun, we were kids messing around. I imagine those early times were a bit like Freshers Week in university, only without the alcohol.

There's something crazy about your first love, your heart feels like it's about to explode with excitement. Plus it was the first time I'd ever felt really comfortable being that close to anyone. Most importantly, we laughed a lot and our personalities connected.

We were both sporty and it was just fun to be around one another. We were both due to go to HGV driver training after our basic training ended, even though I desperately wanted to be a PTI. Knowing I was going to be with Lynne eased my jealousy towards all the recruits who were heading out on PTI training from our intake.

It turned out she was seeing a guy before she joined up, but she said it was nothing serious, and that it didn't really feel right with him, which makes sense now. I think part of the reason it was so special is because it was all new – our first experience of being in a same-sex relationship.

We had a halfway break in the middle of basic training where we all went home for the weekend. I loved going back to see my family, Dad, Kev, Stu, Nan and Grandad but I missed Lynne like crazy and couldn't stop thinking about her the whole time.

When I got back to the barracks, to my surprise, she had missed me as much as I had her. Remember there were no fancy phones to get in touch, plus I still didn't know what my emotions meant. I thought she might have hooked back up with her boyfriend or something, but it seems she felt exactly the same way.

Lynne told me when we reconnected through Facebook recently: "I remember missing you and thought, 'what is going on in my head with feelings for you?'" It wasn't just us either, there was a girl in my dorm who was going out with another of the girls, so the four of us got close.

I can't remember when I found out and I had no idea there was a law in the military making it illegal to be gay. I didn't know I was gay when I first joined, I was just a teenager who was exploring her sexuality I suppose so learning about the potential consequences seemed irrelevant. Can you imagine losing your career, being jailed or vilified just because of being attracted to someone?

Looking back, those first eight weeks of training prompted conflicting emotions. I felt the most 'at home' and 'right' I'd ever felt but being conscious that you were breaking the law also felt very confusing. I wasn't the only one. I was lucky that there were lots of other girls in my intake who were going through the same thing, working out their identity. We all just knew to keep quiet, keep our inner feelings hidden and protect ourselves and each other as much as we could.

There were simple things we learnt to do, like never addressing letters to female friends or even our sisters because they got vetted by senior officers and they might think we were writing to girlfriends back home. The same went for diary entries. We knew never to use girls' names or to write anything that might implicate us. There was no privacy and anyone could read your diaries at any time.

We had no idea at the time that LGBT+ rights charity Stonewall had already been fighting to rescind the outdated regulations against same-sex couples in the military since 1986, but it was another 14 years before they finally got overturned by the European Court of Human Rights. In the meantime, we just had to deal with the fear of persecution.

After missing Lynne so much on my first trip home, the next time I took her with me. Mum and I still weren't talking and I knew from Dad's letters that she was still seeing that guy. Mum was still living at the house. Her and Dad were living separate lives, which I couldn't get my head around. I guess it showed how much Mick loved her and that he wasn't ready to let her go and that he wanted to keep things as normal as possible for the boys, but it seemed so wrong to me.

When we arrived back at Hildenborough Dad, Nan and Grandad were waiting, all so proud of me and keen to hear all my stories of my time away. I introduced Lynne as my army friend and no one suspected anything different. Kev and Stu can't even recall me bringing someone home so it must have seemed completely normal, even though my heart was racing the whole time we were there.

I kept my distance from Mum and instead tried to just have a nice time. Dad had a new puppy called Charlie and I remember Lynne and I both taking him out for the day. It felt good just to have her there with me. Kev and Stu loved asking endless questions about what it was like to be a soldier. It was nice to go back home to see everyone, but by the end of the weekend I was ready to return to the barracks, which now felt like home.

Back at Guildford, training stepped up a gear as we prepared for passing out. Non-commissioned Officers (NCOs and Senior NCOs) would bark orders at us as we practised marching on the parade square or went on Combat Fitness Tests, which were an eight-mile run/march carrying full Bergens. I loved the challenge. The only thing I hated was swimming because I've always been petrified of water, but with a bit of encouragement from the other girls, by a miracle, managed the obligatory timed one length of a 25m pool without drowning.

I know there were people of colour in the army in my time, but we were very few and far between. There was one mixed-race girl in training but she left before the end of the course. I recently googled WRAC Guildford and I haven't seen one platoon photo of anyone that doesn't have a white face. I know it's a different institution now but it's crazy to think how I was still the odd one out after all those years.

By the time I passed out, Mum had finally moved out of the family home and was living with the other guy so when Dad turned up in the car, he was with Kevin and Stuart plus they brought Kerrie with them too. I was mortified when he showed up and drove his car straight across the parade square. With everyone taking the piss out of me, I felt embarrassment along with horror and the shame – because it was forbidden! But the important thing was that he was there.

Mum came by herself on the train, I thought she looked awful and it was upsetting as I just thought she didn't care. After the ceremony she got the early train from Guildford, so we barely spoke, but I was determined not to let family drama get in the way of my big day. Dad took the rest of us out for pasta to celebrate the start of my journey in the army that changed my life – the best and worst of times.

At the end of basic training you get sent off to do your specialist training or 'trade training' and for me that meant going off for 14 weeks learning to be an HGV driver.

Life at the Army School Of Mechanical Transport was a completely different experience from Guildford with another whole new bunch of people to get to know, including men. At 5ft 4ins tall, I could barely haul myself up into the cab of the monster trucks and had to sit on cushions to make a bucket seat, so I could see over the huge steering wheel.

I remember the words "double the clutch! double the clutch!" being drilled into me. Once we were trained we were sent out of the barracks compound all times of night and day and in all weathers to practise. One night I remember being terrified as another squaddie and I got lost up on the misty Yorkshire moors for hours.

The biggest change between Guildford and Leconfield was that the barracks were mixed and there were way more men than women, which made the atmosphere really different. I got on well with the blokes and I liked their company even though there was so much testosterone around it could be overwhelming. I'd actually found it all a bit odd being in an all-female environment in basic training after being at a mixed school. The fact we were all thrown in together meant there was much more partying and wild nights at the NAAFI, the resident bar for soldiers.

I'd never been a big drinker when I was at school because I'd always put my running first so while my friends had been going out drinking in the park, I'd been at the track doing time trials with Dave. Now I was only doing my HGV training in the day and had my evenings free, I had a chance to get a taste for pints of cider and dancing til all hours to live bands that would come to visit.

I enjoyed that period of letting my hair down. We would all drink and dance and the straight girls would openly hook up with the guys but of course, for gay men and women, the ban was still in the front of our minds. If we wanted to have a snog at the end of the night we would have to sneak off or give each other secret signals. That was the start of a lifetime learning to hide that part of who I was, but I think it was also the first time I realised how much my childhood had affected the way I saw relationships.

The other culture shock on a mixed base was that sexism was also rife and WRACs, as we were known, were often labelled 'dykes' as an insult, even if they were straight. Some of the male soldiers had a saying that 'you're a dyke or you're WRAC so go against the wall and I'll ride you like a bike' which basically meant if you weren't up for sex with them, you were gay. It was a really toxic environment in some ways but I learnt how to make the best of it and quickly became an expert in avoiding suspicion that I was gay by getting on well with the lads or sticking up for myself and others and calling a lad out by shouting, "piss off you tosser!"

You do what you have to do to get by and, when I was that age, I was at the start of the career I'd longed for since I was 14. I just focused on passing my training so I could get my first proper posting.

I knew I couldn't come out properly in the army but there was one person I really wanted to know that I'd realised I was gay and that I was happy, Dad. He had been there for me through everything and still then he was at home looking after my brothers. I decided to write to him.

'The girl who came to stay with us isn't just my friend, she's my girlfriend,' I wrote. 'I really like her.'

A couple of days later, I rang Dad from the payphone to see if he got the letter. I was nervous when I heard him on the line but he just said: "I got your letter, are you okay? Do you want me to come up there, because I'll get in the car and be with you…"

"No, no, it's fine," I said, cutting him off. I didn't want my bloody dad turning up, 'how embarrassing' I thought. "I just wanted you to know that's all. I'll see you when I come home."

"Well, as long as you're happy," he said. And that was that. He didn't need to say anything else because I knew he loved me for me and would support me no matter what.

In the years since, I've realised just how lucky I was to have that two-minute conversation and that kind of support from my dad and then the rest of my family when I finally told them, because so many people I've met haven't had that.

It was only months later when I went home again that I found out Mum had found the letter I wrote to Dad so she knew I was gay too, even though I didn't want to tell her.

"I can't believe you told your dad and not me," she said, when she confronted me. "What did you think I was going to say?"

"How was I supposed to tell you when we weren't speaking?" I snapped, angry that she'd read the letter and I hadn't been able to tell her on my own terms. I hated that she'd gone snooping around for something I wasn't ready to share with her but in hindsight, it was a relief that Mum, just like Dad, accepted my sexuality for what it was and loved me just the same. For all our ups and downs, I will always be grateful for that and when we became much closer again in later life, I let her know how important it was to me to feel that acceptance.

I think because I'd already had the feeling of rejection from such a young age – it was more important than ever to feel safe and that I wasn't going to lose the people I cared about in my life.

One thing that still makes me so sad today is when I hear stories from people in the LGBTQIA+ community, as it's known now, who haven't had support from their families, or who have even been totally disowned. I've seen people disowned by their families, and for what? Embarrassment, anger, shame?

I know it's complicated and the emotions can be difficult and overwhelming when someone you think you know is different from who you thought, but you can't underestimate how devastating and damaging it can be to reject someone for something they had no choice in, and that they can't change. It would be like disowning your own child or brother or sister for having the wrong colour eyes.

If anyone is reading this now, and doesn't know how to react to a relative coming out, I would say the only answer is to listen and learn. Educate yourself and remember that the person you love is still the same person, it's who they love that makes them seem different or as I say 'unique'. No matter what's happened with my family over the years I always felt that love and security and I don't think I'd be here without it.

* * * * *

Sadly the end of the HGV course was the end of my whirlwind romance with Lynne. We both got posted and we ended up drifting apart. I was sad to be honest because I had been happy at that time, but that's what trying to have a relationship was like in the military, always moving around – even harder if you were hiding everything.

Anyway, I did commit to my training and after 14 weeks I was a qualified HGV driver and was transferred to 17 Port and Maritime Regiment at McMullen Barracks, Marchwood, near Southampton, to work with the Royal Electrical & Mechanical Engineers (REME) under the then 53 Port Support Squadron, as a driver transporting stores to and from the port to the barracks and other places.

The worst part was the 7am start in the morning but I had plenty of spare time in the evenings and this time living in the barrack accommodation blocks, I had a brilliant group of friends around me who made it so much fun.

It was the end of 1988 and Acid house music was taking over the nation – clubbers partying all night with bright yellow smiley faces on their t-shirts and neon glow sticks. We were no different on the barracks and we would often take a small open boat from Marchwood Port to Southampton docks to go out in the bars and clubs.

I never did any drugs but I loved that feeling of totally letting go, dancing and singing with all my mates to the deafening music. It was the complete opposite of the discipline and order that we had to follow back at the barracks. I still love having a good dance now on a night out, it's one of those things that helps you feel totally free – and I don't care who's watching!

It was while I was at Southampton that I did start to secretly explore my sexuality outside of the barracks. I remember one day when I was in town, standing in the newsagents and seeing a gay magazine. I can't remember what it was called but it was mainly men, and I know that I stood in the shop flicking through the pages with my heart racing in case anyone spotted me. I was too scared to actually buy it in case it got found by anyone, but I managed to look up where the gay bars were in Southampton in the directory section and memorise their names.

One night, a few weeks later, I made my excuses and disappeared out into the night all on my own. I figured that if I went as a Civvy and anyone else from the barracks was in there it would mean they were gay too so we wouldn't blow each other's cover.

In dungarees, Kickers, a Paisley shirt and bright red lipstick, I walked up to the entrance of one of the bars I'd read about and went in. It was called Brannigans. I've since found out it's now a branch of Lidl but at the time it felt like one of the most exciting but scariest places on earth. The adrenaline was pumping as I walked through the smoke, with Black Box's *Ride on Time* and *Pump up the Jam* by Technotronic playing.

"Can I have a lemonade please?" I asked as I stood at the bar. I didn't like drinking on my own and I wanted to keep my wits about me too in case anyone asked where I'd been later.

I stood there and looked nervously around the room and just saw loads of couples, all looking so comfortable in their own skin as they drank and laughed. I suddenly felt totally out of place and I was far too shy to approach anyone to talk, but I did see a woman walking towards me and panicked, so I downed my lemonade, and made a swift exit into the night and back to Marchwood. It felt like a total anti-climax at the time but it was my first ever trip to a gay bar and, when I look back, I'm proud of myself for going. I am laughing at myself as I write this – oh, the memories.

After that, though, I decided to stick to having fun with the other girls in my accommodation block. There were quite a few guys who fancied us and a pair of twins in particular who took a shine to me and would always be competing for my attention. I used to enjoy winding them up, by kissing and flirting with them.

In the girls' block we all used to hang out of the bedroom windows singing Chaka Khan's *Ain't Nobody* into our hairbrushes at the group of lads that would gather down below. Even though I didn't find any of them attractive, it felt good to be part of the fun. Unlike Guildford, as far as I knew most of the girls in my block at Marchwood were straight, so I wouldn't have had much chance with them anyway!

Not getting involved in any serious relationships also meant I was able to concentrate on my career and, by complete chance, I got my first opportunity to chase my dream of becoming a PTI. The barracks itself had no female PTIs so when me and the other girls turned up, even though we did the Physical Training with the guys, there was no one there to take female sports like netball, rounders and hockey (what makes me laugh now is that we were never even allowed to try football and rugby).

I loved the assault courses and circuit training and generally keeping fit so I would train in the gym a lot. One day, I asked Ray, the sergeant in charge, whether I could take the girls for PTI. I explained I'd passed the intake test but that the course had been full so I'd done my trade training as an HGV driver but my ambition was still to retrain in physical training.

To my surprise he said yes and I started putting on training, matches and tournaments for the female soldiers and they loved it, we had such a laugh.

One of the PTI Warrant Officers at the gym was none other than the 400m hurdle athletics star Kriss Akabusi. He worked at the gym but then would disappear off for weeks on end to do training for one competition or another and I found out he was competing for Great Britain in the IAAF World Cup and for the army in the Inter-Service Championships.

Hearing him talk about his training made me think back to training with Tonbridge AC. He asked me to go along to see him and Roger Black at Southampton AC where they trained and I went down a couple of times. I was reluctant to do too much, though, as I'd made a conscious decision to give up competitive running when I joined up and my main focus was on getting onto a pre-selection course for my PTI training.

6
—

E.N.D
(Effort Never Dies)

IT'S NO SECRET I HAD A DIFFICULT CAREER WITH more than a few setbacks before I was finally crowned double Olympic champion but I've always believed those failures along the way made me stronger. I believe that rule is true in all areas of life, not just running. I didn't do well at school and I believe failure is your greatest teacher. It all goes back way before my professional athletics career and started when I was in the army.

Everything seemed to be going in the right direction at Southampton as I trained the other girls in the barracks and mixed with the other PTIs. I never experienced the luxury of moving out of the dorms so having my own private room as a perk of taking fitness classes in the morning, at lunchtime and in the evenings, was fab. Ray – the PTI in charge on a day-to-day basis – and Kriss did some research to find out when the next pre-selection course in Aldershot, Hampshire for new PTIs was, and sure enough, in 1989, I was off to take the course. I was devastated when it all came crashing down. I was told they didn't think I was suitable for the nine-month course I would need to pass to get formally qualified as a PTI.

They said I was physically strong enough and could run but my coordination skills let me down, as well as my voice which they said wasn't loud enough to bark the orders. "You should be shouting from your stomach and not your throat," one of the female PTIs said.

Back at Marchwood, even though I failed, the office for the army athletics team had found out about me competing in the Youth Olympics and asked me to join their team to compete in the Inter-Services Athletics Championships. I really didn't feel like going back into competitive sport but I thought if I did that and was successful they might give me another shot at the PTI course, so I signed up, and finally took Kriss up on his offer of training down at Southampton AC.

I was out of practice to say the least but I soon got back in shape with hill runs and time trials and I was selected for the team to compete against the RAF and the Navy. At the championships in Cosford later that year, I won both the 1500m and the 800m and started to make a name for myself in army athletics.

When someone tells you you are not good enough, you can either give up completely or want to prove them wrong. The latter is what I did, getting permission to go on every course I could that would teach me more skills so that I could learn to umpire, coach or referee.

At the end of 1989, after my string of successes and a trip to the rehab centre in Headley Court for a knee injury, another PTI selection course came around and this time I was on top fighting form, and cruising through onto the nine-month training programme.

April 23rd, 1990, was the day my first dream came true. I'd wanted this moment since I was 14, I was now just turned 20 at Army Physical Training school in Aldershot, home of the British Army. I enrolled on WRAC course 81, with 20 female soldiers, two of whom were from Brunei.

We were all various ages, plus there were two senior NCOs and a captain. It was to be a pivotal part of my life because it finally gave me the identity I had been craving, and a chance to be a leader – to show everyone what I was made of. The accommodation we lived in was 10 Coy (company) Duchess of Kent Barracks; a women-only barracks, and it was back to the days of sharing rooms.

I shared with two other girls. I wasn't seeing anyone when I went on my course, but I worked out a few were gay just by using my 'gaydar'. What you have to remember is it was still like a shared secret, sometimes you knew but you didn't need to say and that's how it was. It's very hard to describe but there was an unspoken understanding. You're going through enough shit on a course like that without worrying about dobbing somebody in for being gay, so I felt comfortable enough.

Although I wasn't actually seeing anybody on my PTI course, I probably kissed a couple on drunken nights out. Drinks seemed to be something that we did for fun up in the NAAFI but I never really took those things seriously because we were just young and enjoying ourselves. I think everyone has gone through those stages in life.

There were different phases of this course. The first phase we were all together and it was probably the best phase for me as it was all about our fitness at the PT school. We were then split up into groups and joined up with guys for the second part of the course. That included a trek up Snowdon in Wales, which was hell because of the unbearable weather. But despite that, I actually enjoyed being with the lads because you were pushed harder and I always wanted to hold my own with them.

There were different girls leaving throughout the course either through injury or being taken off for being too quiet or not making the standard. It was always hard to see them go as they had become good friends by now.

* * * * *

By the time we went back to 10 Company in Aldershot for the next phase, I was still loving it but this is where my career was turned upside down totally unexpectedly. I remember this part of my past in particular because I failed this section of the course – and you know by now how much I hate failure. Basically, for some reason when it came to the assessment for this part of the course, I was pulled aside by the commanding officer along with four other girls.

"You need to buck your ideas up," she told us. "You're not going to pass if you continue like this."

Inside I was devastated but I wasn't going to allow anything to get in my way, so I trained even harder. By the time we got towards the end of this section and after seemingly being whittled down, I remember getting called into this room. One of the officers was on my left and the other one straight in front of me, telling me I'd failed. I was devastated and they wouldn't give me the reason or what I had done wrong.

"If you're going to fail me I want to know why!" I demanded, totally losing it in front of the officers, something you are not allowed to do. "You've had it in for me from the start and

I want to know why." But it was no good, I was simply told I wasn't going to make it through the course but that they would encourage me to continue in the army and stay on the athletics and cross-country team. That made me even more angry – they were happy to shatter my childhood dream without giving any good reason but they still wanted to keep face so that I would win them medals for the army. I was not happy.

I will never know why I was kicked off that course. Was it because they found out I was gay? Was it because I was mixed race? I have no idea but what I do know is it was humiliating, it was embarrassing and no one could give me an answer. What I did do was go back into the barracks and trashed my room. I have just been reminded of that as I write this now.

I couldn't face going back to Marchwood a second time or going back to being an HGV driver. If they weren't going to let me fulfil my dream I decided it was time to say goodbye to the army. I was due to go home on leave before the last part of the course anyway, so I packed up my things and went to the personnel office and told them I was going to leave.

"I don't know what I'm going to do, everything's ruined," I told Dad back in Hildenborough. "It's the only thing I want to do."

He tried to comfort me but there was nothing anyone could really say to cheer me up. I went round to visit Mum. Things were still pretty bad between us because now not only had she had an affair but she'd got married to the guy in secret without telling me.

It was as though she hadn't wanted to tell me because she still felt guilty for what she'd done – too bloody right in my opinion. But I missed her and I was feeling so low from failing to pass the course, I thought seeing her might make me feel better. But back at the house, there was another shock waiting for me. There was a message from the Army Training Centre in Aldershot asking me to call them back.

"You need to get back to Duchess of Kent Barracks," the officer in personnel told me when I rang up. "We'll explain everything when you get here but we want you to continue on the course."

I couldn't believe it, the rollercoaster wasn't over yet! I couldn't understand what had happened, the commanding officer had been so clear I wasn't good enough to carry on, but I wasn't going to pass up an opportunity to get back on the course, so I packed my bags and got on the train.

The rest of the girls were now in Wales on the last phase of the outdoor adventure course and they were as shocked as me when I walked back into the dorm two days late, ready to join back in. They were pleased to see me – even they thought it was mad that I'd been let go. No real explanation was ever given for what happened. I was simply told by the Lieutenant Colonel, another officer who outranked the Commanding Officer, that they wanted me back on the course and would just judge me on my performance going forward. I never had anything more to do with the officer who booted me out and I heard not long after that she'd left the PT course team.

Finally I qualified as a PTI and earned my stripes as a Lance Corporal. I was moving up in the world so I didn't allow myself to think about why I'd had such an awful experience – until years later. Now, I'm convinced my failures both at the pre-selection course and on the PTI training course were more than just bad luck.

I was fitter than most of the other women in the group, had experience and was even winning medals for the army and yet two women wanted me out. I've gone through my life saying I've never experienced racism because of the colour of my skin but looking back, while I haven't suffered racial abuse, I can't help wondering whether the fact I was the only mixed-race girl on the course meant there was some discrimination involved. It's horrible to think that about an institution that you love but there has been some bad history of discrimination. In any case, I wasn't going to let anything hold me back any longer. I'd been rubber-stamped as a PTI and I was ready for whatever life threw at me next.

I was also pleased when Mum turned up to see me passing out to the next level of my military career as a PTI. She came with her new husband and their new baby, Penny (my youngest sister). We had grown apart a bit by now but I think maybe it was her way of showing me that no matter what else happened in her new family, she would always love me.

In my later years, I came to realise that although they were stressful and turbulent, those first four years of my life before Mum met Dad and we formed our little family unit, were something really special that she would never share with anyone else. She had three other children with two different fathers but I was the only one who had ever been on their own with her.

My first posting as a PTI was at Imphal Barracks in York, also the home of 2 Signal Regiment and later 21 Signal Regiment; it was just a wonderful place. I love York with The Shambles, Cathedral and city walls and I always think that one day I'd go and live there. I lived upstairs in the Elizabeth block which was not far from the Military Transport section, where I used to go and visit the HGV crew because I still had a connection with the drivers.

I met a girl at those barracks and actually lived out for six months with her, it was really secretive, and there was a huge amount of pressure so it didn't work out and I came back.

I loved being a PTI but it was about to become a very different army because in 1992 the WRAC disbanded and that meant that all the women would be spread out around the different military units, rather than a big congregation of women at certain barracks. During those times it was very difficult being a woman and making decisions about careers and changes.

York barracks was amazing though and I met a load of guys who I was competing in the army athletics team with. I still had the dream of being Olympic champion and I remember watching the Barcelona Games and seeing Lisa York, a girl I'd beaten as a junior in the 3000m and thinking, 'I could do that'.

When I was posted there and after winning an Inter-Services cross-country, there was a guy called Wesley Duncan, who had coerced me to get back into civvy athletics. Luckily for me, he was based in Ealing which was straight down the motorway from Beaconsfield in Buckinghamshire, the location of my second posting as a PTI.

7

—

Raided

I WAS IN GREAT SHAPE DURING MY TIME AT Beaconsfield, as I had plenty of opportunity to train alongside work. The PTI job was everything I hoped it would be and any worries anyone had about my voice not being loud enough were blown out of the water as I was soon ordering platoons of men over assault courses and around the track. Being a corporal and having PTI status, I was respected and had certain privileges, like my own bunk. I didn't go out a lot and had saved up for a TV with a VHS recorder in my room which I would use to watch videos that we passed around the barracks.

One night I was passed a video that had been recorded off the TV. It was a documentary about a gay male couple who wanted to adopt a child. It was the early '90s and even gay marriage was a distant dream in the UK, so it was totally unheard of and everyone was talking about it. I don't think I was given it because anyone thought I was gay, it was just something so unusual that everyone wanted to watch – and I had a video player.

I had mixed feelings watching the show because I'd always assumed I would never have children because of my sexuality, but maybe the world was changing and it would make me feel differently. Even though I love children I've never had a strong maternal instinct – yet it was eye-opening to see how the world on the outside of the army bubble was gradually starting to change.

Life inside the army, on the other hand, was very much still in the Dark Ages and my most traumatic experience happened at that same barracks in Beaconsfield. One morning I got a tip off that the Royal Military Police were sniffing around, back on their mission to seek out anyone in the barracks who might be gay or bisexual.

I'd spent five years looking over my shoulder, never getting into deep conversations with anyone I didn't know well or revealing too much in the NAAFI or at social gatherings. It was well known that the RMP would dress in civvies and get talking to men or women they thought might be gay, then try to lull them into a false sense of security and encourage them to either flirt or confide in them about their sexuality, so I was always on guard. Sometimes, though, they resorted to aggressive and violent bunk raids that left soldiers terrified.

When our barracks got the tip-off that the RMP might be staging raids, I got that same sense of panic I'd had in basic training when the senior officers would come to do random inspections, but now it was much more intense. I remember my heart pounding as I scrabbled around my room, checking every drawer for anything that could give the remote impression that I liked girls.

I gathered up my letters from Kerrie and Lisa and my diaries and put them in a box, took them out to the car park and put them in the boot of my car. Then all I could do was wait. Nothing could have prepared me for the onslaught when the RMP burst into my room.

"STAND BY YOUR BED!" one of them yelled as two others stormed in and started turning everything over.

"You're gay, aren't you?" he went on. "Admit that you're a lesbian!"

I stood physically shaking as two men and a woman went through every one of my belongings, pulling out drawers and emptying them out one at a time, throwing all my clothes out of the wardrobe onto the floor and trampling all over them as they flipped my mattress and steel-frame bed upside down. They brought my wardrobe crashing to the ground to check behind it and went through all my bags and personal belongings. The only way I can describe it is like when you see prison cells being raided on TV. That was how it felt – as though I was a prisoner who had done something terrible and they were there to intimidate me into admitting it.

Just as they started pulling all the furniture away from the walls to check for hiding places, my heart jumped and I felt like I was going to be sick.

I realised that in the rush to clear out all of my belongings I'd left one thing – the VHS of the gay male couple was still in the video recorder. I knew if they found that I would be done for, that would be it. Any little piece of evidence they could seize on would be grounds for discharge. I could lose everything I'd worked so hard for.

I could feel my hands trembling as I watched the search, just waiting for them to hit play on the recorder but by some miracle they didn't.

They found nothing and left my ransacked bunk to move onto the next poor soldier. I felt my heart beating out of my chest as I tried to calm myself down by taking deep breaths. I was a wreck and I started shaking and crying.

The whole experience was terrifying, and yet I knew it was coming, so I couldn't begin to imagine how I would have felt if I'd been caught off guard. 1993 in particular is now known as being one of the biggest military 'witch-hunts' and it is estimated that over 300 service personnel in the military were targeted by RMP because of their sexuality.

It's memories like that which have stayed with me all my life and which instilled such fear into my core as a 23-year-old and made me unable to live my life openly. I wish I could send a message to those people who raided my room that day. Even though I know they were only doing their jobs – and of course it's the government and authorities who were mainly to blame – those individuals caused such trauma to me and hundreds of others.

The thing that hurts me the most looking back is the way I was treated like two different people. On the one hand there was Corporal Holmes, the champion athlete PTI who won medals for the army to be proud of, and trained hundreds of men and women to be the best version of themselves for their roles and careers, physically and mentally; and then on the other hand there was Kelly Holmes who they treated like a second class citizen if they even got an inkling that I might be gay.

It made me feel like a commodity to them that they wanted to use, and then turn on if I didn't follow their draconian rules. Only now do I realise the post-traumatic stress I suffered as a result of having such a mentally damaging relationship with the army.

Thirty years later, whilst looking into the injustice of the Military LGBT ban, I met a woman who was actually discharged after her own RMP raid at the same barracks 10 years before me. Hearing her talk about the fear, shame, horror, abuse and interrogation that resulted in her discharge brought the trauma flooding back and I had to have counselling to deal with it because it was so painful.

Hearing Jean's story made me feel like this was my sliding doors moment. She has never had a good quality of life and her mental health has been hugely affected. I now know, of course, that there are many other former military personnel who suffered and I hope, with the justice that came in the summer of 2023, that others have been able to get closure too.

8

—

One Track Mind

DIFFERENT PEOPLE REACT DIFFERENTLY TO TRAUMA, as I've learnt through my many hours of therapy over the last couple of years. For me, throwing myself into my work, goals and challenges and keeping busy has always been key to getting me through. People sometimes ask me why I move at 100 miles an hour and never sit still, and that all goes back to me using it as a coping mechanism to stop me thinking too much about things that had hurt me. After the RMP raid, I threw myself back into my job as a PTI and athletics as a way of giving me a focus. If I was training and competing I had less time to think about the raid, my sexuality or relationships with other girls in the barracks.

Now training with the wonderful Wes – as I now called Wesley – he encouraged me to take part in a UK championships and, to both our surprise, I won it and recorded the qualifying time for the World Championships in Stuttgart. I used my leave to compete in Germany because I was not allowed time away, being only one of three PTIs in the gym I was in charge of. I have great memories of Stuttgart, breaking the English record for the 800m in the semi-final but not qualifying for the final, and watching Maria Mutola, who was to become my nemesis, training partner and biggest rival.

In between training for the World Championships, I was still working full-time at Beaconsfield and a camera crew was sent to the barracks to film me running PT fitness sessions. The footage shows me yelling at a platoon of male soldiers as they scramble over and under wooden logs on an assault course, and running with them round the track.

It was weird to think that the army was so proud of me and so keen to publicise my great achievements and my Olympic hopes when, behind the scenes, I was being raided by the RMP and held under suspicion by senior officers over doubts about my sexuality. I wondered what Sean Bean, who narrated the documentary, or the thousands of viewers who watched it would think about the fact the army's new athletics star had almost been given a fail on the PTI course or had my bunk ransacked during a raid.

Going to Stuttgart one minute and then patrolling the barracks the next was a bump back down to earth but I loved the fact I was a soldier and also a good athlete, as they went hand in hand, and I was fulfilling both my childhood dreams – not many people could say that. I stayed in Beaconsfield until the beginning of 1994 and then ironically got a posting to Aldershot with 251 Signal Regiment as their PTI. Back to Duchess of Kent barracks that had been the scene of so much grief. I was now juggling both my army career and my athletics after doing so well at the Worlds, but there was one thing missing from my training schedule.

Since I joined the army I'd totally lost touch with Dave but I knew if I wanted to take running seriously again, I was going to need him in my camp. He was the only one who knew how to keep me going and make me improve all the time. I wrote him a letter out of the blue asking if we could talk about my training and he invited me down to see him so on my next leave I travelled down to Tonbridge.

"What's your ultimate goal?" he asked me. And for the first time I think I said it out loud: "I'm going to win an Olympic gold medal." We both laughed and just like that we were back together again.

Dave would come to Aldershot to train me and occasionally at weekends I went to Tonbridge to train with him. I went on to win gold in the 1994 Commonwealth Games in Victoria, Canada, silver in the European Championships in Helsinki and bronze in the European Cup at home in Birmingham and I was really starting to make a name for myself outside the military, but I was still a soldier.

One minute I was running for England or Great Britain, the next I was umpiring a rounder match or taking PT. I spent the next couple of years doing both and still went on in 1995 to win World Championship silver and bronze in the 1500m and 800m respectively. We didn't have long before the 1996 Atlanta Games, so if I was serious about achieving my goal I was going to have to up my game – and get some backing from the army. I applied for leave to train and ended up having a more flexible role with the Army Youth Team so I could concentrate on running.

Getting selected by Team GB for the Atlanta Games in the summer of 1996 was an incredible feeling and I think Dave and I both felt like this was going to be it. The whole country seemed to get behind me too. The impact on my mental health after the Beaconsfield raid didn't come out for years after because I was concentrating all my energy on the Olympics, but I definitely felt like I was only of value to the army because of what I could do for them and that wasn't a nice feeling.

I was so proud to be a part of the army and to serve my country so I never questioned it sooner but I think I knew all those years ago just how desperately change was needed and I promised myself that if I ever got the chance, I would help to bring that change about.

* * * * *

I always knew the Atlanta Olympics in 1996 would be one of the most significant milestones in my athletic career, but I never could have predicted the reasons why. As I prepared to compete in the 800m and 1500m events, I took on a rigorous training regimen that pushed me to my physical and mental limits.

I knew from the start that preparing for the Olympics required dedication, discipline, and a relentless pursuit of success and it wasn't something I was going to take lightly. After all, everything I'd done in my life so far was a challenge and I hadn't given up yet – I wasn't about to start now!

My training schedule was intense, with gruelling track sessions, strength training, and endurance workouts. Each day, I pushed myself to the limit, striving to improve my speed, endurance, and overall performance because I knew everyone else who was qualifying would be doing exactly the same thing.

Under Dave's guidance, I followed a meticulously planned training programme of interval training, long runs, hill sprints, and technical drills to enhance my speed, agility, and race tactics. The training sessions were physically demanding, but

I embraced the challenge, knowing that every effort was a step closer to achieving my Olympic dreams. I also knew that if I was to get anywhere near winning, it would also require mental fortitude and resilience, so I started working closely with sports psychologists to develop mental strategies to cope with the pressure and expectations that come with competing at the highest level.

Visualisation techniques played a crucial role in my mental preparation. I would imagine myself crossing the finish line, feeling the surge of adrenaline and the sense of accomplishment like I'd felt in other races in my career. They said it would help me build confidence and belief in my abilities, enabling me to perform at my best when it mattered most.

As the summer of the Atlanta Olympics drew closer, the anticipation and excitement grew. I knew that this was the pinnacle of my athletic career, and frankly, I felt in better shape than I'd ever been. There was a real feeling that this was going to be my moment and I was determined to make the most of this opportunity. Some army guys saw me off at the airport and I was on my way to Atlanta.

In the days leading up to the Olympics, things started to take a turn.

As I flew to Tallahassee to the holding camp where the rest of Team GB were preparing, I noticed a bruise on my left shin and a shooting pain as I ran on it. I went to the team doctors who did a scan and discovered I had a small stress fracture in my leg.

"You need to go home," one of them said.

"Do I have a choice?" I said, exasperated.

"Yes but you risk breaking your leg completely."

There was no hesitation. "I'm running," I replied.

I was devastated and called my mum who told me to come

home but I wasn't about to throw away all the hard work I'd put in to get there so I just changed my training schedule to keep the weight off the leg as much as I could by cycling and training in the pool instead of on the track. With the support of Dave, my medical team and their unwavering belief in my abilities, I remained focused on my goal but there seemed to be much more risk involved now.

Eventually we moved to the Olympic Village in Atlanta and I got to share a room with none other than Tessa Sanderson, the 1984 Olympic champion who I'd met all those years before on holiday with Mum and Dad at Butlin's. I couldn't believe I was now finally going to be competing for my country just like her and inspiring another young generation of kids back home like me.

Stepping onto the track in the Centennial Olympic Stadium was a surreal and exhilarating experience, despite my anxieties over my injury. The atmosphere was electric, with the world's best athletes gathered in one place, ready to showcase their talents. The weight of the moment was enormous as I wore Team GB's red, white and blue, but I embraced it, knowing that I had worked tirelessly to earn my place among them. I told myself I deserved to be there just as much as everyone else.

Astonishingly, I got through the heats and the semi-finals. As we lined up on the starting line for the 800m final, I felt a mix of nerves and excitement, no one expected me to get this far running with a stress fracture but as the race began, I was purely focused on executing my race plan, relying on the countless hours of training and preparation that had gone into this.

Just before I went out, I was given a pain-killing injection into my leg which hit the bone. The pain was excruciating. Somehow, though, I found that my mind took over and I was there running. As I pushed myself, giving it my all, I felt a sudden agonising dart of pain shoot up my leg – because I had only done my last couple of weeks' prep in the gym and pool, I ran out of gas. I ended up in fourth place at those Games, only being pipped to the line by a tenth of a second which, given the circumstances, was pretty incredible really.

I was still totally gutted as doctors and physios rallied around me, packing and supporting my leg, and taking me off to the medical room. Stupidly, what a lot of people don't know is that I also doubled up at those Games running the 1500m as well and getting to the final but hobbling around in 11th place. People have said I was crazy. Looking back, I was!

It was a long time before I would find the courage to return to compete at that level but in hindsight my journey to the Atlanta Olympics was a testament to the dedication, sacrifice, and resilience required to compete at the highest level. While my appearance at the Games did not go as planned, the experience taught me invaluable lessons about perseverance, mental strength, and the ability to bounce back from setbacks.

Atlanta served as a stepping stone for future successes and fuelled my determination to achieve Olympic glory. It was a reminder that setbacks are not permanent, but rather opportunities for growth and learning. That summer will always hold a special place in my heart. It was a pivotal moment in my career that shaped me into the athlete and person I am today.

I also realised that if I really wanted to continue and fulfil my Olympic aspirations at the next Games, I needed complete focus. I loved the army but it was time for me to turn my attention to running full time.

So I wrote to Lieutenant Colonel McCord, the Chief of Staff responsible for granting leave and discharge to soldiers who wanted to pursue excellence in other areas. She was also the officer who got me back on my PTIs course.

Ma'am,

Following my personal disappointment in relation to my results at the Olympic Games and the overall results of the British Athletics Team in Atlanta, I have carefully analysed the situation.

My individual events were dominated by Russian Svetlana Masterkova, who won both the 800m and the 1500m Olympic titles. Masterkova, like the majority of Olympic champions, carefully and ruthlessly prepared for Atlanta by isolating herself from everything in a single-minded quest to win at least one Olympic gold medal.

Both Masterkova (although she is Russian she resides in Spain during the winter and spring) and Michael Johnson, an American who won the men's 200m and 400m, are ultimate examples of this method of preparation.

I am positive that with the right preparation, both mentally and physically, I can beat Masterkova at this year's World Athletics Championships, which will be held in (*ironically) Athens during August. My wish is to go to South Africa at the beginning of February, returning in May. I would spend a period of time in Pretoria at altitude and then Stellenbosch in the Cape to finalise my preparations at sea level.

When I return from South Africa in May, I will immediately enter into a carefully structured competitive programme which, coupled with training, will lead me to win at Athens.

Unfortunately, we live in a world where success is the only criterion, and I believe I can win a gold medal in Athens, but this will entail me embarking on the programme I have outlined.

I would be grateful if the Army would consider my needs and my aim to become the world's first number one middle-distance runner.

I am Ma'am,
Sgt K Holmes
WO804968

I was delighted when the response came and I was given the time off to pursue my running career. It felt like I was able to pursue my two great loves in life at the same time. Plus, Pretoria in South Africa is the perfect climate and altitude for athletics training so when I had the chance to travel over with Andy Norman, one of the most influential men in British Athletics at the time, and a few other athletes including Fatima Whitbread, the world champion javelin thrower, I jumped at the chance.

A small group of Brits were going to take part in the ABSA Games in 1997. One of the races was in a University town called Potchefstroom which had amazing training facilities, a beautiful sunshine climate and a lovely old town centre with traditional architecture and wide, tree-lined streets. It was a million miles away from Hildenborough but I loved it.

South Africa in the '90s was an exciting place of change, with the release of Nelson Mandela and the abolition of Apartheid and I enjoyed learning about the history of it all. I felt completely at home there in a way I didn't think I would. In fact, I soon set my heart on one day buying a house so I could train there whenever I wanted. By June, though, I had to return to the UK for an Army Athletics team performance.

My wins in civilian races and my travels around the world had given me a new confidence and the army no longer had the same hold over me that it once did. I decided there and then it was time to sever my ties once and for all. I went over to Lieutenant Colonel McCord who had been so accommodating in allowing me to go and train in South Africa and said: "I think it's time for me to part ways with the army for good."

She wasn't happy to see me leave but she could see that if I wanted to achieve my true potential as a civilian athlete I couldn't have the distractions. I think she could also tell by then that I'd lost some of my respect for rank from spending so much time outside the institution, so she saw it was time to go.

I was just a few months off ten years of service when I left and I still remain really proud of that time in my life. When I received my final report, Lieutenant Colonel McCord described my conduct in the army as 'exemplary'.

Of course I was proud to have such a glowing report from my time serving the Crown but I couldn't help wondering at the back of my mind how things could have been so different.

It made no sense to me that I could be praised so highly on my performance as a soldier but that something so personal as my sexuality could have led to me being discharged with disgrace. The main reason for leaving was so that I could focus on my career but I would be lying if I said I wasn't relieved by the fact I would never face the fear, degradation and humiliation of being raided or investigated by the RMP ever again.

* * * * *

After Atlanta I convinced myself that if 1996 was rock bottom, 1997 was going to be my year. Now I was free from my army responsibilities, I could focus completely on my Olympic dream and that meant first going to the World Championships in Athens that summer. From there it would be a straight shot towards the Commonwealth Games in Kuala Lumpur the following year and then the Sydney Olympics in 2000.

I moved back home to Kent so Dave and I could go back to training in Tonbridge just like we had for the five years before I enrolled in the army. While I was serving, I'd saved up pretty much all my money. When I wasn't working, I was off training or competing, so I'd been able to put down a mortgage on a house in Sevenoaks – a three-bed ex-housing association semi with a garden.

It was the perfect base for me to do my training again and it meant I could spend more time with Mum, too. We'd never spent much time together since she remarried and had Penny but I liked being around her more. I would go round to her house and take her dog, Harley D, named after Harley-David-son motorbikes, out for long runs and sometimes Mum would come on her push bike too, which was mainly a distraction and disaster as she was so slow!

Dave and I started training sessions with a couple of other athletes from Tonbridge AC so they could help me keep pace and, to begin with, things were going well. I was in the best shape of my life, unbeaten so far that year and I was running times that were well on track to get me a medal at Athens.

Having beaten the British 1500m record earlier that year, I was five seconds faster than anyone else in the world and was far and away the favourite to win. But a few weeks before we were due to travel over to Greece for the World Championships, my ankle started niggling again.

At first it was just a twinge but then as I continued training a shooting pain would come and go. "I'm worried," Dave told my physio Kevin Lidlow. "I think we need to do something about it now before it gets any worse." I tried to stop myself from panicking too much. After all, the pain was only coming and going and I only needed it to stop long enough for me to get round the 1500m race. But I was also determined not to end up in the same situation I faced in Atlanta, so I booked to see the best specialist in Europe at the Institute of Sport in Munich.

Dr Hans-Wilhelm Müller-Wohlfahrt told me the stress on my Achilles tendon was causing the pain and gave me two injections to try to ease it. Nothing could have prepared me for the pain as I hobbled out of the clinic on crutches. I called my mum from my bedroom that night in floods of tears as the agony in my leg felt like it would never end.

"I think he's made it worse," I cried. "What if I can't run at all now? What if the same thing happens again?"

Mum knew how devastated I'd been by my injury at Atlanta and she hated hearing me so upset. It wasn't the first time I'd called her in the early hours of the morning, consumed in pain and worry, but this time it seemed worse than ever before. Just having her there for me on the other end of the line was the biggest comfort and I believe it actually brought us much closer together.

"Everything will be okay, we all love you and we're so proud of you," she told me. And somehow that was just what I needed to hear. It was a huge reminder to me that no matter how much success I had as a runner, I always needed my family and friends around me. My successes were a team effort and I'm very lucky to have had them and others around me through all the ups and downs of my life.

By some miracle, I woke up the next morning and the pain was gone completely. When I landed in Greece I felt fit as a fiddle and wanted nothing more than to get myself back on track with a big win at Athens.

I woke up on the day of the first heat feeling good and ready for the challenge. Lining up at the start, I told myself not to push too hard and to save myself for the semi-finals. I just had to do enough to get through. But after the second lap I could feel myself running erratically, then suddenly, as I took one step, I felt something that felt like an explosion in my leg and an excruciating pain burst through my body, causing me to leap into the air and yelp.

When I came down, I couldn't go another step and I had no choice but to hobble off the track and drag myself to the railings. My mind was spinning and the pain in my leg was like a searing hot poker being pushed into my calf. I couldn't believe it was happening again; first my Olympic dream in shreds and now my World Championship goal in tatters too. It seemed so unfair, I was devastated.

After I had hobbled down the track to get to the end, the medics and physios rallied around me again but this time it seemed the problem was even more serious. They told me that I'd had treatment on my Achilles tendon and had weakened it, causing it to tear as well as rupturing my calf. It meant the muscle had torn apart, causing intense pain. It was going to take a long time to heal.

I left Greece on crutches and heartbroken. Looking back, what I understand now is that at that time in my life, I put all my value and self-worth in how I performed on the athletics track. I think that's because I couldn't allow myself to live authentically in my personal life but also, because I had a hangover from never feeling good enough, I had this constant need to push myself, sometimes to my detriment. A lot of other athletes when they fell on hard times had partners to support them or could relax between training and competitions by going out and meeting new people, but because of the way the military ban on being gay had become hardwired into me, I was always so scared to relax and I didn't go out much. My entire life until then was trying to prove I could be good at something, all triumph and disaster was dependent on how well I did in my athletics career. Another failure like Athens was a brutal blow to my self-confidence.

Back home on my sofa after a couple of weeks of treatment in Zurich and my leg in a plaster cast, I began to question everything about my life and even wondered whether I could come back from the pain, injury, heartache and humiliation of Athens. I should be known as the world champion and instead I was getting known for my terrible luck and repeated injuries. Perhaps being convinced that I would one day win a gold at the Olympics had been completely naive. Maybe I just wasn't good enough.

I wish back then I could have told myself I would return to Athens seven years later and see all my dreams come true.

9
—

Relationships
and Rumours

HOBBLING ALONG THE PATHWAY TO THE CARAVAN, still on my crutches as the other girls carried my bags, I tried my best to put a brave face on but I felt awful. So much for 1997 being my year... My big plan of leaving the army to pursue athletics full-time had fallen flat just months later. All the training in South Africa, breaking the British 1500m record in Sheffield, all seemed to pale into insignificance after my performance in the World Championships in Athens and what was worse, I wouldn't be able to train again until my ruptured calf had properly healed.

A couple of girls, one from the army I had a brief relationship with, knew how hard I'd taken the blow and when I got home they said I should go with them down to Chichester in West Sussex for a week's holiday. It was better than sitting at home on my own reliving what had happened, so I agreed to meet

Childhood memories As the only mixed-race girl, I was always placed right in the middle of the school photo! (Top) with Mum and baby Kevin and (above) with my afro and school friends Lara, Paul and Kim

First love Lynne with Charlie the dog, Kev and Stu

Wife and wife I played the toothy vicar in our mock wedding ceremony

Service Proudly wearing uniform (top) and pictures from my PTI course

Holmes truths Family is everything. They are the people who love you

Natural talent Hair slowed me down but I still won the English Schools at 17!

'Sarcastic but fun!' Sarah would become my longest relationship

Through the pain barrier Rupturing my calf, ironically in Athens, in 1997

First Olympic medal Celebrating winning bronze in the 800m in Sydney in 2000

True love With my two dogs Whitney and Barney

On track for success Gold at the Commonwealth Games in Manchester in 2002 (left) and silver in the World Athletics Championships in Paris in 2003 (right)

Golden feeling The look on my face says it all as I cross the line in FIRST place in 2004 in the 800m (above). I use this image now in my motivational speeches and it always gets a great reaction. (Right) doing the double! The same celebration after I make it two Olympic golds in Athens with victory in the 1500m

Homecoming Paraded on a double-decker bus with my two gold medals from Athens. The press cameras followed my every move as I worried about what they might uncover

National treasure Mum enjoyed the scenes as I returned to a hero's welcome. But the paparazzi and reporters soon found out where I lived and it was time to move house

On the Parky show They said I flirted with Tom Cruise – little did everyone know...

Special night Being named BBC Sports Personality of the Year in 2004 was one of the best things to happen to me after Athens

Saying goodbye Waving to the crowd after my last competitive race in Sheffield in 2005

them down there. Claire told me to meet one of her friends called Sarah who I'd never met before at Victoria Station as she was travelling down too. As the other two were a couple I just assumed she was gay and I was right. I know now that they were trying to matchmake us but the setting couldn't have been less romantic – me with my crutches and feeling distraught from my loss, her probably wondering why I was in such a bad mood as we both travelled by train together.

Then the morning after we arrived, things got even worse. We woke up and switched on the little telly in the caravan and it was just rolling news.

"Princess Diana has been killed in a car crash in Paris," the newsreader was saying. "She died in hospital after a collision in a tunnel."

We couldn't believe it, and all started to cry from the shock. The Royal Family was especially important to us having pledged to serve the Crown when we joined the army and back then Diana wasn't only a princess but the biggest celebrity in the world. We watched for hours as the news came out bit by bit, that she'd been chased by the paparazzi when leaving the Ritz hotel with her new boyfriend Dodi Al Fayed, and he was also dead.

It was just so sad to think of Prince William and Harry after all they'd already been through with the public divorce of their parents. I think we had a special love for Diana because of what she did for the gay community during the AIDS pandemic in the late '80s and early '90s too. We sat around comforting one another and reminiscing about her for hours that day. It certainly put things in perspective and I started to try to make the most of the holiday.

Sarah, who worked for the MOD and army but as a civil servant, started to really hit it off with me and by the last night of the holiday we were making plans to see each other when we got back home.

We decided to meet up in London, as she was living in Croydon at the time. After chatting I went home and wrote in my diary that she was 'sarcastic but fun', which I think she'd agree with!

We started seeing one another. It was to become the longest relationship I've ever had. I only had one rule and I made it clear from the beginning: "I can be in a relationship but I can't come out publicly, and I never will, so if that's what you need we shouldn't do this." Sarah was cool with it and I knew she was trustworthy because she worked for the army too and could face discipline if anyone found out about her, so we were kind of safe with one another.

I think the key was that we got on so well as friends and she understood just what was important to me. She never complained about me having to be off training or competing, she just wanted the best for me. I loved her company and within a couple of years, she moved in. Sarah was such a strong person and a strong character who didn't suffer fools. You wouldn't want to get on the wrong side of her but I quickly realised she was incredibly loyal and would do anything for the people she loves.

We would bicker like an old married couple. I knew 100 per cent that she had my back all the time and that's what relationships are meant to be about. I knew she also understood when I got my first dog Whitney and my next, Barney, that she came third in the relationship. It was my athletics, the dogs, then her! She took it amazingly well.

It felt good to have my own little family unit for the first time since I'd left home at 17 and now I was with Sarah, I found it easier to come out to other people close to me. She gave me the confidence to feel like it didn't matter what they thought. Up until I was 27 and left the army, Dad was still the only person I'd told I was gay. Mum had found out by mistake of course but that was it, apart from my fellow soldiers who were keeping the same secret.

I decided to tell Kerrie and Lisa together when they came over to meet me at Mum's house one night when Mum wasn't there. It actually wasn't anywhere near as big a deal as I thought it would be. We sat there chatting and I just came out with it: "I'm gay and I'm in a relationship with someone."

They both looked totally unsurprised and smiled at me. I think they were just really happy for me that I'd found someone. They got on really well with Sarah too. They didn't want to belittle my big moment back then but they've since told me they suspected all along anyway. The same with my brothers, who by now were 17 and 20, running about with girls and getting into their own mischief – they weren't bothered either.

We soon had a tight little circle of friends and family in Kent who knew and accepted our relationship and after all the drama of the army and the trauma of the raids, it felt good for a while. I met Sarah's parents Shirley and Alan and her sisters Sandra and another sister, who all became a part of my family.

Sandra even moved in with us for a while before she went off travelling to Australia. They both kept my secret from the outside world and I just felt grateful to have found someone who accepted me for who I am, and that I could be with people I could trust. Life was good. When I look back at the last book I wrote, not long after I retired from athletics, I get a twinge of sadness that I referred to Sarah as a 'close friend' and covered up our relationship by saying that she and Sandra both lived with me.

I suppose I wanted people to think we were housemates rather than in a relationship. That's just one of the things that makes me so grateful for the fact I can now live my life freely but, more importantly, tell the truth about the amazing friend Sarah is to me now, 25 years since meeting. Never once did she break my trust.

Despite 'being in the closet' as it gets described when you are not freely out, I have had several relationships since Sarah. Unfortunately, for a lot of reasons, things have not always been great and they haven't ever lasted long. I have gone out with people because of circumstance and convenience rather than any great lightning-bolt love-at-first-sight. Sometimes they were sporty so I thought we had a lot in common. I also got attached because I wanted to share my successes with people and the thought of always being on my own scared me. But the truth is, with most of them, we should never have been together.

I wish in hindsight I hadn't rushed into things so much. What I do know and admit is that being with me was not easy.

Most of my partners developed an inferiority complex because of my successes, felt invisible because of my commitment to my work or didn't like the limelight. Most of the time, after the initial buzz of being with me wore off and the reality set in, things didn't end well. More often than not was the realisation that I wasn't going to be coming out for them, getting engaged or slowing down my work to spend more time with them. In my defence I have always been totally honest from the start of every single relationship. I told them: "I am not out and not planning to be and will never come out whilst in a relationship."

I haven't been in touch with most of my exes for many years and out of respect I'm not naming them or putting any details about them here because I no longer know their circumstances. I wish I had been strong enough to have been on my own because maybe it would have been better than an unhealthy relationship.

The problem, deep down, was that I never thought I would be able to come out. Even if they said that was fine to begin with, sooner or later it would start to put pressure on the relationship and eventually they would take it as me being ashamed of them or unwilling to give them the commitment they deserved. As I said before, it was never about shame, but I was definitely still scared of the impact having a public same-sex relationship would have on my life and so I invariably chose my safety first.

One thing I'm comfortable with is that I was always completely open with anyone I started a romantic relationship with – it was cards on the table from the start, even if I thought it would scare them away. As it turned out, a combination of my issues with going public about my sexuality and the unresolved childhood trauma that left me scared of abandonment meant that for most of my adult life relationships were pretty disastrous!

Lots of my closest relationships haven't been sexual. I have had some really long-term friendships as well. Kerrie and her mum Sandy who I adore, Lara and Kim my school buddies, Tess who lived across the road from me, Pat who was my hairdresser, and Flo, Jackie and Emma who don't live close to me but I have known for so long now.

There can be a price to fame that is not always great. I had two friends in particular in my life for years who I fell out with. With one, I think we just grew apart and as our own lives changed and different people came into them which caused friction, we just went our separate ways. Another I felt betrayed by; I felt they were using my kindness and financial support for personal gain.

I am disappointed and hurt at losing both of them, but it's all part of life I suppose. All of us will meet people who will come and go throughout our lives, it's the ones who are meant to be in it that stick around.

* * * * *

Since my appearance at Atlanta, even though I didn't win, my name was getting better known and there was more press attention around me. For some reason the one thing everyone was interested in was my personal life, which definitely filled me with anxiety. I'd gone from one homophobic institution in the army to an industry where there wasn't a single openly gay athlete that I knew of, so there were no role models I could turn to.

Of course there must have been other people, like me, who were keeping it secret, but it was never something that was spoken about. Instead I just kept myself to myself and never allowed anyone to get too close to me. I hated the idea that anyone would start asking me about my home life, my relationships or who I fancied. It was just too uncomfortable.

Back home in Kent I felt like the Only Gay In The Village and I wasn't really on the gay scene. Another saving grace for me when it came to publicity about my private life was the great friendship I had with Jason Dullforce. Jason was the same age as me and we'd met a few years earlier at an athletics meet in Manchester where he was also a middle-distance runner competing in the men's 1500m. A tall, mixed-race guy with long eye-lashes and delicate features, we looked quite similar and got mistaken for brother and sister when I was serving, which made us laugh and we hit it off straight away.

Over the following years our careers had crossed paths many times so we'd got to know one another really well and even our families became friends. So, when the press and other people in the athletics community started to assume we were together romantically, I never did anything to stop it. We'd become really close friends and before I met Sarah we'd spent lots of time together but despite the rumours, our relationship was never physical. I suppose in many ways it was convenient for me to allow people to think we were together and he never did anything to shut down the rumours either. I was always honest with him and when I got together with Sarah he was really happy for me but still neither of us openly denied our relationship, which took some of the pressure off me in the early days of my more public career.

When you're trying to win medals and titles and achieve personal bests and break records you need a kind of single-mindedness that helps you to succeed so if you're worrying about someone finding out about your sexuality all the time, that's a distraction that could put you at a disadvantage if you're not mentally strong.

There were more than 20 openly gay athletes in Team GB in the 2020 Olympics in Tokyo so things are definitely changing but other sports like men's football and rugby are still way behind, which is shocking in this day and age.

My coping mechanism was to completely separate my two lives. I had my little house in Sevenoaks with Sarah, Whitney and Barney and then there was the other me, who was on the track, a sergeant in the British Army and a representative for our nation on the world sporting stage. I felt lucky to have both but I wish in hindsight I'd been able to allow the two worlds to collide.

The other impact of the divide was that I often found myself choosing between the two worlds and inevitably, I always chose running. I was open with Sarah from the start because I needed to succeed in my Olympic dream, perhaps now more than ever after the disappointment of Atlanta. Plus, for the outside world it was a distraction from my personal life. I think all of my life I've strived to succeed so there would be something I was known for. If there was something interesting to ask me about in my career or my successes maybe people wouldn't ask me about my relationships or my personal life. No one could judge me for my love of running.

10

Triumph and Disaster

THE UPS AND DOWNS OF A CAREER AS AN ELITE athlete are like a being on a rollercoaster. Somehow once you get past the nausea and fear of the twists and turns, you're back to craving the adrenaline and having another go. With two pretty disastrous events behind me in Atlanta and Athens it would have been easy to give up or let the mental impact of my injuries stop me from trying to reach my goal. But the same Kel that fought to the bitter end to get onto a PTI course and who managed to get through the trauma and fear of 10 years in an army that criminalised my sexuality decided to fight on beyond the world championships and set her eyes on the next goal.

The fact was, if you looked at my performances when I was at peak fitness, I was the best middle-distance runner in the world. I truly believed that all I needed was for my peak form to coincide with the right races and all my dreams would be achieved.

First I had to undergo surgery on my leg to remove the scar tissue from my injury so it wouldn't affect my ability to get back to peak fitness. It turned out to be an injury that has plagued me all my life and I even had to have another op on it a couple of years ago.

The surgery went well and gradually, with the help of Kevin and Dave, I was able to put more weight on my leg, although running was out of the question. I had to do aqua-jogging (or water running as I renamed it) in the pool – something I hated because I still had my fear of water (I absolutely hate cold water) – and gentle walks to get my mobility back. Anyone who knows me knows I'm always on the move, dashing from one place to the next and never sitting still so it was really frustrating for me to have to slow down and just allow myself to heal. But I wasn't going to do anything to risk going backwards so I followed doctors' orders.

I used the spare time I had to arrange a school sports tournament in Kent called the Kelly Holmes Schools Challenge. It was my first attempt at giving something back to kids who might be like me when I was at school – good at sport but not much else! I got 25 schools involved and they all had to compete in loads of different games.

I funded the whole thing myself so I got pretty creative with the props and the challenges involved. I even managed to get hold of a supermarket trolley for one event where they had to push their teammates up and down the school hall, dunking their heads in the flour, then water, to get the apples. I loved going along to watch all the kids have such a great time mucking in and getting involved with sports.

It was another opportunity for me to spend time with Mum too. She was now a single mum living alone with Penny who, being 19 years younger than me, meant that I never really built a strong relationship with at this time. Her only income was a couple of cleaning jobs so I decided to get her to help out with the admin side of things and she loved it too. She got really involved in setting up all the challenges and we had such a laugh, it was exactly what I needed to take my mind off my injury.

It was many months but eventually my ruptured calf was on the mend and I was able to get back to training at a high level and, with the Sydney Olympics now on the horizon, I was totally focused on getting a medal. But first I had to get in shape for the Commonwealth Games in Kuala Lumpur in Malaysia.

It turned out the key to that was marathon runner Paula Radcliffe. I'd got to know her a bit in Atlanta and I knew she'd also had injury problems so when she told me she'd been to a physio in Ireland who she called "the man with magic hands" I had to go and see him. It turned out she was right and as soon as I started seeing Gerard Hartmann, everything changed.

I flew over to see him in Limerick and stayed close by, working on my injured leg. Within six weeks, I was running again – really running. It was an absolute miracle. I started seeing him in May 1998. I could not get ready in time for the Europeans that year, but with the Commonwealth Games on the horizon in September, that became my focus. By the time the new season started in August, I was back on track. I managed to win my first couple of races of the season which really boosted my confidence and by the time I jetted off to Malaysia for the Commonwealth Games, Athens seemed like a distant dream – or nightmare!

The 1500m was always going to be a tight-run thing with

my two main rivals Jackline Maranga and Naomi Mugo from Kenya in peak condition and me only just back from a massive injury. If I could even just make it round the track in a good time it would be a huge improvement on Athens.

I got through to the final and, on the day, as I gritted my teeth and pushed myself to the limit, I won a silver medal. Just months earlier it was unthinkable that I could achieve such a performance. I was so pleased and it was another medal in the bag.

Having Sarah's support during those first couple of years was invaluable and I will always be grateful to her for that. She was always there, looking after me when I was injured then as I started to recover, looking after the house and Whitney and Barney when I was able to go out training again.

The sad thing looking back was that when I was given the huge honour of being awarded an MBE for my military services, Sarah couldn't come with me. I imagine if I'd been straight and been in a relationship and living with a man, I might have taken him along to Buckingham Palace to meet the Queen when I accepted the honour but, of course, that was out of the question.

There are so many things that gay couples miss out on for fear of scrutiny or being outed before they're ready. I've tried to make sure in more recent years that I take Sarah to more events with me because I think she missed out on a lot when we were together. Over the years, having such a close friendship – and because she is my ex – has caused a lot of problems with other relationships I have had. But she has always been there for me – still sarcastic but a great friend!

It was still an amazing experience getting my MBE. I took Mum and Dad with me and they were beside themselves with pride. Mum in particular – how could she, a single teenage mum from a council estate in Kent be joining her daughter at Buckingham Palace to accept an honour? She was so proud and excited. I bought a new cream suit and a navy hat from a shop on the high street and a local limo driver offered to look after us for the day, driving us to and from the reception.

As I was introduced as Sgt Holmes, Prince Charles asked me why I wasn't in my military uniform. I told him I didn't have to wear it since I had now left the army to become an athlete. It probably would have been better if I had worn my uniform as I hate the pictures of me in what I wore. I didn't have much style and I found that one thing about being secretly gay is I never wanted to show too much personality or draw too much attention to myself. I always thought if I went with the kind of steampunk fashion or androgynous outfits and edgy hair-styles that appeal to me now, I would stand out too much. It's probably crazy because I'm sure no one gave two hoots what I was wearing but I always thought there was a risk someone would think I was making a statement or just assume from my style that I was gay, so I kept it as vanilla as possible. There are tons of pictures I look back at where I hate what I look like.

Still, there aren't many people who can say the now king asked them about their outfit!

* * * * *

In the year 2000, as we started a new millennium, the European Court of Human Rights finally lifted the ban on homosexuality in the British Armed Forces. There was a landmark ruling after initially four services personnel fought for justice having been dismissed from the the military on the grounds of their sexuality.

The court ruled that an individual's sexual orientation had no bearing on their ability to perform their duties effectively. It said that the armed forces rely on teamwork, trust, and cohesion, and excluding qualified individuals based on their sexual orientation undermined these essential elements. This marked a change to the future of LGB rights as the ban had been in place for decades and the institution was being dragged into the 21st Century with the rest of the world.

It was a massive milestone in the fight against discrimination for people like me. But I'm sorry to say I had no clue it had even happened. Astonishingly, the story wasn't widely covered in the mainstream media like I'm sure it would be now. Although I spoke to friends from my army days, none of them mentioned it to me, so I had no clue. There was no letter sent out to former soldiers to tell them, it just happened quietly behind closed doors. For me, life went on unchanged.

I was busy training for my next Olympics in Sydney later that year, so I missed out on any sense of relief I'm sure I would have felt from the ruling had I known about it. It was only years later that I realised the ban had been lifted and, even then, there was no information available about what would happen to a soldier who was found to have broken the law before homosexuality was decriminalised – so my fears of retribution remained and I continued to live my life behind closed doors.

What could have been a year of great celebration became pretty bleak as my training for Sydney was once more blighted by injury. A damaged femoral nerve meant I lost all sensation down one side for about five months. It was better than being in excruciating pain but I couldn't believe my luck that it was happening again. It seemed I was just prone to injuries which would knock my training off course at any moment and make everything feel so uncertain. I would lie awake at night willing myself to heal and get back on track but the more I felt the mental impact, the harder recovery seemed to be.

Gerard was able to work his magic again and I flew back off to Potchefstroom to train with some other British and French athletes who were also going for selection to their Olympic teams. While I was there, I sustained another injury. A 12cm calf tear! I thought my Olympic dream was over but I made selection for both the 800m and 1500m based on all my other years of success at major championships.

The team flew out to the Gold Coast at the end of August three weeks before the opening ceremony in September and the camaraderie in the team was amazing. We trained in parks with wallabies and koalas and the whole experience of being in Australia was different from anything I'd experienced before. Andy Graffin, one of the Tonbridge AC guys I'd been training with back home also qualified for the 1500m and I made friends with Kate Howey, a judo player, who was in the team too, so I often relaxed by watching her train. I think in all my Olympic appearances, she was actually the only other team athlete I watched win a medal.

The relaxed and positive vibe in the team really helped me and in those last couple of weeks before the Games opened, my form improved massively. A few days before I was due to run, I was out on the track with Dave and ran one of my fastest times of the season.

I took home a bronze medal in the 800m that year which was a really big achievement given the setbacks and the fact I only had six weeks of running. The rest was about adapting and using the gym as a way of staying at my peak both physically and mentally. Plus it was my first Olympic medal, so I was on a massive high.

I was so happy that I actually messed up the 1500m as I took my eye off the ball. I remember my coach being really unhappy with me as he thought I had let myself down when I missed out on a medal. But the bronze felt like a gold medal at the time. It was enough to prove that I had it in me. If I could win bronze against the best middle-distance runners in the world after the season I'd had, imagine what I could do if I was on form.

The other big landmark that year was my birthday. The actual day, April 19th, I was training in Potchefstroom, so I'd been out to a karaoke bar with some of the other athletes. It was the most bizarre place, themed like the Wild West and I got up and sang Whitney Houston. I didn't drink as an athlete but that night I got really pissed as I was so distraught about turning 30!

Back home in England, Sarah arranged for a night out in London at a posh Spanish restaurant with Lisa and her sisters and, of course, my best buddy Kerrie. We had the best time and Sarah even booked a limo to take us home to Hildenborough afterwards. I felt rather posh for a girl from a council estate.

People sometimes ask me why I never had any friends or family with me at the Olympic Games like some of the athletes but the truth is I always thought they would be more of a distraction if I knew they were out there in the crowd. Not only because I would be focused on them watching me but also because if Sarah came out, I was paranoid the press would start to latch on to the idea we were more than just housemates. I couldn't have that worry distracting from my performance. It was much easier to socialise with other athletes while I was out there as it was only about sport and then come home to my friends and family to celebrate afterwards.

I would always take a few weeks off from training after every big race and Sydney was no different. When I got home to

Hildenborough I spent a few weeks chilling on the sofa with Sarah, Whitney and Barney, visiting Mum and Dad and eating all my favourite naughty foods like Chinese takeaway and chocolate. The medal was the best reward for all my hard work, but that was a close second.

* * * * *

As an over-thinker and a perfectionist, one thing I do after every race, win or lose, is look back and analyse what went well, what went wrong and how I could have shaved off those few precious seconds that could make all the difference. I also do it in my personal life, which is probably less effective, but for athletics, it really works.

After Sydney there was one clear obstacle besides my injuries that meant I won bronze and not the Holy Grail gold medal I'd been dreaming of all those years. That obstacle was Maria Mutola from Mozambique, who took gold. Maria was an absolute legend in her home country, treated like a queen and a national hero as she'd been winning races internationally for years, putting them on the map for athletics.

I'd been coming up against her in races for years, since she won the 800m in the first ever world championships I qualified for, in Stuttgart. But now she seemed to be on top form and I knew that if I wanted to be the best in the world, I needed to be better than her.

Maria was two years younger than me and if I was going to get to the next Olympics in Athens I would be 34 years old – past retirement age for many runners – so I had to keep in shape. I knew Athens would be my last chance and it was never too soon to start my journey.

One thing that brought Maria success, I was convinced, was

the climate of her home country where she could train all year round. I loved training in South Africa but staying in hotels and renting houses for short bursts in the run-up to big tournaments was disruptive and expensive so in 2001, after my post-Olympic slobbing around break, I headed out to Stellenbosch, with the idea of buying my own place so I could train there for more of the year. Dave and I rented a place to begin with while I trained, but I started looking at apartments to buy.

A disappointing performance in the World Championships in Edmonton, Canada, later that year due to having chronic fatigue syndrome a few months before, convinced me even more that I needed to focus on getting back on top form, mentally and physically. With selection for the Athens Games coming round in three years, this was my last chance to really go for it and come home with gold, or forget my dream forever.

A gold medal on home turf at the Commonwealth Games the following year in Manchester and a bronze at the European Champs two weeks later only spurred me on further to believe I could do it at the big one in Athens, but experience had taught me that it wouldn't come without a fight.

Sadly, that fight meant making some difficult decisions.

Firstly, I made the hard decision to move to Potchefstroom full time, leaving Sarah, my family, and Whitney and Barney behind.

It wasn't just that the climate and conditions and facilities were better for training but also because I'd realised it was impossible to focus on the enormity of my dream when I was living back home in Hildenborough.

When you have a partner and a home, it's too easy to get bogged down in sorting out the house, or cutting the trees in the garden or getting into discussions about things that just don't matter. It sounds harsh but I needed that single-mindedness without outside influence or distractions. Yes, it was selfish but I believed, to be Olympic Champion, I just needed to focus on myself.

"We'll never see you!" Mum said when I told her I planned to move for the foreseeable future.

"I'll keep the house here and I'll be back to see you all," I reassured her. "I wouldn't just leave Whitney and Barney would I?!" Plus Sarah was still living there.

While I was in the process of moving to South Africa, I made another big decision. After decades working together I decided to part ways with Dave and get a new coach. It was after a competition in Crystal Palace, at the end of the 2002 season, when I got chatting to a guy called Jeff Fund from Maria Mutola's team. Jeff was her race agent and manager and the ex-husband of her coach Margo Jennings.

He told me Maria had started training with Margo in Johannesburg just an hour away from where I decided to buy another house. I still had my apartment but the house would be in Potchefstroom at altitude whereas the apartment was at sea level being in Stellenbosch. I figured if I wanted to be the best – and beat the best – I needed to train with her too. Dave was completely against the idea of me training with a rival and said he was worried it would mess up my own training schedule but I was determined.

Maria was so strong, confident and without any self-doubt. After all, she had never been injured and was the queen of the 800 metres. She had years of experience behind her and was pretty much unbeaten, so she wasn't about to be bothered by me training with her. In many ways I thought it would help to have a competitor around.

So, after a conversation with Jeff and Margo, she agreed. A few weeks later, back in South Africa, I travelled from Potchefstroom to Johannesburg to join her for her training. It was one of the most gruelling things I'd put myself through, with hill climbs at altitude and relentless reps according to Margo's exacting schedule. At first I felt downtrodden by the fact I was struggling to keep up but I knew it was now or never. I could give up and go home or I could be as focused as Maria.

Two weeks into training, I spoke to Margo on the phone. I explained to her the problems I'd had with injuries and what I was finding difficult in the training sessions with Maria. She said she could help me and train us both as long as my goal was still the Olympic 1500m title. So I told Dave it was time for us to part ways. Of course he was disappointed and I was sad too but I had to give myself the best possible chance.

Sarah flew out to meet me in Cape Town. I just couldn't concentrate at all. I knew we needed some time together but as she tried to tell me about what was going on at home, all I could think about was getting back to training.

"I'm really sorry, I have to get back to Johannesburg," I blurted out suddenly halfway through her trip. "It's just I have this training schedule I need to keep on top of and it's really tough at the moment."

I think I knew, as I packed up my bags and left to go back to our training base, that was the death of our relationship. Sarah stayed with a friend in Cape Town and when we spoke on the phone I just remember saying: "I need to stay. I need to stay in South Africa. I can't do this. I have to do this one thing. If I don't, that's it, the dream is over."

It was the most selfish thing I've ever done and I knew it wasn't nice for her, seeing me choose running over her but she always

11

Black Dog

THE RUMOURS ABOUT MARIA AND ME AND THE split from Sarah took their toll on me to the point where now it was even more important for me to make sure it was all worth it. I didn't want to have made the sacrifices I made only to find myself in another spiral of injuries, disappointment and feeling like a failure. The pressure I put on myself as a result was immense. I guess when all your eggs are in one basket you have to make sure you make it work, otherwise it feels like it will all be for nothing. And when you're focused on a single goal, it's easy to forget all the great things in your life outside of that goal; you hang all your hopes of happiness on it.

Despite my best efforts, after just a few weeks back training in South Africa, the worst happened. Injury struck again. The pain in my leg came screaming back and the physio diagnosed me with something called iliotibial band friction syndrome, which was basically a long complicated name for muscle rubbing on the bone in my knee. If you can't imagine how painful that was, I can tell you it was like fire burning through my leg with every step I took. My injury curse was back and this time I was thousands of miles from home and my family, single again, and had only my competition for company.

The very last thing I wanted was for Maria to see the weakness in me, so I put a brave face on it and carried on. Training was agony and I had to stop every 20 minutes because the pain got so bad I thought I was going to pass out. I laughed bitterly at the fact the press thought I was off gallivanting in South Africa, having some love-in with Maria when, in reality, I was crumbling.

With every training session I had to finish early, as I watched Maria carry on and go from strength to strength, my mental health was spiralling. By the summer I was distraught. This time no amount of physios or chiropractors seemed to make any difference and I was getting desperate. I don't know if you've ever seen a dream slipping through your fingers, but that was what it felt like and I was in a constant state of anxiety.

Despite my worrying state I clung onto the schedule for dear life and when Margo and Maria went to Font-Romeu in the French Pyrenees to train for the 2003 World Championships in Paris, I went too.

We stayed in an apartment with Margo's husband Bobby outside the town centre but while Maria was able to take advantage of all the perfect training conditions I couldn't even get out on the track. I was stuck in the pool again, trying to get the strength back in my leg. The only time I went to the track was to cheer Maria on but inside I was dying. I felt like I'd lost everything and I didn't know where to turn.

One evening I went into the bathroom of the apartment we were all sharing in the little rented apartment and I stared at myself in the mirror. What had become of my life? I'd spent years, decades even, pouring all of my efforts into being Kelly Holmes, being someone.

In hindsight, I know my reasons for hanging my hopes so heavily on Olympic success weren't just about wanting to be a good athlete. It was about proving to myself and to the world that I was worthy, that I was good at something, that I was worth sticking around for. It was about giving myself an identity outside of the sexuality I'd been hiding all those years. It was about making sure I had a life and a career I could be proud of after years in an institution that had chipped away at my self-esteem. Winning was about so much more than a medal.

And now, standing in front of that mirror, I couldn't see a winner. I could see a broken person whose body was giving up on her.

I still don't know what made me do it but I found myself reaching for a pair of nail scissors that were in a glass on the side in the bathroom. I felt the cold metal of them against my skin as I touched them against my left arm and then, after running water from the taps, I pointed the tip against the inside of my bicep and pressed until I saw red. As the blood pooled on my skin, I felt an instant sense of relief.

The pain was nothing compared with the torture of training on my injured leg and if anything it was a distraction. It was like, for a second, all the thoughts swimming around my mind stopped and I had something else to focus on. I was a complete mess and I was having a breakdown. The only way I can describe it is that it was a way to feel something different, to snap me out of the desperate spiral of grief for my career.

To begin with, it was about the injuries and my fear that my athletics career could be over once and for all, so I started making another cut in my arm for every day I'd had to miss training. After that, every day that I couldn't train I would lock myself in the bathroom and do the same thing. Margo and Maria would be chatting and laughing away in the next room, oblivious to the fact I was falling apart behind that locked door. But what started as a breakdown over my physical form quickly opened the floodgates to a much bigger mental crisis.

All my fears and insecurities from the trauma I experienced as a child and in the army started to come to the surface. I found myself obsessing over what I would do if my athletics career came to an end. I couldn't go back to the army now. By then I'd got wind of the supposed changes to army culture following the lifting of the homosexuality ban, but I just didn't believe it was true.

All those same people who tried to sniff out gay men and women, who raided bunks and screamed homophobic slurs in my face were all still there. You couldn't tell me they'd suddenly changed their views on same-sex couples just because of a piece of paper from a court, it takes years for a culture like that to change. So what else was out there for me? Who was I really if I was no longer Sgt Holmes or Olympian Kelly?

My intrusive thoughts soon turned into a full-on identity crisis and up that mountain in France I had no one to turn to. Margo even started to try to keep me away from Maria as she could tell something was wrong and she didn't want my negativity running off on her.

I started to realise that I needed some professional help, because I didn't understand for the life of me what was leading me to hurt myself – weren't my injuries punishment enough? Yet the thought of telling anyone the real reasons behind my breakdown filled me with horror. Sure, I could tell them about the injuries, but how could I make them understand just why the stakes were so high for me without telling them the truth about my past and who I really was? Telling them the truth was out of the question. I knew only too well what the press did when they got hold of even a rumour about my sexuality, so what if I told a medical professional and they tipped them off that it was all true?

Instead I decided to try to deal with my feelings myself. I carried on cutting but did it in such a controlled way, I wouldn't be found out. The last thing I needed was for Margo or Maria to see that weakness as well as my injury so I cut on my arms and on my chest which would be covered by my running vest and t-shirts. I became expert in covering the wounds with little plasters and then, when they healed, pasting make-up over the scars to stop them being noticed.

Over the next couple of weeks, to my surprise, my leg started to get better and I was able to get out of the pool and start running again. There was no time for softly-softly. If I wanted to salvage anything of my last season before the Olympics I had to get stuck straight back in. I did three races in the space of a week in Zurich, Berlin and London and finished fourth, ninth and first. Not perfect but not the disaster it could have been, so when Maria and Margo moved to St Moritz for the last training stop before Paris, I went too.

While I was in St Moritz I went for a sports massage with a specialist and while I was there I plucked up the courage to ask if I could see a local doctor about another private matter. Sitting in the clinic in front of the female doctor, I told her I'd been struggling with my mood. I didn't go into all the details of why or just how low I'd become, because I knew she would assume it was simply linked to my injuries, and that was fine by me.

She told me it was common to have periods of depression when you undergo severe physical and mental stress and said she would ordinarily prescribe me with SSRIs or anti-depressants. But anti-doping was already such a hot topic in the athletics world and you had to be so careful what you put into your body so there was no way I was going to take anything that could be misconstrued and I didn't know if anti-depressants were performance-enhancing, plus I couldn't ask any of my team. Instead the lady recommended some herbal pills made from the cacao plant that she said could help without chemical intervention. It sounded stupid but I was so desperate I was ready to try anything and, as a self-confessed chocoholic, it made sense that it might work.

I'm not sure whether the pills actually helped as I only took two – still worried about what they were – or it was just my improved physical strength that gave me some hope back, but I was soon feeling on slightly steadier ground and decided to go for it in Paris. I just entered the 800m not the 1500m because, with my recent injuries, I thought it would give me a better chance.

Maria was in the same race and by some miracle while she took gold, I took the silver medal. Okay, I didn't beat her but training with Maria had clearly paid off and after the season I'd had I would take second to anyone! On the finish line I was totally overwhelmed with joy and relief and Maria and I hugged each other to congratulate one another. Big mistake.

Jealousy over our joint success and a hungry watching press devoured rumours from other athletes that not only were Maria and I in a relationship but that we'd rigged the race so that we would both get the two top spots. Of course it was total nonsense because there were six other people in the race that could run however they wanted, but this time the rumours hit even harder and I'm really sad to say it spelled the end of my friendship with Maria. She was really upset about the stories. She was a much bigger celebrity back in Mozambique than I was in the UK so she got a really tough time from the media back home.

It got to the point where it was awkward for us to even be seen training together. We just wanted the focus to be on our performances not our personal relationship so, with only one race left in the season, we decided to spend less time together.

The main point of this is not about Maria, it's to highlight that whilst I stood on the rostrum no one knew what was going on with my mental health. I didn't just win a silver medal, I won a psychological battle, no amount of press insinuations could deter from the fact that I had done something pretty remarkable that day. It showed me the power of my mind and that even though I was hurting on the inside, I was still winning.

We all have the power within us to get through the tough times and that's called resilience.

12

If I Ain't Got You

2004: THE YEAR OF THE OLYMPICS IN ATHENS AND my last chance to fulfil my dream. At almost 34, it was now or never. After my third season majorly affected by physical injury and a mental breakdown casting a shadow over the previous year, I could've gone into 2004 feeling pretty hopeless.

The pressures of speculation about my sexuality and accusations of cheating had weighed heavy on me as I recovered from the World Championships but something happened in January of that year that I can't explain.

Out of nowhere, through the shadows of depression, doubt and fear, came a sudden clear and total confidence like I've never known before: I wasn't only going to go to Athens in the summer, I was going to win gold. I can't describe where the feeling came from or why it hit me at that moment. If I was a religious person I might have called it divine intervention but it was such a clear feeling, it was almost a premonition. It wasn't visualisation like I'd practised before to try to get myself in the zone, it was real. I could almost sense that feeling I would have when I crossed the finish line and claimed Olympic glory for the first time.

I even wrote it in my diary to capture that feeling in case it went away. I wrote: 'I have dreamed forever to be the best at what I do. Some dreams have come true, but my biggest ones are still out there and I really want them to become reality. I have gone through a lot to realise my dreams. I have the passion, dedication, willpower and heart to achieve my ultimate goals. I have put my life and soul into this, given up my life to pursue what I know is my destiny. I just pray that for once I can be given the lift to get through this year with no struggles, no injuries and a lighted spirit of guidance. I hope 2004 can bring me more happiness, success, purpose than ever before.'

Now I know I'd had that feeling that it was going to be my year before, and it didn't always end the way I'd hoped, but this time it was last chance saloon. One final roll of the dice, and deep down I knew that all the years of training, physical and mental battles must count for something. Still in the back of my mind somewhere was this feeling that if I won Olympic gold, that would define who I was forever, no one could take it away. I naively thought that if I won, people wouldn't think about my sexuality or who I decided to be with, or try to delve into my mental health issues. I would just be Kelly Holmes, Olympic champion.

Back in Johannesburg, life was pretty lonely at the start of the year as Maria had distanced herself from me after all the rumours, and was now spending lots of time training away. Agnes was going back and forth to Namibia, so instead I decided to pack up and head back to my place in Potchefstroom where there was a community of athletes from all over the world training. I soon found myself in a better place.

In the first few months of that year, I was on fire! I won my 13th British title in the 800m at the indoor AAA meet in Sheffield as well as 1500m in Glasgow and Stockholm. Margo was buzzing every time I spoke to her on the phone or I sent her my times. I was in such good form. My mind seemed to be on an up-curve too and my self-harm was under control most of the time. I would have the odd bad day when things wouldn't go right or when I let myself think about the weight of my hidden sexuality but, for the most part, I was so focused on success I didn't allow myself to dwell on it.

I was reunited with Maria and Jeff in Birmingham where we were both running in a 1000m race ahead of the 1500m event in the World Championships in Budapest in March. I was on cloud nine when I not only won but broke the British and European records. But there was a dark cloud of controversy around the win as Maria had tripped over when she tried to overtake me, and this time there were rumours swirling that I'd tripped her.

Of course I hadn't and even the commentators said she tried to overtake me on the inside where there was clearly no space, but the accusations were hurtful. What was it with the press trying to make drama with our friendship all the time? One minute I was supposedly seeing her and then I was supposedly sabotaging her race. Margo told me to ignore it and let the dust settle, and stay focused on Budapest, so that's what I did, but it was a real insight into the impact rumours can have on your focus and mental health – something I was to learn much more of later that year.

The World Championships were even more dramatic. This time it was my turn to fall, in the 1500m. 500m from the end I decided to make my break for it and try to pass the rest of the field but I tripped and went hurtling to the ground, grazing all down my side and twisting my back. I got back to my feet and completed the race but came in a disappointing ninth position.

Maria and I saw one another for the first time since the tripping scandal as she was there running and I went to cheer her on. I didn't want there to be bad feelings between us so I cheered her round the track. I have to say that for all the nit-picking, in my eyes, she was undoubtedly the best 800m runner in the world, full stop – I was delighted when she took the title yet again. Still, I was gutted about my disaster. I flew home and went to spend a week or two in Kent before going back to South Africa. I just needed to see my friends and my family and they were great as ever, cheering me up and telling me how proud they were of me.

Training in the run-up to the Olympic trials was a lonely journey. I flew out to Oregon, USA, to see Margo. Maria was there too and although it was still slightly awkward, we just got on with training because that was all we were there to do. We all relocated to Madrid along with Jeff ahead of the trials because the climate would be similar to Athens, but it was a bleak time. I was running really erratically since my fall and I no longer had that camaraderie with Maria that made all the training more fun. I sat alone in my tiny bedroom at night, watching DVDs and wishing I was back home with my family and my dogs. Still, in the back of my mind I just kept telling myself: a couple more months and you'll have that medal around your neck.

Even though Dave and I had parted ways and I'd split from Sarah, they were both great during that time. I would text Dave my times and keep him up to date with my progress and message Sarah with funny anecdotes about not being able to speak Spanish and getting stuck trying to communicate in sign language. I felt really supported by them and began to feel more and more distant from Maria and Margo. Understandably, I felt like I was always second fiddle as Margo and Maria had been working together for 13 years. I was still the new girl by comparison. Plus, all the dramas had left a sour atmosphere.

Then came another issue. I was not training with the team anymore but the way I was running, I decided I might want to get selected for both the 1500m and the 800m at the Olympics as I didn't want to ruin my chances of winning a gold by putting all my eggs in one basket. I'd been running great times over the shorter distance, going on to win the 800m at the Olympic trials in Manchester. UK Athletics selected me for both the 800m and the 1500m for Athens as they knew the 1500m was my main focus and I was still number one in Great Britain for that distance.

The problem was that Maria did the 800m as that was her event and she was defending Olympic champion. Margo said she couldn't be in both our Olympic teams if we were going to compete against one another. She told me if I decided to run the 800m, she could not be my coach at the Games.

However, I had already decided that for my mental health, my mindset and for support, I would go with Team GB to the holding camp in Cyprus, where we would do two final weeks of training ahead of the Games. That decision was instrumental in my preparation. I didn't have to make my final decision about which distance I was going for until the last minute so I decided to just focus on my training.

Margo gave me a training schedule which I stuck to religiously and I loved being in Cyprus with the rest of the team. It started to really feel like we were in it together, representing our country, and we wanted to go home with as many medals as possible.

I shared a lovely villa in a new golf resort in Aphrodite Hills with Liz Yelling, a marathon runner, and it was idyllic. The atmosphere in the team was amazing, so relaxed but focused. My team, physio Alison Rose, training partner Tony Whitman and Performance Director Zara Hyde Peters were fantastic and, for the first time, I felt this amazing sense of calm.

Of course it didn't all go without a hitch because I wouldn't be Kelly without a bit of drama. I got bitten by a millipede that I found in my bed – yes, bed! – about a week in and ended up in hospital from the poison. But thankfully the pain passed and didn't affect my running. Insects aside, it was all going to plan.

* * * * *

I'm not a religious person but I've always been a big believer that things happen for a reason and that the universe gives us signs to guide us on our way. I think it all started when I met Lisa in Sainsbury's that day – what were the chances of us bumping into each other like that at that specific time after living down the road all those years? I later realised it had been predicted by a Tarot card reader I'd been to see months before, who told me I was going to meet someone who'd been looking for me. Since then, I have always believed in fate.

The week before I was due to move from Cyprus to Athens for the biggest races of my career, I got two of those signs that have stayed with me until this day. The first was all about my hair. Ever since that summer when I was a kid and Mum took me to the salon to get my massive afro tamed with disastrous results, my hair has been the bane of my life.

My only option back then if I was going to be able to train and run without it getting in the way was to have braids to keep it out of my face. When I went to Cyprus for the Olympics training camp, I decided I would get my braids re-done just before the Games so they would be fresh and tight, ready for my big performance. I guess it was superstition really, but I just wanted everything to be perfect.

Most of the runners up in the mountain villas were in the endurance team but a few sprinters managed to gatecrash our little paradise including Linford Christie, Olympic champion in 1992, Darren Campbell (who went on to win gold in the 4x100m relay in Athens) and Daniel Plummer, his training partner. Daniel told me he could do my hair.

"Honestly, I do my sister's hair back home, it's no problem," he assured me. So I took his word it would all be fine. We agreed he would do it that night.

Later that day, a big group of us went down to the beach after our last big training sessions, for some natural cold therapy (years before it was trendy!). We started messing around and skimming stones when a British woman who was clearly on holiday with her family came over to me and introduced herself as Patricia.

"I never usually do this but just in case you ever need your hair doing, I'm a hairdresser back home in Wembley so you should get in touch."

She left but then came running back down the beach to me and slipped a business card into my hand with her name and phone number on it. What a weird coincidence! I took her card and thought at the time, 'that'll come in handy one day', but I didn't know it would be so soon.

Back at camp that night I sat on a chair with Daniel behind me, afro in full glory, as he tried desperately to part my crazy mane to plait it into braids. The problem was he didn't even have a proper comb and a pen lid wasn't cutting it. Long story short, it was a disaster.

I told him not to worry as I remembered Patricia's card. Could I call her in the middle of her nice relaxing holiday and ask for her help? I was desperate and she had offered. Plus, if I won, I guess she could tell people she was a hairdresser to an Olympic champion! I called her a couple of times before she answered and then when she did, I felt sheepish.

"I'm really sorry but I'm in a bit of a mess and I could really do with your help," I told her.

Patricia turned out to be one of the nicest people I've ever met and I'm convinced she was put on the beach that day just for me. She came over the next day with her daughter Stacia and calmed me down completely, and then did the most amazing job braiding my hair. I felt mentally and physically ready to take on the world, like you do when you have a new hairdo. More importantly, it would be one less thing to think or worry about.

I told her she was a life-saver and I would be back in touch when I got home after the Games. I think she probably thought I was just saying that, but I wasn't. When I finally got back I looked her up and she ended up doing my hair for years and becoming a great friend.

The other sign that week came in the form of one of my absolute idols. Ever since I was a teenager I've absolutely loved Tina Turner. I loved her music, of course, that amazing raspy voice and the don't-give-a-shit attitude, but I also loved everything she stood for.

To me she was the ultimate survivor, after a really tough life and an abusive marriage to being a global superstar, she was so powerful and resilient. In her later years when she moved to Switzerland to be with her new husband she became spiritual, practising Buddhism, yoga and meditation, something that's brought me so much peace in the past few years too.

In Cyprus I was in the back of the car on the way to the track for my last session with Tony and Zara. The countdown was on and I knew I only had 24 hours to make my decision about whether or not I was going to enter the 800m, the 1500m or both, so my mind was racing. I'd been running great 800m times but did I want to lose Margo from my team at the last minute?

Cypriot songs were playing on the radio as I tried to mentally prepare and I was beginning to feel so anxious when I literally said: "I could really do with listening to Tina Turner *The Best* right now". Literally as I spoke, the song came on! I heard that unmistakable: "*Dun... dun, dun... dun...*" come from the speakers. Unbelievable. It was the intro to *The Best* – Tina had come to help me! Tony cranked up the volume and I sang along to the lyrics at the top of my voice.

Give me a lifetime of promises and a world of dreams,
Speak a language of love like you know what it means,
It can't be wrong,
Take my heart and make it strong, baby.
You're simply the best,
Better than all the rest,
Better than anyone,
Anyone I've ever met.

I defy anyone to listen to that track and not feel a massive confidence boost. I know it was meant to be a romantic song but I think, like me, people associate it with strength and achievement. It meant so many things to me too. It was like she was singing to me, telling me I could do whatever I set my heart on and that I was strong enough to do whatever felt right. Everything was going to be okay.

I was so fired up I had the best training session and ran some of my fastest times ever, I felt like I was floating on air. By the end of the day I'd made my decision. I knew I had a chance of a medal in the 800m, so I made the biggest decision of my life – to double up! I texted Dave my times from that day. He had now become a mentor and still my greatest supporter and he messaged back: 'You have to go for it'.

When I called Margo I was nervous about what she was going to say but I'd never been more clear I was making the decision that was right for me. I was pleasantly surprised when Margo said I had to do whatever I thought was best for me and that even though she couldn't be on my team, she would support me in whatever I decided to do. She told me to follow my heart, and that's what I did. Later that night I wrote a press release revealing my intention to run in both the 800m and the 1500m. In for a penny, in for a pound as they say.

I still think it was fate I heard Tina that day and she's remained an idol of mine and a huge inspiration throughout my life. For my 53rd birthday (which I called 39+14 of course!) I went to see the West End show for the second time, with some of my new friends. I absolutely love it. Everyone was up in the stalls singing and dancing along to *Proud Mary* and there was a huge standing ovation at the end. It really showed how loved Tina was and how much she meant to so many people.

When her death was reported earlier this year in 2023, I was really sad but also happy for her that she died peacefully in a place she loved, after living a quiet life of meditation by the lake and in a relationship with the person she loved, out of the way of the prying eyes and judgement of the media or anyone else who had tried to hurt her in the past. I think that's a decent way to end your days on this planet. I have since seen the show for a third time, there was something even more powerful about it after Tina's passing and the fact that I have become friends with Elesha, who currently plays her in the musical, seems another twist of fate!

* * * * *

Being a woman who has spent her entire life trying not to attract too much attention or give anyone reason to probe into her private life, the last thing I needed when I was about to run the most important races of my life was to be at the centre of a media storm. So, when we arrived at the Olympic Village outside Athens ahead of the Games, I was relieved that the descending British press already had one golden girl on their minds – Paula Radcliffe.

Paula was an amazing 10,000m athlete and one of our greatest Marathon runners. I had known her for years, we got on really well and she was touted as Team GB's big hope for gold medals in the endurance races in Athens. Her form was great and she had a consistent record whereas I had a reputation for getting injured or suffering terrible luck just when it mattered. I think everyone knew me as a reliable medallist having won 11 major medals already, but some people were nervous that it wouldn't be third time lucky for me at the Olympics as I'd hoped.

Thankfully for me, because of all the hype around Paula I was able to escape most of the attention and focus on settling into my accommodation. The room was small but comfortable and I pinned up all the good luck cards and notes from my friends and family on the wardrobe. They weren't going to be there to see me race as it was too expensive to travel but I knew they would be thinking of me and again I didn't want the distraction of them being there while I was getting in the zone.

I did one interview with the BBC about why I'd decided to do the 800m as well as the 1500m at the last minute, but I only spoke in broad terms about my ambitions. I didn't want to give too much away about my form in case I jinxed it and I didn't ever talk to the press about my personal life in case they thought that gave them free rein to delve into it and find something I didn't want them to find.

An Olympic village is like something you never experience unless you make an Olympic team and it's an amazing atmosphere. Nations from all over the world come together, sharing the massive food halls, gyms and social spaces, wearing their national team kit and flying their flags with pride. The night before my first heat I laid my kit out on the chair, something that became a ritual throughout my career, and went to sleep early with my headphones in, listening to Alicia Keys, *If I Ain't Got You*, which became my anthem for the Games.

Some people want it all,
But I don't want nothing at all,
If it ain't you, baby,
If I ain't got you, baby,
Some people want diamond rings,
Some just want everything,
But everything means nothing,
If I ain't got you, yeah!

I set off to the stadium early the next morning armed with energy drinks, a ham and cheese roll and my lucky charm, a silver dog tag engraved with the British flag. I kissed it before every race and always made sure to look for the British flag in the stadium the second I emerged from the tunnel onto the track. It was a reminder of the pride and honour I felt in representing my country on the biggest sporting stage in the world. It was a similar feeling to the pride of serving the Crown and my country during my army years and it meant a huge amount to me and still does now.

I cruised through my first heat and won without too much trouble. The semi-final went according to plan too, so I just had to keep my cool on my rest day before the final. During that time we had triumph and disaster in the camp. Hepthathlete Kelly Sotherton came home with a bronze in her first ever Olympics and was elated. I was so pleased for her.

We stayed up talking until 2am because I couldn't sleep, and she was coming down from the huge adrenaline rush. I knew exactly how that felt after my bronze in Sydney. But I also knew what Paula was feeling when she had to pull up in the marathon because of an injury, in what should have been the biggest race of her life. The same happened later in the 10,000m. It was heartbreaking to watch her as she came off the track. I prayed that it wouldn't happen to me again this year.

The night before the final I had another 'sign'. As I was listening to Alicia again on my bed, a massive gust of wind swirled around my neck and I found myself jumping up shouting, "I'm going to do it!". It was the most bizarre moment.

On the day of the 800m final, I was surprisingly calm. When I reached the warm-up track, Margo came over, winked at me and said "good luck", patting me on the back. Maria ran past and touched my hand on the start line and said the same thing. I knew that it was each woman for herself, there were no hard feelings there. Then my mind cleared completely as I lined up in lane three of the track. The gun sounded and, just like in training, I executed each of my tactics; no trips, no falls, no sudden bursts of pain – it was all going just as it should. Ten metres before the end of the track, as I was neck and neck with Maria, I told myself to relax, dropped my shoulders and, in a split second, I was crossing the finish line.

FIRST! Surely not? That couldn't have happened.

I looked up at the big screen and saw the replay, and it was true. I was first, I'd won gold. I was totally overwhelmed.

The iconic picture that everyone remembers of me crossing the finish line – where my eyes are popping out of my head in utter disbelief – still has people cheering when I do my public speaking, and I still well up at the memory. I was on top of the world.

Then, time passes in a blur of press conferences and photographers and doping control before you finally stand on the rostrum and accept your medal. I remember thinking that nothing has ever compared to this; remember this moment, as the Union Jack was raised and *God Save The Queen* rang out around the stadium.

Back at the Village, I would have loved to celebrate but the 1500m heats started the next day so I didn't have much time to recover. The weird feeling was that despite winning gold in the 800m, it was the 1500m that I had dreamed of winning since I was 14. But my family had other ideas… Back home, Mum, Dad, Kevin, Stuart, Lisa, Penny, Danny, along with all my mates (and as I later found out nearly the whole of Great Britain) were partying the night away over my win. They couldn't believe it and kept on calling me to tell me how proud they were of me – each time getting louder and more animated. Although it was lovely to hear them so happy and proud of me, I had to tell them to go and to let me sleep. I had another race to get ready for. I put my medal under the pillow and drifted off.

At the stadium the next day, everyone wanted to talk to me and congratulate me, the press interest was insane. There were photographers and reporters everywhere asking for interviews but I stuck to my usual plan of keeping my head down, only giving one short BBC interview about my win.

Little did I know, the press were going crazy about that. I was their new focus. The team kept it all away from me, but I found out later that I was on the back and middle pages of most of the newspapers and even on the front of some too. I was the new golden girl and now I'd won one, they were rooting for me to bring home another. I'm really glad I didn't know just how mad things were back home because it would have been a huge distraction.

Back at the track that night, I followed exactly the same warm-up routine as I had for the 800m and just tried to remain calm and focused. This time Margo was able to talk to me properly because Maria wasn't running in the 1500m, but she didn't have any changes to my tactics and so I decided to go out there and do what I'd waited a lifetime to do.

Once again, I got through my heat without too much trouble, although I wasn't as fresh as I'd been for the 800m. Sally Gunnell – our 1992 Olympic champion – became part of my post-race ritual. Whether she was interviewing me or not, she was there as I crossed the line to hand me the cashew nuts I'd given her at the beginning of the competition. In the semi the next day, I felt confident and Margo had told me to just do what I needed to get through but not show the opposition my full hand, so I ran a steady race then towards the end hung back and finished second.

There was one more rest day before the final and that was the toughest one. It was a mental challenge to try to psych myself up as if it was my first race of the Games and I hadn't already won a medal. I wanted to feel the same sense of 'now or never' I would be feeling as if I was going for gold for the first time. So I hid my medal and tried to pretend it didn't exist.

On the day of the final, as I lined up for what I knew would probably be my last ever Olympic race, it felt completely different. This time British fans were shouting my name and cheering me as my name was called. Rather than just announcing me as Kelly Holmes, this time the tannoy boomed, "800m Olympic champion Kelly Holmes". I had to block it all out and just concentrate on the race in hand. This was my race, and the gold was the one I'd come to Athens for in the first place.

When the starting gun sounded, it was as though no one else was in the stadium except me and the other runners. I hung back to begin with just as I'd planned and had executed in every other race. On the final lap, another bizarre experience happened. On the back straight with about 250m to go, I felt as though something was lifting me up by my shoulders as I passed other runners in the field. I was floating as though I had wings. I could feel my legs moving but I couldn't feel my feet pounding the track, it was like I was running on air. I was exhausted but the adrenaline was pumping through my veins. About 120m from the finish line, I knew I needed to make a break. I remember looking around to see where the danger may be coming from then, about 50m from the end, I can't even describe it but it felt like something swept me up and lifted me right over the finish line. I was in first place again.

Suddenly reality dawned and I crumbled to my knees, exhausted as the roar of the crowd filled my ears. I had tears in my eyes as the delirium faded and I realised I'd fulfilled my entire life's dream not once but twice. I thought nothing could match the feeling of winning one gold but I can tell you now – doing the double was something else.

The same blur followed, my victory lap, flashing camera bulbs and screaming fans followed by an interview with Sally where I can't even remember what I said. Then it was back to the rostrum for the second time and as I bowed my neck for my hero, Lord Seb Coe to place the medal around my neck, I felt invincible.

Back at the village that night I wanted to go out and celebrate with the rest of the British team, so a few of us tried to get a taxi into town. But it was before the days of Uber and we had no local taxi numbers so after spending some time sitting on a kerb waiting, we gave up and went back into the village to the 24-hour canteen with rower Matthew Pinsent, who was also celebrating his gold medal, and we raided the freezer for ice creams. Not how I envisaged the best night of my life, but it felt incredible.

What I didn't know was that the double gold had truly cemented me in the history books as being the first woman in Great Britain to win two gold medals at the same Olympic Games.

13

National Treasure

AFTER A WHIRLWIND OF EMOTIONS AND TWO historic victories at the Olympics, coming home to Great Britain was a moment I'd waited for all my life. I was returning glorious, with not one but two gold medals around my neck – it was a total dream come true for me, but I never really stopped to think about what it would mean.

I knew there was a buzz about how well I'd done because Mum told me on the phone that I was on the front page of all the national newspapers after my second win. I still have those papers to this day, with that picture of me crossing the finishing line and the one of me draped in a British flag. A couple of them are framed on the wall in my little memorabilia room at the top of my house because they made me proud, of course, but also because they reminded me of what I'd done – I still couldn't believe it!

What I didn't realise was that my wins also made me public property.

As the plane touched down on British soil, I could already feel the anticipation building. Being a medal winner, British Airways had put me and the other Team GB medallists in Business Class, which is always a great perk; I will never turn that one down!

As we landed on the runway, I was asked to lead the team off the plane and as the doors opened we could see a huge crowd of press, officials and BA staff awaiting us. After taking a photo on the steps, we made our way to the arrivals. All the medallists were escorted to a press conference before being reunited with loved ones. But I was not expecting what followed.

Having competed in two previous Olympic Games before, I knew the reception that normally awaits the British teams as we arrive back to the UK. It doesn't matter what sport you compete in or if you medalled or not, the families, friends and fans of the athletes always come out to greet and congratulate you. But the reception that awaited this time was beyond anything I could have imagined.

The hall was packed! People screaming with excitement, cheering fans waving flags and holding banners adorned with messages of congratulations and the press hustling for photos as my mum came over to hug me, crying with pride. As I was reunited with my family it started to dawn on me just how big my wins had been over here.

My dad, Kevin, Stuart, Penny, Lisa and Danny were all there to greet me, it was incredibly overwhelming. There was this big limo waiting to take us all back to Hildenborough, a journey that was a blur of excitement and emotion. What I didn't know was that my wider family and friends had organised a surprise party for me at a local pub called the Hilden Manor where Neil the owner, Claire and Emma my sister-in-law were helping get it all ready. As I walked through the door, the roar of excitement and celebration hit me.

By now I was so exhausted, but the adrenaline of it all carried me through. It was so lovely to share this incredible moment with so many people I loved. The sense of pride and joy was palpable, and I couldn't help but be moved by the genuine warmth and affection shown by everyone, they were so proud of me.

Returning to Mum's house was crazy. She had put red, white and blue flags up outside the house and I saw tents on the grass in front of a hedge. When we got inside and sat down, she drew the curtains.

"What you doing?" I asked.

"It's the paparazzi," she told me. "They're in those tents opposite, they've been there all week waiting for you to come home."

It just felt so strange. It's one thing having my photo taken by a mob of photographers inside the stadium in Athens after my wins, then at the airport with the team, but how did they find out where my mum lived? And why were they there? What were they looking out for? I just didn't get it or the media intrusion as I had never had it before, it felt uneasy.

It made me start to think about the pictures that had gone around the world of me crossing the finish line and standing on the rostrum. Now the entire world knew who I was – or they thought they did. Already in the midst of all the celebrations I had a nervous feeling. The Kelly Holmes who had become a sporting legend and had been beamed around the world into people's living rooms on their TV screens, was still just Kelly from a small village in Kent, a retired soldier who'd made history by going on to win two gold medals.

The real Kelly, who had been hounded and raided in the army over rumours of her sexuality and who was terrified of coming out, was someone completely different. The only thing they would find out about my personal life if they looked back in the newspapers would be a relationship with a man – Jason – which was actually just a friendship. It makes me unhappy to think that's what was going through my mind back then, but at the time I couldn't let those demons ruin what I knew should be the best week of my life so I brushed them to the back of my mind.

The highlight of my homecoming was definitely the parade organised in my honour by Tonbridge and Malling Borough Council a couple of days later. A huge yellow open-top bus was arranged to pick me up outside the scout hut on Riding Lane in Hildenborough, just round the corner from Mum's house, ready to drive me to Tonbridge on a parade route. All my family came on the bus with me as well as Dave, Miss Page, my PE Teacher and, of course, Kerrie. The local newspaper sent a reporter and a photographer. I wore my medals and had a Union flag draped around me as we set off. The atmosphere was incredible.

We'd been told to expect about 40,000 people but it ended up being double that, can you imagine? Unbelievable. Travelling through the streets I used to pedal through on my bike, now I was on top of the bus, being greeted by a sea of smiling faces, waving flags, and cheering at the top of their lungs and chanting my name.

The energy and enthusiasm were infectious, and I couldn't help but be swept up in the sheer joy of the moment. The streets were lined with people of all ages, eagerly awaiting my arrival. Some of them knew me all my life and others were just proud and excited that someone from our little corner of the world had achieved something so amazing. The cheers and applause echoed through the air, creating an atmosphere of celebration and pride. It was a moment that I will always cherish, as I realised the impact my achievements had on the whole nation and especially my home town.

As I waved to the crowd, I couldn't help but reflect on the journey that had led me to this point. The countless hours of training, the sacrifices made, and the unwavering support of my family, friends, and coaches had all culminated in this incredible moment.

It was a testament to the power of perseverance, determination, and the unwavering self-belief. Throughout the parade, I made sure to take in every moment, to lock eyes with the fans who had stood by me throughout my career. Their support had been the driving force behind my success, and I wanted to express my gratitude personally. The smiles, tears, and heartfelt messages of congratulations from the crowd filled my heart.

But the niggling feeling in the back of my mind came back when the press photographer kept snapping me on top of the bus, taking thousands of pictures which I knew would be all over the papers the next day. What if one of the 80,000 people in the crowd or someone looking at the picture in the papers the next day recognised me from one of my rare trips to a gay bar in Slough in my Aldershot heyday, or knew someone who'd had a fling with me in the army? People could make a lot of money selling stories about me to the newspapers and then everyone would know my big secret.

As I looked out into the crowds, I felt myself start to shake with the same fear I'd felt back at Beaconsfield as I waited for the RMP to raid my bunk, terrified they'd find evidence of me being

KELLY HOLMES

gay. I grabbed the camera from the photographer and said I thought I should take some photos, just so the attention was off me for a second. But of course it wasn't, was it!

The homecoming celebrations continued long into the night. The speeches, the laughter, and people sharing stories of inspiration were a reminder of the impact my achievements had on others. Everyone was desperate for an interview with someone close to me, especially as there wasn't much known about me and that's how I wanted it to stay. Thankfully my family and friends never dreamt of speaking to the press behind my back, and, in fact, the only person who did sell a story didn't know I was gay because he hadn't seen me for nearly two decades – 'sperm donor' Derrick. Clearly the money offers were too enticing for him and he gave an interview telling the newspaper that he taught me everything I knew, posing for a photo with a pair of trainers around his neck.

However, I couldn't shake the feeling that I felt more exposed now I was back on home ground. Would anyone want to destroy me and try to out me? In the LGBT community, as it was known then, the worst thing you could do was out someone, and the worst thing that could happen to you was to be outed!

What you have to remember is that society can be so cruel, people's opinions about the way you live your life can be damaging to your soul. Many people from all walks of life have been vilified for just being themselves. They have been hounded, bullied, mistreated and targeted to the point that some sadly have taken their own lives, all because they live life in a way that doesn't suit others' preconception of what 'normal' is. It's normal for me to be attracted to women. I can't help how I feel or what I am. But the fear of being outed, and with my irrational fear of being potentially reprimanded by the military in some way, was enough to always dampen my spirits even while I was on top of the world.

It was the start of a spiral of self-doubt and fear that stayed with me for the next 18 years.

* * * * *

One thing us Brits do well is national pride. In the weeks after I returned home from Athens, the phone didn't stop ringing with people inviting me to showbiz parties, media appearances and awards ceremonies. I was hot property and everyone wanted a piece of the woman who had won two Olympic gold medals after 20 years of trying; the first British woman to win two individual gold medals at the same Games. Only achieved by one other person, Albert Hill, in 1920. I think, as a nation, we also love an underdog so to see me live my dream after so many injuries and setbacks was the perfect fairytale ending that everyone loved – especially the press.

For me, though, it felt totally overwhelming. I had been in the press before and had an element of media attention when they twisted my friendship with Maria and on another occasion after they thought I had accused an athlete, Yolanda Cheplak, of cheating back in 2002 (that wasn't true), but now the interest was on a whole new level. Plus, so far they'd never actually got hold of any real information about my past or my private life and I wanted to keep it that way.

I started turning down a lot of the engagements I was offered, although there were some I just couldn't miss because I knew they would be once-in-a-lifetime experiences. The first week I was back, the call came from the Michael Parkinson Show, asking me to be a guest that Friday night. Parky was huge back then and I remember watching all the big Hollywood stars when

I was growing up. I couldn't turn that down. What if someone amazing was on with me and I missed it? I said yes, but there was one problem. All of my clothes were back in South Africa and all I'd brought with me to Athens was one pair of jeans, a pair of combat trousers and a load of sports gear. I told the producer I had nothing to wear and she asked me what kind of thing I would like, saying that the wardrobe department would be able to sort me out. I told her I wanted something black and preferably not a dress.

Sure enough, when I arrived to have my make-up done at the TV studios, they had an outfit for me. Black bootcut trousers, a sleeveless black fitted top and black boots. With my hair still in Patricia's cornrows – I had no idea what to do with it with two medals around my neck – I waited nervously backstage. I was the last on and the other two guests were Billy Connolly and Tom Cruise! I couldn't believe I was going to be sharing a stage with such showbiz royalty. When Michael introduced me, I took a deep breath.

"Kelly Holmes is only the third woman in Olympic history to win a double gold medal," he announced. "She's a national treasure and a hero. Ladies and gentlemen, our very own Kelly Holmes!"

Then, to my total surprise as I walked out under the lights, the entire audience was up on their feet giving me a standing ovation, even bigger than the superstars got. Even Tom Cruise was up on his feet and clapping and he greeted me with a big kiss on either cheek before I sat down.

The first thing Parky said to me was: "You must be living the dream." I replied that I was and it was just surreal and over-whelming but, in the back of my mind, I was wondering what else he was going to ask. Looking back at that footage, I look like a rabbit caught in headlights. I'm all in black, speaking quietly and politely and I just don't look 'free'.

The thing that makes me sad is that I said in response to one question about the press attention: "I'm expecting people to come out of the woodwork who don't even know me." I tried to make a joke out of it and deflect the attention by adding "… but Tom knows a lot about that!" which made people laugh. But deep down I think I was maybe giving a warning to anyone who was considering calling the press about my relationships in the army and telling them I was ready to deny anything they tried to say about my sexuality. I wish I'd just been able to enjoy the moment and soak up the atmosphere but clearly those fears were already starting to dominate.

What does make me laugh is that towards the end of the interview, Parky made some comment about me and Tom flirting and asked if he and Bill should leave the two of us to it. If only he'd known. I was probably one of the few women in the room who wasn't swooning over him. Tom was a really lovely man, though, and when I got home I got the shock of my life because he'd called and left a message with Mum asking me to go with him to the premiere of his new film *Collateral* in Leicester Square the following week. I was totally flattered but I turned it down. Yes, I TURNED IT DOWN. Oh my God, how bloody stupid?!

In my defence, not only did I have nothing to wear on a red carpet but I thought if I started rumours about me and anyone in the public eye it would be even more carte blanche for the press to go digging around in my past relationships. Plus, big showbiz events and parties were definitely not my thing.

I never went out socialising. I was happy having a Chinese from the local takeaway with Mum and catching up on the

English telly I'd missed during the five months I'd been away training. But it did make me laugh a month later though when I found out there had been an article in *Sports Illustrated* in the US saying I was dating Tom. What a surreal experience.

The rest of the year flew by in a blur of media appearances and training as I still had to finish my season. In between races I was on a string of TV shows, even filming a guest appearance in the *EastEnders* Christmas special. Then there was GMTV, Des & Mel, and another cameo in *The Kumars at No. 42*. I liked doing the funny ones more than the serious interviews because I was less likely to get asked any awkward questions.

Even after winning two gold medals, I still had more races to run. I officially became world number one in the 1500m at the World Athletics Final in Monaco and the last race of the season was the Newcastle Road Mile, the shorter race held the day before the Great North Run. I was delighted when I broke the course record – what a way to end an amazing season.

In October, the official Olympic Parade through London took place and once again there was a sea of people. This time, the whole of Team GB including the Paralympians were there, so the attention wasn't focused just on me and I was a little more relaxed. The media interest didn't seem to be dying down, though. And with the interest of course came some people out of the woodwork, just like I knew they would.

Most of them I had known briefly in my past, who were wanting to wish me well on my success and new-found popularity. Others were more sinister, with threats to reveal details about my past or my private life. I just ignored them. I wasn't about to allow myself to be blackmailed so I had to just keep calm and try to carry on. That period of my life definitely reminded me of how lucky I was to have the tight-knit group of friends and family that knew me and loved me as I was. They were the ones who kept me sane. Kerrie, Lara and Kim as well as my siblings and Sarah and her family were all really support-ive and kept my feet on the ground, being there for me when I needed someone to calm me down and deflect from all the stress of my new-found fame and the anxiety harbouring the truth about my personal life.

One of the best things to happen that year after my wins was when I was announced as the BBC Sports Personality Of The Year. The award was such a prestigious accolade and one that I'd seen lots of great names win in the past so to even be nominated was incredible. Ahead of the awards ceremony I had no idea who had won because it was a public vote announced on the night. Somehow it meant so much more that it was voted for by the British public because the people-pleaser in me that craved acceptance wanted nothing more than to know I was loved by the people I'd been representing in the Olympics.

I was never really a dress person, hence my outfit on Parky, but for this event, fashion designer Scott Henshall offered to make me a bespoke number for the occasion so I accepted. I was nervous at first when I saw the designs because it was short and had big cut-out sections around my midriff, which was far more revealing than anything I would usually wear. At least it was black – my comfort colour!

When Scott arrived at the hotel and I put it on, I loved it. Getting ready for the evening was a mammoth task with a full-on glam squad in my hotel room, it was like nothing I'd experienced before. You don't get dressed up much in the army or on the track! I called Patricia and asked her to come over from Wembley to do my hair. This time, she took out the braids and straightened it into a flicky bob, and a man from the jewellery shop Boodles showed up with diamonds for me to wear. I was never the kind of little girl who dreamt of being a princess, but if I had been, it would have been a dream come true.

On the night of the ceremony, I was so nervous as we awaited the results. Mum, Dad, Kevin and Stuart were all there to support me but they had to sit separately in the audience, while I was next to Steve Cram and Natasha Kaplinsky. They showed a little video about each of the contenders for the award and mine had a string of former British female Olympic gold medallists in it, all sending their messages of luck and support. There was Ann Packer, who won the 800m, Dame Mary Peters, who took the title for the heptathlon and Sally Gunnell, the 400m hurdles champion who I knew so well.

Hearing them all speak about me was so emotional. They were my heroes and they were saying how incredible my achievements were. I wondered whether there would be some young girls sitting at home watching and thinking one day they could join that line-up of incredible sporting women, just like I had.

When they finally announced I'd won I was so choked up I could hardly speak. It meant the world to me to be loved and accepted by the British public. I had my medals, and their approval, and all my family in the audience to enjoy the moment. That was one moment of pure joy in the spotlight that nothing could ruin for me. My life's dreams were complete.

14

Holmes Truths

WHEN I WAS A CHILD, I NEVER GOT TO SPEND MUCH time on my own with Mum. Even though it was just us two for the first four years of my life, being in and out of care and moving around meant I never really had those memories of it being just us at home together. When I moved out to live with Kerrie and her family as a teenager, I'd gone straight from there to basic training, so moving back in with her after Athens was really weird but lovely.

Getting to know your parents as adults can be a strange experience because you appreciate things in them that you never really saw when you were a child or the roles are reversed and you become the parent.

Mum was really loving and caring because she was so proud of me, but she was also so, so nosy. That was one of the things that always made me laugh about her. She couldn't go to the shops or the doctor's surgery or walk the dog without coming back with a story about who was divorcing who or who was moving house or which shops were shutting down. I loved being back in our little village in Kent where everyone knew each other and hearing all her gossip but since the press attention around my wins, the one thing that was tricky was how exposed Mum's house was.

I never quite got over the paps in the bushes and camping in the tents outside when I returned from Athens and we were still getting reporters knocking on the door or waiting for me when I went out for a run, so I knew I needed to get somewhere with a bit more privacy.

"You'll never guess who's splitting up," Mum said when she got back from one of her trips one day. I laughed and rolled my eyes but she told me it was a woman who lived with her husband in a lovely big house at the other end of Hildenborough.

"It'd be perfect for you, Kel," she said. "You should ask her if you can go and have a look."

"I can't do that. It's not even on the market she'll think I'm mad," I said.

But when Mum had an idea in her head she wasn't one to let it go, so off she went to knock on the door herself. I was mortified when she came back to tell me all about it. Mum told the lady she thought I would be interested in putting in an offer and she was delighted, so I went round to see it myself. It had a long private drive and was surrounded by lots of land. It was far more private than Mount Pleasant. The decor inside wasn't exactly to my taste but I could renovate it. And it was close to Mum. I had Dad just up the road too, and the rest of my family all still lived a stone's throw away in Kent.

I put in an offer and it was accepted, so that was that. I was on the move. I couldn't quite believe that, as a kid from a council estate, I now had my own huge place with plenty of land, out-buildings, five bedrooms, a cinema and a massive barn I planned to turn into my gym.

I was looking forward to having a permanent home in England because I wasn't going to need my place in Potchefstroom any longer now I didn't need to train there. I would go back over for holidays, buying an apartment in Stellenbosch, but I'd spent the last 16 years living away a lot either in different barracks or abroad and living out of a suitcase, so I was ready for some home time.

Then one day, fate intervened again. I was out on one of my runs when I passed some farmland. There were three little woolly heads poking out through the fence of one of the fields. I stopped to look at the funny little creatures, not much bigger than lambs but with long necks and curly afros like me when I was a kid. The farmer was in the field with them and I asked what they were.

"They're alpacas," he told me. "Not to be confused with llamas!"

"What do they do?" I asked.

"Well, they run around, eat grass and hedges, that's about it," he replied.

"Will they graze down the field at the back of my house?" I asked, having a brainwave.

He told me that if I wanted to have them I would have to get a few because they're pack animals, but he agreed that they should keep my grass down throughout the year. Plus, they were really cute and I'd already fallen a little bit in love. I agreed to buy two to begin with and they came to live in the field.

At first, it didn't seem like the plan would work. After a few weeks, they were so shy that they just stayed in one little corner of the paddock, eating grass in a little circle. So much for my plans of them keeping the lawn down. So I decided to get another four. Needless to say they didn't become the miracle gardening team I'd hoped for but they did quickly become a big part of my life. I love going out first thing in the morning to feed and talk to them, and giving them a shower with the hosepipe.

One cool thing about being a successful athlete is that you get free stuff. It's usually trainers or sports brands offering to sponsor your running gear. But the coolest thing I was offered came in the same year I got The Boys (as I christened them). A local garden centre wanted to gift me a ride-on mower, just like the one at the big house Mum cleaned when I was a kid. I couldn't believe it and I jumped at the chance. It's funny how things turn out.

When I wrote my first autobiography *Black, White and Gold*, Mum didn't like answering my questions about her past and I didn't like answering hers about my future. She was so desperate for me to be happy. She'd been devastated when she read about my breakdown in France before the Paris championships. She knew I was suffering from injuries but she had no idea just how bad my mental state had become and I think somehow she blamed herself for not knowing, or for not being there.

That's one of the big issues with the stigma surrounding mental health problems like depression and anxiety. Society still looks for someone to blame rather than treating it like a physical illness that has a root cause that needs treating. You wouldn't blame yourself if someone broke their leg but somehow it's harder for friends and family of someone suffering poor mental health to understand.

One thing Mum was definitely right about was that bottling up my fears over coming out was doing me long term damage and no matter what else happened in my life, I would never be truly happy until I was free to just be myself. One of my regrets is that Mum died without ever seeing me as free as I am now but in a way I'm glad that she didn't know the depths of the darkest times I had to go through to get here.

What I now know is that throughout all those conversations we had, I was probably suffering from the delayed trauma of my treatment in the army and so I never told her the full extent of the fear and persecution I suffered back then. It's only been since she died that I've addressed myself just how tough it was to be a gay woman in that institution.

Even though she didn't live to see it, I think Mother Dear would be proud to see how I am now.

* * * * *

No matter how much success I have had in my life, I've never forgotten where I came from or how much I had to fight to get where I am. After Athens, once I was back home where I'd come from, that was clearer in my mind than ever. Most people know me for my Olympic success and now for being on *Loose Women* but a huge part of my life after the Olympics was dedicated to helping other kids like me achieve their potential. That's something that makes me extremely proud.

I always believe one person can make a difference to someone's life like Miss Page and Dave did for me, so it has always been part of me to give back or inspire others and it's still one of the most important things in my life today.

What a lot of people didn't know is that in March 2004, before the Olympics that changed my life forever, I'd already started setting up a scheme for talented young British female runners. I really felt like sport had saved me from some pretty dark times as well as bringing me so much joy and pride, so I wanted other talented young people to have a chance to feel that too. That was when I came up with the idea for 'On Camp With Kelly,' a mentoring and education programme aimed at nurturing and supporting young female athletes on their own journeys to success.

The plan was to provide guidance, inspiration, and practical advice to the next generation. Given my long career, with all its highs and lows, I thought I would be the perfect person to teach them what it took to be a world-class athlete. I hoped then they might go on to achieve great things like I had. What a legacy that would be!

After selecting the first group of girls for the programme early in 2004, I promised I would take them to my training camp in South Africa later that year, barely even registering that I had an Olympic Games to get selected for and hopefully win a gold medal at! That's me all over – always doing 10 things at once and trying to be the best at them all. I never could have imagined how my wins would change my life either. I just assumed I'd be able to fit it all in.

The programme I devised for the selected girls would bring together a team of experienced coaches, sports scientists, and nutritionists to help them reach their potential. I would just be their mentor passing on my years of experiences at the top level of sport and they would hopefully go on to achieve their own goals one day. The idea was that we would work closely with the selected young athletes' coaches and give them everything they needed to get on the road to competing internationally once they left camp and returned to their lives in the UK. But in order to make my vision become a reality, first I needed some cash.

Athletics is amazing, but back then it didn't make you rich.

A lot of the money I had back then was from a bit of sponsorship and my savings from the army. There was no social media for brand collaborations or anything like that back then. There was no cash for posting about protein shakes or sportswear – Facebook only started in February 2004 just before my victories.

Instead, I had to find my own funding. Norwich Union – now Aviva – were the sponsors of British Athletics at the time and so I decided to go and tell them my idea. Even though the Olympics were still to come, I was already a multiple medallist for the Great Britain team so I was well established and mature. I don't know where I got the guts from but I marched into a boardroom with a load of money men and just told them what I wanted. I even asked for my own office in their London building to run the scheme.

Amazingly they were impressed enough to back me and said they would stump up £35,000 to cover the flights, training and insurance for all the young women I picked. And they found me a box room that I lovingly turned into a workspace.

Some people thought I was mad but while I was training for the biggest Olympic Games of my life, I also started the selection process for the first cohort of OCWK participants. I'd been keeping a close eye on regional and national youth events and had already earmarked some great talent. Then we got them all together for a selection process and picked the eight with the most potential. When I went off to Athens, they were already dreaming of my camp in South Africa later that year.

After returning glorious from the Olympics and the world at my feet, everyone questioned why I was still going to take eight giggling girls aged 15-17 halfway across the world. I was at my prime of getting pretty much whatever I wanted, riding high on my success. Appearing at events and having opportunities thrown at me left, right and centre was exciting but I had to stick by my word and give those girls the opportunity I had promised them. I knew what it was like to be let down and I wasn't going to make anyone feel that way.

I decided to take them all out to Potchefstroom for a whole month and give them access to the incredible training facilities, working and training with me. By then I had my five-bedroom house over there and I opened it up to the girls. Two of the female coaches I got on board stayed there with them whilst I moved out for the month to my friend's house.

They loved the whole adventure and I found it so exhilarating seeing these young girls with so much potential, imagining what they could go on to do in the future. The thought of being a part of that gave me far more satisfaction than any of the showbiz parties or events I'd been invited to. This was a chance for me to use my profile to have a lasting legacy.

I chose these girls in particular to be part of the programme simply because I believed they had what it took to go all the way. I had 20 years of training and competing as a female runner behind me and I wanted to share that with other people. After the first training camp in South Africa we replicated the same process in Australia, Spain and India – where a group attended the 2010 Commonwealth Games in Delhi and supported several athletes by taking them too. I had 65 athletes go through the programme over the next 10 years who went on to earn 22 medals at Commonwealth, European or global level. Two girls even competed in the 2012 Olympic Games. What an incredible achievement. I was so proud of every one.

The one thing I wanted was a sporting legacy and to inspire more girls to run the 800m and 1500m. It's another thing I feel extremely proud of now, watching athletics today with the current crop of world-class female middle distance runners. I still believe it takes one person to pave the way and make a difference and I hope I was the one that started that for others to follow.

Over the next decade I started a company called 'Kelly Holmes Education' which included On Camp With Kelly and a scheme called 'Future Stars With Kelly' which was for younger athletes and their coaches. I set up other mentoring and education programmes in the Isle of Man, Gateshead Academy and Jaguar Academy of Sport where numerous other athletes started, still competing to this day. To say I am proud of what I started way before I 'made it big' is an understatement, I just wish I could remind myself more often.

Sadly, however, running On Camp With Kelly for 10 years was yet another reason why I didn't come out during a time when my mental health was suffering again. I used to see so much homophobia in the media and crazy accusations of all sorts against members of the community who decided to work with young people of the same sex. It terrified me.

Acceptance of LGBT + people was still not great and I started to feel paranoia creeping in. I became convinced that if anyone found out I was gay they would think differently about me taking the girls away to training camps. I seriously thought that if anyone suggested something weird was happening or ever accused me of being untoward rather than just giving my hard work, commitment, time and energy, I would want to kill myself.

The sad thing is that people probably wouldn't have thought that at all, I was just so paranoid, I always expected the worst. That's how closeted and fearful the army and society had made me over the years.

Sexuality is such a big part of who you are. It shouldn't define you but if you hide the person you are, you're not fully living and it can have a detrimental effect on your personality and thought processes – it eventually invades your complete headspace. Living with a secret like that is like waiting for a ticking time-bomb to explode. I kept my secret so I could achieve the things I wanted to with those wonderful young athletes.

I've stayed in touch with some of them and I'm even planning a 20-year reunion of the first OCWK bunch next year. I know it will feel so good to finally feel free to be myself around them without fear or paranoia.

* * * * *

Ironically it wasn't On Camp With Kelly that started the rumour mill turning when I got back to South Africa after my golden summer, but another friendship. Amy was a member of the British Olympic Association support team who travelled with the athletes to training camps and stayed with us in the Olympic village while the Games were on. I got on well with all of them but Amy and I in particular became mates during the holding camp in Cyprus.

After the Games, I was writing one of my first books and she came over to South Africa to stay and do some work with me. It was good to have a friendly face around after all the chaos of the summer and she needed a break from it all too. We weren't in a romantic relationship, we were just mates, so I never thought twice about hanging out with her. I was probably busy worrying what people would think about On Camp With Kelly instead!

Then one day a message reached me from my agent in the UK that a newspaper back home had a photo of Amy and me together and they would be running it at the weekend. They said they understood we had "become very close" and asked whether I wanted to comment on the nature of the relationship. I was furious. They couldn't even spell out exactly what they were suggesting but they were going to put it out there for all to see. It was no one else's business.

For a start, there was nothing going on between me and Amy, and secondly, how could they possibly have a photograph of us? I felt totally violated. Had they been following me around even thousands of miles away in South Africa? We decided not to respond to the clear innuendo they were drawing because I didn't want to get into a war with a newspaper in case they went harder on me – so far, everyone had been nothing but kind and supportive since my Olympic success.

The press seemed to see me as a national treasure one day but wouldn't care about my feelings at all when they saw an opportunity for a good headline. It just goes to show how much the media has changed in the last 20 years. If you tried to out someone in a newspaper now you'd be in big trouble, but somehow back then it was fair game.

A story appeared alongside a pixelated picture of me and Amy sitting up on a rocky outcrop at the beach. The headline was 'Kelly: My Rock'. I was laughing as I read it:

'THIS is the 'rock' behind Olympic heroine Kelly Holmes,' it said. The article continued by insinuating we were together, claiming we were staying in a one-bedroom apartment, when in fact we were staying in my three-bedroom apartment. Then they dragged up the Maria Mutola rumours again.

It went on: 'Last night, a source said: "Kelly couldn't be happier. In the summer she pushed on to the next level in her career. Now Amy has helped her push on as a person". What a load of rubbish!

All the bad memories following the rumours about Maria and I came flooding back. This story was much more prominent than that one too, and it totally twisted everything.

The fact is, they should have never run that story, it was clearly a thinly-veiled attempt to out me, causing me anxiety and stress. What if my family hadn't already known about my sexuality? The other point is that when someone else is involved in any report, the papers are basically exposing them too, and I don't think that's right. As I have said before, for people who are not publicly 'out', it is no one else's right to try and make that huge step for them. The consequences could be completely damaging and, in some cases, people have taken their own lives under such enormous pressure.

* * * * *

Luckily, after that story, the rumours seemed to die down. I still had a season to do and was finding the motivation extremely hard. The papers soon went back to being nice to me when I announced my forthcoming official retirement from athletics in August 2005. The story became about my sporting achievements rather than my love life.

My last ever race was on British soil in Sheffield and it was such an emotional day. All my family came on a special bus for the event and there were flares, fireworks and five army helicopters flying in formation over the stadium as I finished my final straight in a black and gold outfit designed especially for me by Reebok.

It was the weirdest feeling knowing that it was all over and I no longer had that big goal to strive for, but I was also probably ready for a bit of a break from competing and some time out of the limelight.

Later on in 2004, I got an official letter from Downing Street telling me I'd been selected to appear in the Queen's New Year Honours List and I was going to be made a Dame Commander of the British Empire. I couldn't believe it, it was just so overwhelming to be honoured in that way, so much was happening to me it was incredible. I was the first woman to be given a damehood for sporting achievements and so again my family, Mum, Dad and my grandad all were so proud of me.

On March 9th, 2005, I was back off to Buckingham Palace to become 'Dame Kelly Holmes' and this time I made sure I wasn't hiding behind an awful hat. I had my hair done by Pat in a funky up-do and wore a slick, white tailored skirt suit by Jasper Conran.

There was one glitch though. When the organisers at the Palace were running through what I had to do when I went up to receive the honour, I expected them to tell me I would kneel before the Queen. A damehood is the female equivalent of a knighthood and the first thing you think of when you hear someone is knighted is kneeling before the monarch and being dubbed with a sword. I was gutted to hear that there was nothing quite so cool for the women who were awarded the same honour – we just had to go up there and curtsy!

I told the Lord Comptroller, who was explaining the protocol, that I wanted to kneel in front of my Queen to get the honour and he almost had a heart attack. It would have been the kind of break from protocol that probably would have caused total chaos, so when it was my turn I dutifully curtsied and accepted my medal with great pride.

I don't know if the Queen recognised me but, years later, I went to the racing at Royal Ascot and she addressed me as 'Dame Kelly'. We had a little chat about how we were both wearing the same colour blue that day and joked that it must be good luck for her horse that was racing so I think she knew who I was!

A bit later that year, I did something totally out of character and swapped my spikes for skates when I took on the challenge of appearing as a celebrity contestant on ITV's *Dancing On Ice*. I'm not sure what made me do it now because I've never really been a dancer but compared with some of the things I was asked to do, it felt like it would suit me because I could approach it like a sport. Unfortunately for my partner Todd Sand I didn't take to it quite as naturally as I did running!

My competitive spirit was in full force but I'd gone from being the gold medallist to struggling to keep up with the spins and heel-toes in the rink. It was hugely frustrating not being able to excel and be the best but I enjoyed the challenge and I ended up staying in for five weeks before I got booted off. The other issue is that I didn't understand the TV world and found it really hard to 'play the game' so I probably didn't show the best of myself at that time. I was also always so tense and on guard that I didn't allow myself to have fun. Looking back on my transition from sport, I found it extremely hard.

What I have learnt about myself is that, if I know how to do something then I am so confident, but when put outside my comfort zone I can get extremely anxious of showing myself up, feeling not good enough or embarrassed of what people might think.

I get asked all the time whether I would do *Strictly* or *I'm A Celebrity Get Me Out Of Here* or any of the other reality TV shows and, up until now, I've always said no but since coming out I do feel like I have a new lease of life, so never say never. If the time was right, you never know you might see me back on telly in a sequin outfit.

No title can make you better than anyone else but it can mean that you become established for more than just one thing. My damehood has opened doors, that I know for sure. But it has also given me a voice to speak up for the causes that are close to me.

Since 2005 I have been given even more honours and titles. Firstly, I have received around 12 honorary doctorates and fellowships and then I was made an Honorary Colonel in the British Army in 2018, so with my MBE for services to the British Army, my official title is now Colonel Dame Kelly Holmes MBE (mili)! Who would have thought that a mixed-raced girl with an afro from Kent would do so well?

After the Damehood I once again started getting more and more requests for interviews and TV appearances. I said no to a lot of them but when the call came from Piers Morgan's *Life Stories*, I knew I had to consider it. It was a bit like a modern-day rite of passage like *This Is Your Life* in the old days with the big red book.

Having opened up more about my past through my work with the DKH Trust and my mental health initiatives, I felt like now might be my time to tell my story. So long as I didn't have to talk about my personal relationships I could keep my sexuality out of it and hopefully just tell the inspiring story of how I got to where I am.

It was a huge milestone for me to feel confident enough to do it. I'd grown so much since that shy girl who appeared on Parky fresh back from Athens. Surely that was a good thing? Mum didn't agree.

"I don't think you should do it," she said, when I told her. "You're going to make me look like a terrible mother, why would you want to air your dirty laundry in public like that?"

She feared that when people heard about me being put in a children's home and then finding out about Lisa and Danny when I was a teenager, people would judge her and our family and people would gossip about us. But I didn't see it like that, and her reaction made me even more determined to do it because I had a right to tell my own story.

I accepted the offer and although I was nervous as hell, I got through it and did myself proud. I even appeared on the episode after Roger Moore, James Bond of all people. I was up there with 007! I had no regrets about doing it but it did cause a rift between me and Mum again and it took us months to get back on good terms.

It's easy to have regrets about arguments you have with loved ones after they have gone and to regret the time wasted by being in a rift with them but we are only human and I'm glad I stuck to my guns because, in hindsight, it was something I needed to do for myself. I hope deep down, in some way, Mum was proud I was strong enough to fight for it.

15

—

Champion in
My Corner

ONCE AN ATHLETE, ALWAYS AN ATHLETE, I SAY, AND
sometimes there are no exceptions, even when you're competing
with the Royal Family! At least that was the case when I played
none other than the Princess of Wales at noughts and crosses,
when she visited one of my charities young people programmes
in Bristol with The Royal Foundation. It was a huge day and
validation of the great work my charity the Dame Kelly Holmes
Trust does to transform young people's lives and so exciting
for my amazing Trust team, the schools, and the young people
involved.

I've always wanted to inspire young athletes to achieve
greatness but while that's a huge passion of mine, there are
many kids out there who may not be cut out for a sporting
career who also need help, guidance, and inspiration to
succeed.

I think, because of my own background, I was always determined that if I ever got the right platform, I would also work hard to give those underprivileged kids opportunities outside of the sporting world.

I've done so much charity work over the years and I think it's really important for people in the public eye to do so. Not for money or gratitude but for love and compassion. I have also had numerous roles that I fought for myself. I was Ambassador for the Youth Sports Trust, National School Sports Champion under Gordon Brown's Government for three years, and I have supported cancer charities, military charities and mental health initiatives over the years. But I'm most proud of my own charity – the Dame Kelly Holmes Trust.

Sitting in a conference room at Bramall Lane football ground in Sheffield earlier this year, it hit me just what we have achieved and I felt an enormous sense of pride. My trust is now 15 years old and there in front of me in that room were all these young people and athletes that had been a part of it.

But how did it all start?

Well, if you look at the statistics on the life chances for children who have been in care and grown up in areas of deprivation or from underprivileged backgrounds, they are far more likely to end up struggling in adulthood with unemployment, addiction problems, mental health issues and even crime.

I was no genius at school and struggled to find my place in the world. It was only really because I happened to have people who believed in me like Miss Page and the inspiring careers officers from the recruitment office in Tunbridge Wells that I managed to get myself on track and have a successful career. When I look back at my life, it could have turned out so differently and, in a way, I am just so lucky my talent for running was identified.

I founded the Dame Kelly Holmes Trust in 2008, with the target of giving young people with challenging backgrounds a chance to believe they had a brighter future. The idea was to assign each of them a mentor who would believe in them, no matter where they came from and no matter what their dream.

After I retired from athletics, I knew of other sports people who reached the end of their careers and also were searching for a purpose in life. Retiring from any kind of intense career is tough because you get a sense of lost identity that can make you question your worth or positioning in society. My idea was to put these people together with the children who needed that support and to let them work together. It was a huge success.

At first, setting up a charity seemed like a mountain to climb but I knew it could work, so I started contacting former athletes I knew from my competing days and I was amazed at how many were keen to come on board. I registered the Trust as a charity and employed a tiny team of admin and organisational staff to begin with, funding it out of my own pocket. The Trust was born.

We targeted schools in deprived areas, young offender institutions, social services, Jobcentre Plus, youth clubs – anywhere we thought could give us access to vulnerable young people who needed our help. Kids from across the country who had been in care, or suffered difficult family situations, grown up in areas of deprivation or been young carers themselves all started to join our programmes.

Some of them had been in trouble with the police or started to go off the rails and others were just completely lacking in confidence from trauma they'd experienced as children. Some amazing organisations like football clubs lent their spaces for free so we could arrange days for groups of kids to meet up for workshops and training sessions and just to meet other people like themselves so they felt less alone.

It was amazing to watch them gradually come out of their shells and tell us about what had brought them to us. I remember one young boy whose mum had been in and out of prison for most of his life so he'd been from home to home, never able to settle properly or focus on his studies or what he wanted from his own life. It turned out he actually had loads of ideas for businesses and was a budding young entrepreneur but he just had no capital and no direction so the trust helped him to build a business plan, apply for grants and set himself up in a way he never could have done by himself. He managed to get a home of his own and the kind of stability he'd craved all his life. There were hundreds of stories like his and every one I heard was different.

As I heard their stories, I was taken right back to my feelings of fear, abandonment and displacement all those years ago and probably for the first time in my adult life I spoke openly about what happened to me too. They were always astonished to hear my background and how I started out in life and I think hearing how I managed to make such a success of my life from such humble beginnings gave them the inspiration to want to do it for themselves too.

I'm extremely proud of my trust and everyone who has ever worked with us throughout the years, the teachers, carers, social workers, sponsors, businesses and of course the young people and so grateful to every athlete who has become a mentor, working on our programmes or running the sessions. I'm the person who started the Trust but they are the people that now continue my legacy and they make my heart feel so warm.

Over the last 15 years, we have helped thousands of young people through various programmes helping many on their road to success and self-confidence. After my gold medals, along with On Camp With Kelly, it's probably one of my proudest achievements.

* * * * *

While I was building the charity those first few years it was a really inspirational time because I'd also worked on the London 2012 Olympic bid and now that was coming to fruition, so I was involved in the preparations for that. I had mentored young athletes who would later go through the selection process for Team GB.

Finally I was going to an Olympic Games with no worries about bringing my own medals home – my only responsibility was giving our brilliant athletes support and belief and to create a wonderful sporting legacy for the nation.

The two weeks in August 2012 certainly didn't disappoint. The opening ceremony directed by Danny Boyle was incredible and made me so proud to watch. It was a celebration not only of sport but of our nation, its people, the military, the NHS, Shakespeare, Elgar, the Beatles and all that makes us who we are. The fact 27 million people watched it on telly shows what an enormous moment it was for us as a nation and I will never forget it.

I was selected as an ambassador of the Games along with six other sporting legends. Our biggest role was to be inspirational figures to the younger generation but we also had the honour of handing the torches to seven young athletes who would go on to light the Olympic cauldron at the opening ceremony to start London 2012 – another 'pinch-me' moment.

That same year, I received another sign from the universe that I had to follow. Back in Hildenborough, I'd always had this dream of buying the little sweet shop where I'd worked as a teenager before I joined the army. I always remembered the local people coming in to chat and they were some of my happiest memories, being a part of that community. I'd tried to buy it before but the timing and the price had never been right. But in 2012, after the Olympics, I got a call from the estate agents telling me it was up for sale again.

I'd always told myself that if it ever became available when I was older and I had the money, I would buy it. So that's what I did! Most people impulse-buy expensive shoes or a car but I got myself a building in the heart of a sunny Kent village without much of a plan of what I was going to do with it. I quickly decided I wanted to turn it into a little café, a meeting place for the community where they could come together and socialise.

What I didn't realise when I bought it, was that it was going to take a lot of work, time, energy and money. But I do like a project, and a challenge, so I wasn't deterred. I got in contractors and builders, structural engineers and set about knocking down the walls of the building on Florence Place. I started to create a massive 100-seater coffee house, more fitting for a trendy London street than a blink-and-you-miss-it rural village. It was a labour of love – and stress – but after a year of being project manager, hod carrier, foreman and tea-maker on the site of the old sweet shop, in 2014, finally it was ready to open its doors to the public.

I christened it Café 1809 after my bib number in Athens. I also had tattooed *Run 1809* on my foot so I could never forget those four special digits. I was so proud of everything. The decor, which I designed with a local guy, featured cool indus-

Honoured
Wearing black – my comfort colour – as I meet the Queen at Buckingham Palace in 2004 and (below) receiving my DBE with Grandad Geoff and my dad Mick

We've done it!
(Above) celebrating in 2005 as London wins the right to host the Olympic Games in 2012

Giving back
On Camp With Kelly, 2004 to 2014. Mentoring before it was trendy

Always with us (Left) at Mother Dear's bench with Kev, Penny and Stu and (above) Kev, Danny and Stu – all grown up now

Special bond With my sister Lisa

I love you Dad At his beloved Tonbridge FC

We are family My wonderful nieces and nephews who I hope will always understand acceptance. Numbered in birth order so I don't lose track! (Above) nieces 5,6,7,4 and nephews 2 and 1 and (right) nieces 2,1,8,3

Forever friends Enjoying the company of Debs, Kerrie, Lara and Kim – 42 years together

Four-legged family
(Above, left) 'The Boys' (without Fudge) had their own reality show during lockdown. (Right) Mum came back... as a donkey?!

Simply the best
My lockdown antics as Tina Turner

You can do it Gok Wan gave me confidence and (right) Alan Carr calmed my nerves

Finding the real me With Kelly Hoppen and (right) Dr Tania Pilley, who helped me so much

Telling the world my story Filming the *Kelly Holmes: Being Me* documentary

On parade Enjoying the Trooping of the Colour as an Honorary Colonel

Palace party At the Platinum Jubilee celebrations with Sally Gunnell and co

Read all about it With Emeli Sandé (above) and (right) with Dawn Butler and Linda Riley

Troopers With some of my Military in Motion gang. They gave me a lifeline during lockdown

Support With Kerrie in 2021 during my burnout (left) and (right) the Princess of Wales visiting a Dame Kelly Holmes Trust project in Bristol, with The Royal Foundation

The inner circle clan If you know, you know

New experiences
Learning to be
Loose with these
wonderful women

Righting the wrongs With veterans in the
House of Commons, after the Prime Minister's
apology for the mistreatment and unethical,
historical ban on LGBT serving personnel

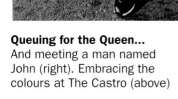

Queuing for the Queen...
And meeting a man named
John (right). Embracing the
colours at The Castro (above)

With Lou When you can finally feel free, you can be yourself and happy! (Below) celebrating with Lou after I won the DIVA Media Personality of the Year. (Bottom) being me! Brighton Pride in 2023

trial furniture, steel beams and lighting. In the apex roof were huge photos of me crossing the finishing line in Athens. I held interviews and employed some young people from the local community as waiting staff and picked out trendy uniforms. I was still such a stickler for ironing from my army days. I would do a joke inspection when they came in and even taught some of them to iron – yes, really! I remember one girl was once running late and came in looking like she'd just picked the shirt up off the floor and slung it on. I didn't shout, I just gave her 'the look' and sent her home to change it. She came back with it all ironed, fit for an army inspection.

The café was my pride and joy and it felt like home. There was something so special about transforming that building where I'd grafted as a kid to save the money to buy my parents our first tumble dryer then, when I was 16, a scooter and finally my first car. It felt like I'd properly come home to my community and given them something back.

Everyone in Hildenborough knew me. They would come into the café sometimes for a cup of tea or lunch, but more importantly just for a chat to see how things were going. I would get to know the old dears who popped in after getting a perm; the kids who visited on their way home from school or the mums with pushchairs trying to get their babies to sleep as they drank endless coffee. Kerrie had her own little company making amazing cakes and bakes by that point, so I sold them from the counter to make her a bit of extra cash too.

I could get from home to work in less than five minutes and I had a manager who would look after 1809 when I needed to be off travelling for OCWK or the Trust. It felt like the perfect balance between my own little project and giving something back in a wider sense.

The only problem with being back in the heart of the village, in a place where people go to gossip was that everyone knew everyone else's business! At that time I was fully convinced I was the Only Gay In The Village like Dafydd in the sketch show *Little Britain* by Matt Lucas and David Walliams. I would joke about it with my friends. Looking back I'm sure some people knew I was gay and others probably either had no clue or didn't care either way but nonetheless I kept my personal life very private.

The most important relationships to me at that time, though, were my friends and family. Kev, Stuart, Lisa, Danny and Penny all still live in Kent so being able to see my siblings and my nieces and nephews as much as I wanted was a huge bonus. Plus Mum and Dad were around the corner so I had all my loved ones in one place – what more could I want?

16

Broken Hearted

EVER SINCE I WAS SMALL, I'VE BEEN TERRIFIED OF death. I hate ageing, the thought of being old and I can't stand hospitals or being ill. I used to lie awake at night worrying about something happening to one of my parents and my worst nightmare has always been contemplating when one of them might get ill or worse, die. I think it goes back to being a child and being scared of losing Mum again after she left me in the children's home or when I was growing up feeling that she was my one constant. My ultimate fear was that one day I would have to live without her.

One bonus of having a young mum was that I always assumed we would have years and years together. Now I was back in Kent and we could see one another as often as we wanted, it felt like we would have plenty of time to make up for those lost years. After all, her mum, my nan Elsie lived until she was 98!

Towards the end of 2014, I had gone around to her bungalow after her shift at the hospital and she was complaining of a back ache, which she'd never mentioned before. She was an active woman who'd had jobs requiring her to be on her feet all day for years and never complained before. She seemed to be run down and exhausted, which wasn't like her.

Me being me, I thought she must have just pulled a muscle so I started massaging her over the course of a couple of weeks. But the pain wasn't relenting and as she was working at a hospital anyway, I persuaded her to go to the doctor.

For months she said she was fine and it was just old age catching up with her but she was only 61, so I kept nagging her. I knew from my own experience with my many sporting injuries that the longer you leave a niggle without getting it checked out, the worse it will get. Mum was adamant, though, and carried on as normal. When she did go to the GP, they didn't think it was anything serious so we all agreed to just keep an eye on her.

As she seemed to be struggling a bit, I tried to see Mum as much as I could and I would often go over to the bungalow where she was living with Penny and order a Chinese while we watched telly. She loved sweet and sour chicken balls and egg fried rice with chips. I always tried to get her to change her order to something more adventurous but she would say: "I know what I like," and I would laugh.

We would watch crap TV for hours and sometimes, if I wanted company, I would sleep on her sofa even though I had a five-bedroom house up the road. By now, we had got past our row about Piers Morgan and things were back to normal. We were soon seeing each other almost every day when I was in Kent. There was something special about time spent with her on my own.

Then one day, when Mum came over, she said that she'd spoken to one of the consultants at work who suggested that she have a scan to see what was causing her back pain. Immediately I went into panic mode. A scan didn't sound like good news. I'd had enough of them myself to know they usually pick up a problem and as Mum was a 61-year-old woman and not an elite athlete, I guessed it would pick up something more serious than a muscle injury.

As it turned out, the scan was inconclusive so the doctor insisted on some specialist blood tests and the following week asked Mum back in for the results, and to take someone with her. Kevin, Stuart, Penny and I all went. We knew they wouldn't have called her in if there was nothing to worry about. I remember sitting in the cramped little doctor's office as he told us Mum had a rare form of cancer called myeloma, a sort of lymphoma that attacks the blood cells and bone marrow. We all listened in stunned silence as he said those words you dread hearing: "It's incurable."

I felt my heart start to race. I felt sick rising in my stomach but I knew I had to keep a cool head. I was already thinking about how we could get her to see the best doctors and what I could do to help – to keep her alive. I just couldn't even bear to think about life without her – I couldn't let it happen. But before I could speak, the doctor said that while there was no cure, there was treatment Mum could have and that she could have it there at Pembury and at Maidstone Hospital down the road. So we all agreed she would start the treatment as soon as possible to give herself the best chance of extending her life for as long as possible.

Back home, Mum tried to put on a brave face and we talked about dividing up the hospital appointments and trips to the pharmacy to collect the tons of different pills she'd been prescribed.

Penny would look after her at home while she was off work and we would take it in turns to take her for her chemotherapy which she was due to start straight away. She had a blood transfusion too, to try and kickstart the production of new healthy blood cells and regenerate her bone marrow. It was a huge shock to get the diagnosis but I think we were all just so focused on making sure the treatments available worked, we pulled together as a family and hoped for the best.

Even though Mum worked in a hospital, she hated being a patient. After years of being a nursing assistant, it felt unnatural for her to be on the receiving end of the poking and prodding, plus it was hard for her to be seen in a weak and vulnerable state by her colleagues. I was amazed at how brave she was. As she sat shivering with the chemo coursing through her veins, she never complained. (I also couldn't believe the amount of drugs cancer patients have to take, I can't even take a Benadryl without suffering from the side effects!).

Remarkably after that first round of chemo, further blood tests showed it had worked and she was significantly stronger than she'd been before. Her blood was regenerating and the cancer seemed to be losing its battle with the drugs. "I told you I'd be okay," she told me, as though I'd been fussing over nothing. Within a couple of months, she was back working on the X-ray ward. We couldn't believe it.

For a while she seemed much stronger and life went back to normal but the following year, she began to complain of exhaustion, pain and tiredness again.

More tests showed the cancer was back with a vengeance. I remember standing by the bed squeezing her hand as she had a painful marrow extraction from her pelvis – that was brutal! I knew from the look on her face and the pain she was in that day that she knew it was serious. Months passed and she underwent more chemo and her prescriptions from the pharmacy seemed to come in bigger bags every week. She had to give up work permanently and gradually found it harder to move around.

One morning, two years after the diagnosis, I arrived at the bungalow early in the morning and Mum didn't even have the strength to get out of bed and use the bathroom. Her complexion was grey and she looked really unwell. I got her to the toilet and she collapsed. I panicked and called an ambulance to take her into hospital.

It was the first of two long stints on a ward. She was suffering from pneumonia which had hit her hard because her immune system was so low. Seeing Mum like that was awful. The next few months she was in and out and eventually Dr Wyke, her consultant, suggested she go to a hospital in Maidstone for some tests and to see if they could do anything.

"What's the point of me being here if I'm just in and out of hospitals," Mum cried. "I just want to be at home and to see my chickens."

On the June 14th, 2017, the doctor gave us the result of her latest tests and confirmed that she only had months to live. Once again we were all there when she got the news and we were in total shock. I could see the boys trying to be brave. I felt somehow as the eldest that I should be the strong one. In a situation like that it's hard not to let the emotions get the better of you though. I can't remember if I cried there and then, but I know when I got back home that night I was a wreck. The thought of being without Mum was just unbearable. I wasn't ready to lose her.

* * * * *

After weeks of sitting at Mum's side in the hospital, she'd finally turned a corner and the doctors had even allowed her to go home to the bungalow I'd bought for her a few years earlier. She'd been begging to get off the ward since the moment she was admitted because she hated being the one that needed looking after – that was *her* job.

Mum and I got closer than ever during that time she was on the ward. I would get up early and cycle from my place in Hildenborough across to the hospital in time to spend the day sitting at her side.

We would laugh and joke about her times working in the hospital. She would tell funny stories about giving elderly patients enemas and then them farting and giving her a shower! It was also the same hospital where she'd had me years earlier and we would talk about my younger days too, though she always found it hard to speak about the time we were on our own, before Mick and the rest of the family came along.

Most of all, she just wanted to get back to her own home. So when there was a break in her chemotherapy and the doctors deemed she was well enough to leave, we were over the moon. Penny was living in the bungalow and could look after her while she was there and the rest of us would take turns to visit. Even Dad was on hand to help out when we needed him. After all those years and so much water under the bridge he still cared so much for Mum, you could see it.

I'd been umming and ahhing over whether to go away on a short break to Greece with a girl I'd been seeing to get some sunshine and a bit of a break from all the hospital visits. When she was given the green light to go home, Mum was adamant that I should go. "Just go and enjoy yourself," she said. "I'll be fine."

Running through the airport in a blind panic, I could feel my heart racing. I just needed to get on a plane and get home as soon as I could. I'd been in Greece for less than 48 hours when Kevin had called. "Something's happened, Mum's back in hospital," he said. "You need to come back."

It wasn't clear on that phone call exactly what he meant but I knew straight away that I needed to get on a flight home. The problem was that the villa I was in was on a little island; a boat ride away from the mainland and where the airport was – and the crossings were few and far between. I felt totally helpless as I desperately tried to think of how I could get back. I actually spoke to my mum, telling her to hang on as I was on my way back. But there was nothing I could do. It was nine hours before I could get to the airport and hopefully get onto a plane.

In a total panic, I ran to the bathroom and locked myself in, I picked up some nails scissors as I had 11 years ago and cut myself on the leg. What the hell was I doing? I was going back years in my recovery from self-harm. I wanted to take away the pain I thought my mum was in, but I had a sudden revelation that no matter how deep the cut, Mum would still be lying in a hospital bed potentially dying and I would still be here. The phone rang again and I rushed out in hope of some better news, but my greatest fear became true. Stuart told me Mother Dear had died.

My world suddenly went into slow motion and I felt a physical pain tear through my body as though someone was actually reaching into my chest and ripping my heart in two. All I could think was 'no, don't let it be true'. But it was.

By the time I got to the hospital, Mum was in the chapel of rest. It turned out that the morning I'd left, she hadn't got out of bed as usual, and Penny had struggled to wake her. She had called Kev and Stu, and they tried to take her to the bathroom but Mum didn't even have the strength to stand and had to use the commode left there since the last bad turn she'd had. Mum lost consciousness in the ambulance and passed away soon after she got to hospital.

As I went into the room where she was peacefully laid out, I couldn't believe she'd actually gone as I held her hand and kissed her on the head, speaking to her for the last time, telling her I loved her, telling her I was sorry I hadn't been there.

She was only 65, it was so unfair. Our relationship in those last few years had become closer and better than ever. That's the thing about losing people you love, it's so finite you don't just lose a person, you lose a part of yourself.

Mum was the most important person in my life since I was a baby and, despite all of our ups and downs, I felt like our souls were bonded together. It wasn't just that she was my only full blood relative, but it was that it was just us in the beginning, the only person who had been there through my entire life. I genuinely feel like the part of me that died that day will never come back.

After Mum died I barely functioned. For three weeks I could only sort funeral arrangements. I stopped work as I was so consumed with grief. I missed Mum so much that I found it hard to do anything. I know some people need to throw themselves back into routine but I couldn't. It was one of those critical moments in my life when I truly needed my friends and family the most.

17

—

Letting Her Go

IN THE DARKEST OF TIMES YOU HAVE TO FOCUS ON the things you have control over and one of those, for me, was the way we would say goodbye to Mum. It was three years from diagnosis to her passing away and one thing I am grateful for is that we did have plenty of time to talk about exactly what she wanted for her funeral.

Having grown up in Hildenborough village you seemed to know everyone and sadly, one of the ladies I had known for years died. Earlier in 2017 we attended her funeral and getting there late, we sat at the back of the crematorium.

When Mother Dear saw the coffin, a big wooden box, she said: "I don't want one like that." I didn't know what other kinds of coffins there were, but she whispered, "put me in a wicker casket, otherwise I am coming back to haunt you!"

We were both laughing as I told her to stop being stupid and to 'ssshhh!'

I had previously had a really hard conversation with her

about wanting to be cremated, not buried. If I have any advice to anyone going through a similar traumatic experience, please have the hardest conversations you will ever have with a loved one about what their wishes are. To be honest, out of all the heartache, this is one thing I am so happy I did; knowing what she wanted.

On the morning of my mum's funeral, I went to my hairdresser Luci, who had been doing my hair for years. As I sat in the chair I asked her to shave my head on one side just leaving a bit more length on the top. It was the look I'd always wanted but avoided in favour of braids or a straightened bob through the years. It sounds like a stereotype but I was convinced if someone saw me with an undercut they would take that as a sign I was gay. But now Mum was gone, I didn't care what anyone thought.

In the years before she left us, Mum would often say how much she wished I could just be open about who I was and live my life without caring so much about what other people thought. She was desperate for me to be happy and to be myself.

Now, in a little act of defiance, and in tribute to her, that was what I decided to do. There was a bloody long way to go, but looking back, that was the first step on my five-year journey to being me.

You hear about people from the LGBTQIA+ community who wait until their parents pass away to come out because they feel like they would be hurt or ashamed of them but, for me, it was the other way around. Mum wanted that freedom for me and now I felt like I owed it to us both to try to free myself from the shackles that had held me for so long.

For the funeral arrangements, I made sure Mum's wishes were adhered to and that each of us chose a song that was special to us. Mine was *This Woman's Work* by Kate Bush. The lyrics are so full of emotion and the words describe exactly how I felt during the time she was ill.

I know you've got a little life in you left,
I know you've got a lotta strength left,
I should be cryin' but I just can't let it show,
I should be hopin' but I can't stop thinkin',
All the things we should've said that are never said,
All the things we should've done that we never did,
All the things we should've given, but I didn't.
Oh darlin', make it go,
Make it go away,
Give me these moments,
Give them back to me.

I knew that as soon as I heard the first bars of it I would be a complete wreck and I was. I'd also agreed, as the oldest, to do a reading on behalf of the four of us kids. I regularly spoke to huge rooms full of people for my work because I was a motivational speaker, but now, the thought of standing in front of a room of people while I was so emotional, filled me with dread.

On the morning of the funeral, dressed in black, along with Kev, Stu and Penny, six of us carried the wicker casket on our shoulders into the crematorium, to say our final goodbyes. After the humanist did her address, I read – or tried to read – a poem I'd written for Mum, mentioning all the happy things I remembered about her.

I wanted to include her love of nature, birds and horses and how special she was to me. Standing in front of the congregation, the tears came and I swallowed hard, choking them back as I was determined to read the poem for her.

My heart gallops like a racehorse charging down the furlong,
My head pounds like the beat of a drum,
My body falters with every walking step as my eyes fill and blur,
My heart skips a beat each time I breathe,
The growl in my voice has lost its bark,
but I lie with the sound of your voice around me
like the morning lark,
I think I can see you but then you disappear,
like a piece of my heart that went when yours stopped.
I can't believe you are gone but the biggest gift you gave me
was the strength of your mind to carry on.

One of the things that really hits my core, the same as when my grandparents all passed, is that when the curtain slowly surrounds the coffin or it's taken away, that's it. But one thing that gives me peace with my Mother Dear passing is that I know she would have at least been happy with her send-off.

When I look back at that day, I think we made Mum proud. But as time went on, in moments of crises, grief can drive us to act out of character. I believe massive change in our lives can also help us to connect with our inner spirit; one we may not even know is there.

Soon after the funeral I got a tattoo of a jigsaw puzzle piece over my chest to symbolise what I feel is a missing piece of my heart alongside a clock face to show that there's no time for healing and an eye to show I will always be searching for her.

People have asked me in recent times why I started getting tattoos. They were around for me long before my mum passed away. Mine actually started when I was a young recruit in the army. One of my first rebellions was going with some of the other girls to this house of a guy who did tattoos. We ended up getting a tiny tattoo on our hips of different fruits! I got a bloody strawberry – why?! I didn't realise how tattoos would have a deeper meaning as I got older. For me they are an expression of my thoughts, a show of identity and purpose, to signify a moment in time, a memory or a belief.

After the strawberry, they became more prominent for me when I was an athlete; I loved the thought of having powerful words on my body permanently. Before my Olympic wins I had already experienced success in my army career which was a fight for identity, purpose and respect. I also had success as an athlete, both in the military and in world athletics, so I found a Chinese symbol – that used to be the in-thing in the '90s – the meaning was 'Strength and Power'. It was just a small insignia on my right shoulder. Of course, I thought I was invincible back then!

As time went on, I left the army and had my battles with injuries on the track as well as health issues and gynaecological problems (bloody periods and women's issues drove me crazy – just another setback I didn't need). So I added another Chinese symbol underneath that translated to 'Will to Win'. Little did I know it would later become my mantra!

In a strange twist of fate a year after my Olympic double, I was visiting China for an awards ceremony. After finishing a run, a local man stopped me in the street and pointed at the tattoo. There was no way on this earth he knew who I was as he swept up the pathway outside his humble little shack.

I thought it was a bizarre moment because when I asked him what it meant (hoping he wouldn't say something completely unrelated) he spoke in very broken English 'extraordinary victory'. I was stunned! Still processing what I had achieved the year before, it felt like another sign to me and always makes me believe that my gold medals were meant to be.

I believe Mother Dear comes to me in certain ways when I need her and to give me strength.

After she passed away, I began seeing butterflies at the most unusual times; one even landed on my shorts when I was on a charity trip to Malawi. We had just pulled into the shore after kayaking on Lake Malawi. I was lying in the sun, wishing I could have called Mum and showed her where I was, like I used to every time I was away, when a butterfly came towards me. A single butterfly. It hovered above me before landing on my shorts. I thought it was going to just fly off but it didn't, I swear it stayed there for 10 minutes and I even had time to take a photo of it. That's why my next tattoo was a butterfly above the puzzle piece, another reminder she is always here.

Tattoos for me have become more than just art or an act of rebellion to conforming, they have become symbolic of my life journey. Each time I have got a tattoo (apart from the bloody strawberry I got on my hip in the army!) it has been about a reflection of my state of mind or a stage in my life that has had some life changing impact.

Thinking back on my horrific night without sleep, pinning my body in my bed whilst my spirit was wandering down to the kitchen to reach for the knife drawer, I realised that I had a moment of power; a resistance to go downstairs in the midst of my deep despair.

I felt so emotional about that period of my journey I was compelled to get the word L;fe on the inside of my left wrist. I had the 'i' down as a semicolon, because it represents a personal strength to overcome internal struggles.

It's a reminder on my dark days that "I chose Life "

In the past five years I have added numerous tattoos that have been part of my own spiritual and mental health journey. They symbolise many aspects and different stages of my life, like; growth, healing, positivity, hope and life. I have a quote on my arm which says:

> *'Strong enough to stand alone,*
> *Smart enough to know when I need help and*
> *Brave enough to ask for it'*

I'd written it to remind me that even in the darkest of times, through grief, there is always help out there. Maybe it can help you too.

Three years after Mum died, I wrote:

'Three years ago today, my mum 'Mother Dear' passed away. That day was the worst time of my life. My heart broke in pieces. That day was also the last time I self-harmed. I knew it would not bring her back and it definitely would destroy me. Loss is horrendous! But we never talk about it – why? Everyone deals with it in different ways, I cried for three weeks solid leading up to her funeral, I became a bit of a recluse. My friends and family were my lifeline.

The pain and loss is still there and I miss her so much but you learn to deal with it as life carries on. I changed the day of Mother Dear's funeral – I know I did. For me, probably for the better. I am a private person to some degree. I know people probably wonder exactly 'who I am' but I don't care anymore because I am who I am! I am waiting for a butterfly to come down – maybe she is sleeping. I want to be free like a beautiful butterfly but so far my life, whilst glorious and special, has sometimes felt like being a moth in a cocoon. I want to one day be free from this anguish but I don't know how...

'One of the hardest things about losing Mother Dear is that she is not around to see how I have changed my life, but what is important now is whilst I am walking on this earth, I must actually live my life. REST IN PEACE, MUM'

* * * * *

It wasn't just the type of coffin she wanted that Mum had told us about. Firstly, no way on earth did she want to be buried. "I'm claustrophobic," she said. "You won't know, you'll be dead!" I would joke. She was cremated. I wasn't taking the risk of her threats to come back and haunt me – no way!

In the later stages of her illness, she told me she dreamt of buying a camper van with her pension money and travelling around the country to visit some special places.

Unfortunately, by the time she had a chance to buy one, it was too late and she was far too poorly. So in the year after she died, Kevin, Stuart, Penny and I decided to make our own pilgrimages to each of the places and to scatter her ashes where she could rest in peace forever.

We started closer to home at the lake in Haysden Country Park. Mum used to go to walk her dogs over the years and one of her wishes that I had spoken to her about was to have a bench placed there in her memory. It had always been a place to enjoy the countryside, so we decided to take her back there too.

I called the local council and told them I wanted a bench dedicated to her, overlooking the lake where she felt so peaceful and they said we could. Mum also said she wanted, 'Take a pew and enjoy the view' as the inscription, so that's what we had engraved on a silver plaque. Now there are some little holders either side of the armrests where we can leave flowers when we visit.

Stuart, Clare, Kevin, Emma and Penny went down to the lake with the kids, but we had no idea what the protocol was for scattering ashes in a public place. What if there were some health and safety rules or we got caught? It sounds ridiculous now, but we were all giggling as I took the cardboard container with the ashes from the crematorium in, hiding it under my nephew Finlay's coat, and we scattered them like you would a Shake n' Vac!

We each took a handful and walked around the whole lake. What I couldn't believe was how much was left when we got back. I'd never had any idea the amount of ashes there would be.

The first road trip to scatter more of the ashes was to the New Forest, the place Mum wanted to go to most of all. She was a huge lover of horses and loved seeing the white horses in the forest roaming free on the open heathland. For this trip we all took our bikes which was a task in itself given we had all the kids, but it was a laugh as we went searching specifically for the white horses, not brown, black or grey, it had to be white! Sounds easy, but it was only after an hour of searching, and going round in circles we finally came across some.

We stood in a row and each took a handful to scatter. Just at that solemn moment, the wind whipped up. We all fell about laughing, wiping the ashes from our jackets and faces. It wasn't the perfect peaceful send-off I'd imagined but it was very much about doing it as a family and we were all there together, that was what mattered. That spot became a really special place for our family after that, and we still go back to visit. Three years later I wrote on my Instagram:

'Had an amazing day with my family down at the New Forest. My Mum 'Mother Dear' wanted to go there and I had told her I

would take her a couple of weeks after she came out of hospital for a break. But sadly she died before that. My family and I had gone down a couple of months after for her and found this wonderful place – Hatchet Pond.

'Three years since Mother Dear left us, we went again. Now there are wild horses, donkies, cows everywhere... this donkey befriended me, it stayed staring me out for ages and just didn't move! It even sneezed over me, it felt that comfortable. I had a good chat with it as I stared into its eyes. I know my Mother Dear is around in spirit, but as a bloody donkey??!'

Next stop on the ashes tour was the Isle Of Wight. We never went on holiday much as kids but I do remember one year Mum and Dad took us to the Isle of Wight for a proper seaside holiday. We stayed in a caravan park, went to Blackgang Chine or to Alum Bay to collect the multi-coloured sands, just like I'd imagined other families did or school kids had on end-of-year trips.

It was obviously a happy memory for Mum too because it was one of the places she wanted to go back to. Sadly she never got the chance but instead, the whole family and I piled into our cars and drove down to the ferry and booked caravans on a campsite for the weekend.

One night we decided to get a Chinese takeaway (Mum's favourite) in her honour, but first it was bingo! Penny always moaned that she never won anything but we all told her that we just had a feeling she was going to win and that Mum would help her. By some bizarre turn of events we were right – she hit the jackpot! With her winnings she treated us all to Mum's favourite: egg fried rice, sweet and sour chicken balls and chips.

The next day, the craziness continued. We went to the end of the pier to scatter her ashes. It was set to be another comedy scattering as we threw handfuls into the sea and, just like the New Forest, a gust of wind came from nowhere and the ashes ended up in our faces. We didn't mind though. We agreed Mum was probably having a laugh with us as she watched us spitting her out of our mouths.

I definitely knew she was around when, after having walked through the arcade back to the cars, I realised I had lost my glasses – yet again. I ran back to find them but couldn't. Thinking they were lost, I walked to the entrance just as Penny came in to find me. Out of the blue some young lad, who was playing on a slot machine, turned around and just handed me them. Penny and I stared at each other in disbelief; instantly we both knew it was Mum!

Almost a year after Mum died, with the last of her ashes still in the box, it was time to let her go. The final resting place we'd chosen was a place called Cleeve Hill in Gloucestershire. Mum had always wanted to go to the Cotswolds and Cleeve seemed perfect as it overlooked the famous Cheltenham racecourse.

Mum loved the races, hence the reference in my poem, and we knew she would be happy there, looking down on the gee-gees. After a three-hour journey, the weather was awful and, to cut a long story short, we had to head back home. It wasn't for another six months that just four of us returned and finally laid her to rest.

While we were travelling around, scattering Mum's ashes, it felt like the final chapter of her life was still ongoing. Once we had finished, I expected the heartache would all be over, but it wasn't. Having suffered from mental health problems in the past, I knew only too well what depression felt like, but this time it was different. While before my depression and anxiety and self-harm had seemed irrational in hindsight, this time it made perfect sense to me; I felt like the world was ending. I'd lost my mum, the person I loved most in the entire world, my one constant throughout life.

I went through the motions and focused on working, paying the bills and just praying that one day soon, things would feel better. Over the following 18 months, I still felt utterly consumed with grief; I missed Mum so much that I found it nearly impossible to go out with my friends and have fun or find joy in anything, really. Just when you think you've found ways to manage and move forward, things can take an unexpected turn and the world, and my life, was just about to go bonkers!

18

When the World Stopped

"THEY'RE SAYING IT'S GETTING WORSE IN ENGLAND too, you know," said Kate as we chatted over dinner in a Manhattan restaurant in New York. "I read that hundreds of people are being taken to hospitals now."

I looked around us, and it was definitely quiet for a spot in the middle of the city that supposedly never sleeps. It was March 2020 and I'd taken a much-needed break from work for a few days to visit the Big Apple. Kate and I had dated for about six months the previous year, we'd split, but stayed good mates so she came along with me. We'd been planning the trip for ages. Now it didn't seem like quite such a good idea.

Around Christmas time we'd started hearing about some weird deadly virus in China that was killing people and there was no cure. They called it Coronavirus to begin with, then Covid-19 and it sounded like some crazy conspiracy theory from a disaster movie. I hadn't taken much notice of it to begin with but then I heard Brits from Wuhan, the town where people started falling sick, had been evacuated back to RAF Brize Norton and it seemed pretty serious.

Anyone coming back from China had to be quarantined, so we did check about flights and they were still going from London to New York and most places around the world. How bad could it be? Very bad, it turned out!

The first night we arrived in New York, we were looking around a packed Times Square. Then these messages started to appear on the huge billboards saying that Broadway was shutting. You could hear all the murmurs and saw the disbelief because people were actually queueing for the shows.

Over the next two days, our hotel restaurant announced it was closing; restaurants were boarded up and the streets were emptying. I'd taken a picture on the Manhattan Bridge with no one in sight and later, when I was sitting on the subway, it was completely empty. It was like a scene from a movie where suddenly they heard something awful was going to happen and everyone locked themselves indoors. What was so strange is that it all happened so damned quickly, it was eerie.

Back at the hotel I had a very uneasy feeling and started checking the news on my phone. That's when I saw there had been an announcement in the UK that they were planning to close the borders and stop people from outside Europe coming back – TOMORROW!

"We have to get to the airport and get on a flight," I panicked, already throwing my things into a bag. "No way I am getting stranded over here. I have work, the house and The Boys to get back to. Come on, let's go!"

We jumped in a yellow cab and dashed to JFK, desperately

trying to change our flights on the way. When we got there, it was chaos with people from all over the world panicking as they tried to get back home to their families. Thankfully we managed to get on an early flight. I called Dad and told him we were on our way but things were already moving so fast – he said they were already talking about the country going into 'lockdown'.

What the hell was that?! I started to hear that some other countries like China had begun stopping foreigners going into their counties and people were not allowed to go out. It all just seemed crazy! There was no way I would have ever believed that our government was actually going to make it law in the UK for you to stay in your house.

By the time we hit the tarmac in London, the wheels were already in motion. Constant news bulletins told us the nation was going into lockdown from the very next morning.

Rushing back to Hildenborough, we tried to work out when Kate could go back home. However, her parents being an elderly couple, they were unsure what to do and thought it best if she didn't return to the house. I had no clue it would end up being months!

My phone didn't stop pinging with messages from people asking if we got home alright; it was as if New York had become a war zone. I started getting emails from my PA Andrea who works for my company Double Gold Enterprises and arranges my diary and speaking engagements. The diary had been full of bookings for the spring and summer and suddenly they were cancelling left, right and centre.

The next morning I got up and went out to feed The Boys at 7am as I did every day. Outside seemed even quieter than usual, no distant sounds of cars trundling through the village, no trains and no planes, just dead silence. Back indoors the breakfast TV was showing pictures of central London looking completely deserted, without a single person on the streets. This was getting serious.

Anyone who knows me knows that when I'm stressed or when things seem to be going wrong, I have to keep busy. And with no work to do and the NYC trip cut short, there was nothing much else to do except exercise. I flicked through Instagram and psyched myself up to go outside and do a core workout. I saw more people than ever sharing what they were doing on their stories and grids. No one could go out, so suddenly everyone was online instead.

So one day, when I went out to feed The Boys, I filmed it and introduced each of them in turn to the camera. The comments went wild with everyone saying how cute they were and asking me questions about them. It seems no one had a clue I had six big fuzzy alpacas living out the back of my house.

Over the next few weeks they became celebrities in their own right: Polo, Liquorice, Toffee, Crème Caramel, Truffle and Fudge (who later passed away during lockdown and now his ashes are buried in that same field where his life with me began) with people messaging saying their kids were obsessed with them and wouldn't start homeschooling until they'd seen them in the morning. I got requests to see more of them and to watch them coming into my garden or getting a shower from the hosepipe. To be fair, it's pretty mesmerising because it's so weird!

A few days later I decided to go live and film myself doing my workout. I figured if they were coming online in the morning then perhaps I could encourage them to do some exercise with me too.

I'm sure some people thought I was mad at first just talking to myself and shouting into my iPhone as I counted through my reps but I was surprised to see quite a few people joining and making comments, cheering me on or saying how cool it was to see how an ex-elite athlete trains. It gave me a bit of a boost to be honest, whether they were doing the exercise or not, it was just about connecting with people through the doom and gloom. I decided to document my life through the weird times, not just to share it with my followers but to look back on it too. It felt like this was going to be one of those periods in your life you would not want to forget.

Each morning I filmed The Boys followed by my workout. Over the next couple of weeks, people watching my 'lives' went from a couple of hundred up to about three thousand at one stage, while I was doing my workouts. It was actually an amazing time. I was outside working out, the weather was incredible, the birds were singing like a choir. By now, Joe Wicks was doing YouTube workouts for kids, so I decided to do something a bit different.

I was getting so many questions about what type of training I did now I had retired and what were the best exercises to keep fit. I decided to go back to my PTI days and film some video classes people could follow.

Then, in one of my Instagram stories, I mentioned I would set up a live Zoom for anyone who wanted to join and I would send the entry code to anyone who DM'd asking for it. That evening, instead of going live on Instagram, I logged onto my computer and, one by one, little squares popped up on my screen. Some cameras were off so I said I needed them on as it would help me support them and correct any technique; I also didn't just want people perving and not participating!

Dressed in their sports gear all ready for a workout were all these strangers, young and old, men and women. I had no clue who anyone was and it wasn't my business to pry into their personal lives. I just wanted to connect. It was like my computer screen was a telescope into the living rooms, garages and gardens of all the people who'd been watching me but I had never seen, and now we could actually talk to one another. I went through the exercises and pushed them all to the end.

After one particularly successful session, I said I was going to treat myself to a gin and tonic. To my surprise, a lot of them stayed on and did the same and we all got chatting, getting to know each other. There were people from all over England, Scotland, Wales and Ireland, even France and South Africa, the place I call my second home. Andrea and a couple of friends I knew joined too, so it wasn't too weird and we all just had a laugh like we would have done with friends if the pubs were open.

Lockdown didn't turn out to be the couple of weeks we all thought, did it?! While the novelty of being stuck at home wore off pretty quickly for me, my fitness classes certainly didn't. As the community started to grow, I decided to call it 'Military In Motion', something I had started doing prior to lockdown actually, but at live health and fitness events.

One thing apart from running I think I am good at is being creative, so to switch things up, I started 'Nightcrawl' on a Friday night. My house became like an Amazon depot as each day I ordered wigs, outfits, accessories and props to make the workouts more fun and entertaining.

I figured we could all do with a bit of cheering up and the routines became more and more elaborate, with costume changes off-camera between songs, sometimes as many as eight times a night! Kate would be standing just out of view ready to whip me out of one outfit and into the next.

I think I ended up driving her crazy during those Fridays, repeating and perfecting every routine I was making up for that night. From John Travolta in *Saturday Night Fever* and *Grease*, Tina Turner strutting to *Proud Mary*, to the bearded lady from *the Greatest Showman* and so many more, I was shattered by the time I started at 7pm! Getting to know that community got me through the first lockdown when everything was so uncertain and the world felt like it was spinning out of control. Everyone was dealing with life changes in different ways and so was I.

In August, I was called in for an operation I had been waiting for. It was touch and go whether it would happen because like everyone, appointments were getting cancelled and hospitals were turning into Covid centres. I was extremely lucky to get my Haglund's sorted – a growth on the heel bone – because by now, with all the jumping up and down like a madwoman, it was killing.

Despite this physical setback I didn't stop taking the core in the mornings on Instagram even with my crutches. I adapted the sessions I was doing. Work started to come back and my public speaking engagements moved on to Zoom too. Do you know what? I actually started to really enjoy being at home for once. I missed Mum, of course, and it made me sad that I could only see my family on a screen, even 'celebrating' my 39 plus 11 birthday on my computer but looking at what was happening in hospitals and care homes up and down the country, I felt pretty lucky.

* * * * *

In October it hit me. Lying on the sofa, shivering, I pulled the blanket over me as my head was pounding. I didn't have a cough, but every breath felt like someone was punching me in the chest, it was so tight, and I just couldn't seem to catch my breath or fill my lungs with oxygen. After six months of lockdown and endless measures to try to stop the pandemic, Coronavirus had finally got a grip on the world and had got me! I felt horrendous.

I turned on the TV to see Boris Johnson standing there with his scientists again, peering over the wooden lectern with a very serious face. STAY AT HOME>>PROTECT THE NHS>>SAVE LIVES, the words screamed from a luminous yellow plaque in front of him. The lockdown had eased for a while but now we were back in the thick of it and I'd tested positive.

My temperature was through the roof and I hadn't slept properly for days as Covid-19 had taken over my body. I was in so much pain, I felt so weak and I could hardly walk around the house, let alone go out for fresh air. It had been a week since I'd seen those little red lines on the plastic test. I was getting worse, not better, and I was starting to panic.

"The number of admissions to hospital of people with coronavirus has increased again, I'm afraid to say," Boris told us as scary-looking graphs of the death toll flashed up on the screen.

"Next slide please," Chris Whitty, the man who seemed to have all the answers asked. "You will see this line shows deaths from Covid-19 in the last seven days," he said calmly. But the line on the screen showed a terrifying picture of the death toll from this mystery illness.

Just a few months earlier, life had been normal. I'd been travelling all over the world for work, speaking to rooms full of thousands of people, catching up with family and friends. But now as I lay there on the sofa in a cold sweat.

Now I was infected, I couldn't do anything, no Zooms, no workouts. Even worse, I was concerned because I'd had problems with asthma since I was a child, something I've always had to fight through in the army and during my professional athletics career. It was one of the reasons I'd always kept so fit and healthy through diet and exercise and generally caring for my body.

When we first heard about the virus, one of the things they said was that people who'd had underlying health conditions or lung conditions would have to be extra-vigilant because it could become very serious for them. Weirdly, though, we were finding out that really fit people were dying too – it was becoming crazy! Now I had the virus, there was nothing I could do except wait and hope it passed.

As the days went on, I lost all my taste and smell, plus my troubled breathing didn't seem to lift. There were times in the night when I was in so much pain, I worried I should go to hospital, but everything you read seemed to suggest you were safer at home.

For three weeks, I just battled through. As the physical symptoms didn't lift, Covid and being in isolation started to take its toll on my mental health too. Alone with my thoughts, I had nothing but time to relive things that still haunted me. I thought about Mum and how such a huge part of my heart still felt like it was missing. I knew you couldn't put a time on grief but at that point I felt no better than the day I found out she was gone, and wondered if I would ever feel normal again.

When I was rushing around working and seeing friends I could keep my mind off the dreadful feeling of loss some of the time but now I just wanted her there with me.

The worst thing was watching the TV and hearing about all the deaths, not just from Covid but because of other conditions that were not being treated during lockdown. It's no exaggeration to say there were moments when I thought, 'what if I don't make it through?" and started to think about my own mortality.

I imagined my friends and family being at my funeral, saying how sad they were for me because I'd never managed to truly find peace with myself and be proud of who I was inside. And what was there to stop someone going to the newspapers and telling them about my private life after I died?

It made me start thinking that it was MY right to talk about that part of my life.

I was honestly so low, I worked myself into tears so many times in those dark few weeks. It just made me so sad that I'd lost Mum and promised myself I would start living my truth on my own terms, yet here I was still a prisoner of my own silence.

Thankfully, after ten weeks, the physical symptoms of Covid started to improve. I finally got my taste and smell back and I began to build myself back up; at first just by walking as I was still recovering from my operation, and then gradually getting back into the gym. But while my physical strength was returning, I found myself firmly in the clutches of my spiralling mental health.

We now know that there was a huge spike in people suffering from anxiety, depression and other mental health problems during the pandemic. Perhaps it was the isolation, the uncertainty about the future and the time to reflect on the past or just sit with your demons, for me it was one of the darkest times of my life. That was when I realised just how bad things had become for me. Little did I know they were about to get worse.

After my previous breakdowns, I was no stranger to the feelings of helplessness and lack of control that go along with emotional and mental turmoil. But having promised myself on the day Mum died that would be the last time I would self-harm, my coping mechanisms, no matter how destructive, were no longer there as a crutch. I refused to resort to the bathroom scissors again or the relief I felt by piercing my skin and watching the blood flow. But my other coping mechanisms had all been robbed from me in the pandemic too.

You're probably getting the impression by now that I'm a 100-miles-an hour person. I need to be doing things all the time. I need goals and challenges and to be spinning plates in the air, that's how I've always been. That's just who I am – nothing by halves. It's probably the reason I managed to become an elite athlete while holding down a full-time job in the armed forces for such a long time, and how I'd managed to build a success-ful business, charity and public speaking career. I was rarely alone with my thoughts and when I was, that was when things started to go wrong for me. In the middle of the pandemic, with lockdown restrictions changing every few weeks, stopping us all from seeing our loved ones, working normally, travelling and doing all the things I usually relied on to keep me sane, I was lost.

Military In Motion felt like the only thing that kept me going. My 'Troopers' as I now called them, were amazing, sending me gifts and well wishes. I didn't let them know how bad things were for me, as I had only known them a relatively short amount of time. Yet they were my source of happiness and light during the days.

It was the nights that heightened my despair. As I felt myself plummet, I thought maybe I should try and get some profes-sional help. It was clear now that this wasn't just something that happened when I was under immense pressure or in the shock and grief of loss, but something that was a part of who I am, and a result of my experiences over many years. I thought back to those little chocolate herbal tablets the doctor had given me all those years ago in France, the anti-depressants that my local doctor Paul had prescribed me during the years after retiring when I felt so lost and he diagnosed me with clinical depression. I didn't want tablets but wished I could see someone now. But the same fear was still there, holding me back. What if I went to see someone and they leaked it to the press, or worse, contacted the British Army to inform them? Would they have a duty to pass the information on if I had told them I'd broken the law? So irrational I know, but by now these were my deep-rooted fears.

I should say for anyone reading this who has the same fears: doctors and counsellors are all bound by a code of practice which means they can not share your personal information with anyone else unless you give them permission. I should also say that you can't face court-martial for something which happened while you were serving the military as it is no longer 'a crime'. In fact it hadn't been since 2000 when the ban had been lifted.

I wish more than anything I just had the courage to compute this, because I would have saved myself years of anguish. But for over 30 years since I'd enrolled in the British Army, there I was, still terrified and ruled by those draconian, homophobic rules. I wished more than anything that Mother Dear was still around for me to talk to but she would never come back, plus she would have absolutely hated these times, it would have driven her crazy.

After my symptoms had eased and my fears of giving way to Covid had subsided, the feeling of weakness endured. I started going back into the gym, doing my workouts again, and getting the Military In Motion gang back together but off-camera I would feel completely drained. The same with work – I would get up and put on my make-up, choose a nice top, while keeping my PJs or leggings on under the table, trying to be all smiles and full of motivation for my audience for the hour they booked. Then I'd have to go for a lie down as I'd worn myself out. I just kept telling myself if I carried on eventually things would go back to normal. But once I felt physically fit again, something still wasn't right. That dark cloud of depression had got a grip on me again and I was really struggling to shake it off.

Perhaps this time I wouldn't, and that thought terrified me the most.

19

—

Rock Bottom

WHEN WINTER CAME AROUND, THE NIGHTS GOT shorter and everything was dark and grey, it became even harder to keep my head above water. When we first went into lockdown it was incredible; beautiful sunshine, exercising outside, sunbathing in the garden, but in the winter months it was pretty bleak.

Then one night I was lying in bed, unable to sleep when I found myself completely hopeless. I still can't pinpoint what exactly drove me to the brink but I began to envisage myself creeping out of the bedroom and into the kitchen, and going into the cutlery drawer where I kept the sharpest knives. I'd promised myself I would never self-harm again, but this time it wasn't a compulsion to cut myself to relieve the pressure and jolt myself back to reality.

I knew it was more serious and, for the first time, I thought if I had that knife in my hand, I could end my life. It's a terrifying realisation for anyone to get to that point where you feel like there is no other option, no way out of how you feel.

Lying in my bed that night I felt the muscles in my arms tense, pinning the duvet down either side of my shaking body as I stared into the darkness barely seeing through the tears. What was happening to me? Only months earlier I'd been petrified of dying from Covid and now I was imagining taking my own life. It made no sense.

The risk of asking for help now seemed somehow much less, when faced with the other alternative. It was as though the shock of thinking what I might be capable of jolted me into reality, just like self-harming once used to.

I reached for my phone and typed in 'celebrity psychologist'. It seems like such a weird search term doesn't it? I didn't type it in because I think of myself as a celeb! I did think if I spoke to someone who had experience of treating people in the public eye I could probably trust them. Maybe someone who made their living out of being discreet would be more invested in helping me keep my sexuality hidden.

The first thing that came up in my Google search was the psychologist who treated Jesy Nelson from Little Mix when she had her breakdown. I remembered a year earlier that she'd done a BBC documentary about her mental health struggles caused by the bullying on social media she suffered from being in the public eye.

Her situation was completely different from mine but we had a lot of the same symptoms in the end – feelings of hopelessness and wanting to just disappear from this planet. I thought if she'd managed to get help it was worth a try to see if this person could do something for me too, so I wrote an email, for the first time in my life, asking for help.

Even hitting 'send', I was terrified, but if it was a choice between that and slipping into a state where I wasn't strong enough to stop myself from opening that knife drawer, it had to be done. Even if it was 1.30am.

The rest of that night felt like an eternity until the sun came up and I forced myself to get out of bed, get dressed and log on for work. I still can't believe how I managed to keep going through such dark times but maybe it was years of practice. The same drive that made me cover my self-harm scars with make-up and get out there on the track or made me log on and give my all to the clients who had booked me to talk to their employees.

Since the start of the pandemic, all my speaking engagements and corporate training gigs had gone online just like everything else in the world it seemed. It was strange to have hundreds of faces in little boxes staring back at me or looking at myself in the screen, knowing they were all watching me with their screens turned off and volume muted, instead of standing on a stage and being able to see them all in the room with me; seeing their facial expressions, using my energy to inspire and motivate and feel that buzz and sense of accomplishment. But I had no choice if I wanted to keep my business going, just like so many other people who were adapting what they did to get by.

It's funny really, for someone who suffered so much anxiety and self-doubt in their personal life, but being on a stage transformed me into another person. It's like over the years I have become an expert at putting my game face on and doing the best job possible. Perhaps it goes back to my life as a PTI when I was calling the shots and shouting at groups of male and female soldiers in PT. Or perhaps it was just years of learning how to hide my true self that made me good at performing when I needed to.

Either way, usually I loved my job, meeting new people from all over the world in all different industries and sharing my experiences with them to help with their wellbeing and success. But now it was all online, just faces in boxes on a screen, it got harder as it wasn't the same. I still did my very best though, like running a race to get to the finish line, but when I logged off, I was back to feeling horrendous.

Thankfully, the same day I sent my email, the psychologist I'd contacted got back to me and suggested that we have a phone call to talk more about what I felt I needed and wanted from her help. I knew something had to change.

By now the world was burning anyway. Covid was showing no signs of stopping, civil unrest and global protests were sweeping the world after George Floyd's murder in the US earlier that year and it felt like there was no real hope of an end in sight.

So maybe now was time to just rip off the plaster and see what happened. We spoke on the phone for about an hour as I told her how I'd emailed in the early hours of the morning because I'd been worried about my mental health and frightened I might harm myself. I told her I'd lost Mum, that I'd had a history of self-harm and depression and that the global pandemic had brought it all to a head. Saying it all out loud actually helped in itself because it made me realise that actually it was no surprise that I was feeling this way when there was so much going on.

But there was that one big underlying secret that loomed like a shadow over everything else. 'F**k it', I thought, 'just say it'. And so I did. "I'm also gay but I don't feel like I can be open about it because I'm so scared!"

I had a few more sessions with her but it wasn't necessarily helping me decide what to do next. Instead of going any further with therapy at that point, I did what I knew best – I threw myself back into work and exercise. All my life, being busy and being successful have been the two things that have kept my head up, even in the darkest of times, and I thought if I could just keep my head above water like other people were trying to do during the pandemic, I would get through.

By now I was focused on another company I had started, creating a corporate health and wellbeing app with a guy who is no longer a friend after 14 years. I won't belittle him in my book but basically it showed a downside of mixing friendship with business. I was also running a lot of virtual medal events and challenges for Military In Motion and, apart from looking knackered, I am not sure they really knew what was going on. I wanted to keep them going as much as I could.

Logging onto another Zoom engagement one day in April 2021 I could feel my heart pounding. I felt like I was already on the verge of tears but I did what I always did – put a brave face on to get the job done.

On this particular day, I was asked to talk about mental health in the workplace. It was something that almost a decade after I first started championing it, was now becoming a bit of a buzzword in the corporate world. Talking about feelings and psychological wellbeing was no longer a taboo but something most businesses were having to do in order to stay competitive and keep their staff happy. There are awards for that sort of thing now and it has become a big PR tool for big corporations to prove they are doing the right thing and leaving the hard management and tough love of the past behind.

Usually I was well up for talking about it and I was always ecstatic that it was being taken more seriously and that people wanted to learn from what I had to say. But on this particular day, my own mental health was getting the better of me. I suppose there's kind of an irony there but as I sat in my office preparing for the call, I could feel the symptoms of self-doubt and I was procrastinating. Being cynical about my ability to do my job well. I was exhausted from not sleeping properly and my body was full of tension.

I felt sick to my stomach and shaky as I dialled into the call and tried my best to smile and put the Dame Kelly Holmes work face on. It's a good job it wasn't in person on a stage because it would have been more obvious how jittery I was.

But as I was introduced to the group by the session host, I just felt an overwhelming urge to be honest. It would have been so hypocritical of me to stand there and pretend I had it all figured out and had all the answers when in reality I was suffering right in that very moment.

"I'm here to talk about mental health," I started, wondering if they would be able to hear my wavering voice, "but I have to tell you, I'm not in a good place this morning. I'm really struggling."

I wondered as the words came out whether it was a huge mistake and I would be burning bridges with the company that had hired me to impart my wisdom to its staff, but I carried on and the more I talked, the more engaged the people looked. The more I spoke, and heard my own feelings out loud, the more I realised what I was going through and that something had to change. I had physical burnout.

That's the thing about poor mental health. First of all, it affects everyone in some way or another because we are all human. Secondly, it can hit you at any time. It's not like there is some magic cure or an off-switch. It doesn't matter how much success, money, love or time you have. It doesn't discriminate and doesn't stop you from ever suffering again.

That morning, I knew I needed to take a break. So as I shut my laptop, I knew that would be my last engagement for a while. Ironically, the feedback from the booker was amazing. They loved that I had been so raw and honest about the way I was feeling and given an insight to the people on the call about how mental health can affect even a Dame of the British Empire with two Olympic gold medals!

I texted Kerrie to tell her I needed to talk. She is amazing at that and I feel so blessed to have her in my life, even now after all these years. Just one message in the middle of a chaotic work or family time to tell her I need 'friends time' and she knows what to do. So the next day we met at Mum's bench.

"You have to take a break," Kerrie said as she looked at me and I told her about what had happened. "It's time to just focus on you for a while, you're completely burnt out and you won't get better until you stop."

I felt the tears pricking my eyes and I knew she was right. Here I was at 51 (ouch), with an amazing career, successful charity work, great friends and family but still the pain and fear of not being able to live authentically – to be who I am – was getting to my core.

As we sat on the bench I thought, 'what if Mother Dear could see me now?' She would hate how torn up I was over it all and that made it hurt even more. Back home that night I wrote a very hard post on Instagram and added a clip of me and Kerrie on Mum's bench. I wrote:

'Yesterday I met my amazing and lovely friend Kerrie, who has been my best friend since day one of secondary school (a long, long time). But she is someone who knows me so well, and knows everything about me!! (No, she won't tell). Anyway, we went to meet at my mum's bench and after a run we had a good chat... I think it's important to share. So this post announces that I will be stepping back from all my corporate and commercial work to

find 'me' at least until the end of May! Time out, doing jobs that have long been left, trying things that I haven't done, spending time with family and friends, setting myself physical challenges, doing my house and garden up, changing things that need to be changed, grabbing more me-time.

'This is one of the boldest, hardest, scariest decisions I have made since I retired from my athletics career (15 years ago). ACTUALLY I AM REALLY SCARED. But it's time and it's got to be done! I have had a few bad weeks of emotional dilemma and feel that I am not heading in the right direction. My mental health has deteriorated and I am scared I will regress to where I don't want to go. Whilst I am 'away' I will still be doing some stories but mainly about what I am doing, not necessarily about me. So, over and out on here for a little while.'

The two weeks I had in my head turned into ten months as I called off speaking engagements and other work to focus on getting myself better, but somehow things only got worse.

My mental health was at its lowest point during lockdown. During the 10 months that I took away from my commercial work, I was suffering both mentally and physically. My body was shutting down. My glands were up and I was getting cold sores on my face on a regular basis. When we were allowed out for exercise, I ran. In the past, running has brought me a sense of release and relaxation but now I was using it as a tool to punish myself.

One day I got out my weighted vest from my gym. The vest was 20kg! I put it on and ran down to Mum's bench. It's 4.5 miles each way, but I needed to get out. The constant narrative in my head was causing me to be consumed with the need to be free from my demons and, most of all, to be happy. Mum's bench became my place of solitude, as did the hills of Knole Park. My energy was so low after getting Covid, but I pushed myself so much. It was all just self-sabotage. I needed to get help. I was as scared as I had been all these years and yet the alternative of remaining silent and not using my voice was becoming more and more painful.

Because I couldn't speak publicly, I started recording voice notes on my phone. Maybe that seems silly as they were only for me to hear but I just had this overwhelming urge to use my voice and speak my truth even if I couldn't do it for all to hear. The notes became increasingly erratic as time went on and when I listen back to them now it makes me cry to hear just how desperate, trapped and helpless I felt.

"I need to use my voice, I need to speak up and finally be free to live as who I am. It's 2021 and I have kept this hidden for 33 years. I need to find a way."

* * * * *

I believe, if you let them, the right people come into your life at the right time and there is always a reason for it. Whether it was Sarah on that holiday in Chichester when I was feeling broken by my injuries or Pat on that beach in Cyprus when I needed my hair doing – or even the wonderful people brought into my life by Military In Motion thanks to the pandemic – I believe they all have reasons for being led into my world.

After my chat with my first therapist I realised that although I'd made the enormous step forward by asking for help, I hadn't quite found the right person and I couldn't let her in. A relationship with a therapist is a bit like a romantic relationship in that you have to have a certain chemistry for it to work; it's no criticism of anyone if you don't quite find the right match straight off. That was the case for me. I thought if I'd spent such a long time psyching myself up to tell someone my most personal problems and to try to get well again, I owed it to myself not to settle for the first person that came along. Then I struck absolute gold.

Dr Tania Pilley was not a therapist to the stars but there was something about her that just drew me in when I had the opportunity to speak with her on a Zoom. I felt instantly at ease with her. She was a straight woman about my age, who wore a pair of crazy multicoloured glasses on her smiley face.

She told me she used alternative methods as well as traditional talking therapies to help people achieve their goals, improve their mental health and wellbeing. I've always been the kind of person who prefers talking face-to-face so when Tania invited me down to see her in person to talk about things in more detail, I was nervous but felt positive. I got in the car and drove down from Kent to Dorset to meet at her home. When we saw one another, I knew almost instantly that we were going to hit it off.

We spoke for a couple of hours about what I had been going through and she asked me what had forced me to a crisis point when I decided to get help. I told her about the night when I almost relapsed into self-harm. She asked why I thought that was. I found myself talking more easily than I had done for years and gave her a brief overview of my personal story over recent years.

Tania diagnosed that I had childhood trauma, unresolved issues with Mum and with my time in the army, as well as the problem of keeping my sexuality out of the public eye. It was overwhelming to hear someone tell me all the things they feel might be causing so much pain but I felt seen and understood.

On my first day there, she suggested we do some work on my emotional state by doing Brainwave Therapy, or Neurofeedback as it's also known. I'd never heard of it before and it sounded a bit wacky but, to be honest, at that stage I was happy to try anything.

I felt strange sitting there in her little office at her house, with electrodes stuck to my head as she watched the brainwaves in my muddled mind. I imagined they would be going out of control with everything that had been swirling around in my head for months or even years but when she looked at the results, she just said: "You're flatlining."

I had no idea what she meant but she explained that I had become so exhausted and reached such a point dealing with my own stress and trauma that my mind had started to shut down on me to protect itself. She called this 'emotional flatlining'. The only time I'd ever heard the term flatlining before was watching medical shows on the telly and they never seemed to end well! But Tania assured me she could help.

I was only going to stay a night but that turned into almost a week. I talked to her about my earliest memories of Mum, St George's, and how I was terrified she would never come back. We talked about the feelings of fear and loneliness that came with realising I could have lost my career, and my failed relationships. And of course we talked about losing Mum.

It wasn't just the talking that helped, it was her mad personality and she made me laugh out loud, something I hadn't done in so many years. Tania was even delusional and insisted on coming on a run with me – let's just say, she never runs. I'm not sure she knew what she was letting herself in for but we had such a laugh, with her puffing and panting her way along the river banks, she said she thought she was having a heart attack!

Back at her house I found myself organising her kitchen cupboards and doing fridge management. We both found it funny that she was organising my brain and I was reorganising her kitchen.

At some point before the end of the week, after so much talking, we discussed what I thought I wanted from my life going forward and how I thought I could achieve it. It's such a big question for anyone to answer and in the past I never knew how to answer it, but I knew in my mind at that point that the only way I was going to be truly happy was to be honest about who I really am.

"I want to be free to be me," I said. I knew that meant one day I was going to have to come out and at last that felt OK.

20

—

I'm Coming Out

A FEW YEARS BEFORE I MET TANIA I'D MET A MAN called Emanuele Palladino at an event for British sporting heroes in London. By chance, I was seated on a table with him and his client, Welsh rugby legend Gareth Thomas. Gareth was equal parts inspiration and source of envy to me as he had bravely been one of the first international sports stars to come out.

In 2009, after his fourth Rugby World Cup, he became the first openly gay rugby player in the world. He then did an amazing documentary revealing that he was HIV positive and attacking the stigma attached to gay men in his position.

I have worked with a few different agents in the past including a wonderful lady, Bev James, who I had a close working relationship with, but sometimes it's just hard mixing friendship with business – although I am pretty sure our paths will cross again – and then others who I didn't feel comfortable being open with.

At the time, coming out seemed like a complete pipedream

that would never happen. I didn't even want to think about it. But after my breakthrough with Tania, I started to wonder whether I needed to get an agent who would at least understand some of the complexities around sexual orientation and 'coming out' so I emailed Emanuele and we arranged a meeting at The 1809 Hub, my former coffeehouse, Café 1809-turned-events space.

There we could talk openly about what I was going through. I explained to him that although many people had made assumptions about my sexuality, I had never felt able to live my life authentically in the public eye being a gay woman.

Sitting under the eaves of the Hub, with my victory pictures looking down on me, I discussed how I thought doing a documentary would be a step forward, enabling me to articulate some really sensitive subjects, whilst tackling the demons that I carried in my head; ultimately to move towards finally being true to myself and happy. I'd been on one tough journey, blighted by injuries and setbacks before fulfilling my dream as an Olympic champion, but an even harder one trying to fit within society, knowing that it would never be an easy task.

More and more I felt the need to publicly come out. I would swing between feeling desperate to do it and then being terrified. Growing up in the '80s there was a huge stigma around being 'gay' or 'bisexual' and I suppose I had seen over the years both the continued bigotry and judgement about people's sexuality if it didn't conform to the so-called 'society norm'. I also felt jealous of the relaxed way the younger generation were able to just come out with a single post on Instagram and then go on living their lives in a true and authentic way. I knew that could never work for me. My story was far more deeply rooted for that.

There was so much time that had elapsed since I first decided to keep my mouth shut about the people I loved that I felt I needed not only to come out, but also to explain why it had taken me so long. The last thing I wanted was for people in the LGBT+ community to think I was ashamed of being gay or that I thought there was something wrong with it. I needed people to understand that there was a very real and rational fear surrounding my silence.

The thing is, I actually don't think many people in society even knew a ban on being gay in the armed forces even existed. And definitely not that the European Court of Human Rights had ruled the ban on being LGB in the military to be unlawful in 2000 and that restrictions had been lifted. Also, in sport, how many world class gay athletes do you know that were out before 2004? Exactly?!

So, thinking again about Gareth and Jesy, I realised that maybe the only way to really deal with this was to tell my story in full by doing a documentary – a raw and honest look at what it was like to be me. And maybe then, as well as freeing myself from the burden, perhaps I would be able to help other people in the same position as me.

I had privately started to tell just a couple of people my idea and then Emanuele mentioned we could ask Gary Lineker's production company Goalhanger for a meeting about doing a documentary. I knew his company had produced some really hard-hitting programmes in the past so I had a feeling they might be interested, yet I knew there was one big hurdle if I wanted to even get them on board: I would have to actually tell them my story.

The idea of saying the words out loud still filled me with dread, but I was getting better at it, I had to keep telling myself that. If I wanted any hope of ever being able to go public, I knew I needed to be able to at least tell a producer. Plus, it wouldn't be the first time I'd been in a documentary, so I knew what to expect from the process to a degree and that helped keep me from completely losing it!

In 1996, as I trained for my first Olympic Games in Atlanta, USA, I'd taken part in a documentary narrated by Sean Bean, of all people. A film crew came to the barracks where I was still working as a PTI while training for the Games.

They filmed me putting a group of male recruits through their paces across an assault course, shouting orders as they scrambled over giant nets and ran around the field. I look back at that footage and smile at how strong and centred I seem doing the job I love.

It's strange to think that while I was excelling at work and in my sporting career, I was already hiding the secret that would come to haunt me so much in my later life. At that point I was just laser-focused on being a success, both in the military and as a runner. I was at the beginning of what would become an 18-year journey to finally getting my double gold and now I was at the start of another journey that I couldn't afford to take as long.

Luckily, my hopes of having a compassionate and trusting team around me were realised, when I met the Executive Producer Tony Pastor, Producer Jonathan Gill and Director Lucy Rogers. We met in the café of a big art gallery in central London. We had a discreet table in the corner of the room.

The place was buzzing with conversation and the clinking of cutlery and glasses. I still felt anxious when I had to say out loud: "I'm gay, I've just never felt able to say that publicly," but as soon as I'd said it, I felt more relaxed. It's such a strange feeling to tell people you're gay and get no reaction, when you've spent your whole life worrying about how people will respond. Of course it was brilliant to see how much the world has changed but it still blew my mind every time I said it out loud and no one flinched.

I spent an hour or so explaining to Lucy about the military ban on homosexuality and basically how I had lived a life of different traumas and the need to start to change that. Lucy and her team were astonished by my experiences and were keen from the get-go to tell my story in a documentary they planned to pitch to a TV channel. But before we could get the show commissioned, they needed to know if we could have access to the army of today; to interview serving soldiers and to go to the barracks where I could talk more about my life in the military.

It became clear from that first meeting that the only way to get my story out there would be to confront the very institution that had suppressed me and set me on a spiral of self-destruction, but one which I also loved and was still very much a part of since I was made Honorary Colonel. "I'm going to have to think about how I do this," I told them.

I also said that if we were going to work together, I needed to have full editorial control – this was finally my chance to tell the truth about my life and I wanted it to be in my own words, no one else's.

* * * * *

Back home in my office in Hildenborough, I started researching on the internet about what would happen to someone who came out as gay now, but had served in the army under the ban, but it just wasn't clear. Just like civilians didn't even seem to know the ban had ever existed, the consequences didn't seem to be discussed anywhere – perhaps because others in my position also felt too scared to speak up.

Instead I turned to Instagram and I came across the LBGT+ British Army Network page. As I scrolled through the pictures on their feed, I saw men and women proudly carrying rainbow flags while wearing their uniforms, and marching on parade at Pride events. There was even a picture of them laying a wreath at the Cenotaph on Remembrance Day and all of this was interspersed with photos of everything I love about the military – Queen Elizabeth, the stories of brave veterans, fallen heroes and shining medals.

I felt a pang of jealousy as well as happiness for the way things had moved on and they were allowed to live their lives so freely. It was almost incomprehensible how much things had progressed since I left in 1997. I knew the law had changed but I couldn't believe how open and positive the army now was about the very same people who just two decades earlier had been shunned, punished and ostracised. But most of the people smiling in the pictures were much younger than me and would have enrolled in the army long after the ban was lifted, so they were in the clear. I still didn't know what the consequences of coming out would be for someone in my position who broke the law of the time.

One woman who appeared to be central to the LGBT+ community was Colonel Clare Phillips, soon to be Brigadier. As a senior officer, and after reading a few of her posts, I guessed she was likely to have been in the army before the ban was lifted. Yet here she was still serving at a very high rank and openly celebrating all the diversity that makes up the forces now. For some reason I knew instantly, if I was going to tell someone once and for all, she was the one.

I kept turning over in my mind how she would react and how I would cope if she told me I could still be in some kind of serious trouble with the military. In my most paranoid moment, I envisaged the RMP knocking on my door and filling me with the same panic and terror they had when they raided our barracks rooms when I was 22! But what was worse – facing the consequences of what had happened 32 years earlier or living another 32 with it still hanging over my head? The truth was, I feared if I didn't do something radical I might not even be here to see the next ten.

I sent Colonel Phillips a message, but didn't tell her what I wanted to talk to her about, just that I was making a documentary and wondered if she could help me. She replied by giving me her phone number and organised a call to discuss more. Now there was no turning back.

As I waited nervously in my office for the time to tick around, I wondered whether I was making a huge mistake but I really was on a mission now. When I decide to do something in life, I don't stop until I get there, no matter how many hurdles I have to cross or how difficult it might be.

When she answered the phone, Clare sounded pleased to hear from me and addressed me with my military rank, as I did her, immediately making me feel that sense of belonging and pride that I'd loved so much during my time serving. I told her how I'd found her profile and explained I was planning to make a documentary about my life. Then I had to say those words again: "I'm gay and I was gay when I was in the army for nearly ten years but I have always kept it hidden because of the ban. If I come out now, what will happen to me?"

There was a brief pause on the line and then she said: "Nothing at all. Nothing will happen to you. The ban was lifted over 20 years ago and the army is a completely different place now." I should have felt a wave of relief wash over me, but to begin with I just couldn't quite take in the words. I asked the same question again and again, making sure she understood what I was saying and asking her if she was completely sure nothing could happen to me, but each time the answer came back the same – I was safe, I was free, no one could do anything to me now.

"I'm actually horrified that you thought you could still be punished now after all these years," Clare said. "I had no idea there were still people living with that fear, it must have been so difficult for you."

I felt my eyes well up as she told me she had also been forced to live two separate lives when she joined the army in 1995, and how she suffered many of the same fears and anxieties that I had.

We talked about the raids and the RMP investigations, hidden relationships and derogatory nicknames; all the things I'd buried in my past. It felt so good to talk to someone who had been through the same thing as I had, and to see that she's not only survived beyond the ban but that her career had thrived.

She told me that just a year earlier in 2020 she'd been invited to join the LGBT+ Network as a Co-Chair. She explained how the network aims to support army soldiers and officers who are members of the LGBT+ community and the army's chain of command. They even had equivalent networks in the RAF, Royal Navy, civil service and across the MOD, which blew my mind. It seemed it wasn't all just PR spin, the institution really had changed.

I knew if I wanted to tell my story, to really explain what had happened to me and so many others, I needed to gain access to serving personnel of all different ranks; to talk to them about their experiences – as well as people like me who had served in the bad old days under the ban. Colonel Phillips couldn't give me permission to do this, it had to come right from the top, Major General Neil Sexton.

I now had the assurance that I wasn't putting myself at risk of legal action or public shaming. My confidence was growing so I requested a meeting with him. The date came through for a Zoom meeting and this time as I logged on, I felt a sense of strength. I knew it was going to be much harder talking to a high-ranking, straight, white male officer who had served during the time when someone like me would have been vilified, but he had what I needed and I was determined to get it.

To my total surprise, as I started to explain the documentary, he seemed intrigued. I started to explain to him how frightened I had been throughout my adult life and that I could not take living in fear any more. I told him about the raids and the humiliation I had endured but also some of the deep mental health problems that it had led to.

He said he was sad to hear my story and ashamed of the way I'd been treated, but more so how it had affected my life. He told me he had no idea just how bad it had been for some serving soldiers who had endured this and even worse kinds of humiliation, but that he hoped it was much better in the military now and that he wanted to help me.

"You will have as much access as you need to the barracks, the serving personnel and anything else you need," he told me. "And after I'm gone from this role, I will make sure whoever comes next will allow you the same access until your story is told."

To hear him being so compassionate and supportive confirmed just how important my story was to tell. It was no longer just about me but about all the other loyal military servicemen and women who were victimised during their careers. A chance to speak for them too.

* * * * *

Three months after I decided to come out once and for all, at a meeting in a quiet bar at the Hilton Hotel in London Bridge, the dream became a very scary, but exciting reality. Emanuele and I met up with the Director of Sport, Niall Sloane, from ITV.

He listened to my wishes and all the access I'd managed to get from the army and he loved the idea. He commissioned a 45-minute one-off documentary to be aired on ITV1 later that year, the title being 'Kelly Holmes: Being Me.' It was my platform at last to tell the world who I really was. Not just a soldier, or an Olympian or a Dame but a proud gay woman who wanted to help other people just like me.

So that was it. I told my close friends and family what I planned to do and they were amazingly supportive. All any of them – Mum included – had wanted, was for me to be happy, safe and comfortable in my own skin and free to be me. As the filming got going, I asked Dad, Kevin, Stuart, Lisa and Kerrie, to come around when the filming crew were there. We all stood around the large kitchen island, reminiscing about when I first came out to them. I asked Dad for the first time how he had really felt when I sent him that letter from trade training to tell him I was gay.

"I just thought if she's happy enough then why not? It don't bother me!"

He's a man of few words in his best common Kent accent, but sometimes they are just the right ones! Hearing him say that again all those years later made me well up, as I had when he'd called asking to come to the barracks and see me. I realised how lucky I was to have my loving family and friends around, who have always supported me and I also realised my story could have gone a very different way, especially knowing how devastating it can be for many of the LGBT+ community who get rejected by their families.

During filming I decided to talk to a couple of veterans who had been kicked out of the military. I went down to Bournemouth to meet a lady called Emma Riley who'd joined the Royal Women's Naval Service in 1990 to follow her dream of a military career. She told me that even though she was celibate, she was reported to the Navy's Special Investigation Branch just for telling someone she thought she might be gay.

"I thought she was a friend so I confided in her how I was feeling and then the next morning at 6am I was woken up and told to get up, get dressed, get downstairs, you're under arrest."

The 'friend' Emma had confided in had called the police to report her for even thinking she might be gay, let alone having a relationship with anyone. It showed just how deeply ingrained homophobia was in the culture of the military and it made me so sad to hear that she'd lost everything, her job, her future prospects because of it.

It was hard not to imagine how easily I could have been in that same situation myself if someone had chosen to dob me in, the same way Emma was betrayed and I started to feel my anger grow. I must highlight here that Emma has now become a good friend and we have been on a tough, but rewarding journey together since we met.

Another veteran I met, David Kelsey, who later became Mayor of Bournemouth, had been 'discharged with dishonour', marched out of his barracks and forced to leave his medal behind when he left. These people were willing to put their lives on the line for Crown and Country and yet they were treated like animals when they were found out simply for liking someone.

As a complete contrast, when I went back to barracks to talk to serving personnel about life in the army now, I finally got to meet with Clare, now Brigadier Phillips (for those that don't know about rank, a brigadier is a high-ranking officer). Anyway, for those who watch my documentary, you will see the huge sense of connection and gratitude I have for her. Speaking to the soldiers was so surreal as the parallels of our journeys were worlds apart, but it was heartwarming to know how much the world and the forces have moved forward.

I found it hard to get my head around how something so extreme could have really changed so much in the space of just a couple of decades, so I wanted to see it for myself. I knew from social media and the sporting community that there was one highly successful sporting couple who had been open about their same-sex relationship throughout their careers.

Lauren Price and Karriss Artingstall both won medals at the summer Olympic Games in Tokyo 2020 (taking place in 2021 due to the pandemic) for boxing but Karriss is also a former member of the Royal Horse Artillery, where she started her sporting career. The pair are openly gay and have supported each other to their huge successes which I think is incredible but so hard to comprehend how different life can be now for young sporting talent.

While filming, Lucy and I went to visit them in training at the English Institute of Sport in Sheffield and they seemed so happy and at ease with one another in front of the cameras as they spoke about their relationship and their careers. It was unimaginable to me just a few years ago that it could even be possible and I felt a twinge of sadness that I hadn't been allowed the same opportunities. It's easy to think about what would have happened if life had been different for me, but it wasn't, so I was intrigued to talk more.

To my surprise, Karriss never knew there had been a ban in the army and both of them were totally shocked to the point of welling up when I explained my journey. It is a very different experience for the sporting elite now. They come back from the Olympics and have the world at their feet, with social media deals and reality TV shows making them overnight celebrities.

I didn't have that same exposure in the early days but with what I had achieved, I do sometimes wonder what I could have done with that fame had I really embraced the opportunities that had come to me back then. The truth is I didn't know how to just be me and that was the biggest barrier I had.

* * * * *

As the release date for the documentary drew closer, I started to feel the fear and trepidation of the past coming back to haunt me and although I was excited at the prospect, the reality of the film going out to millions of viewers was pretty terrifying. Once it was out there, there was no taking it back, so it took all my strength to stick to my guns, not just for me but for all the other people I could be a voice for.

In one moment of doubt I FaceTimed the wonderful and hilarious Alan Carr, who I had met through world-renowned interior designer Kelly Hoppen, someone who had become a friend over the years and had invited me to her CBE celebration party in London. I had seen Alan perform in Belfast too and that was where I had originally told him about my doc.

So, back home sitting on my sofa, I explained I was finally

doing it, and filming was under way but that I was still terrified about the reaction of the public and what they would think about me hiding the truth for so long.

"Listen, Kel, not everyone's going to like it and that don't matter. If they have a problem with it, they weren't worth having around in the first place," he said. "You have to do this now, it's time. And when you do, you will feel like a weight has lifted, I promise."

Alan had a similar story to mine in that lots of people assumed he was gay before he found the courage to come out. He told me it was 'the worst kept secret in Northampton' when he told his friends and family but said that, just like me, he had to say it in his own words and on his own terms in order to really feel that freedom. I knew when I came out some people would say, "oh, of course she's gay, we've known that all along," but that didn't matter because I would be owning it and that felt like the most empowering thing.

Soon, I didn't have any choice because the wheels were in motion. The date, June 26th, 2022, was written on my calendar and seared into my memory as the day the documentary would air and my 34-year journey to freedom would be over at last. Then, a few weeks before D-day, I got a call from Emanuele.

"I don't think you should wait for the documentary to come out, I think you should do just one big newspaper interview coming out, and then tell the full story in the documentary after that," he said. "You'll be able to raise awareness and it will drive interest in the programme, and get the viewing figures up, so as many people as possible would get to hear your story, directly from you"

But I'd psyched myself up for the 26th! I thought I had more time to prepare in my head and now there was the opportunity of a big sit down tell-all interview and photoshoot with the *Sunday Mirror* the week before that. Emanuele told me he knew the editor, Gemma Aldridge, and had worked with her on the story of Gareth Thomas revealing his HIV diagnosis. He promised me she would make sure the story was told in the right way and wouldn't print anything without my permission. I knew the press would pick up on the drama of it all as soon as the documentary hit TV screens anyway and I envisaged sensational headlines about 'Gay Dame Kelly' screaming from the front pages, which was the opposite of what I wanted. Instead I wanted to come out in my own words, on my own terms, before the documentary aired, so I agreed.

It was a surreal experience sitting in a hotel suite on London's South Bank with sun streaming through the window and telling a journalist the story they'd all wanted me to tell since my victory parade in 2004. It felt like I was doing the one thing I'd spent my life avoiding. Amy Sharpe was a lovely young female reporter who put me at ease but I still couldn't stop from crying as I relived the journey I'd been on. I told her everything from the dawn raids to the first kiss in the laundry room, the fears, the mental health battles and why now at the age of (you get the picture – yikes!) I was finally coming out.

The nerves were out of control and my mind was racing. Would the paper turn on me and ignore how I wanted it said, or twist my words to sell more papers? What if I was making a huge mistake? It wasn't so many years ago that mainstream media was openly homophobic, just like the army, using language that would make anyone wince now.

But it was a risk I had to take. It was time.

Gemma rang me as I was in the middle of Selfridges in London, just before they were going to print. She told me the headline they were planning was 'Dame Kelly: I'm Gay' and it stuck in my throat as I repeated it back to her. Of course that was what I was saying but it was so direct and I thought it reduced my story to something much less complex than it really was. It wasn't just that I was gay, it was that I had been a prisoner of other people's opinions about sexuality all my life; it was that I'd been frightened into silence and not had a voice for so long.

"That's what I think the headline should be," I said, when I explained how I felt. 'Dame Kelly: I'm Finally Free to be Me'. Just as promised, they changed it and put a rainbow-coloured strap line above it, saying: 'Olympic heroine comes out'.

Gemma sent me a copy of the front page and there it was, in black, white and rainbow colours

While I waited for the story to hit the website and social media that night, I played Emeli Sandé's song *Read All About It* at top volume on repeat, practically screaming along to the lyrics as I kept refreshing the *Mirror* website on my phone to see whether it had been published yet.

I wanna sing, I wanna shout,
I wanna scream til the words dry out,
So put it in all of the papers,
I'm not afraid,
They can read all about it,
Read all about it…

As I sang those words, that was exactly how I felt. I knew once the story hit the newsstands there was no going back. Everyone would know and my life would be changed forever: I was ready. But I never could have imagined just how big a change it would be.

The article went up online late on Saturday night and, within minutes, my phone started to blow up. First of all it was messages from my friends and family. They all said how proud they were of me, that the article came across really well, which made me feel reassured that I'd done the right thing.

I decided to try to get some sleep before the big day on Sunday but then things started to go really crazy as I was sucked into this whirlwind of attention. Every few minutes my phone was pinging with DMs from people I'd never heard of, congratulating me on coming out, telling me I was an inspiration and wishing me luck with my new life as an openly gay woman.

People were telling me about their own experiences of coming out – some young, some older like me. Many were out and proud but others were still living in the darkness of fear, unable to be honest about their sexuality. At first I read every one, and realised there were so many people in the same situation as I had been; crippled by fear and suffocated by what I thought other people would think. Well, now I knew what people thought – they thought it was great!

With each message that landed, I felt my nerves ease a little but 1 had no chance of sleeping that night and as more people read the article, the harder it was to keep up with the messages.

I put the front page and a link to the article on my Instagram stories with a soundtrack of the Emeli Sandé song that was playing in the background, and hundreds of people started replying to that too. As the nerves began to subside, I felt like I was going to explode with relief and pride and excitement for my new life.

That was when things went really mad. Athletes who had worked with me years before got in touch to say congratulations. Sally Gunnell, who was always a huge inspiration and a friend to me in our Team GB days was one of the first. I'd kept the secret from her for decades as she stood on the sidelines with cashew nuts and drinks for me to get me through my rounds in Athens.

I'd only told her a few weeks earlier when we were at the Queen's Platinum Jubilee, that I was working on the documentary because I didn't want her to find out in the press. But when she saw the front page for herself, she sent me the kindest message, saying how happy she was that I could finally be myself in public and wishing me all the luck in the world; one thing to put into perspective is to remind you that I had NEVER told anyone during my 12-year athletics career about my sexuality so this was a massive deal to me.

Other famous faces followed. The bubbly Davina McCall who had been on my podcast *Mental Health and Me*; Fearne Cotton was one of a handful of public figures I confided in and said she would help me tell my story on her amazing podcast *Happy Place* if and when I was ready; Gok Wan and Tessa Sanderson who were also at the Jubilee and of course, the wonderful Alan Carr. Ironically, I had been on a reality show the month before called 'Cooking With The Stars', not saying a word about my documentary but then Dr Ranj, Josie from *This Morning*, my fab chef Ronnie and the rest of the team all congratulated me. The list goes on – it was crazy and overwhelming the support I got.

Over the next 24 hours, I just kept waiting for the backlash, the trolls or the negative reaction that had hung over me like a threat for so many years. I expected cruel jibes and nasty names like I'd read about from other people in the public eye, but thankfully they never came.

21

—

Loose Women and a Man Named John

FOR THE FIRST FEW DAYS AFTER THE *SUNDAY MIRROR* article came out, I was shell shocked to be honest. I had built up a lot of anxiety, thinking life was going to suddenly change, I felt like I'd thrown a grenade and then run and ducked for cover.

I couldn't bring myself to leave the house to begin with. Social media was one thing but I had no idea how people would react in person, so I told myself I would stay home until after the documentary aired.

There was a huge amount of interest from the media and the LGBT+ community, which was overwhelming. I had every TV show wanting me on their sofas and invitations to celebrity events I would never have even considered going to before starting to fill my inbox.

It was a media storm that wasn't going away, one that I could try to ignore, or embrace.

I'd come this far. I couldn't hide, so my first appearance was on the sofa of *This Morning* with Holly and Phil. I don't actually know how I got through that interview, I felt so much emotion running through my veins. The simultaneous build-up of anxiety and relief was overwhelming. I was shaking like a leaf; a mix of embarrassment and pride. It was a little too much and I took a while to contemplate what I had done after all these years.

Later that week I was asked to be a guest on *Loose Women*. This was my first real interaction with 'national treasure' Linda Robson who I had watched on the sitcom *Birds of a Feather*. I had been told how she is a real gossip, something I learned for myself later that night! She and the other ladies were so kind; more about 'Loose' later…

Earlier that week after the story dropped, someone approached my team from the British LBGT Awards asking if I could attend on the Friday night, as a special guest and to present an award. It was the kind of thing I never would have considered before because I had always purposefully avoided the 'scene'. I am not sure people realised that, for me, any association at all with the LGBT+ community had been like a spotlight picking me out in the middle of a dark concert. Basically I avoided at all costs for fear of the association. But now this was a chance to begin to embrace it.

Over the years, I have been to many events, places and countries for work. Sometimes I would have the opportunity to take a 'plus-one', to support or help with logistics and travel and so on, but because I wasn't 'out' I would always introduce people as my 'friend' or 'PA' – I was soon to learn that admitting this was a big mistake!

I bought a canary yellow dress by Ruedi Maguire for the night. It had a pleated skirt with a split up the thigh and cut-out panels at the waist. A proper showstopper. I had my hair and make-up done before making my way to a stunning venue called The Brewery. I was ready to go when I got a call from my partner, Louise (yes partner, how refreshing not to have to hide or lie – you have no idea?!).

She was due to fly over from Northern Ireland to join me but her flight was delayed. "Noooooo, what are you talking about, delayed?! I can't go by myself," I totally panicked and quickly wondered if it was too late to cancel because it was my first time EVER at an LBGT+ event, my first public outing since I came out and my first time appearing in public with Lou. Too many firsts on this occasion, so I was already a bag of nerves.

Little did I know, Lou was already all over it. She called Kathy, who I must mention here, has become a really close and loyal friend. I met her also through Military In Motion during lockdown when she asked if I needed help with the community and ever since we have helped each other out in work and personal situations. I know she will be a friend for life.

Anyway, by the time I arrived at the event, I had been assured by Lou that Kathy and Andrea were on their way. Andrea had been with me for eight years and I think she knew that out of all the times I needed her support through the years, this one was a must! "Don't panic, we will be there, and have already sorted the train to London. We can be with you until Lou arrives. It'll all be great. You can't pull out now. I've got your back," said Kathy. I was so relieved.

So, I went as planned. Cameras flashed as I arrived and when I look back at the pictures now, I see how much I embraced the attention and openness that I could now portray. I was taken into a room away from the event as I was a 'surprise' guest. Kathy and Andrea arrived and we waited for Lou but when the event started, I had to send Kathy to the table and told her to tell Linda she was a friend of mine.

Suddenly, fright struck me – shit, Linda! Remember I said I used to pretend my partners were my PA or friend? Well, that was OK when people didn't know about me, but now it was a different story. The last thing I wanted was for people to assume any woman I'm with is my girlfriend – especially mates! The panic set in and as soon as Lou arrived I sent her up to the room with Andrea. Yep, exactly as I thought, Linda had already introduced Kathy as my girlfriend – OMG – to not one, but two tables of people. Then proceeded to say to Lou, "I think I have some gossip to withdraw." Moral of the story… don't tell Linda anything!

The crowd roared when I went on stage to present the award and that was the first time I uttered it out loud: "Freedom is my voice."

I had a ball like I never could have done before. The room was filled with influential people from the LGBT+ community, impressive business leaders and even politicians. It was like this whole world opening up to me, celebrating the very thing I had been hiding from all my life. I'm not going to lie, though, it all felt a bit surreal, outside of my comfort zone and I was taken aback with thoughts of, 'how did I not know these events even existed?!'

The next day, 24 hours before the documentary aired on ITV, I'd hired out a screen at the Curzon Soho cinema for a private screening, and invited 50 of my closest friends and family. We served popcorn and cocktails and all watched 'Kelly Holmes: Being Me' together. There wasn't a dry eye in the house as they all saw for the first time the journey I'd been on. I think some of them knew what I'd been through but had never seen or heard me talk out loud about it in so much detail and they were shocked and saddened by what I, and people like me, had to endure. But the overriding emotion seemed to be pride. I was proud of myself too, and we finished the evening by partying in Soho until the early hours. I let my hair down properly for the first time as 'me'; drinking shots, dancing with some of my school friends, new friends and even my Troopers. The night ended in a complete blur. As per usual I was poured into the back of a taxi home. Put it this way, I don't go out much, but when I do, it generally ends up messy!

* * * * *

Who would have thought I would ever be a loose woman?!

"We think you should be a Loose Woman," said Judi Love and Linda Robson when I saw them at the ITV rooftop party prior to appearing at Pride in 2022.

"I'd love that" I said, with an *I can do anything now* attitude. Before I knew it, I was having a meeting with *Loose Women* Editor Sally Shelford and Deputy Editor Yiljan Nevzat and Emanuele at Soho House White City, across from the ITV studios

The week after Pride, Lou and I went away for three weeks. To be honest, I needed to process the emotions that had built up over the past year, bad and good. The reaction and response I got from strangers as well as people who had known me for years was overwhelming. And that continued for weeks and weeks after the newspaper article and my doc came out.

Once again, I had thrust myself into the limelight, the media interest in me and my experiences hit another high. Now I wasn't only a Dame, an Olympic medallist and an honorary colonel but I was becoming, more and more, a voice for the LGBTQIA+ community and for mental health awareness.

It was uncomfortable in some ways because – I'm the first to say – I was not yet an expert about gay rights issues because I've shied away from that world all of my life. I have so much to learn. But there was no question, I had a story to tell and experiences to share, which I thought might be comforting to other people.

So I jumped at the chance to go for a meeting with ITV about joining the *Loose Women* panel, as a regular member of the team. I was equal parts terrified and excited.

Sitting there in the meeting, we had a discussion about what I could bring to the mix and what I would and wouldn't feel comfortable talking about. We agreed that it would be a good fit but I wanted to think about it because the idea of actually being open and opinionated and totally 'loose' about my thoughts and feelings in front of a studio audience and live on telly was daunting.

The whole concept of Loose was really out of my comfort zone as I've spent my entire life being super guarded and private around people who aren't in my inner circle. Speaking candidly about emotions and feelings or elements of my personal life doesn't come naturally to me. But I was also aware that it was a great opportunity to use a platform to give my opinions and raise awareness for things that matter to me.

Plus, as a mixed-race gay woman, I think representation and visibility is important and to have someone who looks like me, lived like me and struggled like me, on a mainstream TV show like Loose can only be good for people watching, who share some of those characteristics, and I hope I help them feel seen and heard.

I try not to have regrets but one of the things I do think is a shame is the number of opportunities I've felt I had to turn down because they might put me too much in the limelight, make me fair game for the press, or people, who have known me in the past, could potentially reveal my sexuality before I was ready. Now that I've come out on my own terms, that fear is gradually easing, and I'm learning to say yes to things instead of no. So, even though the idea of going on Loose was scary, I felt like I owed it to myself.

My first appearance was in September and I was fretting over what the subjects of the day might be and what I would have to think about but then something happened that blew everything out of the water.

The day before I was due to go on the show for the first time, I was on the red carpet for the *Daily Mirror* People's Pet Awards at the swanky Grosvenor Hotel in Mayfair, with cameras clicking everywhere. Judi Love from Loose was presenting and I spotted Linda there too. There had been murmurs from around lunchtime that something was wrong with our Queen and for me, like so many, it was a news none of us ever wanted to hear, with notifications buzzing on everyone's phones: The Queen had died.

I walked up to the top of the carpet, saw Linda, grabbed her and sobbed. I couldn't stop crying! Everyone around was in total shock and disbelief, there was a commotion as I think the organisers were not sure what to do next. I didn't know if the event was going to continue and felt bad walking into the function, make-up running down my cheeks. It felt really personal.

I'd met the Queen so many times and spoken to her on a personal level, as well as her family, and I felt a deep respect and admiration for her and everything she did for our country. Having pledged allegiance to the Crown and served Queen and Country for a decade of my life, having once been a driver in the army as she had and currently being an Honorary Colonel of the Royal Armoured Regiment she'd been my boss – effectively.

As head of the Commonwealth, to which I had won two golds and one silver medal in my athletics career at the Games and winning multiple medals flying the British flag, she had been a huge figure throughout both my career and life. I felt the loss as though she was a member of my own family and I think a lot of people felt that.

Through so many ups and downs over all those years, the Queen was our constant and our strength as a nation. She saw us through conflicts and economic crises and the pandemic, not to mention the tragedies she faced in her own personal life along the way, so to face the future without her felt daunting and incredibly sad to me. I was deeply privileged to speak on various news platforms about my fond memories of meeting the Queen.

Loose Women was cancelled the day after the Queen passed to make room in scheduling for rolling news and tributes to her from around the world. A week after she died, a special edition of the show was scheduled and the producers wanted me on the panel. In some ways, the fact I had so much insight into the royal family and such respect and knowledge of the Queen herself made my first appearance on Loose very fitting, as I knew I would be talking about something that mattered to me deeply.

At the start of the show, we played one of the Queen's favourite songs, *We'll Meet Again* by Dame Vera Lynn and already I was holding back the tears. Ruth Langford, who was presenting, had to pass me a tissue as they flashed pictures of me meeting with Her Majesty after Athens in 2004.

It was such an emotionally charged atmosphere and everyone on the panel and in the audience was in tears. Each of the panellists, Linda Robson, Brenda Edwards and Jane Moore, spoke about their individual experiences over the years; meeting the Queen and working with the royal family and it was a really special tribute which I feel very grateful and proud to have been a part of.

It was in the second half of that first show that the conversation became more personal, when we had a conversation about dealing with grief. Of course whenever someone as high profile and well-loved as the Queen passes away, it can become very triggering for people who have lost loved ones themselves and it can intensify the feelings of grief and loss.

We spoke about the pain, shock, anger and intense sadness that can cripple you in the wake of losing someone you love and it brought back all those feelings I'd had about Mum, which was incredibly difficult. The Queen was of course the head of state and monarch, and Commander in Chief of the Armed Forces but she was also a mum, a gran and a great gran, and I couldn't help thinking what her entire family must have been going through at that awful time.

Although it was out of my comfort zone, I'm so glad we spoke about that because the reaction to the show was huge and I think so many people were watching and going through their own issues with grief. Such major events in our life can act as a catalyst for change. It was a very personal loss of my own that would provide the trigger for me to take those first tentative steps towards a brave new life as the person I was always meant to be.

* * * * *

The second *Loose Women* show I did was for the Queen's funeral in September 2022, which was another hugely emotional day but once again I had so much to talk about because in the interim period I'd been one of the thousands of people who queued up to see the coffin lying in state at Westminster Hall in London.

I can't describe what it was that made me go but I was in Liverpool for the National Diversity Awards which was held in the incredible Anglican Cathedral. That night, I was the recipient of the Celebrity of the Year Award. I had a fantastic night partying with some wonderful people until the early hours, after days watching the incredible outpouring of emotion on live TV. I couldn't get away from the feeling of wanting to pay my respects.

The queue had been taking people up to 14 hours at one stage and I had been messaging my mate Kathy all day. "How long's the queue now?" I'd keep asking. "I really want to go." I was due to travel to Belfast in the morning but this feeling didn't go away throughout the awards.

At 22:39, I sent some voice messages: 'Wanna meet me in London and join the queue? I SO WANT TO GO!!!"

I amplified my voice through the messages. Then back in my hotel room after the event, I just couldn't sleep. I knew there were only a couple of days left for people to join The Queue and get their chance to say a final goodbye.

At 02:21 I messaged: 'Still want to go'. The next thing I got a message back. 'Me too, I cannot sleep'.

Kathy was awake as she had been tossing and turning because we had both been saying for days that if we didn't go it would be the biggest regret we would always have. I don't want to live with regrets, and she felt the same way.

The 'need' consumed my thoughts, so I booked the 10.30am train back to London. I arranged for Sarah, who was by now one of my most loyal friends since we split up back in 2002 to meet me at Charing Cross with some clothes appropriate for queueing a potential 16/18 hours by now. A quick change in the smelly loos and I was ready. Sarah went back home on the train, Kathy met me on the station concourse, and the next thing we were off on a train to London Bridge. We pretty much ran to the start because there had been whispers of them closing it. "NO WAY!"

We joined the back of what was to become the longest queue I will ever wait in. It started in Southwark Park, snaking up and down the lines of barriers. It turned out to be more than just a queue though.

I began talking to a wonderful guy, a former serviceman called John who, at 95 years old, was planning on walking the whole way too and told me a story of the time he was on parade as a young lad and had got a glimpse of the King; no, not our current King – King George VI! He was there with his daughter. We chatted to the loveliest people around us from all walks of life who later became our 'queue buddies'. We were given our wristbands, I did a quick interview for TV and we began our pilgrimage.

It took us along Bermondsey, China Wharf, up towards Tower Bridge, onto the Embankment, past Shakespeare's Globe Theatre, Millennium Bridge, Tate Modern, National Theatre and Royal Festival Hall.

Everyone in the queue was sharing food with each other

throughout the day, but by now we were gagging for something hot, so we bought chips with curry sauce, and Kathy and I started drinking gin which all went down a treat! We walked over to the other side of Westminster Bridge and back down on to Embankment.

Earlier that day, I had started a chain reaction as Kathy and I were also part way through a Military In Motion Press-Up Challenge that I had set up for my 'Troopers' that month. So, to keep ourselves occupied, we had started doing them back in Bermondsey. Each hour I would encourage more and more of the queue to join us and even managed to convince some policemen and women to join in along the whole route!

Passing the Palace of Westminster across the river, looking at all the flags at half-mast, we started feeling emotional as we were finally getting closer. The sun was setting by now, as we passed the Covid Memorial, and did another set of press-ups as the temperature had rapidly dropped.

Finally after nearly seven and half hours, the first-aiders came and said that they could take John ahead of the queue.

"No, it's OK" he said "I will stay with you all."

"No way, you need to get to the end now and you have been an inspiration to us all," we said, feeling relieved that finally he would get to pay his respects and get somewhere warm.

I gave him a huge hug and a kiss goodbye and, through the power of social media, someone who had been following my stories on Instagram had managed to capture him walking into Westminster. That was so heartwarming.

Then, over Lambeth Bridge, we did our final set of press-ups. We dumped off all the food we had for the scouts to send back down the line or for the foodbank.

In Victoria Gardens, I got mobbed by people wanting photos,

which in some way felt weird but in another felt like a shared, lived experience and everyone was happy being there together, even if complete strangers. We got changed in the Portaloos. Then we did another dump of all liquids and so on – Kathy has reminded me that I was not happy as I had to bin my new bottle of Michael Kors perfume and MAC make-up!

There was a mass of X-ray machines and security – at that point the mood changed and was totally sombre, and silent. We went up the stairs into Westminster Hall, and despite watching the live feed of the queue the days before, it was totally overwhelming; the sheer size, and how magnificent the building was, you could hear a pin drop with the silence.

The coffin looked so small on top of the catafalque. We paused momentarily as we were so moved by it all; we went down the right-hand side, giving each other space. When we got to the front of the catafalque, I bowed my head, and said 'thank you'. I walked on out in tears, but stopped at the door to look back. Kathy had remembered a volunteer telling us to look back before we left the hall as it would all happen so quickly, and what good advice that was.

Our queue buddies were all in tears when we got out and we just hugged and cried. It was an enjoyable, long day with such an emotional end. They were memories that last a lifetime and to share them with a mate was very special.

I had also worked for a couple of news channels on the day of the funeral, having been situated literally outside Westminster Abbey watching the incredible military procession march past with the Queen's coffin carried on the state carriage. Reliving that day and the gravitas of my experiences on *Loose Women* was another emotional show.

Those two shows were a baptism of fire for my journey on

Loose but in hindsight I'm really glad I did them; it made me realise what a lifeline the show can be for people going through difficult times and how I really can make a difference and a contribution. It's not all about telling your personal stories or airing your dirty laundry, or being controversial, it can be about compassion and making people feel less alone, and that's really important.

I've loved meeting the ladies who have been the stalwarts and backbone of the show and the newer panellists who come from different worlds to mine.

Meeting the different audiences, I've spoken openly about my complex life. My experience as a perimenopausal woman I hope has helped others in that position as the symptoms can be really confusing, hard to deal with and they're not spoken about enough. I have been given a platform to support the LGBT Veterans Campaign led by Lord Etherton, where we recently had the Prime Minister apologise in the House of Commons, for the mistreatment and unethical, historical ban on LGBT serving personnel.

I find it extremely hard to talk about my personal relationships – I mean, let's face it, you have read about them and this is the most I have ever said in this book, let alone saying it all on live TV!

The thing is, I still get anxious every time I go on the show because it is ingrained in me to worry about what people think and the judgement that I am open to by being on TV. But what matters is that I have been given an opportunity to grow and, as I write this, I am celebrating a year on the panel. I have been given new life experiences and, for that, I am truly grateful.

This is a new chapter of my life. Who knows how the story will unfold but what I do know is that I will take up as many opportunities as I can, especially on TV, as there's so much more I want to do. When people shout, "Are you ready?", I shout back, "Born ready!"

22

Love is Love

WHEN I WAS YOUNG I THOUGHT MY INDIVIDUALITY and differences from other people around me was a superpower. I hated the thought of being put in a box. In the army and then in the sporting world, I found my uniqueness comforting, until I found it a burden.

After I came out publicly as being gay, one thing I did find scary was finding my place in this wonderful, vibrant, new community that I suddenly found myself immersed in. The past 15 months since I first stood on that stage at Pride, has been one of the biggest learning curves of my life. I feel as though I have missed out and have half a century of catching up to do when it comes to learning about the LGBTQIA community. Before I went public, I never engaged with it, I actively distanced myself from anything to do with it in case it would blow my cover.

In some ways it feels amazing that I'm now surrounded by people who have shared experiences with me and who understand elements of what I've been through as well as the challenges that come with being gay and coming out. In others, I feel sad that a massive part of my life has been wasted, hasn't been as fruitful and definitely hasn't been as colourful or happy as I am now.

One thing that is really important to me is that I can learn about the community. Over the years I have seen the transition and growth within the community while watching from afar from what I knew growing up, LGB – 'Lesbian, Gay and Bisexual'. Out of all the letters in the acronym LGBTQIA, the 'L' was the first to come into existence.

For centuries, the word had been associated with the works of Sappho, an ancient Greek woman from the island of Lesbos who wrote poems about same-gender passion. The interesting thing is that I have always hated the word because, growing up in the army it always had derogatory connotations – you were called 'Lezzo' or 'Lezzer'. So I have always referred to myself as a gay woman (in my private life, of course). So who would have thought I would become friends with 'Head Lesbian' – as she's affectionately known within the community – Linda Riley, publisher of DIVA Magazine!

She befriended me backstage at Pride and we instantly hit it off. Linda has been instrumental in the community for years and has helped me navigate this colourful new world I now live in. I am not afraid to challenge some of her ideals, even to the point of saying I prefer to identify as a gay woman because that terminology sits far more comfortably with me, mainly because the word Lesbian was so derogatory in the past. But I have learnt it is each to their own and that's what acceptance is. She has introduced me to so many fantastic people who have taught me so much already, and I want to continue to learn.

I don't know how I feel about the idea of being some kind of gay icon, but I was very proud when I appeared on the front of DIVA magazine and have been so grateful to have appeared in so many LGBTQIA influencer lists.

I have also been lucky to win so many other awards in the short time since coming out. Including 2022 Hello! Inspiration Awards – Trailblazer of the Year, where I met the legendary Joan Collins! 2023 DIVA Media Personality of the Year and 2023 Rainbow Honours, Celebrity LGBTQIA Champion of the Year. What has been the most rewarding part of coming out, apart from being so happy, is that I can use my platform to be a voice for those who don't have one.

Just like I wanted to help underprivileged young people through my charity The Dame Kelly Holmes Trust after my Olympic success, I am using my voice to amplify the messages around the importance of psychological safety, equal rights and the need for people to feel heard. To connect people and be instrumental in the fight against any bigotry and discrimination. I used to laugh at the extension of the community 'alphabet', not understanding the need for so many letters, until I realised it's important to have a sense of belonging. It's been an emotional journey of exploration for me as I find my feet in my 'new' world, but I am loving the freedom it gives me too.

Perhaps the most important thing for me, though, has been my involvement in Lord Etherton's review into the treatment of LGBT veterans. He chaired the review to try to settle once and for all what really happened to the thousands of men and women who were persecuted in the military because of their sexuality, and to make amends.

After *Being Me* aired and he saw the people I'd spoken to in the making of it, he was keen to get me involved, and I wanted to help in any way I could. The problem they had was that they were struggling for people to come forward and give their testimonies, so I decided to use my platform to try to get people to contact the review team. I did interviews in the press, shouted about it on *Loose Women* and posted on my social media to try to get people to get in touch, and they did, in their hundreds.

A few months ago we achieved the most amazing victory for thousands of veterans, including myself. Prime Minister Rishi Sunak gave an apology in Parliament, for the way that LGBT veterans were treated, not only during their time serving their country but also because of the long-term damage it caused so many of us after we left. Hence my deeply-engrained fear of coming out.

The Government read the report from Lord Etherton's review, which has 49 recommendations for 'righting the wrong'. We got to go to the House of Commons to listen to former Secretary of State for Defence the Rt Hon Ben Wallace MP give his passionate statement following the publication of the Independent Review into the service and experience of LGBT veterans who served prior to 2000. Basically the mistreatment and injustice suffered at the hands of a barbaric ruling and law – and this was acknowledgement at last that the way we were treated was wrong.

It was such an emotional but rewarding day. The recommendations in the review will make real change in the armed forces and hopefully mean that all veterans can now be proud of serving and start to rebuild their lives.

I was invited with other veterans to represent more than a thousand brave men and women who submitted testimonies of our experiences in which between us we were arrested, raided, interrogated, dismissed, bullied, sexually abused and jailed. In some cases, losing the right to a career they loved, having medals stripped, pensions taken away and, for everyone, mental health trauma

The charity, Fighting for Pride, and Emma Riley from my documentary were instrumental in campaigning along with other charities and individuals like myself, *Loose Women* and the *Sunday Mirror* who also supported the campaign. Being there when LGBT+ veterans were heard and cared about in Westminster was such a momentous occasion for me and for everyone involved.   .

A couple of years ago, when I was on my journey to freedom, I decided I wanted to mark that in some official way. Not many people know this but 'Unique' isn't just something I use as a mantra, it's actually officially now part of my identity – legally!

Having spent years hiding parts of myself but also struggling with my identity in some ways, I decided to change my name by deed poll to have 'Unique' as a middle name. I might sound absolutely nuts, but during lockdown when I felt like I was 'losing the plot', I'd thought about changing my name many times.

I considered many times over the years about changing Holmes to Dad's name Norris and to distance myself from the 'sperm donor' but everyone who knows me and has supported and celebrated my achievements over the years knows me as Dame Kelly Holmes, so it would seem strange to change that now. But adding middle names to my legal title seemed like a great way to be reborn in a way as a new me and to celebrate all the different and wonderful things about my life and my identity.

I have carried the name 'Unique' with me most of my life, as a protective shield, and now as a celebration of everything I am. So when I got the form from the deed poll office, I didn't hesitate to fill it in.

The second name I chose because it's just as special to me. When I lived in South Africa there were beautiful birds of paradise; they were so bright, colourful, and resilient. The native birds also symbolise freedom and the bird-of-paradise plant which looks just like the bird itself, with bright yellow flowers and beautiful blooms, was named in honour of Nelson Mandela's long fight for freedom during the Apartheid era.

So my name now is Kelly Unique Paradise Holmes. Some people may think I am strange, different, mad but guess what? I LOVE ME! And you never know, I may need a stage name one day – ha!

* * * * *

Standing in the pouring rain, looking out over a misty-grey cove on the west coast of Ireland, with the wind whipping around the hood of my poncho, I couldn't believe it was the middle of bloody August. But while the weather was a total disaster and I had no idea where I was going to sleep for the night, I wouldn't have been anywhere else in the world if you'd paid me. I guess that's how you know you really love someone – when the only thing that matters is being with them.

Of course, a tropical island in the blazing sunshine would have been nice, but since I have been seeing Lou, I knew I was in for a few trips to the Emerald Isle instead and, to be honest, I was all-in. She's an Irish lass through and through, so it comes with the territory: rain!

People who follow me on social media have probably seen Lou's face pop up more and more over the past year, but we've never gone 'Insta-official' and I deliberated long and hard over whether to talk about my relationship in this book. Yes, relationship! I don't want to go all soft and, as you know, it takes a lot for me to talk about personal relationships, but finally, after decades of failed flings, relationships that have not been successful and a life that has been lonely at times, I've found someone to share my world with, and I'm happier than I have been for a long time.

I'm not going to say too much about Lou here because if she ever wants to talk about being in a relationship with a runner-turned-Dame and telly presenter, that will be her story to tell. But I couldn't let this book come out without acknowledging how happy I am to have her in my life right now.

It's true what they say that it's when you're least looking for someone that they can just walk into your life. In the depths of lockdown when we were in a global crisis and I was still grieving for Mum while trying desperately to hold things together, Lou was one of the many amazing people who joined Military In Motion, my little fitness community that became my lifeline.

We didn't even meet one another for over a year because we were in lockdown and we hardly chatted in the group as there were people much louder and more prominent than she was.

When lockdown restrictions started to ease, I met up with my wonderful 'Troopers'. Even the first few times we met, Lou and I rarely spoke to each other: she was in a relationship and she never bloody spoke to me anyway! Maybe because I was 'Troop Leader' but she now says it's because she was shy!

Over the following few months, the community as a whole kept getting stronger and closer. Even though we both had people that were part of our lives during lockdown, I think our stars aligned.

It was after we met again as a smaller group that I got to know her more. I personally think things happen for a reason. Lou's relationship broke down and gradually, over time, we seemed to connect more and more and here we are now.

She lives in Northern Ireland and our lives couldn't be more different but she's kind and trustworthy and we have so much in common. She's got the fitness bug too and we love running, hiking, paddle boarding and generally getting out in the great outdoors together and having fun – with a few gins and cocktails thrown in for good measure, of course.

For the first time in years I feel totally comfortable and have no doubts about her wanting to be with me for my achievements or my titles; she just loves me for me, the mad, crazy, frantic, workaholic me, and that feels great.

After the enormity of 'coming out' and going to Pride, I went on holiday for three weeks with Lou. There was a lot of emotion, both cheers and tears, so I needed to get some headspace.

Feeling liberated, Lou and I visited San Francisco's Castro District, commonly referred to as The Castro, in Eureka Valley. The Castro was one of the first gay neighbourhoods in the United States and boasts an iconic giant flagpole and oversized rainbow flag as a proud symbol of the LGBT community.

We did one of those free audio tours and walked about the streets, passing the lively bars like Moby Dicks, taking pictures amongst all the colour and vibrancy. I was fascinated by the story of Harvey Milk who was an American politician and the first openly gay man to be elected to public office in California. It was his strength of standing up for others that paved the way for LGBT movements across the world. I would NEVER have gone to a gay area on holiday before, so whilst it was a bit scary, it also felt awesome to be free.

I won't go on about our relationship any more, because I've realised that it's our story, and hopefully one to elaborate on another time. But we are enjoying life between sunny Kent and rainy Northern Ireland, and I hope we have many happy years together ahead of us. Only the future will tell what happens next but I'm incredibly grateful that we met.

Love really is love, no matter who it's between, and there is so much worry and stress in the world, we have to make the most of the good times when they come our way and celebrate love where we find it – even if it's in the least-expected places.

It's taken me a long time to realise that there are many different kinds of love in the world and, throughout my life I've been lucky enough to experience many of them: The love of my best mates Kerrie and Sarah who have stuck by me through thick and thin and who know me better than anyone. My home and school friends who have only ever known me as just Kel. The love of the siblings I grew up with – and the ones I missed out on as a child but have grown to feel they were always part of my life. My wonderful nieces and nephews, who I hope will always understand acceptance. The love of my loyal dogs and, of course, The Boys.

I've had a first love. The love of my dad, who took me on as his own from the day he met my mum. Then, of course, Mother Dear. I still miss her every day and I'm forever grateful for how losing her started me on my five-year journey to being free to be me. I wish she'd lived to see me so happy being free, but I believe she's around. I still see the odd butterfly, a white horse or feather to remind me she's here.

Then there's been the love of the British people and sports fans around the world that I felt so strongly when I won my two Olympic gold medals – for them – and finally, the new friend- ships I have made who have come into my life in recent months and who have embraced the 'new' me. I LOVE YOU ALL.

I'm sure there's plenty more love in the world, for me and for you. Our lives are made up of different pieces of a puzzle and love should be one piece that's in place. It should not matter where it comes from or who it's with, whether you're straight, gay, trans, bisexual, black, white, rich, poor, big, small or anyone who fits within the glistening spectrum of light that comes from a diamond. Everyone deserves love and to live without fear or judgement, every love deserves the same respect. It's what gets you through the darkness and makes the highs of your life so much higher. Having love and acceptance is a safety net and a comfort and brings so much joy, so let's embrace it. Love is love. And remember, every love is UNIQUE.

I want to leave you with a few words from a song that I heard that makes me feel proud and for anyone else who needs strength, you might like it too:

Wyn Starks

I've been closing the door
All my life, held it in but not anymore,
Got two feet on the floor,
This is it, I'm stronger than before,
Pardon my imposition,
But this is my conviction,
I need to get this off my mind.

I gotta be me, gotta be I
Gotta be who I know I am inside
Can finally breathe, taking it in,
Look at me flying!
It's always been there,

LOVE IS LOVE

It just took me a minute to find it,
If I were to be anybody else,
I'd just be hiding
Who I am
Who I am

Acknowledgements

MY FIRST THANKS GOES TO EVERYONE WHO HAS bought this book and those who have followed me for years. You may not know me personally but have watched me grow, go through the highs and lows of my athletics career and life. I may never get to meet you or to say thanks personally, but I truly respect your dedication, your love and support, whoever you are.

To my Dad Mick. Your love has been unconditional since you took me into your life. I Love you x

To my bestie Kerrie and Miracle Woman Sandy (Kerrie's mum). Your love is undeniable, you will always be classed as my family. I love you from the bottom of my heart, always and forever.

To Debbie, (P.E. Teacher) and Dave Arnold (first coach in the sky), I hope your spirit can see me now. Without your guidance and belief in me as a little girl, I may never have had the courage to be who you knew I could be.

To my ever-growing family. Siblings; Lisa, Kevin, Stuart, Danny, Penny. Nieces and nephews; Honey, Archie, Lola, Rosa, Olivia, Lily, (future Lioness) Finley, Martha (Marmite) Poppy and Ada-Mae (another Lioness); Siblings in-law; Clare, Emma,

Dion and Danny's partner Kelly. No matter how we started or what we have done together, my love for you will be there until my dying day. Stay proud, work hard and never stop believing x

To Lara, Kim, Sarah, Sandra, Jackie, Dobo (who's in the sky), Wes, Flo, Emma, hairdressers Pat, Barbara, Trevor and Luci, make-up Emilie and Pilates Sandrine. You have been a huge part of my life at different times – thank you x

To my WRAC friends, you pushed me, and laughed with me. Whether I loved you or not, you are a big part of my early adult life. To Clare, Cathy, and other military comrades I have worked with in the past and recently, thanks for your acceptance and opportunities, they definitely added to my stories!

To Tess, Simon, Jo, Sheila and wider family, thanks for being part of my childhood, there were some great times.

To my 'inner circle' Kathy (side-kick), Polly, Kate, Suzanne-BG, Tracy. Beauty girls – Maria, Nicola, Belli, you all make me smile and I love our fun times together. Thank you for helping me trust people.

To Andrea my 'real' PA, thanks for putting up for me for over nine years. You have had the hardest job of all sticking with me through my recent life transitions. Thank you for all your support, it means more than I probably have told you!

To those I have worked with including Rockwater Luke, Ying, Ed, and to everyone who has worked for my charity The Dame Kelly Holmes Trust, or those that I had a romantic connection with in the past; however short or long. I believe people come into our lives to support, connect, fulfil, or challenge what we really want. I hope yours is now fruitful, safe and happy.

To ALL my 'Troopers' from my fitness community, Military in Motion. I can't write all your names as I don't want to miss anyone out, but YOU know who you are; you saved me! Your total belief in me during lockdown and your support keep my heart going. I will never forget you!

My new friends from the LGBTQIA community, allies and of course *Loose Women* and all the team that make it happen, I have loved getting to know you all. Thanks for helping me navigate this part of my life, it's been a journey.

Thank you to all the organisations for my 12 doctorates (so far) awards and accolades, in recognition of my dedication to the British Army, sport, community and charity over the years. I am truly grateful. A special shoutout to Polly and the team at The Pickering Cancer Drop-in Centre – I love you x

To my previous managers thanks for being part of my life journey. Including Emanuele for being with me on this one; remember, a challenge is to raise up on top of the podium – gold!

To Gemma, Amy, Paul, Mirror Books, Reach Plc, ITV, Lucy, Tony and Jon from Goalhanger for allowing me to share my deepest life struggles and successes, giving me a safe place and the freedom I always wanted, in this book and in my documentary *Kelly Holmes: Being Me.*

Kelly, 2023

P.S – If I've missed anyone I will add you to my next book x
P.P.S To Lou – will you???

Gastrointestinal
System

Series editor
Daniel Horton-Szar
BSc (Hons)
United Medical and Dental
Schools of Guy's and
St Thomas's Hospitals
(UMDS),
London

Faculty advisor
Paul Smith
MD, FRCP
Consultant Physician
and Honorary Clinical
Teacher,
Llandough and Cardiff
Hospitals,
Wales

Gastrointestinal System

Elizabeth Cheshire
LL. B. (Hons)
United Medical and
Dental Schools of Guy's
and St Thomas's
Hospitals,
London

Mosby

London • Philadelphia
St Louis • Sydney • Tokyo

Publisher	**Dianne Zack**
Managing Editor	**Louise Crowe**
Development Editors	**Filipa Maia**
	Marion Jowett
Project Manager	**Peter Harrison**
Designer	**Greg Smith**
Layout	**Marie McNestry**
Illustration Management	**Danny Pyne**
Illustrators	**Kevin Faerber**
	Robin Deane
	Amanda Williams
	Mike Saiz
	Annette Whalley
Cover Design	**Greg Smith**
Production	**Gudrun Hughes**
Index	**Janine Ross**

ISBN 0 7234 2994 4

Copyright © Mosby International Ltd, 1998.

Published by Mosby, an imprint of Mosby International Ltd, Lynton House, 7–12 Tavistock Square, London WC1H 9LB, UK.

Printed in Barcelona, Spain, by Grafos S.A. Arte sobre papel, 1998. Text set in Adobe VAG Light; captions in Adobe VAG Thin.

Cataloguing in Publication Data
Catalogue records for this book are available from the British Library.

The publisher, author, and faculty advisor have undertaken reasonable endeavours to check drugs, dosages, adverse effects, and contraindications in this book. We recommend that the reader should always check the manufacturers' instructions and information in the British National Formulary (BNF) or similar publication before administering any drug.

Preface

Most medical students and junior doctors join firms which specialise in a system. We therefore need to know the anatomy, physiology, embryology, and pathology of that system, and how to examine it properly. Medical textbooks usually cover only one or two of these disciplines, and to learn about any particular system we have to refer to many different sources. Well, not with this book!

This *Crash Course* title has been designed to bring together everything students need to know about the gastrointestinal system to pass their Finals successfully—and to enjoy life on a gastrointestinal firm! This is all done in an up-to-date, comprehensive format that is small enough to be carried around and referred to during teaching and on the wards.

Crash Course: Gastrointestinal System also aims to provide a useful revision text for junior doctors.

I hope you find it useful!

Elizabeth Cheshire

This text is designed with the new medical curriculum in mind and interlinks basic science with clinical medicine. It has been written by Elizabeth Cheshire, a final year medical student, and I have revised the text from the viewpoint of a faculty advisor.

There are over 100 illustrations in this book and the text is concise, incorporating all the required core material. *Crash Course: Gastrointestinal System* should become a constant companion to the student both during revision and on the ward. Questions are included in every chapter which are designed to check the student's understanding of the information in the text. There is also an additional section of MCQs, short-answer questions and essay questions at the end of the book. Difficult and essential facts are emphasized in the text to assist in memorizing them easily. The text is fully comprehensive and any student mastering this book should pass Finals with ease.

Paul Smith
Faculty Advisor

Preface

OK, no-one ever said medicine was going to be easy, but the thing is, there are very few parts of this enormous subject that are actually difficult to understand. The problem for most of us is the sheer volume of information that must be absorbed before each round of exams. It's not fun when time is getting short and you realize that: (a) you really should have done a bit more work by now; and (b) there are large gaps in your lecture notes that you meant to copy up but never quite got round to.

This series has been designed and written by senior medical students and doctors with recent experience of basic medical science exams. We've brought together all the information you need into compact, manageable volumes that integrate basic science with clinical skills. There is a consistent structure and layout across the series, and every title is checked for accuracy by senior faculty members from medical schools across the UK.

I hope this book makes things a little easier!

Danny Horton-Szar
Series Editor (Basic Medical Sciences)

 **Acknowledgements**

Figure Credits

Figures 4.6, 4.10, and 4.11: courtesy of Dr W Marshall. *Clinical chemistry* 3rd ed. Mosby, 1995. Figures 4.18, 5.17, 5.15B, and 5.19: Berne R, Levy M. *Physiology* 3rd ed. Mosby Year-Book, St Louis 1993. Figures 8.4, 8.5, and 8.6: courtesy of Dr JJ Misiewicz, A Forbes, AB Price, PJ Shorvon, DR Triger, GNJ Tytgat. *Atlas of clinical gastroenterology* 2nd ed. Mosby-Year Book Europe Ltd 1994.

Contents

To my family

x

DEVELOPMENT, STRUCTURE, AND FUNCTION

1. Overview of the Gastrointestinal System

ANATOMICAL OVERVIEW

The gastrointestinal tract (Fig. 1.1) is a true system in that it develops from a single, continuous structure, and the entire tract, including the ducts, is endodermal. Its basic structure is the same throughout (Fig. 1.2), with a mucous layer, submucosa, muscular layer and adventitia or serosa, and intrinsic submucosal and mucosal nerve plexuses (Meissner's plexus and Auerbach's plexus), the activity of which is moderated by extrinsic innervation.

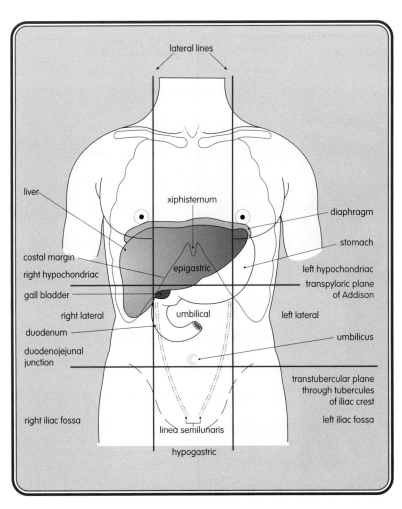

Fig. 1.1 Anatomy of the gastrointestinal tract showing its surface markings. The transpyloric plane of Addison passes midway between the jugular notch and the symphysis pubis, and midway between the xiphisternum and the umbilicus. It passes through the pylorus; the neck of the pancreas; the duodenojejunal flexure and the hila of the kidneys.

The gastrointestinal (GI) tract takes in, breaks down, and absorbs food and fluids. Different parts of the system are specialized to perform these different functions.

Food is moved through the tract by gravity and peristalsis. Peristalsis propels food by the coordinated contraction of muscle in one area and relaxation in the next. A series of sphincters prevent reflux (Fig. 1.3). Reflexes operating between different parts of the tract, together with hormonal and neuronal factors, determine the speed of food movement through the tract. In general, the contents only move through the tract at the rate at which they can be processed.

FUNCTIONS OF THE GASTROINTESTINAL TRACT

The principal function of the gastrointestinal tract is the intake, breakdown, and digestion of food and liquid to provide energy and nutrients, and to create a store of energy for use during short periods of abstinence.

Food and drink are generally not sterile. The gut is therefore presented with a large number of bacteria and other potentially harmful substances on a daily basis. The tract has a number of mechanisms to deal with these:

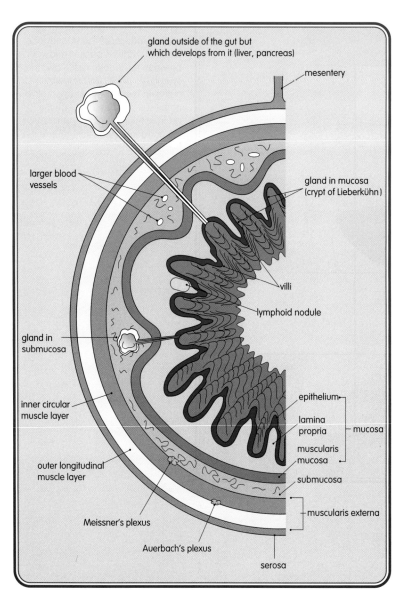

Fig. 1.2 The basic structure of the gastrointestinal tract.

- Sight and smell often alert us to the fact that something is contaminated. A vomit reflex exists to eject harmful material from the gastrointestinal tract.
- The stomach is an acid environment; most bacteria swallowed in the diet are killed by the acidity.
- Aggregations of lymphoid tissue (part of the body's immune system) are present in the walls of the tract, in the form of Peyer's patches. These counteract antigens present in the diet.
- A number of gastrointestinal hormones (mainly peptides) are produced in the gut (Fig. 5.11) and many of these have local as well as systemic effects.

Excretion of waste products is another important function of the gut.

CONSTITUENTS OF FOOD

The body needs food to provide energy. Vitamins and minerals are necessary to maintain good health. The main food groups are carbohydrate, fat, and protein. These are oxidized to generate high-energy bonds in ATP (adenosine triphosphate) and also to provide materials for building new tissues.

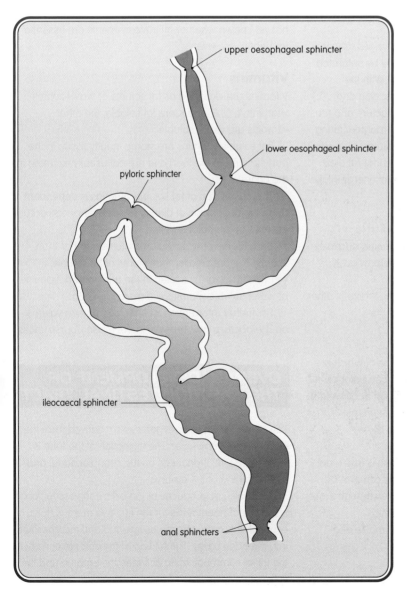

Fig. 1.3 Sphincters of the gastrointestinal tract.

upper oesophageal sphincter

lower oesophageal sphincter

pyloric sphincter

ileocaecal sphincter

anal sphincters

Excess food, stored as fat, leads to obesity and associated diseases such as ischaemic heart disease and non-insulin-dependent diabetes. Men and women have different patterns of fat distribution in the body. When deprived of food, an average 70 kg man may survive for 5–6 weeks on body fat stores provided he is able to drink water. Blood glucose levels drop during the initial few days, then rise and stabilize (the brain needs a constant supply of glucose, although other organs are better able to utilize other forms of energy). During prolonged fasting, the body will also break down muscle, including heart muscle, to provide energy. This may lead to death from cardiac failure.

Fat

Dietary fat is chiefly composed of triglycerides (glycerol plus esters of free fatty acids, which may be saturated, monounsaturated, or polyunsaturated). With the exception of essential fatty acids, linoleic acid and α-linoleic acid, which we cannot manufacture and must obtain from our diet, we are efficient at manufacturing fats (triglycerides, sterols, and phospholipids) and will lay down subcutaneous stores, even on low-fat diets. Fat intake should be less than 35% of total energy intake.

Carbohydrate

The carbohydrates found in food are starch (a polysaccharide), some disaccharides (mainly sucrose), lactose, and non-starch polysaccharide (previously called fibre).

Excess of carbohydrates may limit the intake of other forms of food.

Protein

Protein is composed of amino acids, nine of which are essential for protein synthesis and nitrogen balance.

We need 0.75 g protein per kilogram of body weight per day, but in developed countries most people exceed this. Excess protein may lead to bone demineralization.

In developing countries, where protein is less readily available, combinations of certain foods can provide enough of the essential amino acids even though those foods, on their own, are low in amino acids.

Examples of good combinations are maize and beans, and baked beans on toast!

Water

Water in the body comes from fluid intake and the oxidation of food. We need about 1 L of water per day to balance insensible losses (more in hot climates).

Excess water is excreted by the kidneys; inadequate intake leads to dehydration.

Minerals

Minerals are chemicals that must be present in the diet to maintain good health; over twenty have so far been identified.

Trace elements are substances that, by definition, are present in the body in low concentrations (less than 100 parts per million) and include some minerals. It is not yet known whether all trace elements are essential for health, however.

Vitamins

Vitamins are classified as fat soluble or water soluble; vitamins A, D, E, and K are fat soluble, the other vitamins are water soluble.

Fat soluble vitamins are stored in fatty tissue in the body (mainly in the liver) and are not usually excreted in the urine.

The absorption of fat soluble vitamins is dependent upon the absorption of dietary fat: deficiency can occur in cases of fat malabsorption.

Body stores of water soluble vitamins (other than vitamin B_{12}) are smaller than stores of fat soluble vitamins. They are excreted in the urine and deficiencies of water soluble vitamins are more common.

For further information, see the companion volume on *Metabolism and Nutrition* in the *Crash Course* series.

OVERALL DEVELOPMENT OF THE GASTROINTESTINAL TRACT

The GI tract is the main organ system derived from the endodermal germ layer. The formation of the tube is largely passive; it depends on the cephalocaudal and lateral folding of the embryo.

The yolk sac produces blood cells and vessels, and is the site of haemoeisis for the first two months from conception. Later, it becomes inverted and incorporated into the body cavity. The folding of the embryo constricts the initial communication between the embryo and the yolk sac.

The remnant of this communication is the vitelline duct which normally disappears *in utero*. Where it persists (as it does in about 2% of the population) it is known as a Meckel's diverticulum.

The gut tube divides into foregut, midgut and hindgut, each of which has its own blood supply (Fig. 1.4). The superior mesenteric artery is in the umbilicus. The gut tube starts straight but twists during development and the midgut grows rapidly, with the developing liver occupying most of the space.

There is not enough room in the fetal abdomen to accommodate the rapidly developing gut. The gut herniates between weeks 7–11 of gestation, continuing its development outside the abdominal cavity.

It undergoes a clockwise rotation of 180° and what was the inferior limb becomes the superior limb (and vice versa). It then undergoes a 270° turn anticlockwise so that the caecum lies under the liver. The tube then elongates again so the caecum points downwards. Sometimes the caecum remains pointing up instead of down which makes diagnosis of appendicitis difficult!

The falciform ligament lies in front of the liver and the lesser omentum lies behind the liver. The liver and pancreas develop from endodermal diverticulae that bud off the duodenum in weeks 4–6 (Fig. 4.16).

Much of the mouth (including the muscles of mastication and tongue) and the oesophagus develop from the branchial arches.

The muscles of mastication, mylohyoid and anterior belly of digastric develop from the first (mandibular) arch, supplied by the trigeminal nerve (V).

The anterior two-thirds of the tongue develop from three mesenchymal buds from the first pair of branchial arches. The posterior belly of digastric develops from the second arch, supplied by the facial nerve (VII).

Stylopharyngeus develops from the third arch, supplied by the glossopharyngeal nerve (IX).

Cricothyroid, the constrictors of the pharynx, and the striated muscles of oesophagus develop from the fourth and sixth arches, supplied by branches of the vagus nerve (X). The fifth arch is often absent.

- Summarize the basic organization of the gastrointestinal tract.
- What are the gastrointestinal tract's main functions? Where in the tract do these occur?
- Name the major food groups.
- Describe the embryological origins of the gut.

Divisions of the primitive gut tube		
Divisions of gut	**Blood supply**	**Components**
foregut	coeliac artery	pharynx oesophagus stomach proximal half of duodenum gives rise to: liver gall bladder pancreas
midgut	superior mesenteric artery	distal half of duodenum jejunum ileum caecum ascending colon proximal two-thirds of transverse colon
hindgut	inferior mesenteric artery	distal one-third of transverse colon descending colon sigmoid colon proximal two-thirds of anorectal canal

Fig. 1.4 Divisions of the primitive gut tube.

2. The Upper Gastrointestinal Tract

ORGANIZATION OF THE MOUTH AND OROPHARYNX

Regional anatomy

The oral cavity extends from the lips to the oropharyngeal fauces. It contains the tongue, alveolar arches, gums, teeth, and the openings of the salivary ducts (Fig. 2.1).

The oral cavity is divided into the vestibule, anterior to the teeth, and the oral cavity proper which is posterior to the teeth.

The blood supply of the oral cavity and oropharynx is principally from branches of the external carotid artery and its innervation is from branches of the cranial nerves.

Tongue

The tongue consists of intrinsic muscles (longitudinal, transverse and vertical), which have no attachments outside the tongue itself, and external muscles which attach both to the tongue and to points outside it.

The external muscles are:
- Genioglossus, which attaches to the mandible in the midline.
- Hyoglossus, which has an external attachment to the hyoid bone.
- Styloglossus, which, as the name suggests, attaches to the styloid process.
- Palatoglossus, which attaches to the soft palate.

Genioglossus, hyoglossus, and styloglossus are innervated by the hypoglossus nerve (XII), palatoglossus is innervated by the accessory nerve (XI) through the pharyngeal branch of the vagus nerve (X). The nerve supply of the tongue is summarized in Fig. 2.2.

The blood supply of the tongue is from the lingual artery (a branch of the external carotid); lymph drains to the deep cervical, submandibular, and submental nodes. The tongue contains numerous taste buds (Fig. 2.3).

Fig. 2.1 The oral cavity.

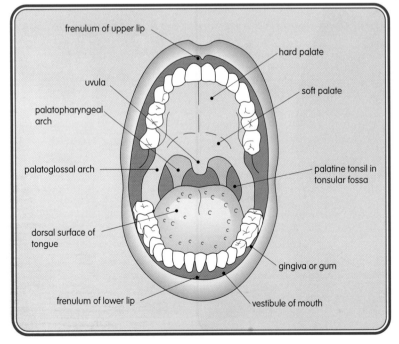

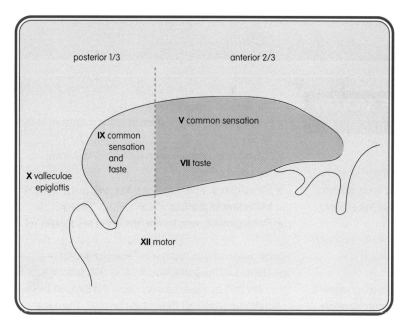

posterior 1/3   anterior 2/3

V common sensation

IX common
sensation
and
taste

VII taste

X valleculae
epiglottis

XII motor

Fig. 2.2 Nerve supply to tongue and epiglottis. V = lingual nerve (from mandibular division of trigeminal). VII = chorda tympani (joins the lingual nerve to be distributed).

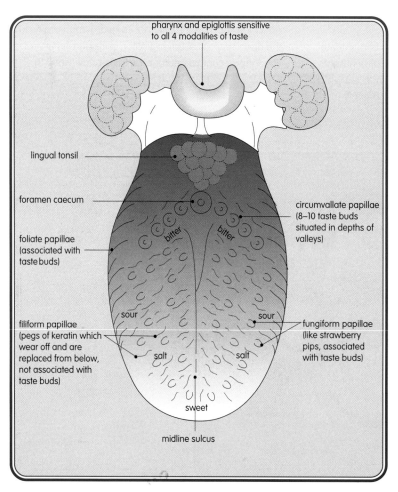

pharynx and epiglottis sensitive
to all 4 modalities of taste

lingual tonsil

foramen caecum

foliate papillae
(associated with
taste buds)

bitter   bitter

circumvallate papillae
(8–10 taste buds
situated in depths of
valleys)

sour   sour

filiform papillae
(pegs of keratin which
wear off and are
replaced from below,
not associated with
taste buds)

salt   salt

fungiform papillae
(like strawberry
pips, associated
with taste buds)

sweet

midline sulcus

Fig. 2.3 The tongue and taste buds.

Soft palate

The hard and soft palates form the roof of the mouth and separate it from the nasal cavity. The oral surface of the soft palate contains many mucous glands. The soft palate is a mobile, muscular aponeurosis attached to the posterior border of the hard palate. It is covered with mucous membrane continuous with that on the superior surface of the nasal cavity and on the oral surface of the hard palate.

Its free border lies between the oropharynx and the nasopharynx and forms the palatoglossal arches anteriorly and the palatopharyngeal arches posteriorly. The palatine tonsils lie between the arches, in the tonsillar fossae.

The muscles of the soft palate are:
- Levator veli palatini.
- Tensor veli palatini.
- Palatoglossus.
- Palatopharyngeus.
- Tensor veli palatini.

All are supplied by branchial motor fibres carried to the pharyngeal plexus by the vagus, except tensor veli palatini, which is supplied by the mandibular nerve.

Muscles of mastication

The muscles of mastication (masseter, temporalis and the lateral and medial pterygoid muscles) develop from the mesoderm of the first branchial arch. Their motor supply is from the mandibular division of the trigeminal nerve. They all arise from the skull and insert into the mandible, causing movement of the mandible at the temporomandibular joint (Fig. 2.4).

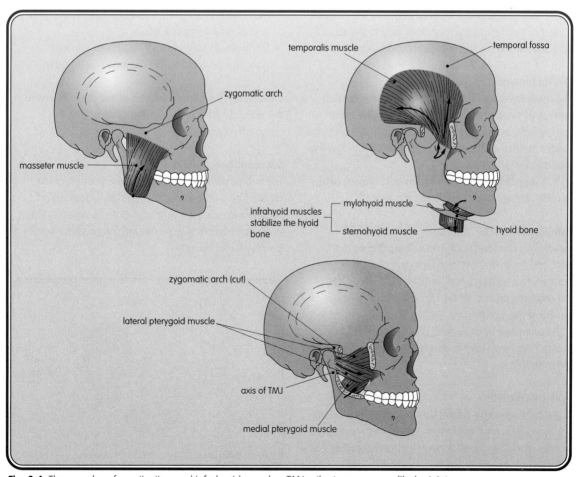

Fig. 2.4 The muscles of mastication and infrahyoid muscles. TMJ = the temporomandibular joint.

Masseter muscle

The masseter arises from the lower border and medial surface of the zygomatic arch and attaches to the lateral aspect of the angle and lower half of the ramus of the mandible. It is a powerful elevator of the jaw. It is supplied by the masseteric branch of the mandibular nerve, which passes through the mandibular notch of the mandible.

Lateral pterygoid muscle

The lateral pterygoid has two heads, both innervated by the lateral pterygoid branch of the mandibular nerve:
- The upper head arises from the inferior aspect of the greater wing of sphenoid (the roof of the infratemporal fossa). It closes the mouth and stabilizes the temporomandibular joint when chewing.
- The lower head arises from the lateral surface of the lateral pterygoid plate and opens the mouth.

The heads merge and narrow to attach to the anterior aspect of the neck of the mandible, and to the capsule and articular disc of the temporomandibular joint.

Medial pterygoid muscle

The medial pterygoid arises mainly from the medial surface of the lateral pterygoid plate. Its fibres run downwards, backwards, and outwards to attach to the medial surface of the angle of the mandible below the mandibular foramen.

It is supplied by the medial pterygoid branch of the mandibular nerve and it elevates the jaw.

Temporalis muscle

Temporalis is a fan-shaped muscle arising from the temporal fossa and overlying temporal fascia. It narrows to a tendon which attaches to the borders of the coronoid process of the mandible and the anterior border of the ramus.

It is supplied by deep temporal branches of the mandibular nerve and its action is to elevate and retract the mandible.

Salivary glands

There are three large, paired salivary glands (the parotid, submandibular, and sublingual glands) and numerous smaller glands scattered throughout the mouth (Fig. 2.5).

Parotid gland

This is the largest salivary gland and produces serous saliva. It lies between the ramus of the mandible and the mastoid and coronoid processes, and its anterior border overlies the masseter. An accessory lobe may be found above this muscle. The facial nerve passes through the parotid gland.

The parotid duct is about 5 cm long, pierces the buccinator and opens into the mouth opposite the second upper molar tooth. This opening can be felt with the tongue.

The parotid gland is supplied by branches of the external carotid artery; venous blood drains to the retromandibular vein. It is innervated by both the sympathetic and parasympathetic systems. Parasympathetic innervation is secretomotor (causing production of saliva), sympathetic innervation is vasoconstrictor (causing a dry mouth).
- Parasympathetic fibres are carried from the glossopharyngeal nerve through the otic ganglion and auriculotemporal nerve.
- Sympathetic fibres from the superior cervical ganglion pass along the external carotid artery.

Lymph from the superficial part of the gland drains to the parotid nodes and from the deep part to the retropharyngeal nodes.

Submandibular gland

The submandibular gland lies in the floor of mouth, covered by a fibrous capsule, and produces mixed serous and mucous secretions. Both its superficial and deep parts communicate around the posterior border of the mylohyoid muscle.

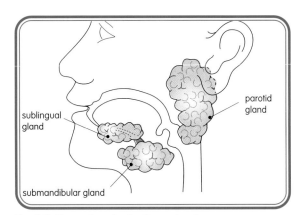

Fig. 2.5 The main paired salivary glands.

Its duct passes forwards between the mylohyoid and hyoglossus muscles to open onto sublingual papillae at the base of the frenulum. The duct is crossed by the lingual nerve.

The gland is supplied by the facial and lingual arteries (branches of the external carotid arteries); venous drainage is by the facial and lingual veins.

It is innervated by both the parasympathetic and sympathetic systems.

- Parasympathetic fibres are conveyed from the facial nerve through the chorda tympani and submandibular ganglion.
- Sympathetic innervation is from the superior cervical ganglion, with fibres passing along the arteries of the gland.

Lymphatic drainage is to the overlying submandibular lymph nodes.

Sublingual gland

This is situated below the mucous membrane of the floor of the mouth and produces mainly mucous secretions which pass into the submandibular duct or directly into the mouth via 15–20 small ducts. Its innervation, blood supply and venous and lymphatic drainage are similar to the submandibular gland.

Pharynx

The pharynx is a muscular tube approximately 14 cm in length, extending from the base of the skull to the level of C6 (the lower border of cricoid). The pharynx communicates with the nose, middle ear (by the auditory tube), mouth, and larynx. Distally, it is continuous with the oesophagus (Fig. 2.6).

It provides a common entrance for air, food and fluids, and mechanisms exist to ensure food and fluids pass into the oesophagus and air passes into the lungs (although some air is swallowed with food).

The pharynx is divided into the nasopharynx, oropharynx, and laryngopharynx and its walls have mucous, submucous, and muscular layers.

The muscular layer of the pharynx consists of:
- Superior, middle and inferior constrictors.
- Salpingopharyngeus.
- Stylopharyngeus.
- Palatopharyngeus.

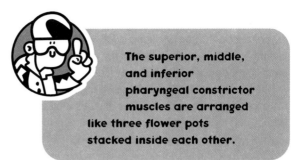

The superior, middle, and inferior pharyngeal constrictor muscles are arranged like three flower pots stacked inside each other.

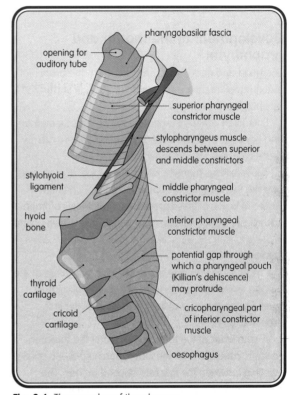

Fig. 2.6 The muscles of the pharynx.

Cricopharyngeus forms the upper oesophageal sphincter (Fig. 2.6). Stylopharyngeus is supplied by the glossopharyngeal nerve; the other muscles of the pharynx are supplied by the vagus through the pharyngeal plexus on the outer surface of the middle constrictor.

The muscular coat is deficient superiorly where the submucosa thickens to form the pharyngobasilar membrane, attached to the base of the skull.

The pharyngeal tonsils, or adenoids, lie submucosally in the nasopharynx. The palatine tonsils lie between the anterior and posterior arches of the fauces in the oropharynx (Fig. 2.1).

The epiglottis lies in the laryngopharynx and closes the entrance of the larynx during swallowing. The piriform fossae lie on either side of the epiglottis and are a common site for fish bones to lodge!

The blood supply to the pharynx is from branches of the ascending pharyngeal, superior thyroid, maxillary, lingual, and facial arteries. Venous blood drains to the internal jugular vein via the pharyngeal venous plexus.

Lymph from the nasopharynx drains to the retropharyngeal lymph nodes. Drainage from the remainder of the pharynx is to the deep cervical nodes.

Development of the mouth and oropharynx

The head and neck derive primarily from the branchial (pharyngeal) arches—mesenchymal tissue separated by pharyngeal pouches and clefts.

Each arch contains an artery, nerve, muscle element, and cartilage or skeletal element. Initially there are six arches, but the fifth disappears.

The maxillary, mandibular, and frontonasal processes give rise to the mandible, upper lip, palate, and nose. Failure of fusion of these processes is relatively common and causes abnormalities such as cleft lip and cleft palate.

Tongue

The mucous membrane of the anterior two-thirds of the tongue forms from endoderm of two lateral midline swellings on the floor of the pharynx over the first branchial arch.

A small part of the tongue, in front of the foramen caecum, develops from the tuberculum impar—a midline swelling between the first and second arches. The posterior one-third of the tongue forms from the copula—a midline swelling over the third and fourth arches.

The muscles of the tongue develop from suboccipital myotomes, which migrate forwards, carrying their nerve supply, the hypoglossal nerve, with them.

The parotid gland develops as a tubular ectodermal outgrowth from the inside of the cheek, and the submandibular gland as an endodermal outgrowth from the floor of the mouth.

Tissues

Mucosal surface

The gingiva and hard palate are covered by masticatory mucosa They are firmly bound to the underlying bone and consist of stratified squamous epithelium (keratinized, parakeratinized, or non-keratinized) and lamina propria.

The lips, cheeks, alveolar mucosa, floor of the mouth, undersurface of the tongue, and the soft palate are covered by lining mucosa which distends with movement of the underlying musculature. It consists of stratified squamous epithelium, lamina propria, and a submucosa of collagen and elastic fibres that binds the lining mucosa of the lips and cheeks to the muscle, and prevents the mucosa folding and being bitten when chewing.

The mucous layer of the pharynx is continuous with that of the nose, oral cavity, auditory tube, larynx, and oesophagus. The nasopharynx is lined with respiratory epithelium (ciliated mucous membrane with goblet cells). The oropharynx and laryngopharynx are lined with stratified squamous epithelium to withstand abrasion from the passage of food.

Taste receptors

We can detect four types of taste: sweet, sour, salt, and bitter. Receptors for these are found in separate areas of the tongue (Fig. 2.3). Most of our 'taste' is actually smell!

Salivary glands

The salivary glands consist of parenchymal and stromal components. Each parenchymal unit is called a salivon, which consists of an acinus (from the Latin word for grape) and a duct (Fig. 2.7). The duct of the salivon modifies the secretions of the acinus. The striated segment of the duct is continuous with the excretory part of the duct.

Acini consist of serous or mucous cells. The parotid gland has only serous acini, the sublingual gland contains mostly mucous acini, and the submandibular gland contains predominantly serous acini. The minor salivary glands are mucous, except for Ebner's glands and those in the tip of the tongue, which are serous.

Lymphoid tissue

The lingual tonsils (the lymphoid tissue beneath the mucous membrane of the pharyngeal part of the tongue), the palatine tonsils, the pharyngeal tonsils (the adenoids), and smaller aggregations of lymphoid tissue (such as the tubal tonsil) form a ring of lymphoid tissue around the oropharynx and nasopharynx which is known as Waldeyer's ring.

ORGANIZATION OF THE OESOPHAGUS

The oesophagus is a muscular tube approximately 25 cm in length, extending from the pharynx to the stomach. Its primary function is to convey food and fluids from the pharynx to the stomach during swallowing.

Regional anatomy

The oesophagus begins in the neck at the level of the cricoid cartilage, where it is continuous with the pharynx, and passes into the thorax just to the right of the midline.

In the superior mediastinum, it lies in front of the upper four thoracic vertebrae, behind the trachea, left main bronchus, and left recurrent laryngeal nerve, to the left of the azygos vein, and to the right of the aortic arch and the thoracic duct.

- Describe the regional anatomy of the oral cavity, salivary glands and pharynx.
- Discuss the development of the mouth and oropharynx from the branchial arches.
- Name the tissues of the oral cavity and pharynx.
- Describe the location of the taste buds in the mouth.
- Describe the histological structure of salivary glands and the mechanism of secretion.

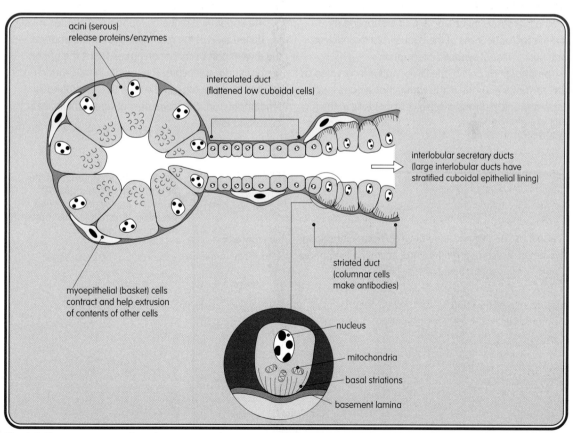

Fig. 2.7 The components of a salivon.

The oesophagus moves forward and to the left at T5, accompanied by the right and left vagus nerves, and descends behind the fibrous pericardium and in front of the descending aorta. It leaves the thoracic cavity through the muscular part of the diaphragm at the level of T10.

The distal 2 cm of the oesophagus is below the diaphragm (and is lined by columnar epithelium). It joins the stomach at the cardiac orifice at the level of T11.

Blood supply
Blood supply is from the inferior thyroid artery, branches of the thoracic aorta, and branches of the left gastric artery ascending from the abdominal cavity.

Venous drainage
Venous drainage is to both the systemic circulation (by the inferior thyroid and azygos veins) and the hepatic portal system (by the left gastric vein). It is a site of portosystemic anastamosis.

Innervation
The efferent innervation to muscle is by the vagus nerve (X).

Striated muscle in the upper part is supplied by somatic motor neurons of the vagus from the nucleus ambiguus, without synaptic interruption.

The smooth muscle of the lower part is innervated by visceral motor neurons of the vagus that synapse with postganglionic neurons, whose cell bodies lie in the wall of the oesophagus.

Development
The respiratory (tracheobronchial) diverticulum appears at the ventral wall of the foregut at about week 4 of gestation. It becomes separated from the dorsal part of the foregut by the oesophageal septum (Fig. 2.8).

The dorsal portion becomes the oesophagus (which is short initially, but lengthens rapidly with the descent of the heart and lungs); the ventral portion becomes the respiratory primordium. The muscular layers of the oesophagus develop from mesenchyme. Congenital abnormalities are described in Chapter 9.

Tissues
The layers of the oesophagus are essentially the same as in other parts of the gastrointestinal tract (Fig. 1.2).

The serosa covers the oesophagus inside the abdominal cavity and the adventitia is a connective-tissue covering that blends with the surrounding connective tissue in the neck and thorax.

The muscularis externa consists of an outer longitudinal and an inner circular layer (the opposite arrangement from that in the urethra).

The upper third of the oesophagus is striated muscle (a continuation of the muscular layer of the pharynx — the lowest part of cricopharyngeus forms the upper oesophageal sphincter). The middle third is made up of striated and smooth muscle, and the lower third is smooth muscle. The lower oesophageal sphincter is described later.

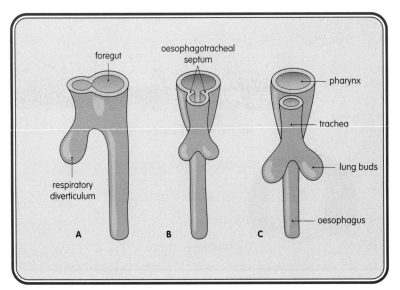
Fig. 2.8 The development of the pharynx and oesophagus. (A) Development by end of week 3 of gestation. (B) and (C) Development in the course of week 4.

The submucosa contains numerous branched tubular glands, more abundant in the upper region, which produce mucus to lubricate the oesophagus.

The mucosa is lined by non-keratinized, stratified squamous epithelium and has a lamina propria similar to that in other parts of the body, but the muscularis mucosa is thicker than in the rest of the digestive tract. Numerous mucous glands are usually present in the uppermost part and mucus-producing 'cardiac glands' (resembling the glands in the cardiac region of the stomach) are found in the lowermost part.

The lumen appears branched in cross-section, because the oesophagus is usually collapsed.

Oesophageal metaplasia

As in other parts of the body, metaplasia can occur, more commonly in the lower third of the oesophagus when gastric contents reflux through the physiological sphincter. Metaplasia may undergo further indirect transformations to dysplasia and then to neoplasia.

Factors predisposing to reflux include a defective lower oesophageal sphincter (caused by smoking, fatty meals, delayed gastric emptying, pregnancy, or following cardiac sphincter surgery in achalasia), increased intra-abdomimal pressure (caused by tight clothes, obesity, big meals), and drugs (e.g. tricyclics, anticholinergics).

The oesophagus does not have the structural adaptations necessary to cope with the acid contents of the stomach. Reflux causes cell injury and increased desquamation, which is compensated for by increased proliferation of basal epithelial cells (basal cell hyperplasia).

Ulcers form if basal cell formation cannot keep pace with cell loss and these may haemorrhage, perforate, or heal by fibrosis (sometimes forming a stricture) and epithelial regeneration.

In long-standing reflux, squamous cells may be replaced by columnar ones, a premalignant and important condition known as Barrett's oesophagus.

Read the information on dysphagia in Chapter 6—this will help you to understand the functions of the oesophagus, what can go wrong, and how you can identify possible causes of dysfunction.

- Describe the regional anatomy of the oesophagus and its embryonic development.
- Name the layers of the oesophagus and the gastrointestinal tract as a whole.
- Discuss the cell types found in different parts of the oesophagus, and the significance of these in the formation of ulcers and neoplastic change.

FUNCTIONS OF THE MOUTH, OROPHARYNX, AND OESOPHAGUS

Food intake and its control

The control of food intake is complex and the hypothalamus plays an important role.

Young people burn off excess intake as heat and maintain a relatively constant weight, but this ability reduces with age, leading to middle-aged spread.

Animals force-fed to obesity voluntarily reduce their food intake until their weight has returned to normal. Starved animals naturally increase their intake until their weight returns to its prestarvation level.

Signals that affect appetite

Glucose levels in the blood activate a glucostat in the brain. Amino acids in food raise body temperature: starving people feel cold even in hot surroundings.

Fat ingestion releases cholecystokinin and slows stomach emptying, making us feel full. Injection of cholecystokinin into the hypothalamus decreases appetite, suggesting a central as well as a peripheral role. Calcitonin decreases appetite.

Deposits of body fat may control food intake by releasing neuronal or hormonal signals that are relayed to the brain. Cold environments stimulate appetite; hot environments depress appetite.

Distension of a full stomach inhibits, and contraction of an empty stomach stimulates, appetite. Interestingly, however, denervation of the stomach and intestines seems to have no effect on food intake.

Central controls

There is a satiety centre in the ventromedial hypothalamus, stimulation of which causes aphagia. Lesions of the ventromedial hypothalamus result in hyperphagia.

Experiments show that local microinjections of glucose cause an increase in neuronal activity.

Glucostats measure the utilization of glucose: diabetic patients feel hungry despite high blood-glucose levels because insulin deficiency means utilization of glucose by cells is low.

There is a feeding centre in the lateral hypothalamus that is not specific for hunger. Its stimulation, however, increases eating and lesions result in aphagia.

Cortical and limbic centres

Habit and conditioning play a role.

Diurnal variation

We principally metabolize carbohydrates during the day and fats at night. The hypothalamus is responsible for the switch between the two.

Disorders of food intake

In Fröhlich's syndrome, a hypothalamic tumour causes obesity through excessive intake.

Anorexia nervosa is a potentially fatal psychiatric disorder, primarily of adolescent girls, in which patients persistently perceive themselves as overweight and, although obsessed with food, voluntarily starve.

Bulimia nervosa is a psychiatric disorder characterized by binge eating and compensatory vomiting, purging, or both.

Mastication

Mastication breaks up large food particles, mixing them with salivary secretions and aiding subsequent digestion. Molecules dissolve in salivary secretions and stimulate taste buds.

The muscles of mastication cause movement of the mandible at the temporomandibular joint.

The digastric and mylohyoid muscles open the mouth and the infrahyoid muscles stabilise the hyoid bone during mastication.

The teeth, gums, palate and tongue also play an important role, manipulating food and immobilizing it between the crushing surfaces of the teeth. The tongue then propels the bolus of food along the palate towards the pharynx, initiating the swallowing reflex.

Salivation

The components of saliva vary according to the rate and site of production—the main components are water, proteins, and electrolytes. The average rate of secretion of saliva is 1–2 L/day.

Primary secretion in the acini produces an isotonic fluid that is modified in the ducts (Fig. 2.9).

Control of secretion

Chemoreceptors in the mouth and oropharynx are activated by smell and taste: amyl nitrate and citric acid produce copious secretion.

Parasympathetic cholinergic stimulation produces a watery secretion which is blocked by atropine. This is given before surgery to reduce the risk of aspiration of saliva.

Sympathetic adrenergic and noradrenergic stimulation produce thick mucoid secretion.

Denervation causes dribbling. This is known as Canon's law of denervation hypersensitivity. Normally receptors are localized at neuroeffector junctions, but if nerves are cut, receptors spread all over the gland and it becomes excessively sensitive to circulating acetylcholine, producing copious amounts of saliva.

Salivary electrolytes

Saliva contains Na^+, HCO_3^-, Cl^- and K^+, the concentrations of which vary according to the rate of flow (Fig. 2.10). Levels of Na^+ and Cl^- in saliva are hypotonic, but levels of HCO_3^- and K^+ are hypertonic at higher rates of flow. Saliva is hypotonic overall (about 200 mmol/L), and alkaline, although the exact pH varies with flow.

Salivary proteins

Salivary proteins include amylase, ribonuclease,

R protein (which protects vitamin B_{12} as it passes through the duodenum, jejunum, and ileum), lipase (important in cystic fibrosis when pancreatic lipase is lost), lysozyme, secretory IgA, IgG, and IgM.

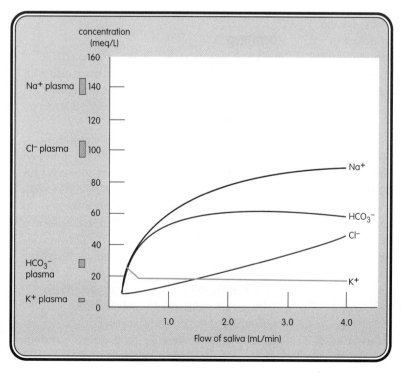

Fig. 2.9 Secretion of saliva.

Fig. 2.10 Salivary composition against flow rate. (Redrawn with permission from: Thaysen JH *et al.* Secretion control in salivation. *Am J Physiol* 1954,**178**:155.)

Functions of saliva and the salivary glands

The functions of saliva and the salivary glands include:

- The secretion of digestive enzymes especially α-amylase (ptyalin) which attacks 1,4-linkages in starch and cleans the oral cavity after food.
- The lubrication of the buccal cavity by mucus-secreting units of glands (under sympathetic and parasympathetic control).
- The secretion of the antibacterial enzyme known as lysozyme that protects teeth.
- In most people but not all, the secretion of IgA by plasma cells in connective tissue that has immune and other, poorly understood, functions. The secretory component is synthesized by striated duct cells.
- The moistening of the buccal cavity for speech, breast-feeding (saliva forms a seal around the mother's nipple), and cleansing.

Oral absorption

Most drugs are administered orally, but this is the most complicated pathway to the tissues and exposes drugs to first-pass metabolism in the liver.

Drugs given orally must dissolve in the gastro-intestinal fluids and penetrate the epithelial cells lining the gastrointestinal tract by passive diffusion or active transport. Some drugs are poorly absorbed orally or are unstable in the gastrointestinal tract.

Sublingual administration allows diffusion into the systemic circulation through the capillary network, bypassing the liver and avoiding first-pass metabolism. Lower doses can therefore be given. Glyceryl trinitrate used in angina treatment is commonly given this way.

Oral defences

Salivary defences

The alkaline pH of saliva neutralizes acid in food, or gastric contents following vomiting. Calcium and phosphate in saliva protect teeth by mineralizing newly erupted teeth and repairing pre-carious white spots in enamel.

Salivary proteins cover teeth with a protective coat called 'acquired pedicle'. Antibodies and antibacterial agents retard bacterial growth and tooth decay.

Swallowing

Swallowing is controlled by medullary centres and consists of voluntary and involuntary phases. The involuntary reflex is initiated by the voluntary action of the propulsion of contents towards the back of the pharynx.

The reflex is triggered by afferent impulses in the trigeminal, glossopharyngeal, and vagus nerves. Efferent fibres pass to the tongue and pharyngeal muscles through the trigeminal, facial and hypoglossal nerves. The upper oesophageal sphincter relaxes and involuntary waves of contraction in the pharyngeal muscles push the contents into the oesophagus. Respiration is inhibited and the epiglottis is closed by a reflex to prevent both food passing into the lungs and aspiration pneumonia.

We swallow about 600 times a day: 200 times while eating and drinking, 350 times while awake (but not eating or drinking) and 50 times while asleep.

A primary wave of peristalsis sweeps down the length of the oesophagus at the start of swallowing and (together with gravity) propels food towards the stomach. Secondary peristalsis occurs locally in response to direct stimulation (e.g. by distension of the oesophagus) and helps clear food residues. Tertiary waves are common in the elderly, but are not peristaltic or propulsive.

The lower oesophageal sphincter relaxes through hormonal and vagal mechanisms when swallowing is initiated, ahead of the peristaltic wave, to allow food into the stomach. Defects in the lower oesophageal sphincter are described below.

Vomiting

Vomiting is one of the most common symptoms of illness, especially in children (when it is associated with almost any physical or emotional illness), pregnancy, alcohol dependency, and some metabolic disorders (e.g. uraemia).

Vomiting centres (Fig. 2.11) in the lateral reticular formation of the medulla are stimulated by:

- Chemoreceptor zones in the area postrema, which are themselves stimulated by circulating chemicals, drugs, motion sickness (induced by prolonged stimulation of vestibular apparatus), and metabolic causes.
- Vagal and sympathetic afferent neurons from the gut, stimulated by mucosal irritation.
- The limbic system—less is known about these circuits, but sights, smells, and emotional circumstances can induce vomiting.

Lesions of the chemoreceptor zones abolish vomiting

induced by some emetic drugs, uraemia, and radiation sickness, but not gastrointestinal irritation.

Stages of vomiting

- A feeling of nausea is often accompanied by autonomic symptoms of sweating, pallor, and hypersalivation (which protects the mucosa of the mouth from the acid contents of the stomach).

> To quote a surgeon: 'it doesn't matter how many times you do it, vomiting only has one 't'.'

- Reverse peristalsis empties the contents of the upper intestine into the stomach and the epiglottis closes, protecting the lungs and trachea.
- The breath is held in mid-inspiration, fixing the chest, and the muscles of the abdominal wall contract, increasing intra-abdominal pressure.
- The oesophageal sphincters relax allowing expulsion of gastric contents through the mouth by reverse peristalsis.

Emetic drugs

Emesis is sometimes induced if the patient has swallowed poison and gastric lavage would be difficult (for example, small children are given paediatric ipecacuanha). More usually, vomiting is an unwanted side effect of drugs given for other reasons (e.g. cytotoxic drugs and opioids).

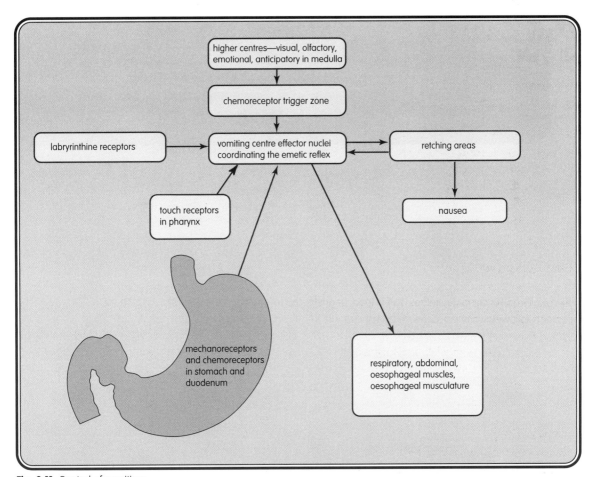

Fig. 2.11 Control of vomiting.

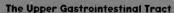

Antiemetic drugs

These should only be prescribed when the cause of vomiting is known, otherwise they may delay diagnosis.

The oesophageal sphincters

The oesophagus has two sphincters:

- The upper oesophageal sphincter is a striated, muscular sphincter and part of the cricopharyngeus.
- The lower oesophageal sphincter is a physiological sphincter, contributed to by the lower 4 cm of oesophageal smooth muscle, the intra-abdominal segment of the oesophagus which acts as a flap valve, and a mucosal rosette formed by folds of gastric mucosa, which all help to occlude the lumen of the gastro-oesophageal junction.

Failure of relaxation of the lower oesophageal sphincter (achalasia) may cause dilation, tortuosity, incoordination of peristalsis and hypertrophy of the oesophagus. It often presents in the third decade with progressive dysphagia, reflux from the contents of the dilated oesophagus and aspiration pneumonia. Malignant change may occur.

An incompetent lower oesophageal sphincter results in reflux, oesophagitis, ulceration, scarring, stricture formation, and the premalignant Barrett's oesophagus (described in Chapter 9).

- **What are the processes that regulate hunger and satiety?**
- **Describe the purposes of mastication and the muscles of mastication.**
- **How do salivary electrolytes compare with those in plasma?**
- **Describe the processes involved in swallowing and vomiting.**
- **Discuss the upper and lower oesophageal sphincters.**
- **Describe the complications of reflux into the oesophagus.**

3. The Stomach

ORGANIZATION OF THE STOMACH

The stomach is a muscular organ that mixes food with digestive juices to form chyme. It receives food and fluid from the oesophagus and releases its contents into the duodenum. Gastric contents are broken down both by the churning action of the stomach and by being squirted through the narrow pylorus.

The stomach wall is impermeable to most substances but alcohol, water, salts, and some drugs may be absorbed through it. Most other substances are absorbed from more distal parts of gastrointestinal tract.

Regional anatomy

Anatomically, the stomach is divided into 3 parts (Fig. 3.1):
- Fundus—lies above an imaginary horizontal plane passing through cardiac orifice.
- Body—the largest part, lies between the fundus and the antrum.
- Antrum—lies to the right of the incisura angularis and tapers to the right to join the pyloric canal.

The stomach lies between the oesophagus proximally and duodenum distally. It is mobile, muscular and can expand considerably after the intake of food or fluid.

The physiological lower oesophageal sphincter protects the oesophagus from reflux of the acidic contents of the stomach. The pyloric sphincter controls the flow of gastric contents into the duodenum.

The cardiac orifice of the stomach lies behind the 7th costal cartilage about 2.5 cm to the left of the median plane. The pylorus lies 1 cm to the right of the midline, in or below the transpyloric planes and is joined to the cardiac orifice by the lesser curve. The position of the greater curve varies greatly.

The shape of the stomach varies according to the shape and size of the individual. It is usually 'J-shaped' in tall thin people and 'steer horn' shaped in shorter fatter people.

The anterior and posterior surfaces of the stomach are covered by peritoneum and meet at the greater and lesser curvatures. The peritoneum is reflected at the greater curvature to become the greater omentum—a double layer of peritoneum suspended from the greater curve. It looks like a plastic bag hanging off the stomach and has a remarkable ability to stick to damaged or

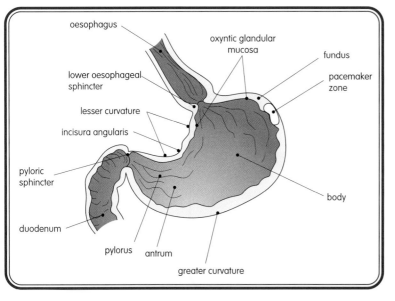

Fig. 3.1 Structure of the stomach.

oesophagus

oxyntic glandular mucosa

fundus

lower oesophageal sphincter

pacemaker zone

lesser curvature

incisura angularis

pyloric sphincter

body

duodenum

pylorus   antrum

greater curvature

perforated parts of the gastrointestinal tract, sealing off leaks and giving some protection against peritonitis.

Excess fat may be stored on the greater omentum, especially in men (who have different distributions of fat from women)—the infamous beer belly!

The peritoneum is reflected at the lesser curve to form the lesser omentum.

It is easiest to learn the blood supply from diagrams.

Relations

The anterior surface is in contact with the diaphragm, anterior abdominal wall, and left and right lobes of the liver. The spleen lies posterolateral to the fundus.

The diaphragm, left suprarenal gland, upper part of the left kidney, splenic artery, pancreas, transverse mesocolon and, in some people, the transverse colon, lie posteriorly forming the 'bed of the stomach'. They are separated from the stomach by the lesser sac.

Blood supply

The stomach has a very rich blood supply (Fig. 3.2). The arteries supplying the stomach are direct or indirect branches of the coeliac artery, the first midline branch of the abdominal aorta.

Venous drainage

In common with most of the alimentary system, the stomach drains to the hepatic portal system (as do the abdominal oesophagus and small and large intestines).

- The veins accompany the gastric arteries and drain into the portal venous system.
- The right and left gastric veins drain into the portal vein itself.
- The short gastric and gastroepiploic veins drain into the splenic vein.
- The right gastroepiploic vein usually drains into the superior mesenteric vein.
- Oesophageal tributaries of the left gastric vein form an important portacaval anastomosis with tributaries of the azygos vein in the thorax.

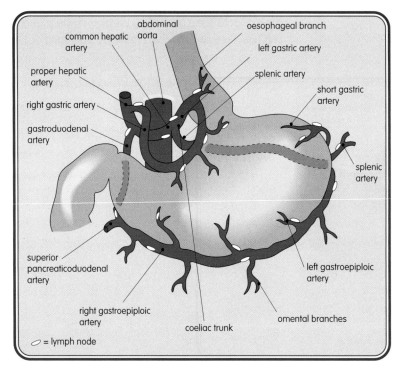

Fig. 3.2 The blood supply and lymphatic drainage of the stomach.

Nerve supply
The stomach is supplied by both sympathetic and parasympathetic systems.

Sympathetic supply
The sympathetic supply is from autonomic plexuses on nearby arteries (the coeliac plexus and superior and inferior mesenteric plexuses); it is vasomotor to gastric blood vessels and carries pain fibres from the stomach.

Parasympathetic supply
The parasympathetic supply is from the vagus (X). Anterior and posterior vagal trunks from the oesophageal plexus pass through the diaphragm with the oesophagus and divide into anterior and posterior gastric branches on the anterior and posterior surfaces of the stomach. Posterior branches contribute to the coeliac plexus.

Gastric branches form Auerbach's and Meissner's plexuses, described below. Postganglionic fibres control muscular activity and secretion.

Lymphatic drainage
The lymphatic drainage follows arteries.
- Those following the right gastric artery drain to pyloric, hepatic, and left gastric nodes.
- Those following the right gastroepiploic artery drain to right gastroepiploic and pyloric nodes.
- Those following the left gastroepiploic and splenic arteries drain to pancreaticosplenic nodes.
- Those following the left gastric artery drain to left gastric nodes.

These nodes all drain to preaortic nodes and then to the cisterna chyli. From the cisterna chyli, lymph drains to the thoracic duct, which is the largest lymphatic vessel in the body and, unlike most of the lymphatic system, is visible to the naked eye. The thoracic duct passes superiorly through the thorax and opens into the junction of the left internal jugular and subclavian veins.

Hepatic and pyloric nodes are close to the biliary system and may obstruct the common bile duct and cause jaundice if they enlarge because of tumour.

Throughout the alimentary system, the lymphatic system takes up finely emulsified fat absorbed from the diet.

Development
The stomach develops from a fusiform dilation of the foregut which appears at about week 4 of gestation (Fig. 3.3). Its appearance and position change greatly during development as it rotates around both:
- A longitudinal axis.
- An anteroposterior axis.

The posterior wall grows faster than the anterior wall and forms the greater and lesser curvatures.

Tissues
All parts of the stomach have the same basic structural layers (Fig. 3.4):
- Mucosa.
- Submucosa.
- Muscularis externa.
- Serosa.

Mucosa
The mucosa and submucosa form rugae (longitudinal folds) when the stomach is empty.

Mucous surface cells (simple columnar epithelium) line the stomach and the gastric pits (foveolae), which open onto the inner surface of the stomach. Gastric glands open into the bottom of the pits.

The lamina propria contains numerous cells of the immune system, migrant cells from the blood, and resident connective tissue cells. The muscularis mucosa consists of two thin layers of muscle.

Submucosa
This is the same as the submucosa of the rest of the alimentary system.

Muscularis externa
This consists of three layers of smooth muscle:
- An outer longitudinal muscle layer (absent from much of the anterior and posterior surfaces of the stomach).
- A middle circular muscle layer (poorly developed in the paraoesophageal region).
- An inner oblique muscle layer.

Serosa
This is the same as the serosa of the rest of the alimentary system.

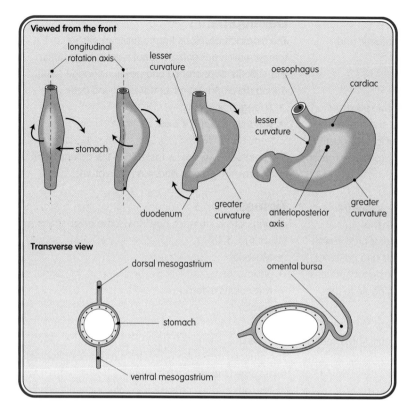

Viewed from the front

longitudinal rotation axis

lesser curvature

oesophagus

cardiac

stomach

lesser curvature

duodenum

greater curvature

anterioposterior axis

greater curvature

Transverse view

dorsal mesogastrium

omental bursa

stomach

ventral mesogastrium

Fig. 3.3 Formation of the stomach. (Redrawn with permission from: Sadler, TW. *Langman's medical embryology* 6th ed. London:Williams & Wilkins; 1990.)

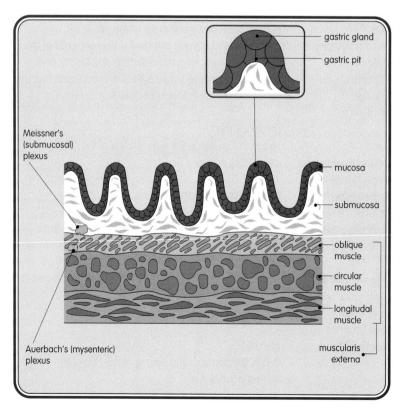

gastric gland

gastric pit

Meissner's (submucosal) plexus

mucosa

submucosa

oblique muscle

circular muscle

longitudal muscle

Auerbach's (mysenteric) plexus

muscularis externa

Fig. 3.4 Cross section of the stomach wall.

Glands of mucosa

There are three groups of glands, named after the region in which they are found.

Fundic (gastric) glands

These are the most numerous and contain several types of cells:

- Mucous neck cells—these are found just below gastric pits and contain mucinogen granules, well-developed Golgi apparatus, and rough endoplasmic reticulum.
- Parietal (oxyntic) cells—these are interspersed with mucous neck cells. They look distinctive, being triangular in section, with the apex pointing towards the gland lumen and have a spherical nucleus. They are sometimes binucleate. Their internal appearance changes when food has been eaten (Fig. 3.5). They

secrete HCl and intrinsic factor and contain numerous mitochondria to provide energy for HCl production. Parietal cells are absent in achlorhydria ('absence of acid'); thus, no intrinsic factor is produced in this condition. Histamine, gastrin, and acetylcholine all stimulate HCl production (Fig. 3.6).

- Chief (zymogen) cells—these are found in the deepest part of gastric glands and are typical protein-secreting cells. They secrete pepsinogen, the inactive precursor of pepsin (a proteolytic enzyme), which is converted to pepsin by acid.
- APUD (amine precursor uptake and decarboxylation) cells—there are several different types and they are found in the basal portion of the epithelium (the cell often does not reach the surface).
- Undifferentiated cells—undifferentiated cells are located in the neck region.

Fig. 3.5 Morphological changes in parietal cells.

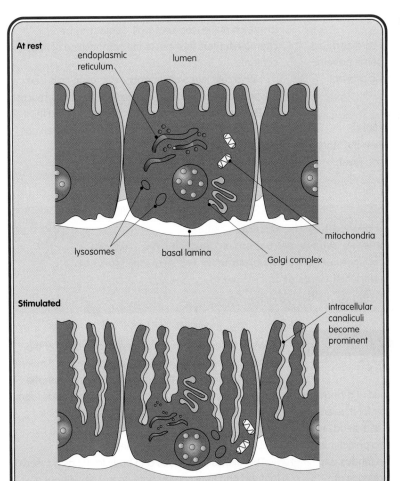

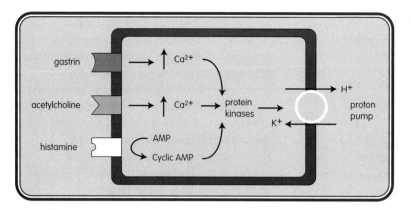

Fig. 3.6 Stimulation of secretion of HCl by parietal cells.

Cardiac glands

As the name suggests, they are found in the cardiac region. They are mostly mucus secreting, coiled tubular glands (but may be branched). Some undifferentiated cells are present in the neck region and APUD cells are scattered throughout. Some parietal cells may also be seen.

Pyloric glands

Pyloric cells are coiled (but less so than cardiac ones) and contain mucous cells. Sometimes some parietal, APUD, and undifferentiated cells are also present.

Nerve fibres

There are two major networks of nerve fibres:
- Auerbach's (myenteric) plexus between the inner oblique and the middle circular muscle layer.
- Meissner's (submucous) plexus between the inner oblique muscle layer and the mucosa.

Both plexuses are interconnected and contain nerve cells with processes that originate in the wall of the gut or mucosa.

Mucosal receptors are mechanoreceptors sensitive to stretch of the intestinal wall. Some may be chemoreceptors that sense the composition of intestinal contents.

Nerve cells innervate hormone-secreting cells (see gastric functions) and all the muscle layers in the mucosa.

The plexuses are sometimes described as a third division of the autonomic system, the enteric nervous system.

- Summarize the anatomy of the stomach.
- Describe the arterial supply and venous drainage of the stomach.
- Discuss the development of the stomach from the primitive foregut.
- List the layers and cell types of the stomach.

GASTRIC FUNCTIONS

Storage of food

We often consume large quantities of food at a single meal and the stomach acts as a reservoir for it, releasing the gastric contents into the duodenum at a steady rate.

Relaxation of the lower oesophageal sphincter is followed by a receptive relaxation of the fundus and body of the stomach, mediated by the release of vasoactive intestinal peptide from the vagus (Fig. 3.7).

Muscle contraction in the fundus and body of the stomach is normally weak. The muscle wall is thinner in the fundus and body than in the antral area and the smooth muscle cells have a low resting potential (about −50 mV). The cells are partially contracted at their resting potential, but hyperpolarization induced by inhibitory nerve fibres causes them to relax.

This allows the fundus and body to act as a reservoir for food and to accommodate up to 1.5 L without a marked increase in intragastric pressure.

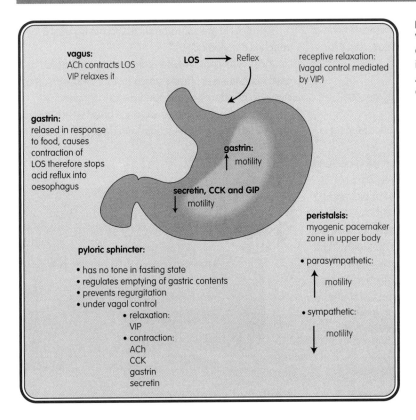

Fig. 3.7 Gastric motility. VIP = vasoactive intestinal peptide; CCK = cholecystokinin; GIP = gastric inhibitory peptide; ACh = acetylcholine; LOS = lower oesophageal sphincter.

Within the figure:

vagus:
ACh contracts LOS
VIP relaxes it

LOS → Reflex

receptive relaxation:
(vagal control mediated by VIP)

gastrin:
relased in response to food, causes contraction of LOS therefore stops acid reflux into oesophagus

gastrin:
↑ motility

secretin, CCK and GIP
↓ motility

peristalsis:
myogenic pacemaker zone in upper body

pyloric sphincter:
• has no tone in fasting state
• regulates emptying of gastric contents
• prevents regurgitation
• under vagal control
  • relaxation:
    VIP
  • contraction:
    ACh
    CCK
    gastrin
    secretin

• parasympathetic:
  ↑ motility

• sympathetic:
  ↓ motility

Gastric muscle contraction in the antrum is vigorous. Food is mixed rapidly with gastric secretions to aid digestion and the antral contents are squirted into the duodenum. Smooth muscle in the antral area has a higher resistance to stretch than that of the fundus and body.

Food may remain in the stomach, unmixed, for up to 1 hour. Fats form an oily layer on top of other gastric contents and are emptied later. Liquids empty more quickly.

Gastric secretions and their control
Secretions of the stomach
The average adult produces 2–3 L of gastric juice every 24 hours.

Resting juice
Resting juice is an isotonic juice secreted by the surface cells. It is similar to plasma but has an alkaline pH of 7.7 and a higher concentration of HCO_3^-.

Mucus
The alkaline mucus of the stomach is a thick, sticky, mucopolysaccharide. It plays an important role in the protection of the stomach against its acid contents.

Mucous is secreted by goblet cells of the surface epithelium, mucous neck cells of the body of the stomach, and by the pyloric cells of the antrum.

Pepsin
Pepsin is secreted from the chief cells in the gastric pits in the form of its precursor, pepsinogen. HCl activates pepsinogen (42 kDa) by cleaving nine amino acids to form pepsin (37.5 kDa).

Pepsin is an enzyme that acts on proteins and polypeptides, cleaving peptide bonds adjacent to aromatic amino acids.

Lipase
Gastric lipase is an enzyme that acts on triglycerides to produce fatty acids and glycerol but is of little physiological importance except in pancreatic insufficiency.

Hydrochloric acid
HCl is produced by the parietal (oxyntic) cells.
The concentration of HCl depends on:
• The rate of HCl secretion.
• The amount of buffering provided by the resting juice,

ingested food and drink, and the alkaline secretion of the pyloric glands, duodenum, pancreas, and bile.
- Gastric motility.
- The rate of gastric emptying.
- The amount of back diffusion into the mucosa.

The pH of the contents of the stomach after feeding is normally about 2–3.

The functions of HCl include killing ingested bacteria, aiding protein digestion, providing the required pH to activate pepsin, and stimulating the flow of bile and pancreatic juice.

Its secretion by parietal cells is stimulated by histamine, acetylcholine, and gastrin (Fig. 3.6). It is also stimulated by caffeine (through the activation of cyclic AMP).

Secretion is inhibited by vagotomy (which removes acetylcholine stimulation), by blocking the histamine receptor on the parietal cells by drugs or, more effectively, by blocking the proton pump with a drug (e.g. omeprazole).

Intrinsic factor

Intrinsic factor is made in the parietal cells of the stomach and is a protein vital for the absorption of vitamin B_{12} in the terminal ileum. Without intrinsic factor, vitamin B_{12} is digested in the intestine and not absorbed.

R protein in the saliva protects vitamin B_{12} until it reaches the stomach.

Most diets contain excess vitamin B_{12} and stores are built up in the liver. These stores last for 2–3 years; thus, it takes considerable time for a dietary deficiency to produce symptoms. However, once body stores have been used up, pernicious anaemia develops.

When learning the risk factors for ulcer formation and the drugs used to prevent it, look at the diagram summarizing the control of gastric secretion (Fig. 3.8).

Control of gastric secretion

There are three phases of stimulation—the cephalic, gastric and intestinal phases (Fig. 3.8).

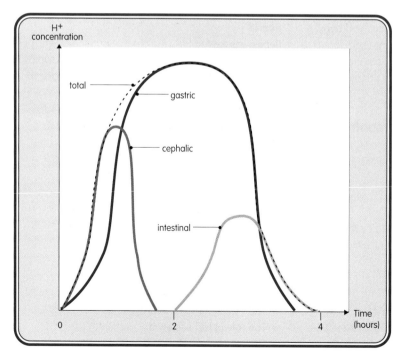

Fig. 3.8 Three phases of gastric secretion.

The cephalic phase

The cephalic phase is initiated by the sight, smell, and taste of food. It is mediated entirely by the vagus nerve—if the vagal innervation of the stomach is ligated, the cephalic phase is abolished.

Acetylcholine released from neurons of the intramural plexus causes secretion of acid:

- Directly, by stimulation of the parietal cells.
- Indirectly, by causing release of gastrin from G cells in the antrum and duodenum and release of histamine from cells in the gastric mucosa.

The gastric phase

The gastric phase is initiated by the presence of food in the stomach, in response to distension of the stomach and the presence of amino acids and peptides resulting from the action of pepsins. Most acid secretion in response to a meal takes place during the gastric phase.

Distension of the body or antrum of the stomach stimulates mechanoreceptors that cause local and central cholinergic reflexes.

Amino acids or peptides (but not intact proteins) in the stomach act directly on G cells in the antrum to cause release of gastrin. Tryptophan and phenylalanine are particularly potent stimulators.

The intestinal phase

The intestinal phase is brought about by the presence of chyme in the duodenum. When the pH of gastric chyme is above 3, the intestinal phase is stimulatory, but it becomes inhibitory once the pH falls below 2.

The stimulatory phase is primarily endocrine mediated. The presence of amino acids and peptides in the duodenum causes release of gastrin from G cells in the antrum which stimulates parietal cells to produce acid.

The inhibitory phase is mediated by:

- The presence of acid in the duodenum, which causes release of secretin into the bloodstream. This both inhibits the release of gastrin by G cells and reduces the response of parietal cells to gastrin. Gastrin secretion is also inhibited by the presence of acid in the antrum.
- Fatty acids (produced as a result of triglyceride digestion) in the duodenum and proximal jejunum which cause the release of gastric inhibitory polypeptide and cholecystokinin, which both inhibit the secretion of acid by parietal cells. Gastric inhibitory polypeptide also suppresses gastrin release.

Protection of the gastric mucosa

The concentration of hydrogen ions in the stomach is up to a million times that found in the plasma and is sufficient to cause tissue damage. Several factors protect the mucosa from the acid contents:

- Mucus, secreted by neck and surface mucus cells in the body and fundus and similar cells elsewhere in the stomach, forms a flexible gel that coats the mucosa (Fig. 3.9). Prostaglandins stimulate mucus production.
- The surface cells secrete HCO_3^- which, together with the mucus, forms an unstirred layer.
- The surface membranes of the mucosal cells and the tight junctions between them protect the cells.
- Prostaglandins (especially prostaglandin E) inhibit acid secretion.

Several factors cause a breakdown of the mucosal protection or an increase in acid production and predispose to gastric irritation and peptic ulceration:

- Acid secretion from the parietal cells is stimulated by histamine, acetylcholine, and gastrin (Fig. 3.6).
- Ethanol, vinegar, bile salts, and non-steroidal anti-inflammatory drugs (NSAIDs,) such as aspirin, disturb the unstirred layer.
- NSAIDs also reduce mucus secretion, increase acid secretion, and decrease bicarbonate secretion by inhibiting prostaglandin production.
- In Zollinger–Ellison syndrome, gastrin-secreting adenomas result in marked hyperacidity. The adenomas are usually found in the pancreas but may be present in the stomach or duodenum. The syndrome is rare.
- *Helicobacter pylori,* a gram-negative bacterium that may infect individuals and live on the surface epithelium beneath the mucus layer in the stomach (but not further down the alimentary tract), has been isolated from about 70% of gastric ulcers and about 95% of duodenal ulcers. It attacks the surface cells causing an acute inflammatory reaction.
- Hyperparathyroidism predisposes to ulcer formation because increased levels of calcium stimulate acid production.
- Chronic exposure to nicotine from smoking causes an increase in acid secretion.
- Stress and obesity may also result in ulcer formation.
- Gastric and duodenal ulceration are common and a number of drugs have been developed to reduce acid secretion or increase mucosal protection.

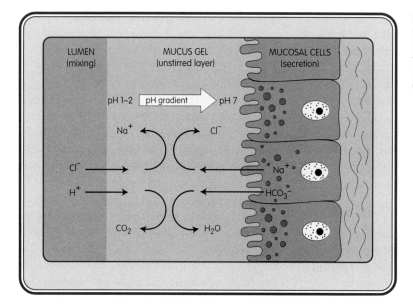

Fig. 3.9 Protection of gastric mucosa from low pH by mucus layer. (Redrawn with permission from: Underwood, JCE. *General and systemic pathology.* Edinburgh: Churchill Livingstone; 1992.)

Acid secretion reducers

H_2 histamine receptor antagonists (e.g. cimetidine and ranitidine) reduce acid secretion, relieve the pain, and increase the rate of ulcer healing.

M_1 muscarinic receptor antagonists (e.g. pirenzepine) selectively block M_1 receptors, reducing acid secretion with fewer muscarinic side effects than non-selective blockers, such as dry mouth, blurred vision, and urinary retention.

Proton-pump inhibitors (e.g. omeprazole) irreversibly inhibit the proton pump, reducing the transport of H^+ ions out of parietal cells. Proton pumps are the most powerful inhibitory drugs available.

Mucosal strengtheners

Sucralfate forms a polymerized, sticky gel in acid conditions of less than pH 4 that adheres to the base of ulcers. It has very few side effects.

Bismuth chelate has a similar mechanism of action to sucralfate and may eradicate *H. pylori.*

Prostaglandin analogues

Misoprostol is a synthetic prostaglandin analogue which can prevent NSAID-associated ulcers. It is contraindicated in pregnancy and breast-feeding.

Helicobacter pylori eradication

Triple therapy regimes provide higher eradication rates than dual ones and result in long-term ulcer remission. Current regimes include the following:

- Amoxycillin, metronidazole, and omeprazole.
- Clarithromycin, tinidazole, and omeprazole.

Metronidazole should be avoided during the first trimester of pregnancy.

Gastric motility and emptying

Gastric motility and emptying are carefully regulated to ensure that chyme is delivered to the duodenum at a rate at which it can be absorbed.

Gastric motility

When food is swallowed there is a reflex receptive relaxation of the stomach which allows food to enter it, caused by vagal impulses arising both centrally and from receptors in the pharynx and oesophagus (Fig. 3.7).

The layers of the stomach are shown in Fig. 3.4. The stomach consists of three muscle layers (the inner, oblique muscle is incomplete in parts) with a submucosal and a myenteric plexus.

The plexuses are networks of nerve fibres and ganglion cells, with incoming axons from both the sympathetic and parasympathetic systems. They innervate gland cells in the mucosa and submucosa, intramural endocrine and exocrine cells, and smooth muscle in the muscularis mucosa and muscularis externa. Interneurons connect intrinsic afferent sensory fibres with efferent neurons to smooth muscle and secretory cells so that gastric activity is coordinated even in the absence of external innervation.

The muscularis externa of the stomach is thicker in the antrum and most gastric motility takes place here, with food being broken into smaller particles and mixed with gastric secretions before being squirted into the duodenum at a controlled rate.

Cholinergic stimulation from the vagus causes an increase in gastric motility in the antral area and an increase in gastric secretion, whereas adrenergic stimulation from the coeliac plexus has the opposite effect.

The presence of amino acids, peptides and hydrogen ions in the duodenum combine with distension of the duodenum to initiate the enterogastric reflex. This causes a neuronally mediated decrease in gastric motility.

Gastric emptying

The rate at which the stomach empties depends on:

- The type of food eaten. Carbohydrates are emptied most quickly, proteins more slowly, and fatty foods even more slowly to ensure that food is released into the duodenum at a rate at which it can be absorbed. Fatty acids or monoglycerides in the duodenum decrease the rate of gastric emptying by increasing the contractility of the pyloric sphincter. The presence of acidic contents with a pH of less than about 3.5 in the duodenum also slows gastric emptying, as may amino acids and peptides.
- The osmotic pressure of the contents of the duodenum. Duodenal osmoreceptors initiate a decrease in gastric emptying in response to hyperosmolar chyme.
- Vagal innervation. Vagotomy results in a marked decrease in the rate of gastric emptying.

The antrum, pylorus and upper duodenum function as a unit with contraction of the antrum being followed by a wave of contraction in the pyloric region and the duodenum. This coordinated contraction ensures that food travels down the digestive tract and prevents reflux.

Gastric defences against infection

Pepsin and the acid conditions in the stomach kill aerobic flora (bacteria that need oxygen) and other ingested bacteria, providing an important defence against infection. Large numbers of anaerobic flora exist in the ileum and colon. Rupture of the lower gastrointestinal tract may lead to peritonitis.

- What is the role of the stomach in the storage of food?
- What are the secretory and other functions of gastric mucosa?
- How does the body control gastric secretion?
- How does the body protect the gastric mucosa from enzymatic and acidic damage?
- List the main drugs used for mucosal protection.
- Summarize the process of gastric motility and emptying.
- How does the stomach protect the body from infection?

4. The Liver, Biliary Tract, and Pancreas

ORGANIZATION OF THE LIVER AND BILIARY TRACT

The liver is the largest organ in the body and is vital to life.

The biliary system removes waste products from the liver and carries bile salts to the intestine where they aid digestion.

Regional anatomy

The liver is a wedge-shaped organ lying under the diaphragm, mainly in the right hypochondrium (Fig. 1.1). It weighs approximately 1.5 kg.

The diaphragmatic surface is related to the diaphragm (as the name suggests!).

The bare area is related to the inferior vena cava and the right adrenal gland.

The visceral surface is related to the abdominal oesophagus, fundus and body of the stomach, the lesser omentum, the gall bladder, the superior part of the duodenum, and the transverse colon (Fig. 4.1).

The liver is attached to the anterior wall and diaphragm by four folds of peritoneum:

- The falciform ligament (the remnant of the ventral mesentery of the abdominal foregut), which attaches the anterior and superior surfaces of the liver to the anterior abdominal wall and the diaphragm.
- The coronary ligament which connects the posterior surface of the right lobe to the diaphragm.
- The right triangular ligament (an extension of the coronary ligament).
- The left triangular ligament, which attaches the posterior surface of the left lobe to the diaphragm.

The liver is divided into left and right lobes by the falciform ligament and each lobe receives its own blood supply (Fig. 4.1).

Blood supply

The blood supply to the liver is very rich and comes from:

- The hepatic artery (a branch of the coeliac trunk), which divides into left and right branches to supply the left and right lobes.

- The portal vein (Fig. 4.2).

An accessory left hepatic artery, often arising from the left gastric artery, may be found.

Nerve supply

The innervation of the liver is from both vagi (through the anterior gastric nerve) and the coeliac plexus.

Lymphatic drainage

Lymphatic drainage is to deep and superficial plexuses.

The deep plexus drains to the posterior mediastinal nodes (with the hepatic veins and inferior vena cava) or to nodes around the porta hepatis (with the portal vein).

The superficial plexus drains through the diaphragm to the anterior mediastinal nodes and, on the visceral surface, to nodes around the porta hepatis.

Development

The liver develops from the liver bud (hepatic diverticulum) that appears as an outgrowth of the endodermal epithelium at the distal end of the primitive foregut in the middle of the third week (Fig. 4.16).

The gall bladder

The gall bladder is a pear-shaped sac that acts as a temporary reservoir for bile from the liver. When stimulated, it releases its contents into the duodenum through the cystic and biliary ducts.

The gall bladder is related to the visceral surface of the liver and is partly covered by peritoneum which is reflected off it. It is also related to the duodenum and the transverse colon. It has a fundus, body, and neck, which narrows to blend with the cystic duct (Fig. 4.3).

The cystic duct joins the common hepatic duct to form the bile duct, which opens into the duodenum through the sphincters of Boyden and Oddi at the ampulla of Vater (the duodenal papilla). The position at which the cystic duct joins the hepatic duct varies considerably.

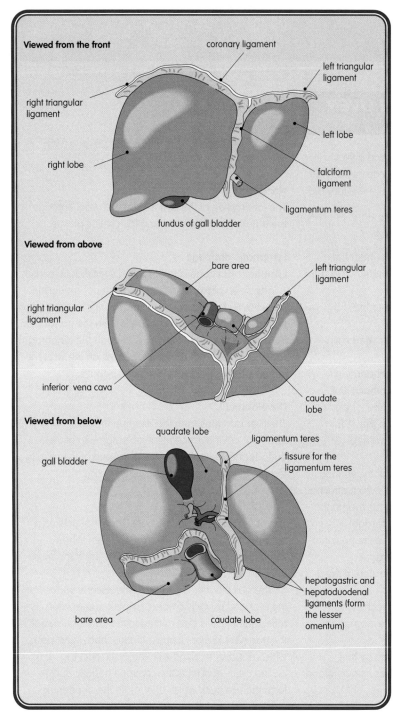

Fig. 4.1 Three different views of the liver.

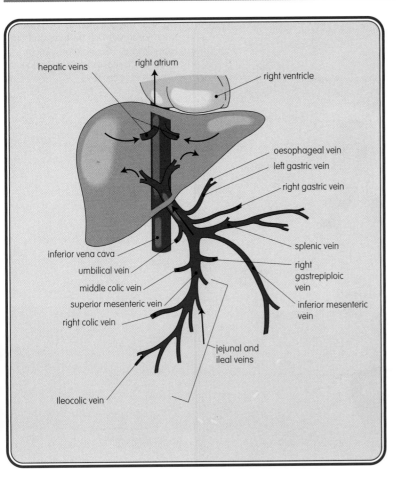

hepatic veins

right atrium

right ventricle

oesophageal vein

left gastric vein

right gastric vein

splenic vein

inferior vena cava

umbilical vein

right gastrepiploic vein

middle colic vein

superior mesenteric vein

inferior mesenteric vein

right colic vein

jejunal and ileal veins

ileocolic vein

Fig. 4.2 The hepatic portal venous system. (Redrawn with permission from: Hall–Craggs, ECB. *Anatomy as a basis for clinical medicine.* London: Waverly Europe; 1995.)

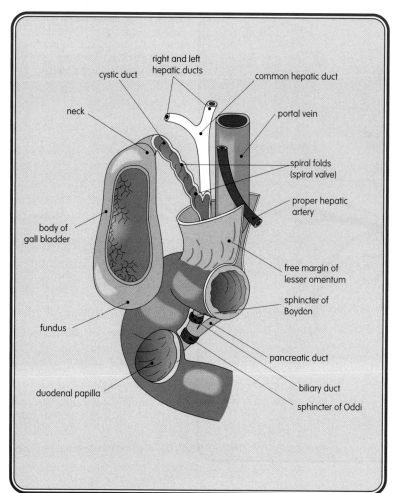

Fig. 4.3 The gall bladder and biliary tract. (Redrawn with permission from Hall–Craggs, ECB. *Anatomy as a basis for clinical medicine.* London: Waverly Europe; 1995.)

Blood supply

The blood supply to the gall bladder is from the cystic artery (a branch of the hepatic artery); venous drainage is directly into the liver.

Lymphatic drainage

Lymph from the gall bladder passes to the hepatic nodes.

The biliary tract

The biliary tract conveys bile from the liver to the duodenum. The left and right hepatic ducts join to form the common hepatic duct which descends in the free edge of the lesser omentum and joins the cystic duct to form the bile duct.

The bile duct is approximately 8 cm in length. The duct descends in the free edge of the lesser omentum. It continues its descent behind the superior part of the duodenum and head of the pancreas to open into the duodenum through the sphincter of Oddi at the duodenal papilla, 10 cm beyond the pylorus. The main pancreatic duct opens into the duodenum at the same point.

Tissues of the liver and biliary tract

Traditionally, there are three ways of describing the arrangement of the liver (Fig. 4.4):

- Classic lobule.
- Portal lobule.
- Acinus.

Classic lobule

Each lobule may be thought of as a hexagon with a central vein at its centre and a portal triad at its outer corners. A portal triad consists of a branch of the hepatic artery, a branch of the portal vein, and a bile duct.

Fig. 4.4 The arrangement of the liver.

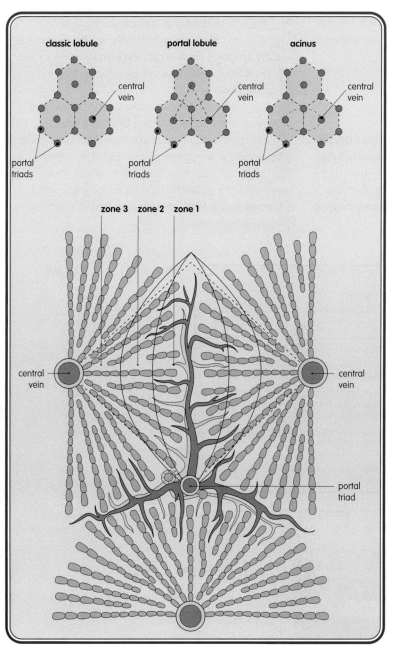

Portal lobule

This views the liver as being made up of a series of triangles with a central vein at each corner and a portal triad at the centre and emphasises the exocrine function.

Acinus

This is an elliptical arrangement with a portal triad at the centre and a central vein at each pole and emphasises the endocrine function. It reflects the gradient of metabolic activity found in the liver and is divided into three zones for descriptive purposes.

Most oxygenated blood is found in the centre of the acinus around the portal triad (zone 1); this zone is most susceptible to damage from toxins carried to the liver in the hepatic portal vein. Most of the metabolic activity of the liver takes place here.

Conversely, zone 3, being furthest from the portal triad and closest to the central vein, is most susceptible to ischaemic damage.

Cell types of the liver
These are summarized in Fig. 4.5.

Sinusoids, spaces of Disse, and bile canaliculi
Networks of capillaries (sinusoids) are found between the cords of hepatocytes, separated from them by the space of Disse (perisinusoidal space) (Fig. 4.6). The sinusoids radiate out from the central veins into which they drain.

The sinusoids have an incomplete lining of endothelial cells and Kupffer's cells; soluble substances in the sinusoids travel across this lining into the spaces of Disse from where they are taken up by the hepatocytes.

Two surfaces of each hepatocyte face a space of Disse, and two surfaces face a bile canaliculus (Fig. 4.7).

Bile canaliculi are made up of small canals formed by grooves in two opposing cells (Fig. 4.7); microvilli from hepatocytes project into the canaliculi. The canaliculi are sealed by zonulae occludentes, which prevent the contents escaping into the adjacent intercellular spaces.

Fig. 4.5 Cell types of the liver.

Cell types of the liver	
Cell type	**Function**
hepatocytes	phagocytosis
Kupffer's cells	perform most of the functions of the liver (Fig. 4.8)
ITO cells	replace damaged hepatocytes and secrete collagen
endothothelial cells	scavenger cells for denatured collagen, harmful enzymes and pathogens
haemopoietic cells	haemopoiesis in the fetus, and in adults with chronic anaemia

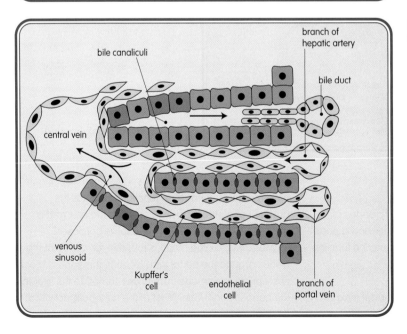

Fig. 4.6 Cords of hepatocytes radiating out from the central vein.

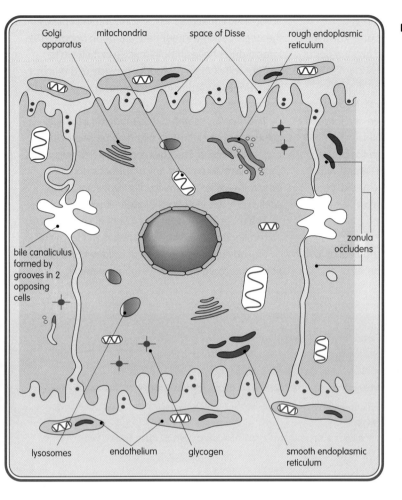

Labels (clockwise from top left): Golgi apparatus, mitochondria, space of Disse, rough endoplasmic reticulum, zonula occludens, smooth endoplasmic reticulum, glycogen, endothelium, lysosomes, bile canaliculus formed by grooves in 2 opposing cells.

Fig. 4.7 Lumen of sinusoid.

The canaliculi form rings around the hepatocytes and make up networks draining into small bile ducts (canals of Hering), which drain into the bile ducts of the portal canals. This arrangement allows hepatocytes to take up soluble substances from the spaces of Disse and secrete bile into the biliary system.

In the fetal liver, spaces of Disse contain islands of haemopoietic cells and these may reappear in the adult in chronic anaemia (extramedullary haemopoiesis).

Portal canal and limiting plate
The portal canal consists of the portal triad (hepatic portal vein, hepatic artery, and bile duct) surrounded by connective tissue.

A small space (the space of Mall) exists between the connective tissue covering and the surrounding hepatocytes. Lymph is thought to originate in the space of Mall.

The limiting plate, a plate of hepatic cells surrounding the portal tracts, may be breached in certain forms of liver injury. Breaching of the plate is usually followed by cirrhosis.

Nerves
The liver is innervated by both the sympathetic and parasympathetic systems.

Nerves enter the liver at the porta hepatis and travel in the portal canals with the vessels of the portal triad.

Sympathetic fibres innervate blood vessels.

Cell bodies of parasympathetic neurons may be found near the porta hepatis. Parasympathetic fibres innervate large ducts with smooth muscle in their walls and may innervate blood vessels.

Blood vessels

The liver receives blood from the hepatic artery and the hepatic portal vein, both of which extend into the portal triad.

The hepatic artery has a smaller lumen than the hepatic artery and a thicker, muscular wall. It supplies oxygenated blood to the connective tissue, the larger portal canals and the sinusoids.

Blood flows from the smaller vessels in the portal triad into the sinusoids and drains to the central vein. From there, it flows into the sublobular vein and the systemic system and is returned to the heart.

Tissues of the biliary tract

The intrahepatic bile ducts are lined by cuboidal or low columnar epithelial cells. Increasing amounts of fibroelastic connective tissue surround the epithelium as the ducts become larger near the porta hepatis. The largest ducts have smooth muscle in their walls.

The wall of the gall bladder consists of a mucous membrane, muscular layer, adventitia, and a serous membrane.

The mucous membrane is made up of simple columnar epithelium and a lamina propria of loose connective tissue. The columnar epithelial cells have many microvilli on their apical surfaces and are absorptive cells. The mucosa is thrown into folds, particularly when the gall bladder is empty.

The muscularis consists of layers of smooth muscle with collagenous elastic fibres between the layers.

The adventitia is made up of collagen and elastic fibres and contains a rich lymphatic network.

- **Summarize the anatomy of the liver and biliary tract.**
- **Describe the development of the liver and biliary tree.**
- **What are the lobular and acinar views of the liver?**
- **Discuss how some parts of the liver are more susceptible to damage from certain agents.**
- **List cell types of the liver.**
- **Name the tissues of the biliary tract and gall bladder. What are their functions?**

METABOLIC FUNCTIONS OF THE LIVER

Overview of liver metabolism

The liver is the largest organ in the body; it is vital to life and has a substantial capacity to regenerate after injury. Its main functions are summarized in Fig. 4.8.

The liver receives about 25% of the cardiac output through the portal vein and hepatic artery, and plays an important role in the detoxification of ingested substances.

The portal vein drains blood from the stomach, intestines, pancreas, and spleen and delivers about 1L of blood per minute to the liver.

On reaching the liver, the portal vein divides into branches which lead to specialized venous channels (sinusoids) (Fig. 4.6). Nutrients and other substances absorbed from the alimentary tract are taken up from the sinusoids by liver cells where they are metabolized, or detoxified and excreted.

Sinusoidal blood drains to the hepatic veins which return it to the systemic circulation and back to the heart.

Functional heterogeneity of hepatocytes

The acinar architecture of the liver was previously described in 'Organization of the liver and biliary tract'.

Zone 1 of the acinus (the periportal area) is adjacent to the portal canal (Fig. 4.4) and receives more oxygenated blood from the hepatic artery and blood from the hepatic portal vein. It is, therefore, particularly susceptible to damage from toxins absorbed from the alimentary tract and carried to the liver in the portal system, for example in paracetamol poisoning.

Zone 3 (the perivenous area) is furthest from the arterial supply and particularly vulnerable to ischaemic damage, for example in cardiac failure. These zones are contiguous and liver cell necrosis affecting this zone is often confluent.

Carbohydrate metabolism

In the normal individual, blood glucose levels are carefully regulated. The liver plays an important role in glucose homeostasis (Greek for 'staying the same').

Blood glucose levels rise transiently after a meal but the liver takes up the glucose and converts it to glycogen.

In the fasting state, glycogen is converted to glucose (glycogenolysis) (Fig. 4.9) and released into the blood stream to keep levels within the range 3.5–5.5 mmol/L.

The liver contains approximately 80 g of glycogen. This is enough to keep blood glucose levels within the required range for approximately 24 hours at rest, but for less time during heavy exercise.

The peptide hormone, glucagon, produced in the pancreas, regulates the level of glucose in the liver and the liver's metabolism of free fatty acids.

A feedback mechanism operates; hypoglycaemia causes an increase in plasma levels of glucagon whereas insulin inhibits its secretion.

Glucagon stimulates the production and release of glucose, free fatty acids, and ketoacids (the presence of which suppress its secretion) and stimulates the conversion of amino acids to glucose.

Carbohydrates and amino acids (but not fats) are used to make glycogen. Its synthesis is catalysed by glycogen synthetase.

Main functions of the liver	
Process	**Function**
protein metabolism	synthesis and secretion of albumin, prothrombin and fibrinogen
	formation of urea from ammonium in the urea cycle
fat metabolism	synthesis of fatty acids, bile acids and lipoproteins
	synthesis of excretion of cholesterol
	ketogenesis
	25-hydroxide of vitamin D
carbohydrate metabolism	gluconeogenesis
	synthesis and breakdown of glycogen
hormone metabolism	metabolism of polypeptide hormones
	metabolism and excretion of steroid hormones
	metabolism and excretion of bilirubin
	metabolism and excretion of drugs and foreign compounds
storage of	glycogen
	vitamins A and B_{12}
	iron and copper

Fig. 4.8 The main functions of the liver and hepatocytes.

Glycogen is also present in muscle, but its sole purpose there is to provide energy for muscle contraction—it makes no direct contribution to blood glucose levels. Glycogen is a highly branched polysaccharide and is made exclusively from α-D-glucose with α-1,4 and α-1,6 linkages. Branched chains are added to existing glycogen remnants in cells (primers).

A number of enzymes are involved in the synthesis and breakdown of glycogen and defects in one or more of them lead to glycogen storage disorders (e.g. Pompe's disease, McArdle's syndrome, Hers' disease, Cori's disease, and von Gierke's disease).

Glycogen phosphorylase cleaves the α-1,4-glycosidic bond, glucosyltransferase transfers residues to other branches and further enzymes act to release glucose.

As the synthesis and degradation of glycogen has an effect on blood glucose levels, both are carefully controlled, principally by cyclic AMP.

As might be expected, adrenaline inhibits synthesis and activates breakdown of glycogen in the liver and muscle—in fight-or-flight situations we need normal

blood glucose levels and do not want to make it into glycogen for storage.

Glucagon has a similar effect on glycogen in the liver (but not in muscle). Conversely, insulin increases synthesis of glycogen.

In diabetes, the utilization of carbohydrates is impaired and ketone bodies are formed in the liver from β-oxidation of fatty acids.

Ketones are released from hepatocytes and carried to other tissues where they are metabolized.

In prolonged starvation, ketone bodies and fatty acids are used as alternative sources of fuel, and body tissues (except the brain) adapt to a lower glucose requirement.

Lipid metabolism

Most of the fat in the diet is in the form of triglyceride (long-chain saturated and monounsaturated fatty acids esterified to glycerol).

The essential fatty acids (linoleic, linolenic, and arachidonic acids), must be included in the diet. They cannot be synthesized in the body and are needed to

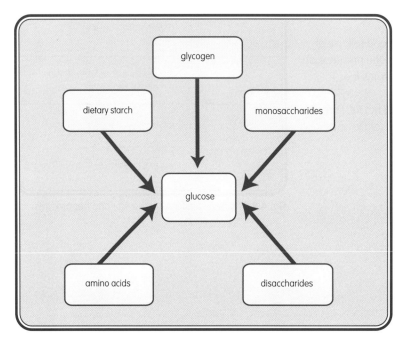

Fig. 4.9 Sources of glucose.

make components of cell membranes and prostaglandins.

Non-essential fatty acids can be made and there is no requirement for them in the diet.

In developed countries, the fat component of an average diet is excessive, leading to an increased incidence of atherosclerosis and obesity.

Cholesterol is needed for the manufacture of steroid hormones and bile acids and can be synthesized in the liver. It is also a component of most diets.

The digestion and absorption of dietary lipids is described in Chapter 5.

Lipids are insoluble in water and are assembled into lipoproteins (complexes of lipid and protein) in the liver, for transport in the blood (Fig. 4.10). Depending on their composition, lipoproteins are classified into chylomicrons (the lowest density), very low density, intermediate density, low-density, and high-density lipoproteins (Fig. 4.11).

Low-density lipoproteins have been implicated in atheroma and their level in the plasma should be kept low. Conversely, high-density lipoproteins have a

protective function and their levels should be higher.

The apoprotein element of the polar coat is made in the liver and intestine, and defects in its synthesis have important effects on lipid metabolism.

Hyperlipidaemia may also result from a defect in lipid receptors. Alcoholic fatty liver changes are described in Chapter 10.

It is easy to remember the ideal levels of circulating lipoproteins. Low-density ones should be low, and high-density ones should be high!

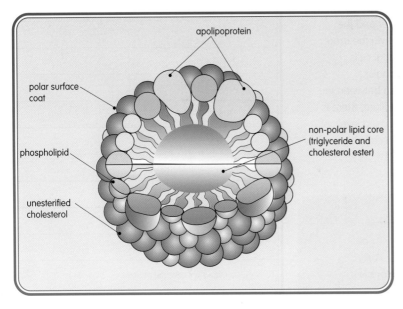

Fig. 4.10 Structure of a lipoprotein particle.

Density classes of plasma lipoproteins			
Class	**Abbreviation**	**Sources**	**Mean diameter (nm)**
chylomicrons	CHYLO	Intestine	500
very low density lipoproteins	VLDL	liver	43
intermediate density lipoproteins	IDL	catabolism of very low density lipoproteins and chylomicrons	27
low-density lipoproteins	LDL	catabolism of very low density lipoproteins	22
high-density lipoproteins	HDL	catabolism of chylomicrons and very low density lipoproteins; liver and intestine	8

Fig. 4.11 The density classes of plasma lipoproteins.

Protein metabolism

The liver synthesizes all the major plasma proteins. These are summarized in Fig. 4.12.

Urea metabolism

Amino acids are deaminated in the liver and the ammonia formed is converted to urea via the urea cycle. This occurs mainly in the periportal cells (hepatocytes adjacent to the portal canals).

Enzymes of the cycle are partitioned between the mitochondria and cytoplasm. In liver failure, there is decreased synthesis of urea and increased levels of ammonia—a toxic product. Ammonia can depress

Proteins synthesized by the liver
albumin
plasma lipoprotein
globulins
transferrin
ceruloplasmin
α_1-antitrypsin
α-fetoprotein
blood-clotting factors
fibrinogen
prothrombin
factors V, VII, X and XII
complement cascade proteins

Fig. 4.12 Proteins synthesized by the liver.

 Lipoproteins are complexes of lipids and proteins. They have a triglyceride and cholesterol ester middle, and a polar coat made up of phospholipids and apoproteins, with some unesterified cholesterol (Fig. 4.10).

cerebral blood flow and cerebral oxygen consumption. Ammonia toxicity is usually due to cirrhosis but is also seen in inherited deficiencies of urea cycle enzymes.

Transamination (interconversion) of amino acids also takes place in the liver.

Vitamins

Vitamins A, D, E, and K are fat soluble; vitamin deficiency may occur in malabsorption of fat, due to a variety of hepatic and extrahepatic causes.

Vitamin B_{12} is absorbed from the diet in the terminal ileum, provided intrinsic factor is made by the parietal cells of the stomach, and enough is stored in the liver to last 2 or 3 years. Deficiency eventually leads to megaloblastic anaemia.

The liver stores folate and converts it to its active form, tetrahydrofolate. Folate is needed as a coenzyme for the transfer of 1-carbon groups and its deficiency also leads to megaloblastic anaemia, sooner than vitamin B_{12} deficiency because body stores of folate are only sufficient for a few months. Folate deficiency in early pregnancy may also lead to neural-tube defects in the fetus. Dietary deficiency of folate is much more common than vitamin B_{12} deficiency and is seen in alcoholics and others on a poor diet or suffering from a severe illness where folate utilization is increased (e.g. in cancer).

In general, deficiency of any substance may result from increased utilization, or excretion, or decreased manufacture, or absorption.

Drug and hormone metabolism

The liver metabolizes drugs by phase I (oxidation, reduction, or hydrolysis) and phase II reactions (conjugation).

- Phase I reactions often produce more active metabolites than the original drug.
- Phase II reactions normally inactivate drugs and their metabolites, making them more water soluble and allowing their excretion in the urine or bile.

Phase I reactions

The mixed function oxygenase system of the smooth endoplasmic reticulum catalyzes oxidation reactions. Several enzymes are involved, most notably cytochrome P_{450}.

Oxidation may also be carried out by other enzymes such as xanthine oxidase and monoamine oxidase, present in other tissues as well as the liver.

Reductive reactions also involve microsomal enzymes but are less common than oxidative ones. Hydrolytic reactions take place in many tissues.

A number of drugs induce microsomal enzymes, affecting the metabolism of other drugs taken at the same time, and this should be borne in mind when deciding what dose to prescribe.

Notable examples of enzyme-inducing drugs include phenobarbitone, ethanol, and phenylbutazone.

Phase II reactions

A number of groups are conjugated with drugs or their metabolites in the liver, including glucuronyl, acetyl, methyl, glycyl, sulphate, and glutamyl groups, of which glucuronyl is the commonest.

Conjugation is important in the metabolism of paracetamol. It is inactivated by conjugation to form a glucuronide or sulphate, but the liver has a limited capacity. If saturated, mixed-function oxidases form a toxic metabolite instead. The toxic metabolite is itself inactivated by conjugation with glutathione, but stores of glutathione are limited. In paracetamol overdose, the saturation of liver enzymes and depletion of glutathione lead to liver necrosis and damage to kidney tubules by toxic metabolites. Treatment is with acetylcysteine, which increases the formation of glutathione, or with methionine.

Paracetamol has a narrow therapeutic index (the difference between a beneficial and a toxic dose is small) and accidental or deliberate paracetamol overdose is common.

Damage to the liver is not immediate and patients often wake up a few hours after large overdoses thinking they are fine, and do not seek help. Symptoms of liver necrosis develop later (often too late for treatment to be effective) and death may follow.

Some drugs are rapidly inactivated by the liver (e.g. propranolol). The amount of active drug reaching the circulation is reduced and the drug is said to undergo significant first-pass metabolism.

Haemopoiesis

The liver is the main site of haemopoiesis in the fetus between months 2 and 7, but this function normally ceases before birth.

It is supplemented by the bone marrow from month 5 onwards.

Between conception and month 2, haemopoiesis takes place in the yolk sac. The liver and spleen can resume their haemopoietic role (extramedullary haemopoiesis) if necessary.

○ **Summarize the metabolic activities of the liver.**
○ **What are the differences in hepatocyte metabolism across the liver acinus, from periportal to perivenous zones?**
○ **Discuss the role of the liver in carbohydrate metabolism.**
○ **Discuss the role of the liver in lipid metabolism.**
○ **Discuss the role of the liver in protein synthesis.**
○ **How does the liver maintain levels of fat-soluble vitamins? Why is this important?**
○ **Discuss the role of the liver in drug metabolism.**
○ **List the sites of fetal haemopoiesis.**

BILE PRODUCTION AND FUNCTION

Overview of bile production

Bile consists of water, electrolytes, bile acids, cholesterol, phospholipids, and the pigments bilirubin and biliverdin.

It is a greenish yellow liquid secreted by the liver and its functions are:

- To carry away waste products formed in the liver.
- To help emulsify fats in the small intestine and aid digestion.

Waste products in bile include the pigments bilirubin and biliverdin, which give bile its colour.

Bile passes out of the liver through the bile ducts and is concentrated and stored in the gall bladder. During and after a meal it is excreted from the gall bladder by contraction and passes into the duodenum through the common bile duct.

Most of the bile acids are reabsorbed from the terminal ileum and recycled by the liver (Fig. 4.13). Bile pigments are normally excreted in the faeces, which they colour dark brown.

Fig. 4.13 Production and fate of bilirubin.

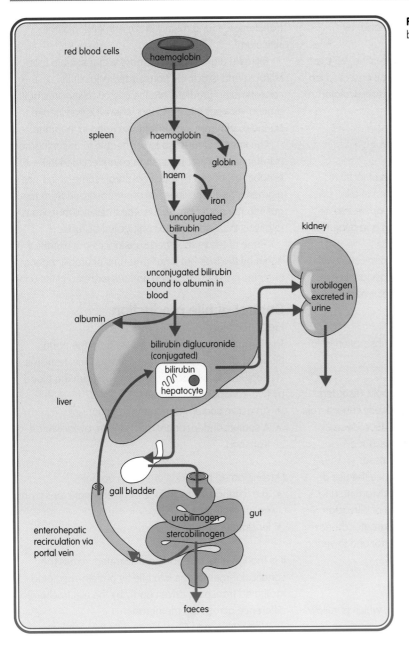

Reabsorption through enterohepatic recirculation means we only need a small pool of bile acids. Normally about 250–500 mg of bile acids are produced a day, which replaces the amount excreted in the faeces.

Bile acids

Bile acids are detergents which emulsify lipids. They have a hydrophobic and a hydrophilic end, and form micelles in aqueous solutions.

Bile acids are synthesized in hepatocytes from cholesterol and excreted into bile. They account for approximately 65% of the dry weight of bile.

The rate-limiting step in the production of bile acids is catalyzed by cholesterol-7α-hydroxylase.

The principal primary bile acids are cholic acid and chenodeoxycholic acid. They are made more soluble by conjugation with taurine or glycine.

Intestinal bacteria convert them into the secondary bile acids: deoxycholic acid (from cholic acid) and

49

lithocholic acid (from chenodeoxycholic acid) by
7α-decarboxylation.

Of the bile acids excreted into the intestine, 95% are
reabsorbed (mostly in the terminal ileum) and recycled
by the liver. The total pool of bile acids is recirculated six
to eight times a day.

Functions of bile acids
The main functions of bile acids are:
- Triglyceride assimilation: with the aid of lecithin
  (which is present in high concentration in bile), bile
  acids emulsify lipids, breaking them down into
  droplets of about 1 μm and providing a large surface
  area for digestive enzymes to attack.
- Lipid transport: bile acids form mixed micelles with
  the products of lipid digestion, increasing the
  transport of lipids to the brush border where they are
  absorbed by the epithelial cells

A deficiency of bile acids results in malabsorption of fat.

Bile acids and hyperlipidaemia
Hyperlipidaemias are a group of metabolic disorders
characterized by high levels of lipids (chiefly cholesterol,
triglycerides, and lipoproteins) in the blood. Several
types of hyperlipidaemia have been described,
depending on which lipids' levels are raised.

Treatment for hyperlipidaemia includes the use of
bile-acid-binding resins (such as cholestyramine and
colestipol). These prevent the re-uptake of bile acids
from the terminal ileum and result in a greater de-novo
synthesis by the liver, using up cholesterol and lowering
its circulating levels.

Bile pigments
The principal pigment in bile is bilirubin, which is yellow
and gives bile its colour.

Most bilirubin is formed by the breakdown of
haemoglobin from worn-out red cells, but about 15%
comes from the breakdown of other haem-containing
proteins such as myoglobin, cytochromes, and catalases.

Bilirubin is insoluble and is transported to the liver in
the plasma bound to albumin. There, most of it
dissociates from albumin and is extracted from the
blood in the sinusoids by the hepatocytes. It binds to
cytoplasmic proteins in the hepatocytes and is
conjugated with glucuronic acid to form bilirubin
diglucuronide (a reaction catalyzed by glucuronyl

transferase, found mainly in smooth endoplasmic
reticulum).

Bilirubin diglucuronide is more water soluble than
bilirubin and is actively transported against its
concentration gradient into the bile canaliculi. A small
amount escapes into the blood, where it is transported
bound to albumin, and is then excreted in the urine.

The intestinal mucosa is permeable to unconjugated
bilirubin and to urobilinogen (a colourless derivative of
bilirubin produced by intestinal flora); some of the bile
pigments and urobilinogens are reabsorbed from the
gut into the portal circulation. The intestinal mucosa is
relatively impermeable to conjugated bilirubin.

Some of the reabsorbed substances are excreted
again by the liver but small amounts of urobilinogens
enter the general circulation and are excreted in the urine.

Control of bile production
Hepatocytes
The hepatocytes take bile acids up from the portal
blood by at least four different transport mechanisms.

Conjugated bile acids are taken up from the blood
by two transport mechanisms:
- An active sodium-dependent mechanism.
- A sodium-independent mechanism, by facilitated
  transport.

Unconjugated bile acids are taken up:
- In exchange for hydroxide or bicarbonate ions by an
  anion exchange.
- By simple diffusion.

It is thought that bile acids are secreted across the
canalicular membrane into bile by protein-mediated
facilitated transport, driven partly by the electrochemical
difference across the membrane.

Water, Na^+, and Cl^- enter the bile through leaky
tight-junctions between hepatocytes.

Intrahepatic bile duct components of bile
The epithelial cells lining the bile ducts produce an
aqueous secretion that accounts for about 50% of the
total volume of bile.

The solution is isotonic, with sodium and potassium
concentrations similar to those of plasma, but with a
higher concentration of bicarbonate and a lower
concentration of chloride.

Control of bile acid synthesis and secretion

Cholecystokinin increases the rate of bile acid secretion during the intestinal phase of digestion.

High concentrations of bile acids in the portal blood stimulate bile acid secretion and inhibit its synthesis during the intestinal phase.

Conversely, low levels of bile acids in the portal blood during the interdigestive phase stimulate the synthesis and inhibit the secretion of bile acids.

Secretin stimulates secretion by the bile duct epithelium and this effect is strongly potentiated by cholecystokinin. Secretin alone has no effect on the concentration of bile acids in bile.

Role of the gall bladder

Functions of the gall bladder

The primary functions of the gall bladder are the concentration and storage of bile.

In the fasting state, the sphincter of Oddi (Fig. 4.3) is contracted but it relaxes, and the gall bladder contracts, releasing its contents, in response to stimulation during and after meals to aid digestion. However, it is not essential for life.

Cholecystectomy is a common operation, following which bile is discharged into the duodenum at a constant, slow rate and allows the digestion of moderate amounts of fat in the diet.

Concentration of bile

The gall bladder stores bile secreted by the liver and has a capacity of about 35 mL (range 15–60 mL).

Stored bile is 5–20 times more concentrated than that secreted by the liver, principally because of the active transport of Na^+ from the gall bladder epithelium into the lateral intracellular spaces (Fig. 4.14).

Gall bladder contraction

Gall bladder emptying begins several minutes after the start of a meal.

During the cephalic phase, the taste and smell of food and the presence of food in the mouth and pharynx cause impulses in branches of the vagus nerve that increase emptying of the gall bladder.

Distension of the stomach during the gastric phase also cause impulses in the vagus.

The highest rate of emptying of the gall bladder occurs during the intestinal phase, mostly in response to cholecystokinin released from the duodenal mucosa as a result of the presence of the products of fat digestion and essential amino acids in the duodenum.

Cholecystokinin enters the circulation and reaches the gall bladder where it causes strong contractions of its wall and relaxation of the sphincter of Oddi.

Gastrin, which has the same sequence of amino acids as cholecystokinin at its C-terminal, may also cause contractions of the gall bladder during the cephalic and gastric phases.

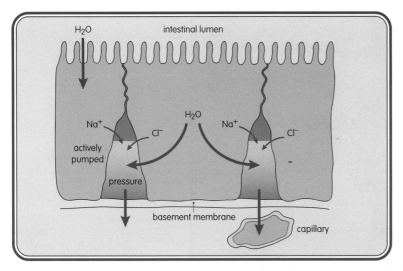

Fig. 4.14 The mechanism by which bile is concentrated in the gall bladder.

- **Summarize the production of bile.**
- **List the structure, synthesis, and functions of bile acids.**
- **Detail the composition of bile pigments.**
- **Describe the control of bile production.**
- **What are the functions of the gall bladder?**
- **How is bile concentrated in the gall bladder?**
- **What is the function of gall bladder contraction? How is this controlled?**

ORGANIZATION OF THE PANCREAS

The pancreas is both an endocrine and an exocrine gland.

Most of the pancreas consists of exocrine tissue in which are embedded islands of endocrine cells (islets of Langerhans). The exocrine cells produce enzymes that play an important role in digestion. The hormones produced by the islets are essential for the regulation of blood glucose.

Regional anatomy

The pancreas is a wedge-shaped organ approximately 15 cm in length, it is lobulated and weighs about 80 g.

It is retroperitoneal and extends across the abdominal wall at about the level of L1, from the curve of the duodenum to the hilus of the spleen.

The pancreas has a head, with an uncinate process (from the Latin meaning 'hook'), a neck, a body, and a tail (Fig. 4.15).

- The head is the expanded right portion and nestles in the curve of the duodenum, anterior to the inferior vena cava and the left renal vein.

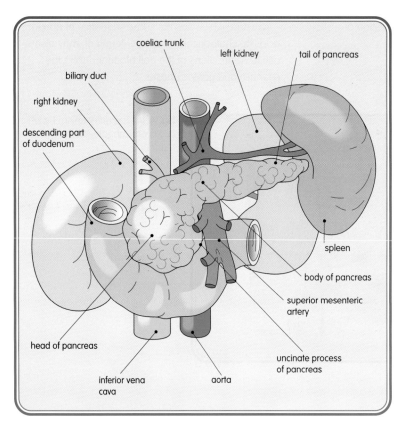

Fig. 4.15 The relations of the pancreas.

- The uncinate process is a small portion of the head tucked beneath the superior mesenteric vein.
- The neck joins the body to the head and overlies the superior mesenteric vessels and the portal vein.
- The body is triangular in cross-section and extends as far as the hilum of the left kidney. It overlies the aorta, the left renal vein, the splenic vessels and the termination of the inferior mesenteric vein. It is crossed anteriorly by the attachment of the transverse mesocolon.
- The tail lies in the lienorenal ligament and ends at the hilum of the spleen.

The main pancreatic duct traverses the gland from left to right and, together with the bile duct, opens into the second part of the duodenum at the ampulla of Vater.

An accessory duct may drain part of the head and, if present, has a separate opening into the duodenum above the ampulla of Vater.

The pancreas is an endocrine organ and therefore has a rich blood supply. The head is supplied by the superior and inferior pancreaticoduodenal arteries.

Branches of the splenic artery supply the remainder of the pancreas (Fig. 4.15).

Venous drainage is to the portal, splenic, and superior mesenteric veins.

Lymphatic drainage is to pancreaticosplenic or suprapancreatic nodes alongside the splenic artery, and to preaortic nodes around the coeliac and superior mesenteric arteries.

The innervation of the pancreas is from the splanchnic nerves and the vagi through the coeliac plexus.

Development

The pancreas develops from two buds (the dorsal and ventral pancreatic buds) that originate from the endodermal lining of the duodenum in weeks 4 and 6 (Fig. 4.16).

The pancreatic islets of Langerhans develop from pancreatic parenchyma tissue in month 3 and are scattered throughout the gland.

Insulin secretion begins during month 5 and fetal levels of insulin are independent of those of the mother. Insulin does not cross the placenta.

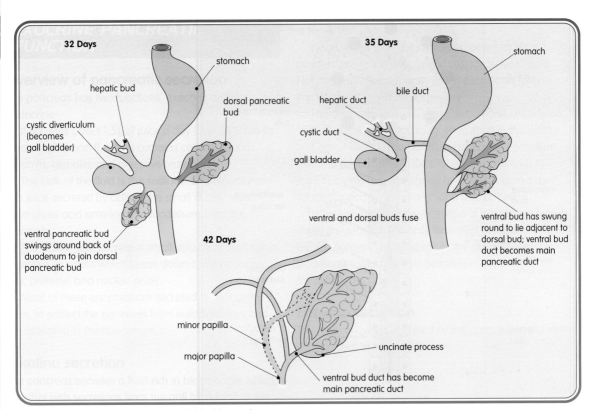

Fig. 4.16 Development of the liver, gall bladder and pancreas.

Several of the pancreatic enzymes are capable of damaging the tissues of the pancreas and are secreted as proenzymes which are activated by substances in the duodenum.

Enteropeptidase (enterokinase) in the brush border of the duodenum (secreted in response to cholecystokinin) converts trypsinogen to trypsin.

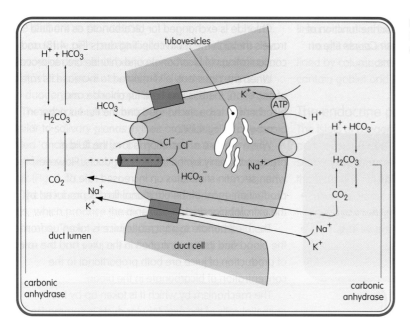

Fig. 4.18 The mechanism by which bicarbonate is taken up by the epithelial cells of the pancreas.

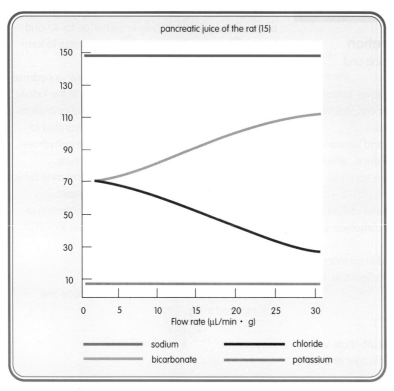

Fig. 4.19 The variation in composition of pancreatic juice with rate of flow. (Redrawn with permission from: *Am J Physiol* 1971, **221**: 496.)

Trypsin then activates other pancreatic enzymes (Fig. 4.20) including its own proenzyme trypsinogen, resulting in an autocatalytic chain reaction.

To protect the pancreas from the chain reaction and autodigestion that would result from even a small amount of trypsin in the pancreas, the pancreas contains a trypsin inhibitor.

In acute pancreatitis, phospholipase A_2 is activated by trypsin in the pancreatic duct and acts on lecithin (a normal constituent of bile) to form lysolecithin, which damages cell membranes and causes disruption of pancreatic tissue and necrosis of surrounding fat.

Circulating levels of pancreatic α-amylase also increase in acute pancreatitis and measurement of levels in the blood are used as a diagnostic tool.

Pancreatic insufficiency

Cystic fibrosis is an autosomal recessive disorder (with a carrier rate of 1 in 25 amongst Caucasians) and is characterized by pancreatic insufficiency and a tendency to chronic lung infections. The underlying defect is an abnormality in the chloride ion transporter.

The incidence of the disease is 1 in 2000 live births amongst Caucasians, but lower amongst Jewish, Asian, and African populations.

Pancreatic enzymes are absent, or secreted in lower amounts than normal, and fat malabsorption occurs. A deficiency in the fat-soluble vitamins A, D, E, and K may also be found.

The cells lining the bronchial tubes are also affected, secreting thick, viscous mucus (predisposing to lung infections). The sweat contains abnormally high concentrations of sodium chloride.

Pancreatic insufficiency also occurs in chronic pancreatitis, which may be due to gall stones, alcoholism or hyperparathyroidism, or may be hereditary.

Control of pancreatic secretion

Pancreatic exocrine secretion is controlled by hormones and by substances released from nerve terminals (Fig. 4.21).

Vagal stimulation enhances the rate of secretion of both enzyme and aqueous components of pancreatic juice.

Fig. 4.20 Pancreatic enzymes.

Pancreatic enzymes		
Enzyme	**Activator**	**Substrate**
trypsin	secreted as trypsinogen, activated by enteropeptidase (and by trypsin)	proteins and polypeptides
pancreatic lipase		triglycerides
pancreatic α–amylase	activated by Cl^-	starch
ribonuclease		RNA
deoxyribonuclease		DNA
elastase	activated by trypsin	elastin and some other proteins
phospholipase A_2	activated by trypsin	phospholipids
chymotrypsins	secreted as chymotrypsinogen, activated by trypsin	proteins and polypeptides
carboxypeptidase A and B	activated by trypsin	proteins and polypeptides
colipase	activated by trypsin	fat droplets

Sympathetic stimulation inhibits secretion, probably by decreasing blood flow.

Secretin and cholecystokinin (released from the duodenal mucosa) stimulate secretion of the aqueous component of pancreatic fluid.

Separate control of the aqueous and enzymatic components explains the variation in composition of pancreatic juice (Fig. 4.19).

Cephalic phase

Gastrin released from the mucosa of the antrum in response to vagal stimulation causes the release of a small amount of pancreatic juice with a high protein content.

Gastric phase

Gastrin released in response to gastric distension and the presence of amino acids and peptides in the antrum continues to stimulate release of pancreatic juice.

Vagovagal reflexes elicited by distension of the fundus or antrum also cause the release of small amounts of pancreatic juice with a high enzyme content.

Intestinal phase

Chyme in the duodenum and upper jejunum stimulate pancreatic secretion.

Acid stimulates the secretion of a large volume of fluid that is rich in bicarbonate (but with low levels of pancreatic enzymes), which neutralizes the acid present. This is mediated by secretin from duodenal and upper jejunum cells.

Cholecystokinin released from duodenal and upper jejunum cells in response to the presence of peptides, amino acids, and some fatty acids (those containing more than 10 carbon atoms) stimulates the acinar cells to release the contents of their zymogen granules and induces the secretion of pancreatic juice that is rich in protein components.

Cholecystokinin has little direct effect on ductular epithelium but potentiates the effect of secretin, which is a weak agonist of acinar cells.

Vagal stimulation is important and vagotomy reduces the response to chyme in the duodenum by 50%.

Secretogogues and their mechanisms of action

Secretogogues are substances that increase secretion from the pancreas. The common secretogogues and their mechanisms of action are summarized in Fig. 4.21.

Somatostatin has the opposite effect and, by inhibiting adenylate cyclase and decreasing cyclic AMP, it inhibits the secretion of acinar and duct cells.

Insulin, insulin-like growth factors, and epidermal growth factor potentiate enzyme synthesis and secretion, through the activation of receptor-associated tyrosine kinase.

- List the major components of pancreatic juice.
- What are the functions of bicarbonate-rich pancreatic fluid in digestion?
- Detail cellular processes involved in the production of the alkaline solution.
- List the pancreatic enzymes and their functions.
- What are the effects of pancreatic enzyme deficiency?
- How is pancreatic secretion controlled?

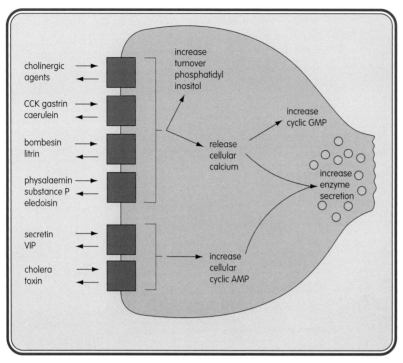

Fig. 4.21 Pancreatic secretogogues. CCK = cholecystokinin; GMP = glucose monophosphase; AMP = adenosine monophosphate; VIP = vasoactive intestinal peptide.

5. The Small and Large Intestine

ORGANIZATION OF THE INTESTINE

The layers of the intestine are essentially the same as in the rest of the gastrointestinal tract (Fig. 1.2). Absorption takes place in the intestine and its mucosa is specially adapted for this.

Regional anatomy
Small intestine

The small intestine extends from the stomach to the colon; it is about 5 m in length in a living person but longer in a cadaver—it relaxes and elongates after death!

It consists of the duodenum, jejunum, and ileum and is responsible for the absorption of most nutrients (Fig. 5.1).

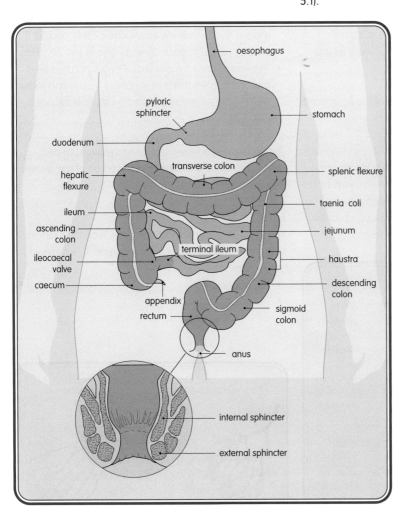

Fig. 5.1 The position of the small and large intestines.

Duodenum

The duodenum is about 25 cm in length and extends from the pylorus to the duodenojejunal flexure. It is divided into four parts:

- The first (superior) part (D1)—this is 5 cm in length and starts at the pylorus.
- The second (descending) part (D2)—this is 8 cm in length and descends to the right side of L3. The ampullar of Vater lies halfway down its posteriomedial wall (Fig. 5.2).
- The third (horizontal) part (D3)—this is 10 cm in length and passes to the left across the posterior abdominal wall before turning upwards to become the fourth part.
- The fourth (ascending) part (D4)—this is 3 cm in length and descends to the duodenojejunal flexure to the left of L2.

The dueodenum becomes the jejunum at the ligament of Treitz.

Jejunum and ileum

The jejunum and ileum are about 2.6 m in length and are suspended from the posterior abdominal wall by a mesentery. They are mobile (unlike the duodenum). The proximal 40% of the small intestine is described as the jejunum and the remaining 60% as the ileum.

- The jejunum is fixed to the posterior abdominal wall at the duodenojejunal junction and the ileum at the ileocolic junction. Between these two points an extensive mesentery joins the small intestine to the wall.
- The fan-shaped mesentery is short at its attachment to the posterior abdominal wall (its root is about 15 cm in length) but much longer at its attachment to the small intestine (about 6 m in length). This throws the small intestine into a series of folds.
- The small intestine is entirely surrounded by peritoneum, except at its attachment to the mesentery.
- The jejunum has a greater calibre and thicker wall, more diffuse lymphoid tissue and closely packed arteries joined to each other by one or two arcades.
- The ileum has a thinner wall, Peyer's patches (well marked aggregations of lymphoid tissue) and more widely spaced arteries united by multiple arcades (Fig. 5.3).

The arcades of arteries supplying the jejunum and ileum are visible at dissection if a section of mesentery is held up to the light.

Large intestine

The large intestine extends from the ileocaecal junction to the anus and is about 1.5 m in length. It consists of:

- The caecum.
- The appendix.
- The colon.

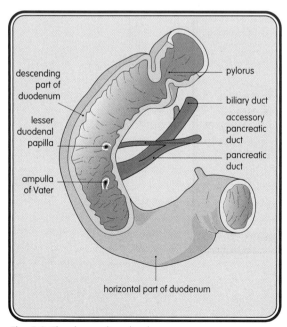

Fig. 5.2 The descending duodenum.

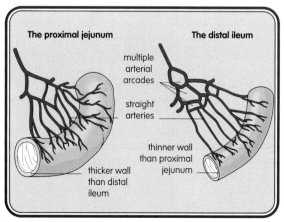

Fig. 5.3 The proximal jejunum and distal ileum.

- The rectum.
- The anal canal.

The colon is divided into the ascending, transverse, descending and sigmoid parts.

The large intestine is larger in calibre but shorter in length than the small intestine.

The outer, longitudinal muscle forms three distinct bands visible at dissection called taenia coli, from the Latin for 'flat band'.

These bands are shorter than the circular muscle layer and gather the caecum and colon into a series of pouch-like folds called haustrations.

The haustra are visible on radiographs when an opaque medium is introduced through the rectum. They do not extend across the entire width and this distinguishes the large intestine from the small intestine which has plicae circulares (Kerckring's valves or valvulae conniventes) visible across the whole width on radiographs.

Fatty tags covered with peritoneum (appendices epiploicae) project from the outer surface of the large intestine.

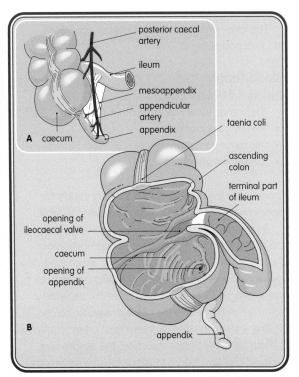

Fig. 5.4 The ileocaecal valve (exterior view [A] and cutaway view [B], and appendix (B).

Caecum

The caecum lies in the right iliac fossa and is a blind sac, continuous with the ascending colon.

It communicates with the ileum through the ileocaecal sphincter or valve (Fig. 5.4).

Appendix

The appendix, or vermiform appendix (from the Latin for 'worm') is about 8 cm in length and protrudes from the posteriolateral wall of the caecum (Fig. 5.4).

It is a blind-ending sac that may become obstructed and inflamed, requiring surgical removal to prevent rupture and peritonitis.

It is covered in peritoneum and supplied by the appendicular artery which lies in the mesentery (the mesoappendix) which connects the appendix to the terminal ileum.

It has aggregations of lymphatic tissue (which may replace the muscular coat in places). The appendix is mobile and, because of the way that it develops (described below), its position is variable. It usually lies behind the caecum or in the pelvis.

Ascending colon

The ascending colon is about 15 cm in length and fixed to the posterior abdominal wall by peritoneum.

It ascends from the ileocaecal valve to the under surface of the liver where it turns to the left, forming the hepatic (right colic) flexure.

Transverse colon

This is about 50 cm in length and extends horizontally from the hepatic flexure to the splenic (left colic) flexure.

The spleen is smaller than the liver and the splenic flexure therefore lies slightly higher than the hepatic flexure. The splenic flexure is attached to the diaphragm by the phrenicocolic ligament, a fold of peritoneum.

It is attached to the posterior wall and to the body of the pancreas by mesentery.

Descending colon

The descending colon is about 30 cm in length and is the narrowest part of the colon.

It extends from the splenic flexure to the pelvic brim in the left lateral region where it becomes the sigmoid colon.

Sigmoid colon

This is about 40 cm in length and lies in the left iliac fossa. It extends from the left pelvic brim to the start of the rectum at the level of S3 and is attached to the pelvic wall by a V-shaped mesentery.

Rectum

The rectum is about 12 cm in length and is continuous with the sigmoid colon proximally and the anus distally.

It starts at the level of S3, in the posterior part of the pelvis, and loops forward to the tip of the coccyx, before widening to form the rectal ampulla.

It has no mesentery but is partly covered by peritoneum.

The relations of the rectum are different in the male and female. In the male, the bladder, prostate, seminal vesicles, and ducti deferentia lie in front of it, in the female it is related anteriorly to the uterus and vagina.

Anus

This is continuous with the rectum and has an internal and external sphincter, the former of which is an involuntary thickened continuation of the circular muscle layer of the rectum.

The internal sphincter is constricted by sympathetic innervation from the aortic and pelvic plexuses and relaxed by parasympathetic innervation from the pelvic splanchnic nerves. The rectum shares the same innervation.

The external sphincter is under voluntary control (allowing us to delay defecation until convenient). It consists of striated muscle and is supplied by the perineal branch of the fourth sacral spinal nerve and the inferior rectal branch of the pudendal branch (S2 and S3). The lower one-third of the anal canal has the same innervation.

The external sphincter and lower one-third of the anal canal develop from the ectodermal anal pit (proctodeum), the rectum and upper two-thirds from the cloaca. This explains the differences in innervation, blood supply and lymphatic drainage of the upper and lower parts of the anal canal.

As might be expected, the relations of the anal canal are different in the male and female.

The anal canal is about 4 cm in length. In the male, it lies behind the prostate and the bulb of the penis, separated from them by the perineal body. Important information about the prostate can be gained from a digital rectal examination. In the female, the perineal body separates the anal canal from the vagina.

In both sexes the anal canal lies in front of the anococcygeal body, levator ani, and the ischiorectal fossa.

It is easy to tell the difference between the large and small intestines on X-rays. The small intestine, being small, has plicae circulares that extend across its entire width. The large intestine, being large, has haustra that only reach part of the way across.

Lymphatic drainage

The upper two-thirds of the anal canal and the rectum drain to pre-aortic, sacral and internal and common iliac nodes.

The lower one-third drains to upper superficial inguinal nodes.

Blood supply

The arterial blood supply is summarized in Fig. 1.4.

The coeliac trunk has three main branches:
- The left gastric artery.
- The common hepatic artery.
- The splenic artery.

Branches of the common hepatic artery supply the duodenum from the pylorus to the duodenal papilla.

Branches of the superior mesenteric artery supply the remainder of the duodenum, the jejunum, and ileum (by the jejunal and ileal arteries, which run in the mesentery and can be seen by holding a portion of mesentery up to the light), the appendix, ascending colon, and right two-thirds of the transverse colon.

Branches of the inferior mesenteric artery supply the remainder of the transverse colon, the descending, sigmoid and lower descending colon, the rectum and upper two-thirds of the anal canal. Venous drainage is to the hepatic portal system.

The blood supply of the rectum

The rectum is one of the sites of portal-systemic anastomoses and varices (piles) may form in portal hypertension.

It is supplied by the superior, middle, and inferior rectal arteries (branches of the inferior mesenteric artery) and drains to the superior rectal vein (via plexuses) and from there to the portal vein.

Middle and inferior rectal veins drain to the internal iliac vein.

Development of the intestine

The proximal portion of the small intestine (from the pylorus to the duodenal papilla) develops from the foregut. The remainder of the intestine develops from the midgut and hindgut (Fig. 1.4).

> To learn the details of Meckel's diverticulum, just remember 2-2-2. It is present in about 2% of the population, is roughly 2 inches long, and found approximately 2 feet from the caecum.

The midgut gives rise to the remainder of the duodenum (that part distal to the duodenal papilla) and to the proximal two-thirds of the transverse colon.

The duodenum is therefore supplied by branches of the artery of the foregut (the coeliac artery) and the superior mesenteric artery (which supplies the midgut).

The midgut is suspended from the dorsal abdominal wall by a mesentery and communicates with the yolk sac through the vitelline duct.

A small portion of the vitelline duct persists in some individuals and forms an outpouching of the ileum known as Meckel's diverticulum.

During development, the liver and primitive gut grow so rapidly there is not enough room in the fetal abdominal cavity and the midgut herniates outside the abdominal cavity at about week 6. It develops in the umbilical cord until the end of the third month when it begins to return to the abdominal cavity.

While outside the abdomen, it rotates approximately 270° around the superior mesenteric artery. Viewed from the front, the rotation is anticlockwise (Fig. 5.5).

The jejunum and ileum form a number of coiled loops, but the large intestine remains uncoiled, and the jejunum is the first portion of gut to return to the abdominal cavity.

The caecal bud appears on the caudal limb of the primitive gut tube at about week 7, and develops into the caecal swelling which is the last part of the developing tube to re-enter the abdominal cavity.

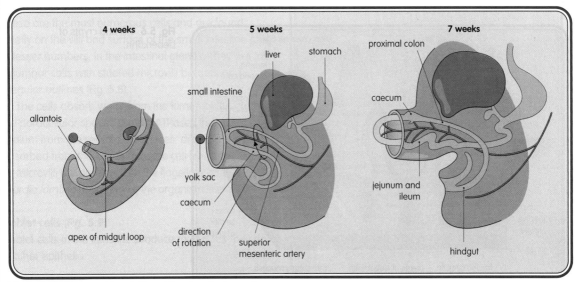

Fig. 5.5 Rotation and herniation of the developing gut.

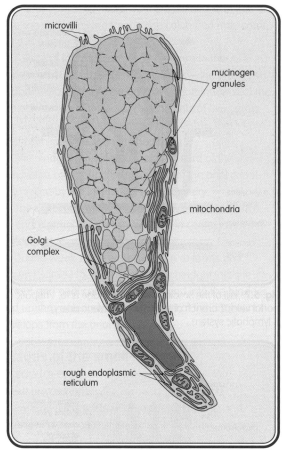

Fig. 5.9 Goblet cell.

They are interspersed between the enterocytes and, like enterocytes, are most numerous on the villi.

Paneth's cells

These are found in the deepest part of the intestinal glands and are typical of cells that synthesize and secrete large amounts of protein.

They are phagocytic and contain granules of lysozyme, an enzyme that digests the walls of certain bacteria. Paneth's cells are thought to play a role in the regulation of intestinal flora.

M cells

M cells are involved in the transport of antigen to Peyer's patches (see below).

Undifferentiated (stem) cells

These are located in the crypts of Lieberkühn and give rise to the enterocytes, goblet cells and APUD cells.

Approximately 1.7 billion enterocytes are shed from the adult intestine each day and are replaced by undifferentiated cells migrating up from the bases of the crypts.

The protein content of the cells lost from the gut each day is approximately 30 g. It accounts for a substantial amount of the daily protein loss from the body.

Peyer's patches

These are present in the mucosa of the ileum, extending into the submucosa, and are characteristically found opposite the attachment of the mesentery.

They consist of aggregations of lymphoid nodules and form part of the mucosal associated lymphoid system (MALT). M cells overlie the patches and absorb and transport antigens to the underlying lymphoid tissue. They may also process and present antigens.

Submucosa

Compound tubular Brunner's glands are present in the duodenum (but not elsewhere).

They secrete mucus, bicarbonate and growth factors such as epidermal growth factor. The last of these promotes the growth and regeneration of tissues.

Tissues of the large intestine
Tissue layers

The layers of the large intestine are essentially the same as those in the rest of the gastrointestinal tract (Fig. 1.2).

However, the walls are thicker, the lumen is larger, and the outer longitudinal muscle layer forms three bands (taenia coli) visible on the outside of the intestine. (Figs 5.1 and 5.4). The large intestine has no villi or plicae circulares.

Most nutrients have already been absorbed by the time the intestinal contents reach the large intestine but the large intestine is responsible for most of the reabsorption of water and electrolytes and plays an important role in electrolyte homeostasis.

Approximately 90% of the water in the faeces is reabsorbed by the colon and faeces become more compact as they travel through the large intestine.

Mucosa

The mucosa contains numerous straight tubular glands that extend through its thickness and consist of simple columnar epithelium.

Columnar absorptive cells are the most numerous cells of the large intestine. They are similar to enterocytes of the small intestine but their principal function is to reabsorb water.

Paneth's cells are present only in the young. Isolated nodules of lymphatic tissue are found which extend into the submucosa.

Anorectal junction

The rectum narrows towards its terminal end and becomes the anal canal.

The upper portion of the anal canal contains vertical folds (anal or rectal columns) separated by depressions (anal sinuses) (Fig. 5.1). They are particularly prominent in children.

The sinuses contain straight, branched tubular glands (anal glands) which produce mucus and extend into the submucosa and sometimes into the muscularis externa.

The ducts of the anal glands open into crypts in the anal mucosa and may become infected or blocked, forming a cyst.

The mucosa of the upper anal canal is similar to that of the large intestine but the lower portion consists of stratified squamous epithelium, continuous with the skin surrounding the anal canal. The middle portion contains stratified columnar epithelium.

The anus contains two sphincters, an internal (involuntary) and an external (voluntary) one, described below.

o **Summarize the anatomy of the small and large intestines.**
o **How do the intestines develop in the embryo?**
o **What are the tissue layers and cells of the small and large intestines?**

The anal columns contain terminal branches of the superior rectal artery in the submucosa. The artery branches may enlarge to form haemorrhoids. Small folds of mucosa (anal valves) are present at the lower end of the anal canal.

CELLULAR FUNCTIONS OF THE SMALL INTESTINE

Overview of small intestine function

The small intestine has a very large surface area and is specially adapted to digest and absorb nutrients, salt, and water. Enzymes and hormones produced in the small intestine complete the digestion that began in the mouth and stomach.

The small intestine has immunological defences against antigens that have been ingested consisting of solitary lymph nodules and Peyer's patches (aggregations of lymphatic nodules).

Gastrointestinal hormones produced in the small intestine play an important role in gastrointestinal secretion and motility.

Defence against antigens is both mechanical, by the production of mucus, and immunological, principally through gut-associated lymphoid tissue, described below.

Epithelial cell turnover

The cells of the intestinal epithelium are described in the 'Organization of the intestine' section above. They have a high rate of turnover and are replaced by undifferentiated (stem) cells which migrate up from the bases of the crypts of Lieberkühn (Fig. 5.10). The cells become partially differentiated and continue to divide as they migrate upwards from the bottom of the crypts (Fig. 5.10).

The average life span of an enterocyte is about 2–3 days, but this is reduced in coeliac disease and as a side effect of some drugs (e.g. prolonged anticancer therapy) and the undifferentiated cells cannot keep up with the increased loss, resulting in a flattening of the villi and malabsorption.

Radiotherapy may have a similar effect (radiation enteritis) depending on the dose and the site at which it is administered. Symptoms usually resolve within 6 weeks of the final dose of radiotherapy but some patients experience chronic radiation enteritis (symptoms persisting for more than 3 months). Radiation damage causes ulceration due to ischaemia, muscle fibre atrophy, and fibrosis which may result in stricture formation and obstruction.

Secretions of the small intestine

The small intestine secretes mucus and gastrointestinal hormones.

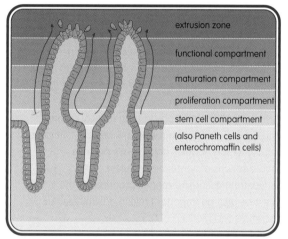

Fig. 5.10 The migration and shedding of cells in the small intestine.

- Mucus is produced by the goblet cells (Fig. 5.9) which are most numerous on the villi. The mucus lubricates the mucosal surface and protects it from trauma as particles of food pass through it.
- Gastrointestinal hormones found in the small intestine are summarized in Fig. 5.11.

The epithelial cells secrete an aqueous solution during the course of digestion but under normal conditions absorb slightly more than they secrete.

Under certain conditions, for example cholera infection, secretion exceeds absorption and secretory diarrhoea occurs.

The immune system in the small intestine

T lymphocytes are made in the thymus, a bilobular organ found in the thorax, and migrate into peripheral tissues such as the spleen and lymph nodes (encapsulated organs). T lymphocytes also migrate to non-encapsulated lymphoid tissue known as mucosa-associated lymphoid tissue (MALT) which gives protection against antigens entering the body through mucosal epithelial surfaces.

The majority of MALT is present as gut-associated lymphoid tissue (GALT), and smaller amounts as bronchial-associated lymphoid tissue (BALT), skin-associated

Main actions of the principal gastric hormones			
Hormone	Gastrointestinal source	Signal for release	Action
CCK	I cells in upper intestine	peptides and amino acids in duodenum	contracts gall bladder, causes secretion of alkaline enzymatic pancreatic juice, inhibits gastric emptying, exerts trophic effect on pancreas, acts as a satiety hormone, stimulates glucagon secretion and contracts the pyloric sphincter
secretin	S cells in upper small intestine	acid and products of protein digestion in duodenum	increases secretion of HCO_3^- by the pancreas and biliary tract, decreases acid secretion, contracts the pyloric sphincter and augments CCK's production of pancreatic secretions
gastrin	G cells in antrum	peptides and amino acids, distension, vagal stimulation, blood-borne calcium and adrenaline	acid and pepsinogen secretion, trophic to mucosa of stomach and small and large intestines, increases gastric motility, may close LOS, stimulates insulin and glucagon secretion after protein meal
somatostatin	D cells of pancreatic islets, intestinal cells	glucose, amino acids, free fatty acids, glucagon and β-adrenergic and cholinergic neurotransmitters	inhibits secretion of insulin, glucagon, acid, pepsin, gastrin, secretin and intestinal juices, decreases gastric, duodenal and gall bladder motility

Fig. 5.11 Main actions of the principal gastric hormones. CCK = cholecystokinin; LOS = lower oesophageal sphincter.

lymphoid tissue, (SALT) and in the genitourinary tract.

B lymphocytes are made in the bone marrow and, in the fetus, in the liver. They also migrate to peripheral tissues, including MALT.

T cells are divided into:
- Helper (CD4) cells which enhance the reaction of the immune system following the presentation of antigen to T-helper cells by antigen presenting cells.
- Cytotoxic (CD8) cells are capable of killing other cells (e.g. cancer cells and cells that have been infected with viruses) and can also down-regulate the immune response.

CD4 and CD8 cells together make up approximately 75% of all lymphocytes. B cells produce antibody and, once they have seen a particular antigen, form memory cells which can undergo clonal expansion (multiply rapidly to form large numbers of identical B cells). B cells then differentiate to form plasma cells which have a relatively short half-life but produce large numbers of specific antibody to particular antigens. Scattered lymphoid cells are also found in the mucosa of the small intestine.

Specialized M cells (so named because of the numerous microfolds on their luminal surface) overlie the Peyer's patches and absorb, transport, process, and present antigens to the lymphoid cells lying between them.

Secretory IgA is then produced by the B cells. There are approximately 10^{10} plasma cells per metre of small intestine, the majority of which (70–90%) produce IgA.

IgA and smaller amounts of IgM are transported across the glandular epithelium into the gut lumen and prevent micro-organisms from entering.

Dimers of IgA bind to a receptor on the membrane of the epithelial cells, the IgA-receptor complex is endocytosed, transported across the cell and into the lumen. Part of the receptor (the secretary component) remains attached to the IgA and protects IgA from proteolytic enzymes in the lumen.

Motility of the small intestine
Functions of intestinal motility
Peristalsis occurs in the small intestine, as it does in other parts of the gastrointestinal tract. It causes forward propulsion of the intestinal contents, mixing them and bringing them into contact with the absorptive surface cells of the small intestine.

Chyme takes between 2 and 3 hours to pass through the small intestine which is the site at which most digestion and absorption of nutrients takes place.

Chyme is mixed in the small intestine by segmentation (contractions of the circular muscle layer) so called because the small intestine is divided into segments by the contractions (Fig. 5.12). This brings chyme into contact with the absorptive cells of the intestine.

Segmentation contractions are more frequent in the duodenum (12 contractions per minute) than in the terminal ileum (9 per minute). Segmentation moves chyme backwards and forwards, bringing it into contact with the absorptive mucosal surface.

Coordinated contractions of adjacent sections (peristalsis) move the intestinal contents towards the distal ends of the gastrointestinal tract. The intramural (Meissner's and Auerbach's) plexuses can control segmentation and short peristaltic movements in the absence of any extrinsic innervation but extrinsic innervation determines the excitability of the smooth muscle and mediates long-range reflexes.

Chyme is moved towards the rectum by peristalsis in response to stretching of the intestinal wall (the myenteric reflex) at a rate of 2–25 cm/s.

Peristaltic rushes (abnormally intense peristaltic waves) may occur when the intestine is obstructed.

Control of intestinal motility.
The motility of the small intestine is controlled by nervous, hormonal and local factors.

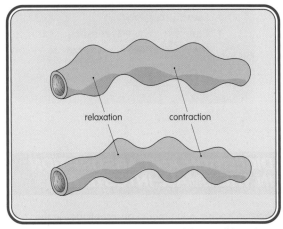
Fig. 5.12 Segmentation contractions of the small intestine.

The ileocaecal sphincter

The Ileocaecal valve (sphincter) separates the terminal Ileum from the colon and is normally closed. However, it opens in response to:

- Distension of the terminal ileum (by a reflex mechanism).
- Short-range peristalsis in the terminal ileum.
- Gastroileal reflex (which enhances emptying of the ileum after a meal).

When the ileocaecal valve opens, small amounts of chyme enter the colon at the rate at which the colon is able to reabsorb most of the salts and water contained in the chyme.

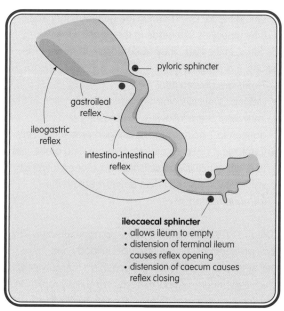

pyloric sphincter

gastroileal reflex

ileogastric reflex

intestino-intestinal reflex

ileocaecal sphincter
- allows ileum to empty
- distension of terminal ileum causes reflex opening
- distension of caecum causes reflex closing

Fig. 5.13 Motility of the small intestine.

- What are the functions of the small intestine?
- Describe the processes of epithelial cell proliferation, differentiation, and loss.
- Name the complications of the high cell turnover in the small intestine.
- Describe the secretory processes in the small intestine.
- Describe the immunological function of the small intestine.
- How is motility controlled in the small intestine?
- Summarize the structure and function of the ileocaecal sphincter.

DIGESTION AND ABSORPTION IN THE SMALL INTESTINE

Digestion begins in the mouth and continues in the stomach, but most digestion and absorption takes place in the small intestine.

General concepts

For food to be absorbed, it must be broken down into small particles which can be transported across the epithelial cells of the gastrointestinal tract and into the blood stream. Substances are then carried to the liver via the hepatic portal system.

As elsewhere in the body, molecules may be transported across the epithelial cells by simple diffusion, facilitated diffusion and by primary or secondary active transport. The properties of these different types of transport are shown in Fig. 5.14.

Factors that control absorption by the small intestine

A number of factors control absorption by the small intestine:

- Sympathetic innervation and adrenaline in the plasma both increase the absorption of sodium and chloride (and therefore water).
- Parasympathetic stimulation decreases the absorption of these substances.
- Aldosterone is a steroid hormone made from cholesterol in the zona glomerulosa of the adrenal glands. Aldosterone's main action is to increase the permeability of the collecting tubules of the kidney and the reabsorption of sodium and chloride. The excretion of potassium and hydrogen ions is increased. It also

Molecule transport mechanisms			
Type of diffusion	Proteins	Transport against or with concentration gradient	Energy required
passive diffusion	no	with	no
facilitated diffusion	yes	with	no
primary active transport	yes	against	yes: hydrolysis of ATP
secondary active transport	yes	against	yes: electrochemical gradient

Fig. 5.14 Molecule transport mechanisms. (Redrawn with permission from: Dr. Rattray, UMDS, London.)

stimulates the absorption of sodium and water by the colon and the secretion of potassium. It is released in response to a decrease in the sodium concentration of the plasma, an increase in the potassium concentration and by the activation of the renin–angiotensin system as a result of dehydration.

- Increased absorption of sodium and chloride in the kidney and gut (and the gastric, sweat and salivary glands) causes retention of water and an increase in effective circulating volume.

Digestion and absorption of different components of the diet
Fat and fat soluble vitamins
Absorption of the fat soluble vitamins A, D, E, and K depend on the absorption of fat and any condition in which fat digestion and absorption is decreased will eventually lead to a deficiency of these vitamins.

Fat is not water soluble and its digestion and absorption is more complex than that of other substances.

Fat in the diet is principally in the form of triglycerides and is only released from the stomach into the duodenum at the rate at which it can be digested. The presence of fat in the duodenum therefore inhibits gastric emptying.

Lipase in the stomach (preduodenal lipase made up of gastric lipase produced in the fundus and, to a lesser extent, lingual lipase from the mouth) hydrolyses triglycerides in the stomach. These are then released into the duodenum. In the duodenum, bile acids form micelles (in much the same way as detergents in washing powder do). A minimum concentration of bile acids is needed to form micelles (the critical micelle concentration).

Micelles consist of 20–30 molecules, arranged so that lipid (nonpolar) molecules lie in the centre,

surrounded by bile acids which are flat molecules with polar and nonpolar sides) rather like a chocolate with a soft centre—the chocolate is the polar component and the soft centre consisting of the nonpolar part of the bile acids together with lipids from the diet.

Lipase (glycerol esterhydrolase), cholesterol esterase and phospholipase 2, all of which are produced by the pancreas, act on fat droplets which have been made smaller by the emulsifying action of bile acids and lecithin in the duodenum.

Pancreatic lipase is inactivated by acid and is ineffective if excess acid is produced by the stomach as in Zollinger–Ellison syndrome, where fat malabsorption occurs.

The products of fat digestion, being lipids, diffuse across the lipid membrane of the brush border of the small intestine.

Different components are absorbed at different rates. Free fatty acids diffuse across rapidly, cholesterol more slowly. The micelles, therefore, become more concentrated in cholesterol as they move along the small intestine.

Under normal conditions, most dietary fat is absorbed before the contents reach the end of the jejunum and any fat in the stools (in the absence of steatorrhoea) is from desquamated epithelial cells and from bacterial flora in the gut.

The surface of the normal small intestine is convoluted (providing a greater surface area for absorption). An unstirred layer is present on the surface, through which micelles must pass before dietary fat can be absorbed by the epithelial cells.

Once inside the epithelial cells, lipid is taken into the smooth endoplasmic reticulum where much of it is re-esterified.

Some lipid is also synthesized in the epithelial cells. Dietary and synthesized lipids are then incorporated into chylomicrons and, provided β-lipoprotein is present, the chylomicrons are exocytosed into lateral intercellular spaces to enter the lacteals. Having reached the lymphatic system, they travel up the thoracic duct and enter the venous circulation.

Apolipoproteins are an important constituent of chylomicrons and are made by hepatocytes and the epithelial cells of the intestine. Their absence leads to the accumulation of lipid in intestinal epithelial cells.

Chylomicrons consist mainly of triglyceride with a phospholipid coat studded with apolipoproteins. They contain small amounts of cholesterol and cholesterol esters in the centre, and their overall size depends on the amount of fat in the diet—following a high fat intake, chylomicrons may have a diameter of up to 750 nm, in low fat diets they may be as small as 60 nm.

Abetalipoproteinaemia is a rare inborn error of metabolism inherited as a recessive trait, characterized by failure of chylomicron formation and an accumulation of dietary fat within enterocytes.

Vitamin A
Vitamin A exists in several forms (retinol, beta-carotene and retinal) with retinol being best absorbed.

Beta-carotene and retinal are both converted to retinol in the intestinal epithelial cells.

Vitamin D
This is absorbed mainly in the jejunum.

Vitamin E
Vitamin E is incorporated into chylomicrons (provided micelles are formed) and enters the lymphatic system.

Vitamin K
This exists in several forms, vitamins K_1 and K_2 enter the lymphatic system, vitamin K_3 the portal blood.

Carbohydrates
Carbohydrates provide most of the calories in the average diet, and the majority is in the form of starch (a polymer of glucose).

Starch contains α-1,4 and α-1,6 linkages: the former are hydrolyzed by α-amylase in saliva (ptyalin) and in pancreatic secretions (pancreatic α-amylase).

This produces maltose, maltotriose, comprising 70%

of the breakdown products and together known as malto-oligosaccharides, and alpha-limit dextrans (the remaining 30%).

Starch is therefore partially digested in the mouth (but not in the stomach—α-amylase is inactivated by gastric acid) and its digestion continues in the duodenum.

Other enzymes exist in the brush border of the duodenum and complete the digestion of starch.

These enzymes further break down starch into glucose and galactose which are actively taken up with sodium. Glucose and galactose then cross the basal membrane into the capillaries by facilitated transport and simple diffusion (Fig. 5.15).

Another monosaccharide, fructose, is also produced and taken up by a sodium-independent mechanism.

A deficiency of enzymes in the digestive system can result in carbohydrate malabsorption, the most common of which is lactase deficiency, which results in lactose intolerance in about 50% of adults worldwide!

Lactase deficiency has a strong genetic component and its incidence varies in different races. Exclusion of milk and milk products relieves many of the symptoms.

Other, rarer deficiencies include congenital lactose intolerance (most cases are acquired), sucrase–isomaltase deficiency and glucose–galactose malabsorption syndrome.

Lactase deficiency is discussed in more detail in Chapter 11.

Protein
The protein requirement of a normal healthy adult is about 40 g/day (to replace the 5–7 g/day nitrogen lost as urea, excreted in the urine).

In the Western world meat eaters usually exceed this, but in the developing world the amount of protein in the diet is less.

We do not have a store of protein in the body (unlike, for example, glycogen). Every protein in the body performs a function and proteins are in a constant state of flux (1–2% of total body protein is turned over daily), being synthesized by ribosomes and then degraded in the body. We synthesize about 300 g/day protein.

Protein in the intestinal lumen comes from protein eaten in the diet and also from desquamated cells, almost all of which are digested and absorbed.

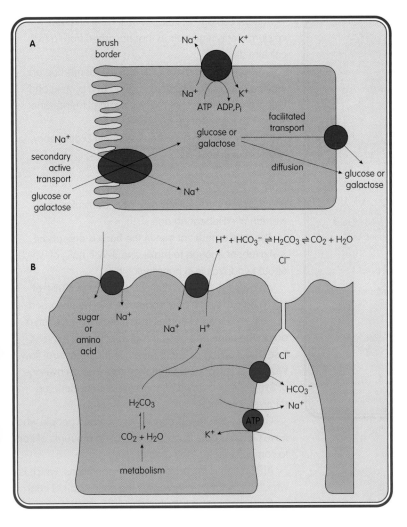

Fig. 5.15 (A) Sugar and (B) ion transport in the small intestine. ([A] Redrawn with permission from: *Nature*, 1987, **330**:379; London, Macmillan Magazines Ltd.)

Digestion of dietary protein begins in the stomach (pepsin hydrolyzes about 15% of dietary protein to amino acids and small peptides). It continues in the duodenum and small intestine where pancreatic proteases continue the process of hydrolysis.

Absorption of the products of protein digestion

Small peptides, particularly dipeptides and tripeptides are absorbed more rapidly than amino acids. They are transported across the membrane by an active mechanism utilizing the electrochemical potential difference of sodium.

Amino acids enter the cells from the lumen and leave it to pass into the capillaries by three mechanisms: sodium-dependent transport, sodium-independent transport, and simple diffusion.

Defects of amino acid absorption are rare but include Hartnup disease and prolinuria, neither of which on their own cause malnutrition.

Water and ions

About 9 L of water per day are absorbed from the gastrointestinal tract under normal circumstances, most of it from the small intestine, especially the jejunum (Fig. 5.16).

Almost all of the sodium in the gastrointestinal tract is reabsorbed (about 99%), mostly from the jejunum in association with glucose, galactose, and certain amino acids.

Sodium is transported across the epithelial cell membrane down its electrochemical gradient and pumped into the intercellular spaces in exchange for

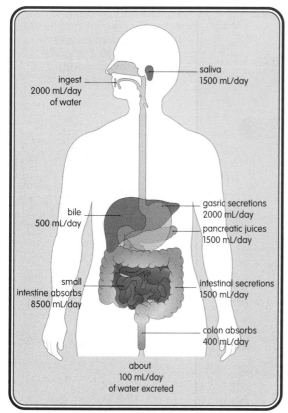

Fig. 5.16 Fluid secretion and absorption in the gastrointestinal tract.

The percentage of calcium absorbed on a low calcium diet is higher than that absorbed from a high calcium diet.

Calcium passes across the luminal membrane and into the cytoplasm where it is bound to a protein and then transported across the basal lateral membrane, some of it in exchange for sodium.

Calcium deficiency is seen in vitamin D deficiency, for example in rickets.

Iron

Iron deficiency is relatively common, particularly in women of childbearing age.

The total amount of iron in the body is only about 3–4 g (about enough to make one 3-inch nail), of which about two-thirds is in haemoglobin.

An average western diet contains about 20 mg of iron a day, of which only about 10% can be absorbed.

Both males and females lose almost 1 mg of iron a day in the urine and desquamated cells and females lose about 50 mg of iron a month in the menstrual flow. Women of reproductive age therefore lose an average of 3 mg of iron a day and iron deficiency anaemia is relatively common.

Growing children, pregnant women and people who have bled are able to absorb increased amounts of iron to compensate for their greater need.

Absorption is increased in acidic conditions (which is why taking vitamin C increases the absorption of iron).

Most dietary iron is in the form Fe^{3+} which is reduced to Fe^{2+} and then absorbed. Anything that prevents this reduction reduces the absorption of iron [e.g. the production of an insoluble complex with other dietary compound such as tannin (present in tea), phytate, and certain fibres].

> **Iron absorption is increased by vitamin C and decreased by tea. Tannin in tea forms an insoluble complex with iron, preventing its reduction to Fe^{2+} and subsequent absorption.**

potassium. Sodium is absorbed against its electrochemical gradient in the ileum and the colon.

Bicarbonate and chloride

Pancreatic secretions contain bicarbonate (which neutralizes gastric acid reaching the duodenum from the stomach) most of which is reabsorbed from the jejunum. However, bicarbonate is again secreted in the ileum and colon (partly in exchange for chloride).

Chloride is absorbed in the jejunum, ileum, and colon.

Potassium

Potassium is absorbed in the jejunum and ileum. It is secreted into the colon when potassium concentrations in the lumen are less than 25 mmol/L.

Calcium

This is absorbed throughout the intestine (especially in the duodenum and jejunum) although absorption is disrupted in vitamin D deficient states.

Fe^{2+} is bound to transferrin in the intestinal lumen, the complex is then taken up by endocytosis and iron is then either released into the plasma where it binds to a similar transferrin molecule or stored in the epithelial cells, bound to ferritin.

The proportion of iron released depends on the body's requirement—a larger amount remains in the cell bound to ferritin when dietary intake exceeds the body's requirement. This iron is then shed when the epithelial cell is desquamated and prevents iron overload.

Excessive amounts of iron are absorbed in haemochromatosis, an autosomal recessive condition leading to deposition of iron in the liver, heart, pancreas, and pituitary and damage to those organs. The disease is commoner in men because premenopausal women are protected by menstruation and childbirth.

Stem cells in the crypts of Lieberkühn can be programmed to absorb more iron, for example following haemorrhage. An increase in absorption may be seen 3–4 days after trauma, and in response to other events causing blood loss (the time taken for stem cells to mature and reach the tips of the villi where most iron absorption takes place).

Water soluble vitamins

At the concentrations present in a normal diet, most of these are taken up by specific transport mechanisms, many of which are sodium dependent.

Vitamin B$_{12}$ deficiency is relatively common after a gastrectomy or ileal resection and amongst alcoholics, as well as in pernicious anaemia. It is important to understand the mechanism by which it is absorbed and the function of intrinsic factor.

Vitamin B$_{12}$

Vitamin B$_{12}$ is bound to R protein found in saliva and in gastric secretions which protects it from digestion in the stomach.

The gastric parietal cells secrete intrinsic factor (IF) and, once vitamin B$_{12}$ has been separated from R proteins in the duodenum by the action of pancreatic proteases, vitamin B$_{12}$ binds to intrinsic factor.

Receptors for the intrinsic factor (IF)–vitamin B$_{12}$ dimer are present in the membranes of the ileal epithelial cells which bind the complex and allow uptake of vitamin B$_{12}$.

Vitamin B$_{12}$ is then transported across the basal membrane of the epithelial cells into the portal blood (Fig. 5.17). It is then bound to transcobalamin II and taken up by the liver, kidney, spleen, heart, placenta, reticulocytes, and fibroblasts.

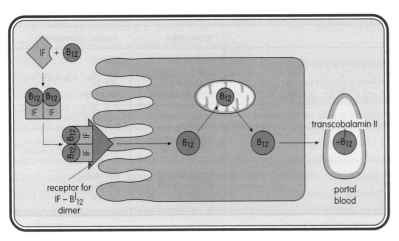

Fig. 5.17 Vitamin B$_{12}$ absorption in the terminal ileum. IF is the intrinsic factor.

cyclase, elevating cyclic AMP and increasing the secretion of sodium, chloride and water into the lumen.

- Summarize the function of mucus secretion in the colon.
- Detail the process of ion transport in the large intestine.
- Discuss the process of water reabsorption and how this is significant in relation to diarrhoea.

MOTILITY OF THE LARGE INTESTINE AND DEFECATION

Motility of the large intestine

Intestinal contents move relatively slowly through the colon, partly as a result of reverse peristalsis in the proximal colon. This allows time for water and sodium to be absorbed. The rate of movement is about 5–10 cm/hour.

Waves of peristalsis in the colon are known as mass movements and only occur about 1–3 times per day, pushing the contents towards the rectum.

Smaller contractions occur much more frequently and their purpose is to mix the contents, bring it into contact with the absorptive mucosa, and allow the transport of sodium and water. These smaller, local contractions divide the colon into a series of segments known as haustra, visible on radiographs.

As in other parts of the gastrointestinal tract, Auerbach's and Meissner's plexuses are present in the walls of the colon (Fig. 1.2). Their activity is modulated by parasympathetic and sympathetic activity.

Parasympathetic stimulation is via branches of the vagus (X) and pelvic nerves from the sacral spinal cord. It increases contraction of the proximal colon, allowing greater absorption of salts and water.

Sympathetic innervation is via the superior and inferior mesenteric and hypogastric plexuses. It decreases colonic movements.

Colocolonic reflexes occur (mediated in part by the sympathetic system) causing one part of the colon to relax if an adjacent part is distended (Fig. 5.20).

The filling of the stomach after a meal increases the frequency of peristalsis in the colon, sweeping faecal contents towards the rectum and anal canal in preparation for defecation (gastrocolic reflex).

Dietary fibre

The importance of dietary fibre in maintaining regular defecation and in reducing the frequency and severity of symptoms in diverticular disease is well recognized.

The incidence of cancer of the colon is also lower in countries where a high fibre diet is the norm.

Dietary fibre consists of those carbohydrates that humans are unable to digest, including cellulose, hemicellulose, lignin, and other carbohydrates with β-glycosidic linkages.

Bread, potatoes, fruit and vegetable are all high in fibre and increase the bulk of the stools by about 5 g for every gram of fibre!

Low fibre foods are less filling and often eaten in greater quantities than high fibre foods, contributing to obesity.

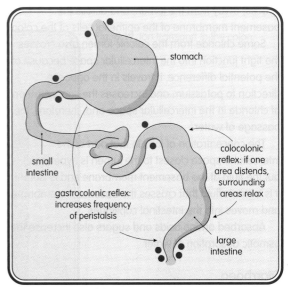

Fig. 5.20 Motility of the large intestine.

Defecation

The anal canal has an internal and external sphincter (Fig. 5.21).

The internal sphincter is made up of a thickened continuation of the circular muscle of the colon and is under involuntary control. It relaxes as a reflex in response to distension of the distal rectum.

Intact Auerbach's and Meissner's plexuses are needed for this reflex relaxation to occur. In Hirschsprung's disease, there is a congenital absence of ganglion cells in these plexuses in the rectum and sometimes in the colon, with the result that the internal sphincter does not relax in response to stretching of the rectum. Faeces remain in the rectum and colon, causing distension of the lower gastrointestinal tract and the abdomen.

This relaxation is only temporary. If defecation does not take place the internal sphincter contracts again and the urge to defecate is lost (until the sphincter relaxes again later).

The urge to defecate is felt because stretching of the rectum causes impulses in cholinergic parasympathetic nerves of the pelvis. These are transmitted to a nerve centre in the sacral spinal cord. A pressure of about 18 mmHg in the rectum is needed.

Impulses are then conveyed to higher centres, allowing an individual to decide whether to defecate; i.e. whether voluntarily to relax the external sphincter or delay doing so. In the latter case, the internal sphincter will recontract and the urge to defecate will subside.

The external sphincter is made up of striated muscle and, like most other striated muscle, is under voluntary control.

If there has been damage to the spinal nerves (and therefore to the control of the external sphincter), the external sphincter will relax when the pressure in the rectum reaches about 55 mmHg.

Tenesmus is an unpleasant feeling that 'something is still there' after defecation. It should be investigated promptly as it may be due to a potentially fatal neoplasm.

The anal canal is a remarkable structure. It can tell the difference between air, liquid, and solid contents, and allow the selective release of air in the passing of flatus.

Normally the rectum is distended as a result of mass movements filling it with faecal material. It may also be distended by a neoplasm or other mass, however, giving rise to tenesmus.

- How is motility controlled in the colon?
- What are the functions of dietary fibre? Why is this important?
- Describe the process of defecation and the different roles played by the internal and external sphincters.

Fig. 5.21 The rectum and anal canal.

levator ani
anorectal ring
internal sphincter
external sphincter

CLINICAL ASSESSMENT

6. Taking a History

Things to remember when taking a history

Most diagnoses are made on the history alone—investigations should confirm the diagnosis arrived at on the history.

Remember that at this stage (when you meet to take the history) the patient has far more information about his or her condition than you do.

Introduce yourself, be polite, listen carefully, and look interested, even if you have been up all night! Give the patient the time and the opportunity to tell you what you need to know and put him or her at his or her ease—many symptoms are embarrassing.

Maintain eye contact (even if the patient doesn't) and watch carefully for clues—how ill does the patient look? Is he or she agitated or distressed? Is he or she in pain, can you notice any tremors? Has he or she lost a lot of weight (cachexia)?

Look around the bedside for clues—inhalers, oxygen, a walking stick or frame, cards from family and friends, sputum pots, reading material and glasses, special food preparations, etc.

The structure of a history

When recording a history, use the headings below. You are less likely to leave things out if your history is structured. It is also easier for others to find the information they need quickly when looking at your notes.

When writing the notes, make sure you include everything, date the entry, and sign your name legibly.

Description of the patient

This should be a brief description giving details of the patient's age, sex, ethnic origins, and occupation. It should allow others who have not met the patient to picture him or her in their mind's eye.

Presenting complaint (PC)

Write one or two lines summarizing the symptoms felt by the patient—not your diagnosis, e.g. 'abdominal pain' or 'chest pain', not 'appendicitis' or 'myocardial infarction'!

History of presenting complaint (HPC)

A complete description of the problem that brought the patient to see you including:

- How and when the symptoms started.
- The speed of onset—was it rapid, or slow and insidious?
- The pattern of symptoms—their duration and frequency; are they continuous or intermittent? How often do they appear?
- If the symptoms include pain, you should spend at least half a page describing it!
- What the patient was doing when it started?
- What does it feel like: a sharp, stabbing pain? Crushing, like a tight band around the chest? Colicky?
- Are there any relieving factors—what makes it better, what does the patient do when it comes on? Does the patient lie absolutely still (as in peritonitis) or roll around? If he or she rolls around it is probably visceral pain (the contractions of a hollow organ such as the uterus, or intestinal spasm).
- Are there any precipitating factors—does anything make it worse, e.g. does exercise bring on chest pain or does eating cause abdominal pain?
- If the pain is abdominal, or retrosternal, ask about its relationship to food.
- Has the patient had it before? Is this exactly the same or a little bit different?
- What happened last time? Did he or she have any treatment (and did it work?) or investigations, or did it go away by itself?
- Why has the patient come to the doctor this time?
- Find out the extent of any deficit—is there any loss of function, anything he or she can't do or any movement he or she can't make?
- Is there anything else the patient thinks might be relevant, however trivial?

Past medical history (PMH)

Has the patient had any medical contact in the past? This question often needs persistence—it is amazing how many people forget operations, spells in hospital or visits to the GP!

- Always ask for symptoms of past complaints—the

diagnosis might be wrong, or misremembered, but patients nearly always remember how they felt.

Ask what previous investigations have been carried out.

Drug history
Ask about all drugs including contraceptive pills and over-the-counter medicines, as well as medicines that have been prescribed.

NSAIDs (non steroidal anti-inflammatory drugs) are commonly taken as over-the-counter medicines and can cause ulcers.

Does the patient have any allergies? It is difficult to defend a compensation claim where a patient has been given a drug to which he or she is allergic!

Lots of people say they are allergic to drugs when what they have actually had is a normal side effect, e.g. diarrhoea after taking penicillin. It is important to establish whether they really are allergic, as you may be denying them the best treatment, but do not give them anything they say they are allergic to unless you are absolutely sure they are not!

Ask about alcohol, smoking, and illicit drug use. Industrial toxins are important in claims for compensation.

The government has set targets for reducing smoking in the *Health of the Nation* document and GPs are now under an obligation to give advice on healthier lifestyles when seeing new patients.

Family history
Ask about the causes of death of close relatives, especially parents and siblings. Practice drawing quick sketches of family trees.

Social history
The purpose of this assessment is to see the patient as a whole and gain some idea of how the illness affects this particular patient, what support he or she has and whether he or she can reduce any health risks.

It should include information about the patient's:
- Marital status.
- Children and other dependants.
- Occupational history—this is especially relevant regarding exposure to toxins, musculoskeletal disorders and psychiatry.
- Accommodation—put yourself in the patient's position. Will he or she be able to cope at home?
- Diet—is it adequate? High cholesterol? Vegetarian?

- Exercise—does he or she take any? Is it appropriate?

Is there any risk behaviour? This overlaps with alcohol, smoking, and drug abuse, but also ask about sexual practices here, if appropriate.

Review of symptoms (functional enquiry)
Briefly go through all the systems of the body and ask specifically whether the patient has experienced any symptoms relating to them.

Going through the systems logically will help ensure nothing is forgotten.

Summary
The history should end with a brief summary, describing the patient again and recapping the most important features. For example:
- Reginald Smith, a 69-year-old retired bank manager, presenting with dysphagia which started about 3 months ago and has become progressively worse. The patient had a hernia operation 3 years ago, but there is nothing else of note in his past medical history. He has smoked 30 cigarettes a day since his early 20s. His father died of cancer of the stomach at the age of 50.

COMMON PRESENTING COMPLAINTS

Belching
This is common, particularly after drinking fizzy drinks and in anxious individuals who involuntarily swallow air.

It is almost always benign, especially if there are no other symptoms, but may occur in obstruction. Air in the gastrointestinal tract cannot get beyond the obstruction and comes back up to be expelled through the mouth.

It is more likely to be pathological if other symptoms such as abdominal pain, vomiting, or weight loss are present.

Dysphagia
This is a symptom of a number of conditions, principally obstruction, stricture, or neurological lesions.

When taking the history, ask whether it is difficult to make the swallowing movement and to swallow fluids as well as solids, whether it is painful, and whether the neck bulges or gurgles when drinking.

⟶ Odynophagia

Difficulty making the swallowing movement is likely to be caused by a neurological lesion (e.g. motor neurone disease or achalasia). The ability to drink liquids but not to swallow food suggests a stricture.

Constant, painful dysphagia may be caused by a malignant stricture. Bulging or gurgling is a symptom of a pharyngeal pouch (Killian's dehiscence).

Heartburn, indigestion, and peptic symptoms

Heartburn is common, especially in developed countries. It is pain behind the sternum (retrosternal) which may radiate up towards the throat. It is worse on bending and lying flat.

It is important to distinguish this from the retrosternal pain of a myocardial infarct (typically described as a central crushing pain, as if someone were tightening a band around the chest).

Indigestion has different meanings to different people and is commonly used to mean any discomfort experienced after eating or drinking. It is important to establish exactly what the patient means by the word.

Nausea and vomiting

Nausea is a feeling that one is about to vomit. It is often accompanied by hypersalivation, which protects the mouth against the acid contents of the stomach.

Some patterns of vomiting are almost diagnostic—for example, the projectile vomiting seen in pyloric stenosis in babies.

The content of the vomit (especially blood or bile), the frequency and amount all give important information. The presence of bile suggests that the lesion is below the ampulla of Vater.

Abdominal distension

This may be caused by one of the five Fs (flatus, fluid, fetus, fat, or faeces).

Obstruction low in the gastrointestinal tract typically leads to distension, obstruction higher up causes vomiting.

Distension may have intraluminal, intramural or intraperitoneal causes.

As with other disorders, the rate of onset (i.e. the rate at which the abdomen distended) is important. A neoplasm, for example, will not produce distension as quickly as gas.

Benign causes are also less likely to cause other symptoms.

Abdominal pain

Because of the embryological development of the gut, pain in a structure that develops from the foregut may be referred to the epigastric region, midgut structures to the umbilical area and hindgut structures to the suprapubic area.

Gastrointestinal bleeding

In general, bright red blood comes from low in the tract and dark, altered blood from higher up. However, profuse bleeding from the upper gut may produce too much blood to be altered on its way through the gastrointestinal tract and may appear bright red.

By far the most common cause of rectal bleeding is piles (haemorrhoids)—patients usually say they notice blood on the toilet paper.

Jaundice

Jaundice is characterized by a yellow skin and sclera (observed in a good light) and is caused when plasma bilirubin levels exceed 35 μmol/L.

The mechanism by which levels may become elevated are described in Chapter 10.

It is classified as prehepatic, hepatic, or posthepatic jaundice.

Diarrhoea and constipation

Severe diarrhoea causes electrolyte disturbances and is a significant cause of mortality worldwide.

It may be classified as acute or chronic. Acute cases are usually due to dietary indiscretion or infections.

Revise Chapter 4, describing the breakdown of bilirubin, to help you understand the causes of jaundice.

In essence, jaundice may be caused by an increase in haemolysis, a decrease in conjugation in the liver, or cholestasis.

Chronic diarrhoea often has more serious causes.

Constipation is a subjective complaint. Some people believe they must open their bowels at least once a day to remain healthy but in fact anything from once every three days to three times a day is well within the normal range.

In the absence of other symptoms, a high-fibre diet may improve things, as long as sufficient fluid is taken with the fibre.

However, constipation may also be due to obstruction.

Flatulence

This often causes great embarrassment, but some degree of flatulence is perfectly normal (about 10–20 releases a day). The sources of intestinal gas are described in Chapter 5.

Excessive gas may cause painful abdominal distension (resulting in a taut, drum-like abdomen) and be due to an abnormal increase in gas from any of the normal sources.

Causes include the incomplete breakdown of food because of an enzyme deficiency. In the absence of other symptoms, simple exclusion of certain foods may relieve the symptoms.

Anorectal pain

This may be caused by spasm of the sphincter, fissures, haemorrhoids, or abscesses.

Fissures are cracks in the anal canal and are intensely painful on defecation (much more so than might be expected from their size). They may be caused by trauma from passing a constipated stool.

Fissures and other acquired anal abnormalities are a common complication of Crohn's disease. Most of them occur in the midline on the posterior margin (90% in men, 70% in women). They may also occur following childbirth, particularly if a perineal tear occurred.

Patients are understandably reluctant to defecate because of the pain and this leads to a vicious cycle of constipation, the passing of hard constipated stools, and further fissuring.

Treatment is by the application of local anaesthetic cream to the fissure (to prevent the pain of defecation) and laxatives if necessary. Anal stretch may also be indicated.

Anal mass

The most important thing to exclude is a malignancy.

Malignancy is by no means the most common cause of an anal mass but it is a potentially fatal one.

Patients often complain of tenesmus (an uncomfortable feeling that something is still there after they have defecated).

The most common causes are haemorrhoids (varices), hypertrophied anal papillae, condylomata acuminata (viral warts), rectal prolapse, rectal abscess, faecal impaction, and neoplasia.

Anal papillae may hypertrophy in response to chronic irritation or inflammation.

Rectal prolapse occurs where the tone of the sphincter is reduced and the pelvic floor weakened. It may be a late complication of multiple childbirth.

Neoplasms include squamous cell carcinomas, malignant melanoma, Bowen's disease, Paget's disease and basal cell carcinoma.

A rectocoele (the protrusion of the rectum through the weakened posterior wall of the vagina) may also occur—the patient may say he or she can feel 'something drop', especially when straining.

It is essential to perform a rectal examination and proctoscopy at the first opportunity to investigate an anal mass.

Faecal incontinence

This may be of faeces or flatus.

The internal sphincter is an involuntary one, relaxing reflexly in response to distension by intestinal contents.

The external sphincter is under voluntary control, allowing us to defer defecation until a convenient moment.

Structural changes such as a loss of the angle of the rectum and anus (which contributes to faecal continence), neuromuscular and neurological lesions may all lead to incontinence.

- List the causes of anorectal pain.
- What is the most important diagnosis to exclude when investigating an anal mass?

7. Examination of the Patient

This chapter describes how to examine patients for gastrointestinal disease.

For a full description of the examination of other body systems, and the diagnostic inferences to be drawn from signs and symptoms elicited, reference should be made to a general clinical text.

GENERAL INSPECTION

The main purpose of a general inspection is to determine how ill the patient is.

Bear this in mind as you introduce yourself and take a history—if the patient is very ill, do not waste valuable time asking questions that can wait until later.

General inspection of the patient		
Test performed	**Sign observed**	**Diagnostic inference**
inspection of skin colour	pallor	anaemia, shock, myxoedema
inspection	yellow skin (and sclera)	jaundice
	pink nodules and/or areas of baldness on scalp (alopecia neoplastica)	metastases from internal carcinoma, usually from gastrointestinal tract, breast, kidney, ovary or bronchus
	dark pigmented flexures, especially armpits and under breasts (acanthosis nigricans)	obesity, endocrine disease, genetic, adenocarcinoma of gastrointestinal tract, or other internal malignancy
	vellus hair over face and body (hypertrichosis lanuginosa)	anorexia, neoplasm
	patient sitting forward on edge of bed using accessory muscles of respiration (respiratory distress)	airways obstruction, anaemia, heart failure, pulmonary embolism, obesity
	abdominal distension	fluid, fat, faeces, fetus, flatus
	large masses	neoplasm, cysts, congenital abnormalities
	telangiectasia	cirrhosis, outdoor occupation
	severe muscle wasting and loss of body fat (cachexia)	severe illness
inspection and questioning	itchy tissue-paper skin (ichthyosis)	lymphoma, drugs, malabsorption, malnutrition
	generalized itching	jaundice, systemic malignancy
	painful tender veins in different sites at different times (thrombophlebitis migrans)	carcinoma of pancreas

Fig. 7.1 General inspection of the patient.

Look at the patient's facial expression—is he or she comfortable, in obvious distress, looking furtive, receptive, hostile?

Assess the patient's body posture and mobility, and his weight and size.

Is he or she appropriately dressed? Very bright and clashing clothes may be a sign of manic depression. An unusual object to which the patient seems to attach a particular significance may indicate schizophrenia (e.g. the patient might believe the piece of string hanging over one ear is a transmitter through which he or she receives messages).

Many diseases and conditions do not have a direct effect on the gut. However, always remember that the patient may be receiving medication for a pre-existing condition, and this may affect the dose of drug you are intending to give for his or her gut condition (e.g. he or she may already be receiving enzyme-inducing drugs for his or her other condition). Current medication might even be producing his or her gut symptoms (e.g. diarrhoea caused by antibiotic therapy).

Finally, treatment for a pregnant or breast-feeding woman needs to be chosen carefully.

HANDS AND LIMBS

Hands and limbs

A surprising amount of information can be gleaned from a careful inspection of a patient's hands (Fig. 7.2).

A proper history should always be taken before a detailed physical examination (unless of course the patient is obviously very ill).

You should have shaken hands at the beginning—this may give you your diagnosis. If the patient takes your hand but cannot release it, you can fairly confidently say he or she has myotonic dystrophy—an uncommon but chronic condition often cropping up in clinical oral examinations!

Physical examination of the patient should start with an inspection of the hands. This is relatively non-invasive and allows the patient to get used to your touch. It also gives you a lot of information.

Skin lesions are described in the 'General inspection' section, above.

When examining a patient, be methodical. Examine the hands and then work your way up the arm to the head and neck (Fig. 7.4).

- What is the main reason for a general investigation?
- What aspects of the patient's behaviour or appearance should be taken into account?

- How does examining a patient's hands and limbs help in making a diagnosis?

Examination of the hands		
Test performed	**Sign observed**	**Diagnostic inference**
inspection of ends of fingers	clubbing (an exaggerated longitudinal curvature, loss of the angle between the nail and nail bed and bogginess)	The causes of clubbing may be divided into gastrointestinal, thoracic and cardiac. Gastrointestinal causes include: inflammatory bowel disease (especially Crohn's disease), cirrhosis, gastrointestinal lymphoma and malabsorption (e.g. coeliac disease)
arms straight with wrists fully extended	hands flap (liver flap or asterixis)	CO_2 retention, cirrhosis, portosystemic encephalopathy
inspection of palms of hands	palmar erythema (redness around the edges of the palms)	cirrhosis, pregnancy or polycythemia
inspection of nails	leuconychia (white nails)	hypoalbuminaemia
	koilonychia	iron deficiency, syphilis, or ischaemic heart disease
	Terry's lines (white nails with normal pink tips)	cirrhosis
	Mees' lines (paired white parallel bands across the nails)	hypoalbuminaemia
	Beau's lines (horizontal grooves across the nail)	chemotherapy, previous severe illness
inspection	purpura (purple lesions which do not blanch on pressure)	clotting disorder, vasculitis, drugs, infections, amyloidosis
inspection of position of fingers	Dupuytren's contracture (fibrosis and contracture of the palmar fascia)	ageing, liver disease, trauma (if unilateral) or epilepsy
inspection	lentigines (small, circumscribed, brown macules)	Peutz–Jeghers syndrome
feel and inspection of skin of palm	excessive sweating	alcoholism, anxiety
pinch a fold of skin up on back of hand	skin fold takes a relatively long time to disappear	dehydration
inspection	dark warty palms (tripe palms)	adenocarcinoma of gastrointestinal tract, other internal malignancy
	calcified nodules	CREST syndrome
	tendon xanthoma	familial hypercholesterolaemia
inspection of palm	simian crease	Down syndrome

Fig. 7.2 Examination of the hands.

Examination of the limbs		
Test performed	**Sign observed**	**Diagnostic inference**
palpation	pulses	information about cardiovascular system
inspection	central dilated arteriole with small red vessels radiating out from it, like a spider (spider naevus)	if more than five or six: pregnancy, cirrhosis, or other chronic liver disease
	scratches	pruritus
	muscle wasting	damage to innervation of muscles, malnutrition, chronic illness

Fig. 7.3 Examination of the limbs.

HEAD AND NECK

Head
Face, scalp, and eyes
Always warn a patient that you are about to look in his or her eyes. You need to get pretty close to have a proper look and this can be misinterpreted!

Stomatitis simply means ulceration of the mucosal surface of the mouth—it can occur in the mouth or at the edges, where the upper and lower lips meet.

When describing any lump in the body, comment on the site, size, shape, surface, smoothness, and surrounding (e.g. tethered or not)—six *S*s!

Examination of the head and face		
Test performed	**Sign observed**	**Diagnostic inference**
inspection of colour of sclera in a good light	yellow	jaundice
inspection of colour of conjunctiva of lower lid	pale	anaemia
inspection	red eye from subconjunctival haemorrhage	bleeding disorder from liver disease or other cause, diabetes, vomiting
	inflamed connective tissue beneath conjunctiva (episcleritis)	Reiter's syndrome (may follow dysentery)
	red eye from conjunctivitis	Stevens–Johnson syndrome
	chronic red eye	cirrhosis, renal failure, hereditary haemorrhagic telangiectasia (Rendu–Osler–Weber syndrome), iron deficiency anaemia, ataxia telangiectasia
	acute swelling of eyelids	adverse reaction to penicillin, bee sting or other allergen, infection
	firm, chronic swelling of eyelids	lymphoma, sarcoidosis
	yellow swelling in periorbital area (xanthelasma)	hypercholesterolaemia, age
	erythematous, swollen eyelids	dermatomyositis
	malar flush	mitral stenosis
	white ring around edge of iris (arcus)	hypercholesterolaemia, ageing
	protruding eye with sclera visible above iris	Grave's disease
	constricted pupils	ageing, drugs (opiates, glaucoma treatment), damage to sympathetic innervation (e.g. Horner's syndrome if unilateral)
	swollen, purple nose and ears (lupus pernio), prominent scars, orange–brown papules, nodules and plaques	sarcoidosis
	patches of hair loss on scalp (alopecia neoplastica)	metastases from internal carcinoma (usually from gastrointestinal tract, kidney, ovary, bronchus, or breast)
	flushing	carcinoid syndrome
	periorbital oedema, erythema of face and neck	dermatomyositis
inspection of cornea	brown rings (Kayser–Fleischer rings) at periphery	Wilson's disease
pupil reaction	pupils constrict to accommodation but not to light (Argyll–Robertson pupil)	syphilis

Fig. 7.4 Examination of the head and face.

Examination of the mouth		
Test performed	**Sign observed**	**Diagnostic inference**
inspection	puckered mouth	scleroderma
	swollen gums	pregnancy, acute leukaemia, puberty, phenytoin, infection
	fissuring at edges of mouth (angular cheilosis or stomatitis)	iron-deficiency anaemia, malabsorption, candidal or other infection
	vesicles on lips and in perioral area	herpes simplex infection
	blue spots on mucosa	hereditary haemorrhagic telangiectasia (Osler–Weber–Rendu syndrome),
	small pigmented areas on lips and on mucosa (lentigines)	Peutz-Jeghers syndrome
	bleeding and necrosis of gums	acute leukaemia
	bleeding gums	vitamin C deficiency
	beefy, raw, red tongue	pernicious anaemia, malabsorption, pellagra
	dry discoloured tongue	gastrointestinal or other infection
	ulcer	carcinoma, lymphoma, trauma, infection (tuberculosis, herpes, Vincent's angina, diphtheria, measles), Stevens–Johnson syndrome, Behçet's syndrome, drugs, pemphigus, bullous pemphigoid
	swellings	cysts, stones in salivary glands, infection
	high arched palate	Marfan's syndrome
	black tongue	antibiotic treatment
	blue tongue and lips	cyanosis
inspection and touch with spatula	white patches that cannot be brushed off (leucoplakia)	trauma, infection (including HIV)
	white patches that can be brushed off	candidal infection (thrush)
smell	halitosis	infection, poor hygiene, hepatic coma, uraemia, diabetic coma

Fig. 7.5 Examination of the mouth.

Mouth

Use a pen torch to inspect the inside of the mouth (Fig. 7.5). If necessary, gently depress the tongue with a wooden tongue depressor. Wear gloves if you need to feel anything in the mouth and ask the patient to remove any false teeth.

○ **What objects should be used when examining a patient's mouth?**

Neck

Inspect both the front and back of the neck.

Then stand behind the patient and palpate for enlarged nodes in the back, front, and sides of the neck.

Examination of the neck		
Test performed	**Sign observed**	**Diagnostic inference**
inspection of JVP (jugular venous pressure)	JVP raised (vertical height of column of blood in internal jugular vein exceeds 3 cm, measured from the sternal angle with the patient lying at 45°)	superior mediastinal obstruction e.g. carcinoma of bronchus (if JVP nonpulsatile), right heart failure, fluid overload, tricuspid incompetence, cardiac tamponade (if JVP pulsatile)
palpation	swellings	infection, carcinoma, bronchial cyst, thyroglossal or other cyst, goitre (iodine deficiency or thyroid disorder)
	enlarged lymph nodes (lymphadenopathy)	infection, carcinoma
	enlarged supraclavicular lymph node on the left (Virchow's node)	carcinoma of stomach
palpation of carotid pulse	character of pulse	information about cardiovascular system

Fig. 7.6 Examination of the neck.

THORAX

Most signs and symptoms in the thorax signal cardiovascular or respiratory disease.

This section is intended as a quick guide to the signs, symptoms, and diagnostic inferences that have particular relevance to gastrointestinal disease. A book on respiratory or cardiovascular medicine should be consulted for a fuller description of the examination of the thorax.

Observation

Undress the patient to the waist.

Be sensitive to the patient, especially if female—do not ask him or her to remove his or her underwear unless and until necessary, and then only for as long as necessary.

Have a chaperone present when examining a female, if you are male.

Stand at the end of the bed and observe the chest for a few seconds before moving nearer to the patient again and having a closer look.

From the end of the bed, assess the rate of breathing (about 12 breaths per minute is normal) and look for any signs of respiratory distress (these may not have been obvious with clothes on).

Check for any signs of asymmetry or abnormality of the chest wall such as a funnel chest (pectus excavatum) or a pigeon chest (pectus carinatum). Check also for a curved spine—scoliosis (combined lateral and rotational curvature), lordosis (abnormally extended spine), kyphosis (abnormally flexed spine), or tilt (lateral deformity) (Fig. 7.7).

Palpation

Feel for the trachea by pressing two fingers gently into the sternal notch—the trachea should be central. Explain to patients that you are about to do this—it is uncomfortable.

Feel for the apex beat with the flat of your hand, i.e. the lowest and most lateral place at which you can feel the heart beat. It is normally in the fifth intercostal space in the midclavicular line.

Place your thumbs together and spread your fingers out around the patient's side. Ask the patient to take deep breaths in and out and see how far your thumbs move apart and whether each thumb moves an equal distance. You are checking for the amount and symmetry of chest expansion.

Percussion

It takes practice to develop a good technique for percussion. Put the middle finger of one hand flat against the patient's skin and hit this finger with the middle finger of your other hand. The movement should come from the wrist.

The clavicle can be percussed without putting your own middle finger over it—simply tap the bone gently with the middle finger of one hand.

Solid organs are dull to percussion (i.e. sound dull

Examination of the thorax		
Test performed	**Sign observed**	**Diagnostic inference**
inspection	enlarged breasts in the male (gynaecomastia)	liver disease, prepuberty, drugs (spironolactone, steroids, digoxin, phenothiazines)
	loss of body hair	cirrhosis
inspection of skin	Figs 7.1, 7.2 and 7.3	
inspection of sputum pot	blood (haemoptysis)	infection, carcinoma or other tumour of lung, tuberculosis, clotting disorder, pulmonary infarction, trauma, vasculitis, foreign body, mitral stenosis
	green or yellow sputum	infection, asthma
	frothy pink sputum	pulmonary oedema
	offensive smelling sputum	anaerobic infection
	clear, white or grey (mucoid) sputum	chronic bronchitis
assessment of expansion	diminished movement on one side	pathology on that side
percussion	hyperresonance	emphysema, asthma, pneumothorax
	dull	obesity, consolidation, fibrosis, collapse,
	duller in upper lobe	old tuberculosis
	stony dull	pleural effusion
auscultation	wheezing	airflow obstruction, asthma, bronchitis, left ventricular failure
	quiet breath sounds	obesity, hyperinflation
	absent breath sounds	pneumothorax, collapse
	fine crackles	fibrosing alveolitis, congestion caused by heart failure
	no breath sounds, but bowel sounds heard in chest	diaphragmatic hernia
	coarse crackles	excess secretions (bronchiectasis)

Fig. 7.7 Examination of the thorax.

when percussed); organs containing air (e.g. healthy lungs) are resonant.

Percuss down both sides, comparing the two.

Auscultation

Remember to put the stethoscope in your ears the right way around (pointing towards the front) and ensure it is switched to the side you are using (the bell or diaphragm). The bell is better for listening to low sounds.

Politely ask the patient not to talk to you while you are listening with the stethoscope!

Medical notes often say 'vesicular breath sounds'—this simply means normal!

Normal breath sounds are louder on inspiration, tailing off in expiration and are caused by the movement of air in the larger airways rather than in the alveoli. Compare breath sounds on both sides.

Crackles sound like the noise you hear if you rub strands of hair together in front of your ears. They may

To remember that the stethoscope bell is better for listening to low sounds, think of 'bellow'.

be fine or coarse (caused by bubbling of air through fluid).

Stridor is increased noise on inspiration, wheezes are louder on expiration (although they may be heard on inspiration if airway narrowing is severe).

- How should percussion of the thorax be performed?
- How should the stethoscope be used during auscultation of the thorax?

THE ABDOMEN

Observation

The abdomen should be examined from the nipples to the knees, but not all at once. Respect the patient's dignity and only uncover as much as you need to at any one time.

Ask the patient to remove his or her clothes and lie flat on the bed or the couch, with his or her head on one pillow and arms by his or her sides.

Cover the patient with a folded sheet or blanket (you can usually find one at the end of the bed or examining couch). It is easy to move this up or down, exposing or revealing different parts, as you complete your examination.

Briefly expose the patient from the nipples to the pubic bone. Stand at the end of the bed to look at the abdomen as a whole and check for :

- Asymmetry.
- Distension.
- Dilated veins.
- Caput medusa (described below).
- Purpura.
- Spider naevi.
- Bruising.
- Visible peristalsis and/or pulsation.
- Masses.
- Scars.
- Striae (Fig. 7.8).

Then have a closer look at individual areas, checking more closely for all of the above. Skin lesions are described above .

Palpation

Make sure you have warm hands and tell the patient that you are about to feel his or her abdomen.

Before you do so, ask whether the abdomen is tender anywhere. If it is, then start your palpation as far away from the tender area as possible.

Ask the patient to tell you if he or she feels anything—this is better than asking him or her to let you know if it hurts. Most people will understandably tense their abdominal muscles if they think you are about to cause them pain.

Never take your eyes off the patient's face while you are palpating. You are looking for any signs of pain or discomfort. Do not hurt the patient!

Gently palpate all four quadrants and then go around again, palpating more deeply. Patients with tender abdomens are naturally apprehensive about having them palpated. When you have been around the quadrants once without hurting them, however, they will often relax their abdominal muscles enough to let you palpate more deeply and feel deeper structures (which is what you need to do).

You should be looking for:

- Enlarged organs (organomegaly).
- Tenderness.
- Guarding (tensing of the abdominal muscles).
- Rovsing's sign.
- Obvious masses (Figs. 7.8 and 7.10).

Inspection of the abdomen		
Test performed	**Sign observed**	**Diagnostic inference**
inspection	nodule near umbilicus (Sister Joseph's nodule)	metastasis of gastrointestinal or ovarian carcinoma through the ligamentum teres
	inflamed indurated lesion (carcinoma erysipelatoides)	lymphatic extension of carcinoma to the skin
	pink nodules on anterior trunk	cutaneous metastases (usually from gastrointestinal tract, kidney, ovary, breast or bronchus)
	central dilated arteriole with small red vessels radiating out from it, like a spider (spider naevi)	if more than five or six, pregnancy, cirrhosis, or other chronic liver disease
	distension	fat, fetus, fluid, faeces, flatus, obstruction
	firm pressure in the left lower area of distension leaves indentations	distension caused by faeces (e.g. Hirschsprung's disease or acquired megacolon)
	visible pulsation	aortic aneurysm
	visible peristalsis from left to right	pyloric stenosis
	visible peristalsis from right to left	obstruction in the transverse colon
	visible peristalsis in the middle (like a ladder)	obstruction in the small bowel
	patient lying rigid, taking very shallow breaths	peritonitis
	distended stomach but thin limbs	Cushing's syndrome, steroids
	discoloration around umbilicus (Cullen's sign)	acute pancreatitis, carcinoma of the pancreas
	discoloration in the flanks (Grey Turner's sign)	acute pancreatitis
	dilated veins (not confined to umbilical region)	obstruction of inferior vena cava
	purple striae	Cushing's syndrome, steroids
	white striae	pregnancy, obesity, previous pregnancy
	veins radiating out from umbillicus (Caput Medusae)	portal hypertension

Fig. 7.8 Inspection of the abdomen.

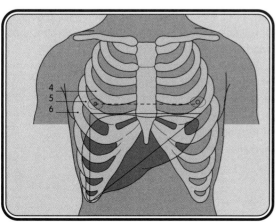

Fig. 7.9 The position of the normal liver.

Remember the five 'F's for the causes of a distended abdomen, and the six 'S's for the description of lumps.

Palpation of the abdomen		
Test performed	**Sign observed**	**Diagnostic inference**
palpation	enlarged liver (hepatomegaly)	malignancy, infection (especially glandular fever and malaria), hepatitis, sickle-cell disease, porphyria, haemolytic anaemia, connective-tissue disease, portal hypertension, lymphoma, leukaemia, glycogen storage disorders, myelofibrosis
	pulsatile liver	tricuspid incompetence
palpation of right iliac fossa	the right iliac fossa is more painful than the left (Rovsing's sign)	acute appendicitis
press on abdomen	pain occurs when you press in and also when you remove your hand (rebound tenderness)	peritonitis
place two fingers over right upper quadrant, ask patient to breathe in	pain on inspiration (Murphy's sign)	inflamed gall bladder
palpation	sausage-shaped mass	pyloric stenosis, intussusception
	mass	carcinoma, obstruction, hernia, faeces

Fig. 7.10 Palpation of the abdomen.

To examine the liver, start at the right iliac fossa and move your hand up, using the long, flat edge of your index finger to feel for the liver edge. The normal position of the liver is shown in Fig. 7.9.

Its edge can usually be felt just below the edge of the costal margin. You need to palpate quite deeply to feel it. Ask the patient to take deep breaths in and out; the edge should be felt moving against your fingers with respiration (Fig. 7.10).

To examine the spleen, start in the right iliac fossa and move up diagonally to the left costal margin—a grossly enlarged spleen can extend into the right iliac fossa! A normal spleen cannot usually be felt.

Most books say the spleen has a palpable notch but many clinicians say they have never been able to feel it!

If you can feel an upper margin, you are not feeling the spleen (you cannot get 'above' the spleen).

Percussion

The liver and spleen are dull to percussion. You can trace their margins (and confirm organomegaly) by percussing in the directions you palpated when examining them both (Fig. 7.11). Always percuss for the upper border of the liver as well as the lower one. The liver may be pushed down by a hyperinflated chest or other respiratory pathology, and hepatomegaly may be wrongly diagnosed if the upper border has not been located.

Auscultation

You should listen for bowel sounds (there should be some and they should not be too loud) and bruits (evidence of disturbed blood flow).

Listen for at least 1 minute over the ileocaecal valve before declaring that there are absent bowel sounds (Fig. 7.12).

You can also use the stethoscope to confirm the edges of an enlarged liver. Put your stethoscope over the liver and gently scratch the surrounding area with the soft part of the end of your finger (not your nail). The sound will be loud when you are scratching over the liver but soft as soon as you go over the liver margin.

You can use the same technique to confirm the edges of an enlarged spleen.

Percussion of the abdomen		
Test performed	**Sign observed**	**Diagnostic inference**
percuss the abdomen from flank to flank, ask patient to roll onto one side and percuss from flank to flank again	flanks are dull to percussion, midline is resonant with patient lying on his or her back, upper flank is resonant but lower flank is dull to percussion with patient lying on his or her side (shifting dullness)	ascites
percussion	hepatosplenomegaly	portal hypertension, amyloidosis, leukaemia, sickle-cell anaemia, thalassaemia, glandular fever
	splenomegaly	lymphoma, leukaemia, portal hypertension, haemolytic anaemia, rheumatoid arthritis, infection

Fig. 7.11 Percussion of the abdomen.

° **What areas of the abdomen should be examined?**
° **How should the liver be examined by palpation?**
° **How do the liver and spleen feel when percussed?**

RECTAL AND GENITAL EXAMINATION

Always wear gloves and make sure your examining finger is well lubricated (Fig. 7.13).

It is absolutely essential to explain that you are going to perform a rectal or genital examination and why you need to do this.

Make sure you have a chaperone of the same sex as the patient when performing any intimate examination.

Many patients find rectal examinations distressing and embarrassing. It is important to establish a rapport with them first and be sensitive to their feelings.

To perform a rectal examination, ask the patient to lie on his or her left side with his or her knees drawn up and gently insert a well-lubricated index finger into the anal canal and rectum.

Gently sweep your finger around the walls to check for any masses or abnormalities.

You should be able to feel the prostate in the male and cervix in the female through the wall of the rectum. The prostate has a shallow central groove.

Withdraw your finger: there should be faecal matter on it but no blood or mucus. Take your glove off cuff first, pulling the glove off inside out, and dispose of it in a clinical waste bag (these are usually yellow).

Genital examination

You should be looking for any signs of infection, gross abnormality and hernias.

It is best to look for hernias with the patient standing and you kneeling down so that you are at the same level as the area you are examining—many hernias disappear if the patient lies down. Hernias are common—about 1 in 100 people will have a hernia at some time in their life. About 70% of hernias are inguinal, 20% are femoral, and 10% are umbilical.

Palpate over the external and internal rings (above and medial to the pubic tubercle) to detect an inguinal hernia and ask the patient to cough. You may feel a lump when he or she does.

Repeat this procedure below and lateral to the pubic tubercle (to check for a femoral hernia) and above and below the umbilicus (for an umbilical hernia).

Perform the same procedure at other points of weakness (e.g. over scars and at the edges of the rectus muscles).

Try to reduce any swelling (gently push it back into the abdominal cavity).

Auscultation of the abdomen		
Test performed	**Sign elicited**	**Diagnostic inference**
auscultation	absent bowel sounds	paralytic ileus
	loud bowel sounds (tinkling)	intestinal obstruction
	bruit	disturbed flow (e.g. atherosclerosis)

Fig. 7.12 Auscultation of the abdomen.

Rectal examination		
Test performed	**Sign elicited**	**Diagnostic inference**
rectal examination and inspection of glove afterwards	bloody mucus	chronic inflammatory bowel disease, ulcerating tumour
	watery mucus	villous adenoma
	pale faecal material	obstructive jaundice
rectal examination	nodular prostate	carcinoma, calcification
	tender prostate	prostatitis
	enlarged, smooth prostate	age-related benign prostatic hyperplasia
	narrow empty rectum and a gush of faeces and flatus on withdrawing finger	Hirschsprung's disease
rectal examination and inspection of glove afterwards	bright red blood and slime	intussusception, colitis

Fig. 7.13 Rectal examination.

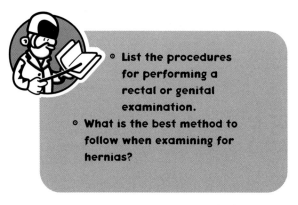

° **List the procedures for performing a rectal or genital examination.**

° **What is the best method to follow when examining for hernias?**

8. Further Investigations

INVESTIGATION OF GASTROINTESTINAL FUNCTION

Oesophageal manometry

Oesophageal manometry measures pressure changes in different parts of the oesophagus and is used to investigate suspected motility disorders.

A fluid-filled continuously perfused catheter is passed through the nose into the oesophagus (in much the same way as a nasogastric tube). Contraction of the oesophagus causes a pressure change which is transmitted up the fluid column and recorded as a trace.

In normal individuals, a pressure wave should pass down the oesophagus to the lower oesophageal sphincter which then relaxes to allow the oesophageal contents to pass into the stomach. Abnormal traces are seen in motility disorders.

Investigation of gastric function

Refluxed acid may overwhelm the normal protective lining of the oesophagus, leading to ulceration. Suspected reflux may be investigated by measuring the pH in the lower oesophagus over the course of 24 hours with a pH-sensitive probe.

A normal trace shows the pH above 4 for most of the time—if the pH is below 4 for more than 4% of the time, significant reflux is said to have occurred.

Disorders of gastric acid secretion may be investigated using the pentagastrin test. The patient fasts overnight and the resting juice in the stomach is aspirated using a nasogastric tube. Pentagastrin, a synthetic analogue of gastrin, is then given to stimulate acid secretion, and gastric contents are again aspirated and analyzed.

A large volume of resting juice suggests gastric stasis, a low pH suggests Zollinger–Ellison syndrome, and a failure to stimulate acid secretion with pentagastrin indicates achlorhydria.

Plasma levels of gastrin (a hormone which stimulates gastric acid secretion and growth of the gastric mucosa) may also be measured.

The levels will be high in Zollinger–Ellison syndrome as G cells in the pancreas, duodenum or, more rarely,

the stomach, secrete large amounts of gastrin in this disorder and cause hyperacidity, leading to ulceration.

Levels will also be high if the patient is taking drugs that inhibit gastric acid secretion and such drugs should be stopped before gastrin levels are measured.

Liver function tests

The functions of the liver are described in Chapter 4. 'Liver function tests' are usually defined as the measurement of serum levels of:

- Albumin.
- Bilirubin.
- Aminotransferase.
- Alkaline phosphatase.
- γ-glutamyltransferase.
- Proteins.

The prothrombin time is a measurement of the clotting ability of the plasma: prothrombin is made in the liver and is a vitamin K-dependent clotting factor with a short half-life. A prolonged prothrombin time gives an indication of the amount of prothrombin synthesized by the liver and therefore of the liver's synthesizing capacity.

However, prothrombin time is also increased in vitamin K deficiency. If there is any doubt about the cause, vitamin K should be given to the patient and prothrombin time measured again after 18 hours. By then it should have returned to normal if the cause was vitamin K deficiency.

Deficiency of vitamin K may occur in biliary obstruction because it is a fat soluble vitamin and bile salts are needed for its absorption.

Serum albumin is a good indicator of chronic liver disease. It is another protein synthesized by the liver and its levels will fall in chronic disease. Its half-life is longer than that of prothrombin, however, and levels may be normal in acute disease.

Biochemical tests

Bilirubin levels increase in liver disease. Aminotransferases (transaminases) are present in hepatocytes and leak into the plasma in liver cell damage.

Alanine aminotransferase is present in the cytoplasm of hepatocytes and its level increases in hepatocellular injury.

Aspartate aminotransferase is a mitochondrial enzyme present in:

- The liver.
- The cardiac muscle.
- The kidneys.
- The brain tissue.

It is less specific than alanine aminotransferase and its level increases in:

- Hepatic necrosis.
- Myocardial infarction.
- Congestive cardiac failure.
- Muscle injury.

Other enzymes of the liver

An isoenzyme of alkaline phosphatase is present in the canalicular and sinusoidal membranes of the liver. Other isoenzymes are present in bone, intestine and placenta.

Levels rise following damage to any of these structures but electrophoresis can be used to determine the particular isoenzyme (and therefore its source).

Hepatic alkaline phosphatase is raised in infiltration of the liver, cirrhosis, and cholestasis (from both intrahepatic and extrahepatic causes). The highest levels are seen in hepatic metastases and primary biliary cirrhosis.

γ-glutamyltransferase is present in the mitochondria of many tissues, including the liver, and raised levels are seen following the administration of phenytoin (an anti-epileptic drug) and the ingestion of even a moderate amount of alcohol.

If γ-glutamyltransferase is raised but alkaline phosphatase levels are normal, the cause of the damage is probably alcohol.

If both γ-glutamyltransferase and alkaline phosphatase are high, the cause may be cholestasis or intrahepatic malignancy.

Immunoglobulins are raised in liver disease. Normally, sinusoidal and Kupffer's cells phagocytose antigens absorbed from the gut, and antibodies are made in the lymph nodes and spleen.

In chronic liver disease, phagocytosis is reduced and lymphoid and plasma cells that infiltrate the portal tracts produce immunoglobulins. IgM is raised in primary cirrhosis and IgG raised in autoimmune chronic active hepatitis.

Additional tests

- α_1-antitrypsin—deficiency of α_1-antitrypsin can produce cirrhosis.
- α-fetoprotein—this is raised in patients with hepatocellular carcinoma and in women pregnant for the fifth (or more) time. Less elevated levels are found in hepatitis, teratoma and chronic liver disease.

Patterns of abnormality are important in diagnosis.

- Raised levels of aspartate aminotransferase and alanine aminotransferase reflect hepatocellular damage.
- Raised alkaline phosphatase and γ-glutamyl-transferase indicate cholestasis or intrahepatic abscess and malignancy.

Endoscopic examinations

Endoscopy is a relatively non-invasive procedure that gives very valuable information about a number of gastrointestinal tract disorders. It is worth going to a hospital's endoscopy suite to see the procedure in action. The results are shown on a television screen and it is possible to gain a very clear view.

Gastroscopy (oesophagogastroduodenoscopy)

Patients are normally told gastroscopy involves 'swallowing a camera' which understandably makes them very apprehensive. They are slightly sedated (normally with a drug that also causes some amnesia), however, the camera is very small, and, although it looks uncomfortable, most people say they can remember little about it afterwards.

Patients must fast overnight beforehand but the procedure may be carried out in the outpatient department.

Gastroscopy is commonly used to investigate upper gastrointestinal disorders. Forceps for taking biopsies can be passed through the biopsy channel of the endoscope.

Endoscopic retrograde cholangiopancreatography (ERCP)

ERCP involves injection of contrast material into the biliary and pancreatic systems followed by radiological screening.

Two different contrasts are used: low iodine for the common bile duct (so as not to obscure gall stones) and a higher iodine contrast for the pancreatic duct.

Diathermy instruments can be passed through the endoscope and used to remove stones in the common bile duct after the ampulla of Vater has been incised (sphincterotomy). Obstructions in the biliary tree can also be relieved using a stent.

ERCP may introduce infection leading to cholangitis and prophylactic antibiotics are usually given. Pancreatitis may also occur.

Always perform a digital rectal examination before proctosigmoidoscopy or colonoscopy. The patient may have a large tumour in the anal canal or rectum and damage may be caused if a scope is inserted without checking first.

Colonoscopy, sigmoidoscopy, and proctoscopy

These procedures give information about the lower gastrointestinal tract.

Proctoscopy is commonly performed in out-patients and involves the use of a proctoscope: a rigid tube with a detachable, disposable end which is used for one patient only and then removed and thrown away. Before the proctoscope is used, an obturator is inserted into its lumen to avoid the discomfort of inserting a hollow tube into the patient's anal canal and the end of the instrument is well lubricated.

The patient is then asked to lie on his or her left side with knees drawn up to the chest, the proctoscope is gently inserted, the obturator is removed, and air is pumped in through the proctoscope to inflate the rectum. It is kinder to explain to the patient that any associated noise is caused by the air being pumped in, otherwise he or she may think it is caused by flatulence and become very embarrassed!

Proctoscopy gives valuable information about the anal canal and rectum but, because the instrument is rigid, it

cannot be used to visualize structures above the flexure.

Sigmoidoscopy and colonoscopy are both flexible instruments and can give information about the anal canal, rectum, and sigmoid colon.

Colonoscopy is also used to visualize the large bowel beyond the sigmoid colon—the whole of the large bowel can be inspected.

The procedure in sigmoidoscopy and colonoscopy is similar to proctoscopy. However, bowel preparation must be commenced 2 days before colonoscopy and patients are given analgesia and sedated for the procedure.

- How should suspected reflux be investigated?
- What is prothrombin time?
- What is prothrombin time?
- What are the uses of endoscopy in gastrointestinal investigations?

ROUTINE INVESTIGATIONS

A number of simple tests are available to confirm (or disprove) diagnoses arrived at from the history of a patient in outpatients or casualty.

A probable diagnosis should have been decided, and appropriate questions asked to support or exclude it while taking the history (unless of course the patient is unconscious and no history is available). The tests ordered should be relevant to the possible diagnoses. Unnecessary or inappropriate tests waste finite resources and are time-consuming.

The results described below are particularly relevant to gastrointestinal disease: other texts in the *Crash Course* series should be consulted for other systems.

Haematological and clinical chemistry tests

The results of the more common tests are described in Figs 8.1 and 8.2.

General haematological tests		
Normal ranges	**Raised**	**Lowered**
leucocyte count 4-11 $\times 10^9$	infection—see below for details	
erythrocyte count men: 4.5–6.5 $\times 10^{12}$ women: 3.9–5.6 $\times 10^{12}$		
PCV (packed corpuscular volume) men: 0.4–0.54 L/L women: 0.37–0.54 L/L	polycythaemia	
MCV (mean corpuscular volume) 76–96 fL	excessive alcohol consumption, vitamin B_{12} and folate deficiency, liver disease	iron deficiency anaemia, thalassaemia
MCH (mean corpuscular haemoglobin) 27–32 pg		
neutrophils 2.0–7.5 $\times 10^9$/L 40–75% of total white cell count	bacterial infections, trauma, surgery, haemorrhage, inflammation, infarction, drugs (e.g. steroids), disseminated malignancy, polymyalgia, myeloproliferative disorders, polyarteritis nodosa	vitamin B_{12} deficiency, folate deficiency, bone marrow failure, tuberculosis, brucellosis, typhoid, kala-azar, septicaemia, hypersplenism, certain autoimmune diseases, drugs (e.g. sulphonamides, carbimazole)
lymphocytes 1.3–3.5 $\times 10^9$/L 20–40% of total white cell count	viral infection, toxoplasmosis, brucellosis, whooping cough, chronic lymphoid leukaemia	HIV infection, marrow infiltration, drugs (steroids), systemic lupus erythematosus, legionnaire's disease, uraemia, chemotherapy, radiotherapy
eosinophils 0.04–0.44 $\times 10^9$/L 1–6% of total white cell count	atopic conditions, parasitic infections, malignancy, polyarteritis nodosa	
basophils 0–0.1 $\times 10^9$/L 0–1% of total white cell count	ulcerative colitis, viral infection, malignancy, polycythaemia rubra, cell-mediated lympholysis, haemolysis, myxoedema	
monocytes 0.2–0.8 $\times 10^9$/L 2–10% of total white cell count	acute and chronic infection, malignancy	
platelet count 150–400 $\times 10^9$/L	inflammatory disease, colitis, Crohn's disease	lymphoma, viral infection, drugs, marrow failure, idiopathic thrombocytopenic purpura, disseminated intravascular coagulation, hypersplenism
reticulocyte count 25–100 $\times 10^9$/L	anaemia, haemorrhage	
ESR (erythrocyte sedimentation rate, mm/h) rises with age, upper limit is: men: age ÷ 2 women: (age + 10) ÷ 2	anaemia, malignancy, infection, sarcoidosis, lymphoma, CT disease, abdominal aneurysm	heart failure, polycythaemia
prothrombin time 10–14 s (often expressed as INR, by definition 1 is normal)	liver disease, warfarin	
activated partial thromboplastin time 35–45 s	haemophilia, Christmas disease	

Fig. 8.1 General haematological tests.

Blood tests		
Normal range	Raised	Lowered
alanine aminotransferase 5–35 IU/L	liver disease (hepatocellular damage), shock	
albumin 35–50 g/L	dehydration	malabsorption, malnutrition, malignancy, liver disease
alkaline phosphatase 30–300 IU/L	liver disease (cholestasis)	
α-fetoprotein <10 kU/L	hepatocellular carcinoma, hepatitis, chronic liver disease, teratoma	
α-amylase 0–180 somogyi U/L	acute pancreatitis	
aspartate transaminase 5–35 IU/L	liver disease (hepatocellular damage), myocardial infarction, skeletal muscle damage	
bilirubin 3–17 μmol/L	jaundice	
calcium ion, 1.00–1.25 mmol/L total, 2.12–2.65 mmol/L	malignancy, sarcoidosis, tuberculosis, hyperparathyroidism	malabsorption, acute pancreatitis, massive blood transfusion, hypoparathyroidism
caeruloplasmin 200–350 mg/L		Wilson's disease
copper 11.0–22.0 μmol/L		Wilson's disease
cholesterol 3.9–7.8 mmol/L	hyperlipidaemia	
creatinine kinase 25–195 IU/L men 25–170 IU/L women	myocardial infarction	
ferritin 12–200 μg/L	haemochromatosis	
folate 2.1 μg/L		malabsorption, alcoholism, drugs, malignancy, haemolysis
γ-GT 0–0.50 μkat/L	alcoholic liver disease, biliary obstruction	
iron 14–32 μmol/L men, 11–29 μmol/L women		iron deficiency anaemia
LDH 70–250 Iμ/L	hepatocellular damage, myocardial infarction	
magnesium 0.75–1.05 mmol/L		diarrhoea, alcohol, total parenteral nutrition
potassium 3.5–5.0 mmol/L	trauma (including surgery), catabolic states, renal failure, transfusion of stored blood, haemolysis	pernicious anaemia treated with B_{12}, diarrhoea, laxative abuse, vomiting, villous adenoma
total protein 60–80 g/L		malabsorption, Ménétrièr's disease, nephrotic syndrome, malnutrition
sodium 135–145 mmoL/L	dehydration	vomiting, diarrhoea, fistulae, ileus, intestinal obstruction, cystic fibrosis
triglyceride 0.55–1.9 mmol/L	hyperlipidaemia	
urea 2.5–6.7 mmol/L	dehydration	
urate 210–480 μmol/L men 150–390 μmol/L women	lymphoma, gout, leukaemia, haemolysis, drugs, alcohol	coeliac disease, Wilson's disease, pernicious anaemia
vitamin B_{12} 0.13–0.68 nmoL/L		malabsorption, alcoholism, pernicious anaemia

Fig. 8.2 Blood tests.

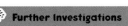

The pattern of deviation from normal levels is more important than individual rises or falls: do not rely too heavily on a single abnormal result. If all the tests were conducted on a healthy person, the chances are that at least one of them would be abnormal!

Microbiology

This is the study of microorganisms and their effects on humans. Bacteria, viruses, fungi, and parasites can cause disease. Various methods exist to identify these different organisms.

Many bacteria, fungi, and parasites can be identified using light microscopy but viruses are too small and other methods (described below) must be employed for their detection.

Samples must be solidified by freezing (in urgent cases) or treated with wax or transparent plastic and thinly sectioned to allow light to shine through and render individual structures visible.

Liquid samples may also be examined under the light microscope by smearing the sample over the glass plate and fixing it.

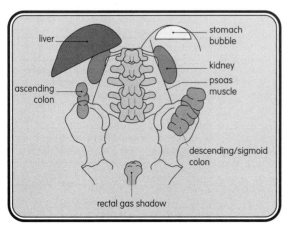

Fig. 8.3 Structures normally visible on plain abdominal X-ray. (Redrawn with permission from: *Oxford handbook of clinical medicine,* 3rd ed. Oxford:Oxford University Press;1993.)

Both solid and liquid samples may be stained to aid diagnosis with the microscope. The Gram stain (designed by a medical student in the 19th century) is particularly useful for identifying bacteria.

Cell culture is useful in deciding which antibiotic is most effective against particular bacteria. Samples are smeared on an agar plate, small areas of which have been impregnated with different antibiotics, and then incubated. Small patches of agar on which no bacteria have grown can be seen around those antibiotics that are most effective against the bacteria in question.

Histology and cytology

Histology is the study of tissue samples taken on biopsy or following surgical removal, usually to confirm whether tissue is malignant or not.

The sample may be examined using light microscopy or electron microscopy.

Cytology is the study of cell samples taken by smears (for example of the cervix) or fine needle aspiration of cystic or other lesions.

The cells are stained and examined under a microscope to detect the presence of abnormal and inflammatory cells.

- **What is the normal range and the normal percentage of white cell count for neutrophils?**
- **How are cell cultures used in assessing the effectiveness of antibiotics?**

IMAGING OF THE GASTROINTESTINAL SYSTEM

Plain radiography and contrast technique

Substances absorb X-rays to different extents, depending on their atomic number—those that absorb most appear white, those that absorb least appear black.

The use of X-rays should be avoided in pregnancy whenever possible.

Borders are only seen at the interfaces between different densities (e.g. the interface between the wall of the stomach and the gastric air bubble), but may be enhanced by the introduction of contrast media, for example, barium.

When commenting on any X-ray, always follow the same order—do not come straight out with a diagnosis!

1. Check the film has been taken properly and the information recorded on it:
   - Look at the name and the date. Is it the correct patient and the X-ray you want to examine? Many patients have lots of different X-rays with their notes, and it is easy to pick up the wrong envelope of films!
   - Is it an AP (anteroposterior) or PA (posteroanterior) film?
   - Check the alignment of the spine (or the clavicles on a chest X-ray)—was the patient straight when it was taken? If not, organs may be displaced and look abnormal even if they are not.
2. Check the outlines of all the structures you would expect to see on a normal X-ray. Are they all visible? Can you see anything you would not normally expect? Is any area more (or less) opaque than normal?
3. Describe the gross pathology that might have caused these abnormalities (e.g. stricture in the oesophagus, rose-thorn ulcers in the ileum).
4. Suggest the most probable diagnosis, and some differential diagnoses.

Abdominal films may be taken with the patient supine (best for seeing the distribution of gas) or erect (better for spotting air under the diaphragm and for seeing fluid levels).

The intestines are lower down in erect X-rays than in the supine position. Before X-rays became available doctors had only seen intestines in supine bodies at dissections and operations and a number of unfortunate people had completely unnecessary operations to hitch up their guts when erect abdominal X-rays were first taken!

Look at the pattern of gas (central in ascites, displaced to the left lower quadrant in splenomegaly). Extraluminal gas in the liver or biliary system suggests a gas-forming infection or the passing of a stone. In the colonic wall it suggests infective colitis.

Air under the diaphragm may be caused by:
- Perforation of the bowel.
- A section of intestine lying between the liver and the diaphragm.
- A gas-forming infection.
- A pleuroperitoneal fistula (tuberculosis, trauma, or carcinoma), following surgery or laparoscopy.
- Giving birth.
- Air being forced up the vagina and through the fallopian tubes (in female water skiers).

Look for opaque areas of calcification, commonly caused by stones (although only 10% of gall stones are radio-opaque), pancreatitis, or atherosclerosis.

A loop of intestinal gas (sentinal loop) can be caused by local peritoneal inflammation resulting in a localized ileus.

Contrast radiographs
These may be single or double contrast (e.g. air and barium). Double-contrast films give a better picture of surface mucosa.

Barium may be administered orally and different parts of the gastrointestinal tract can be visualized using this technique depending on the delay before taking the X-ray.

A barium enema is often used to visualize the lower gastrointestinal tract (Figs 8.4 and 8.5).

Angiography
Angiography is another form of contrast imaging used to visualize blood vessels.

It may show the site of gastrointestinal bleeding (although endoscopy is often the investigation of choice) and the blood supply to specific organs such as the liver (showing architectural abnormalities).

Computerized tomography (CT)
CT scanners have been in use since 1972 and produce computerized images of the body in a series of slices,

based on the amount of X-rays absorbed by different tissues at different angles (Figs 8.6 and 8.7).

They are more effective for imaging soft tissues (including tumours) than radiography, and the level of radiation is generally lower.

CT scans may be plain or contrast—contrast is often used to delineate the bowel.

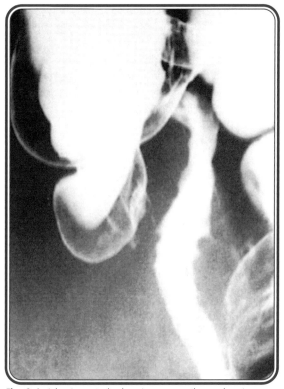

Fig. 8.4 A barium study showing a rose-thorn ulcer in Crohn's disease.

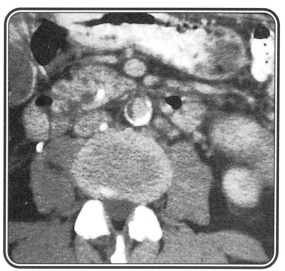

Fig. 8.6 CT scan in calcific pancreatitis.

Magnetic resonance imaging (MRI)

MRI scanners are large circular magnets that align the nuclei of hydrogen atoms in the body so that they lie parallel to each other (normally they lie in random directions).

Fig. 8.5 Explanatory diagram showing main features of a barium study of a rose-thorn ulcer in Crohn's disease.

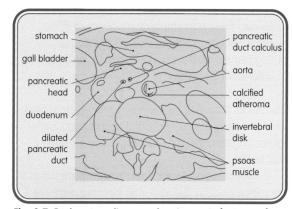

Fig. 8.7 Explanatory diagram showing main features of scan of calcific pancreatitis.

The nuclei are then temporarily knocked out of alignment by radio pulses and emit radio signals as they fall back into alignment.

These signals are analysed to produce sliced images of the body, similar to CT scans.

Fatty tissues contain a lot of hydrogen and produce bright images, whereas tissue such as bone produces dark images.

MRI scans are often preferred in pregnancy as they do not use radiation but they can interfere with pacemakers, hearing aids, and other electrical devices.

Radioisotope scanning

Radioisotope scanning is used to study the uptake of isotopes by various organs.

Different isotopes are taken up by different organs and structures. Hot lesions take up more isotope than the surrounding tissue, cold ones take up less.

Techneconin (^{99m}Tc) colloid is used to scan the liver and ^{99m}Tc HIDA for the biliary tree as it is taken up and excreted in bile. Liver lesions greater than 2 cm in diameter show up as cold spots in scanning with ^{99m}Tc colloid.

Ultrasonography

Ultrasonography has been used since the 1950s and is often the investigation of choice for abdominal masses (Figs 8.8 and 8.9).

Ultrasonographic machines emit very high frequency sound waves, which pass readily through soft tissues and fluids, but are reflected back from bone or gas—the reflected echoes are analyzed to produce images.

Ultrasonographic scans are non-invasive and safe in pregnancy.

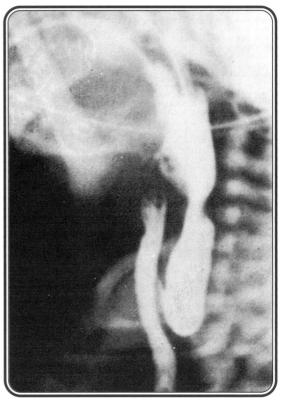

Fig. 8.8 Non-ionic contrast study of oesophageal atresia.

- **How should an X-ray be checked before making a diagnosis?**
- **How is angiography useful in gastrointestinal diagnosis?**
- **What does extraluminal gas in the liver or biliary system suggest?**

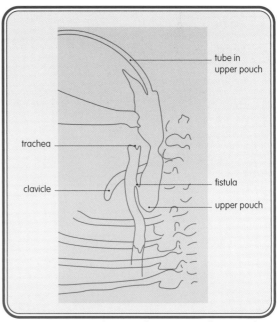

Fig. 8.9 Explanatory diagram showing main features of non-ionic contrast study of oesphageal atresia.

9. Pathology of the Upper Gastrointestinal Tract

Congenital abnormalities

A lateral cleft lip (hare lip) may result from incomplete fusion of the maxillary and medial nasal prominences, and a cleft palate from failure of fusion of the palatine shelves. Cleft lip and palate may occur together or one may be seen without the other.

Overall, cleft lip is more common than cleft palate (1/1000 births compared with 1/2500 births). Cleft lip is more common in male babies than female babies.

The palatine shelves in the female fetus fuse about 1 week later than they do in the male; cleft palate on its own is more common in female babies. Of every nine affected babies, two have a cleft lip, three a cleft palate, and four have both. About 20% of babies with cleft lip or palate also have other malformations.

Genetic and environmental factors have been identified. Trisomy 13 (Patau's syndrome) and a number of teratogens (most notably anticonvulsants such as phenytoin, and folic acid antagonists) are associated with both cleft lip and cleft palate.

Unlike babies with a cleft lip, those with a cleft palate cannot be breastfed (but may be given expressed breast milk or formula milk by a bottle with a special teat).

Repair is surgical and is normally carried out after 3 months in the case of cleft lip and about 1 year in cleft palate.

Median cleft lip is much rarer and is caused by incomplete fusion of the two medial nasal prominences in the midline.

Failure of the maxillary prominence to merge with the lateral nasal swelling causes an oblique facial cleft, exposing the nasolacrimal duct.

Many parents are distressed by the birth of a child with a cleft lip but the results of surgery are usually excellent. It is often helpful to show such parents photographs of other children whose cleft lips have been repaired.

Infections and inflammation

The oral mucosa may be affected by a number of inflammatory disorders, either restricted to the mouth or as part of a systemic disorder.

Herpes simplex virus

Herpes simplex virus 1 infection usually affects the body above the waist and herpes simplex virus 2 below it. Changes in sexual practices, however, have led to an increase in herpes simplex virus 1 infections below the waist and 2 above it.

The primary infection may be asymptomatic or produce a severe inflammatory reaction. Presentation is usually with fever and painful ulcers in the mouth which may be widespread and confluent.

The virus may remain latent in the trigeminal ganglia and be reactivated to cause a cold sore (herpes labialis) in about one-third of people infected with herpes simplex virus 1.

Aphthous ulcers

These are associated with inflammatory bowel disease and coeliac disease but many occur sporadically. They have a grey necrotic base and haemorrhagic rim and usually heal spontaneously within a few days, but often recur.

Oral candidiasis (thrush)

Candidiasis is caused by the yeast *Candida albicans* and looks similar to leucoplakia (described below) but can be scraped off with a spatula.

It causes lesions in neonates, the immunocompromized, and those whose natural flora have been disturbed by broad-spectrum antibiotics. It is common in AIDS patients, in whom it may also cause lesions in the oesophagus.

HIV 1 and 2 are the viruses that lead to AIDS. AIDS can be said to have developed when an AIDS-defining illness has occurred, typically 10–15 years after infection with HIV 1 (slightly longer with HIV 2).

Glossitis

This is seen in certain deficiency states, most notably vitamin B_{12} deficiency, and after trauma to the mouth from badly fitting dentures, jagged teeth, burns, or the ingestion of corrosive substances.

The combination of glossitis, iron deficiency anaemia, and an oesophageal web causing dysphagia occurs in Plummer–Vinson syndrome (Paterson–Kelly syndrome), most commonly seen in women.

Oral manifestations of systemic disease

Infections, dermatological conditions, haematological disorders and other conditions which may lead to oral lesions are described in Chapter 7.

Sialadenitis (inflammation of salivary glands)

This uncommon condition may be caused by infection or obstruction of salivary ducts.

Saliva has antibacterial properties but individuals with reduced amounts of saliva (e.g. in Sjögren's syndrome) are at increased risks of sialadenitis.

Neoplastic disease

As elsewhere in the body, neoplasms may arise from any tissue and be malignant or benign.

Precancerous and benign neoplasms

These include:

- Leucoplakia (hyperkeratosis and hyperplasia of squamous epithelium), a premalignant condition that takes its name from the Greek for 'white patches' and is associated with excess alcohol, poor dental hygiene, and smoking.
- Erythroplakia (dysplastic leucoplakia), lesions which have a higher malignant potential than leucoplakia.
- Squamous papilloma and condyloma acuminata (both associated with human papilloma viruses 6 and 11 and largely benign).

Leucoplakia and erythroplakia are more common in men, particularly those aged between 40 and 70 years.

Malignant tumours

Squamous cell carcinoma are by far the most common malignant tumours (95%); however, adenocarcinoma, melanomas and other malignant tumours may occur.

Alcohol and smoking (and, even more so, chewing tobacco) predispose to squamous cell carcinoma. The risk of a drinker who smokes developing squamous cell carcinoma is about 15 times that of the rest of the population.

Squamous cell carcinoma may arise in areas of leucoplakia and also on the lip, where it is associated with exposure to sunlight.

Neoplasms of the salivary glands

These include:

- Pleomorphic adenoma (mixed tumours accounting for two-thirds of all salivary tumours).
- Marthin's tumour (5–10%).
- Mucoepidermoid tumours.
- Adenoid cystic carcinoma.

○ **What are the common congenital abdormalities that may occur in the mouth? What are the implications of these for the neonate?**

○ **List the common infections and inflammatory conditions that may affect the mouth.**

○ **What are the more common neoplasms of the mouth?**

Hydramnios may also be caused by a failure of development of the fetal neurohypophysis that results in very little or no ADH (antidiuretic hormone) secretion and decreased reabsorption of water from the distal convoluted tubules in the fetal kidney. Treatment of atresia and fistulas is by surgery.

Agenesis

This is the complete absence of an oesophagus and is much rarer than atresia or fistula.

Treatment is surgical.

THE OESOPHAGUS

Congenital abnormalities

The oesophagus and trachea develop from a single embryological tube.

Atresia and fistulas

Atresia is a failure of canalization. A fistula is an abnormal connection between two epithelial-lined surfaces (Fig. 9.1).

Atresia is a common condition, affecting 1/200 births and is caused by a failure of the oesophageal endoderm to grow quickly enough when the embryo elongates in week 5.

In 90% of cases, oesophageal atresia and fistula occur together but either may occur without the other (10% of cases).

In the most common form of atresia, the upper part of the oesophagus has a blind ending but the lower end forms a fistulous opening into the trachea. This means that the infant cannot swallow milk or saliva and the diagnosis becomes apparent shortly after birth. The infant is at risk of aspiration pneumonia and of fluid and electrolyte imbalances.

Atresia should be suspected in a fetus where there is hydramnios (abnormally large amounts of amniotic fluid, i.e. over 2 L). Normally a fetus swallows amniotic fluid and some fluid is reabsorbed into the fetal circulation. Where there is atresia, the fetus cannot swallow, amniotic fluid is not reabsorbed, and excess fluid accumulates causing a distended uterus.

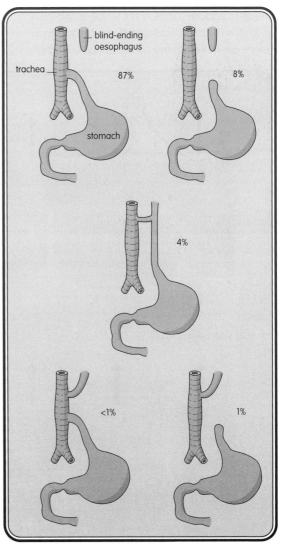

Fig. 9.1 Different forms of oesophageal atresia and fistulas, and their occurence expressed as percentages.

119

Stenosis
Congenital stenosis may occur, but acquired stenosis is more common and is described below.

Inflammation of the oesophagus
Oesophagitis may be acute or chronic.

Acute oesophagitis is more common in immuno-compromised individuals, for example in HIV infection.

Oral and oesophageal candidiasis are common in AIDS patients and may cause dysphagia or retrosternal discomfort. They give rise to white plaques with haemorrhagic margins.

Herpes simplex and cytomegalovirus may also cause focal or diffuse ulceration of the gut. The simplex ulceration is more common at the upper and lower ends of the gastrointestinal tract, cytomegalovirus lesions are more common in the bowel, but either may affect any part of the tract from the mouth to the anus.

Acute oesophagitis may also be caused by the deliberate or accidental swallowing of corrosive substances.

Chronic oesophagitis is most commonly caused by reflux of acidic gastric content through the lower oesophageal sphincter (reflux oesophagitis).

The squamous mucosa of the lower oesophagus is not designed to cope with acid. Reflux causes injury to, and desquamation of, oesophageal cells.

Normally the cells shed from the surface of the epithelium are replaced by basal cells which mature and move up through the layers of squamous epithelium. Increased loss due to reflux is compensated for by a proliferation of basal cells (basal cell hyperplasia) (Fig. 9.2).

Basal cell hyperplasia in reflux oesophagitis causes

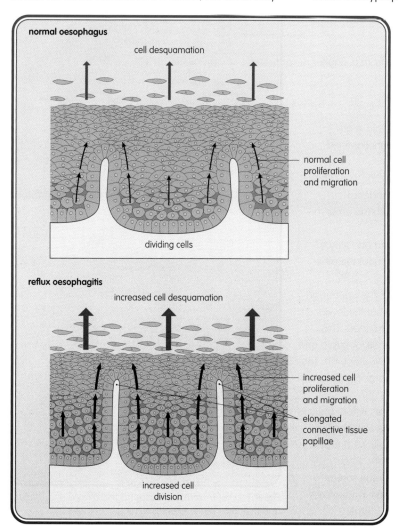

Fig. 9.2 Cell desquamation and proliferation in the normal oesophagus and in reflux oesophagitis.

an elongation of the connective tissue papillae.

A small number of inflammatory cells are usually present and are a normal response to cell injury.

In severe reflux, the increased number of cells lost may not be replaced and ulceration, haemorrhage and perforation may occur, with healing by fibrosis and the formation of a stricture.

A Barrett's oesophagus may result from prolonged reflux and is described below.

Lesions associated with motor dysfunction

Motor dysfunction may be caused by:

- A failure of innervation.
- A defect in the muscle wall of the oesophagus.
- A combination of the two above.

Achalasia

This is an uncommon condition in which the coordinated peristalsis of the lower oesophagus and relaxation of the lower oesophageal sphincter, allowing the passage of food and liquids into the stomach, is lost. The aetiology is unknown.

It may occur as a result of damage to the smooth muscle, for example in scleroderma. It may also be caused by damage to the innervation of the oesophagus, for example in Chagas' disease, where trypanosomes invade the wall of the oesophagus, damaging the intrinsic plexuses.

Diagnosis is by radiography. A barium swallow shows dilatation of the oesophagus, with a beak deformity at the lower end, caused by a failure of relaxation of the lower oesophageal sphincter. Manometry shows an absence of peristalsis and a high-resting lower oesophageal sphincter pressure.

Treatment consists of dilatation of the lower oesophageal sphincter or surgery (Heller's operation) to weaken the sphincter. Reflux is common after surgery unless a fundoplication is also performed.

Oesophageal varices

Oesophageal varices are dilated veins at the junction of the oesophagus and the stomach (the site of portal systemic anastomosis). They are found in patients with cirrhosis of the liver and portal hypertension.

The enlarged veins protrude into the lumen of the oesophagus (visible on endoscopy) and may burst, resulting in haematemesis which may rapidly be fatal.

Prognosis following bleeding varices is poor, particularly when jaundice, ascites, encephalopathy, or hypoalbuminaemia may be present. Overall, mortality from a first bleed from oesophageal varices is 40–70%.

Cirrhosis carries a particularly bad prognosis as clotting factors made in the liver are reduced as a result of cirrhotic damage.

Cirrhosis is the cause of 90% of varices in the UK, but *Schistosomiasis (bilharzia)* is the major worldwide cause.

Never biopsy anything protruding into the lower oesophagus if there is any possibility it may be an oesophageal varix. Massive haemorrhage and haematemesis may occur, resulting in the patient's death.

Hiatus hernia

Hiatus hernia occurs when part of the stomach protrudes through the diaphragm. Such hernias may be sliding or rolling. Sliding hernias are much more common.

They are almost always acquired as a result of the loss of diaphragmatic muscular tone with age.

Diverticula

Diverticula (out-pouchings) may form in the proximal or distal oesophagus, particularly where there is a disorder of motor function in the oesophagus.

A pharyngeal pouch (Killian's dehiscence or Zenker's diverticulum) may form in the area of weakness between the thyropharyngeus and cricopharyngeus (the two parts of the inferior pharyngeal constrictor) (Fig. 2.6). Killian's dehiscence is more common in elderly men. Food may collect in the pouch and later be regurgitated, and dysphagia is common. A swelling may be felt in the neck.

Diagnosis is by barium swallow and treatment is surgical.

A traction diverticulum may form in the lower oesophagus, particularly where fibrosis of the lower oesophagus has occurred.

Mallory–Weiss syndrome

Mallory–Weiss syndrome is haematemesis from a tear at the gastro-oesophageal junction. It is caused by prolonged retching or coughing and a sudden increase in intra-abdominal pressure. It is most common in alcoholics.

Neoplastic disease

As in other parts of the body, neoplasms of the oesophagus may be classified as malignant or benign.

Barrett's oesophagus

Barrett's oesophagus is a premalignant condition resulting from prolonged reflux of the acid contents of the the stomach into the oesophagus through an incompetent lower oesophageal sphincter. It occurs in approximately 11% of symptomatic cases of reflux.

Normally the epithelium of the lower oesophagus is squamous but in cases of prolonged injury the normal epithelium may be replaced by columnar epithelium (a metaplastic change).

This is believed to occur when prolonged injury to the lower oesophagus causes ulceration. Pluripotent stem cells form a replacement epithelium. However, because acid contents are refluxing into the oesophagus, the pH in the area is lower than normal. This causes the stem cells to differentiate into the sort of epithelium seen in areas of low pH—gastric epithelium (found in the cardiac or fundic regions of the stomach) or intestinal epithelium.

Gastric and intestinal epithelium are more resistant to injury from the refluxing acid.

Adenocarcinoma is 30–40 times more likely to occur in a Barrett's oesophagus than in the normal oesophagus.

Benign tumours

These are much less common than malignant tumours and account for only about 5% of all neoplasms of the oesophagus.

Leiomyomas are the most common of benign tumours but fibromas, lipomas, haemangiomas, neurofibromas, and lymphangiomas may also arise.

Benign squamous papilloma

This is an epithelial tumour and may also occur as a result of human papilloma virus (HPV) infection. There are over 70 different HPVs and their role in the causation of cancer is becoming increasingly well understood. For example, HPV 16, 18, and 31 cause particularly aggressive carcinoma of the cervix.

Malignant tumours

The most common type of tumour is a squamous carcinoma (Fig 9.3) which starts as an ulcer (which may haemorrhage) and then develops into an annular lesion constricting the oesophagus and causing dysphagia—the most common presenting complaint.

Adenocarcinomas may be found in the lower one-third of the oesophagus, usually developing from a Barrett's oesophagus.

Unfortunately, by the time symptoms are present, the carcinoma has usually spread and the 5-year survival is only about 5%.

Causes of squamous carcinoma of the oesophagus
Oesophageal disorders chronic oesophagitis achalasia Plummer–Vinson syndrome
Predisposing factors coeliac disease ectodermal dysplasia, epidermolysis bullosa tylosis genetic predisposition
Dietary vitamin deficiency (A, C, riboflavin, thiamine, pyridoxine) mineral deficiency (zinc, molybdenum) fungal contamination of foodstuffs nitrites/nitrosamines in foodstuffs
Lifestyle alcohol smoking

Fig. 9.3 Causes of squamous carcinoma of the oesophagus.

- List the more common congenital abnormalities that may arise in the oesophagus. How do these present and how are they treated?
- What are the causes and consequences of oesophagitis?
- What lesions are associated with motor dysfunction in the gastrointestinal tract?
- Summarize the causes and (potentially disastrous) consequences of oesophageal varices.
- Describe the sequences leading to metaplastic change in a Barrett's oesophagus.
- What other neoplasms may occur in the oesophagus?

THE STOMACH

Congenital abnormalities
Diaphragmatic hernia
The diaphragm develops from:

- The septum transversum.
- The pleuroperitoneal membranes.
- The dorsal mesentery of the oesophagus.
- Muscular components of the body wall.

The pleuroperitoneal folds appear at the beginning of week 5 and fuse with the septum transversum and the oesophageal mesentery in week 7, separating the abdominal and thoracic cavities. This primitive diaphragm then fuses with a ring of muscle that develops from the body wall.

If there is incomplete fusion, the contents of the abdomen may push up into the pleural cavity, forming a diaphragmatic hernia (usually on the left side), pushing the heart forwards and compressing the lungs.

The incidence is about 1/4000 births and treatment is surgical.

Pyloric stenosis
Pyloric stenosis occurs in about 1/4000 births, most commonly in first-born males.

Female babies with pyloric stenosis are more likely to give birth themselves to affected children, suggesting a genetic factor, and 5–10% of babies with pyloric stenosis have a parent who was affected (usually a mother).

Stenosis is caused by hypertrophy of the circular muscles of the pylorus that obstructs the flow of contents from the stomach into the duodenum, and typically presents 4–6 weeks after birth with projectile vomiting within half an hour of a feed. There is no bile in the vomit because the obstruction is above the ampulla of Vater.

Peristaltic waves are visible in the child, a sausage-shaped mass (the enlarged pylorus) can be felt in the right upper quadrant, and the hypertrophied pyloric muscle can be observed using ultrasonography. Treatment is by surgery.

Always ask whether vomit contains bile. Bile joins the intestinal contents at the ampulla of Vater—vomit will only contain bile if the lesion is below the ampulla.

Stenosis may also be acquired in adult life, usually caused by scarring from peptic ulceration or because of malignancy obstructing the outflow. It is diagnosed by barium meal and gastroscopy.

Inflammation of the stomach
This may be acute or chronic.

Acute gastritis
Acute gastritis is almost always caused by drugs (especially NSAIDs such as aspirin) or by alcohol

causing chemical exfoliation of the surface epithelial cells and decreasing the secretion of protective mucus.

The toxic chemicals often inhibit prostaglandins—the latter cause pain but also have a protective function in the stomach.

The degree of damage depends on the amount of toxic substance and the time it has been there. It also varies from erosions (a partial loss of mucosa) to ulcers (involving the full thickness of the mucosa).

Helicobacter pylori has been implicated in both acute and chronic gastritis. Helicobacter pylori was first isolated from the human stomach in 1983 and has been implicated in acute and chronic gastritis, gastric and duodenal ulcers, and non-ulcer dyspepsia. It is found beneath the mucus barrier, where it is protected from the low pH, but may be eradicated by triple therapy.

Vitamin B_{12} is needed for the synthesis of DNA. Normally the nucleus is extruded from red blood cells before they are released into the peripheral blood from the bone marrow. In vitamin B_{12} deficiency, however, maturation of the nucleus is delayed relative to the cytoplasm and macrocytic blood cells are seen in the peripheral blood.

Chronic gastritis

Chronic inflammatory changes in the mucosa cause atrophy and epithelial metaplasia (which may develop into carcinoma). It is classified as:

- Type A (autoimmune).
- Type B (bacterial infection).
- Type C (reflux) gastritis.

Other, less common forms exist, most notably lymphocytic, eosinophilic, and granulomatous gastritis.

Type A gastritis

Inflammation is caused by antibodies against gastric parietal cells and intrinsic factor binding sites. Intrinsic factor is needed to absorb vitamin B_{12}. In its absence, macrocytic anaemia develops once liver stores of vitamin B_{12} have been used up.

Pernicious anaemia occurs where autoimmune gastritis and macrocytic anaemia exist together. It is associated with other autoimmune diseases such as thyroid disease, vitiligo, Addison's disease, and myxoedema. Pernicious anaemia predisposes to carcinoma of the stomach.

Before treatment became available, subacute combined degeneration of the spinal cord was a late complication resulting in damage to the posterior and lateral columns of the cord and peripheral neuritis.

Type B gastritis

Helicobacter pylori infection is present in about 90% of cases of active chronic Type B gastritis. It provokes an acute inflammatory response and the release of proteases which destroy gastric glands and lead to atrophy.

Type B gastritis usually begins in the antrum but may cause atrophy, fibrosis, and metaplasia of the entire stomach.

Type C gastritis

This reflux gastritis is caused by regurgitation of duodenal contents into the stomach through the pylorus and is more common where pyloric or duodenal motility has been compromised.

It may present with dyspepsia and bilious vomiting.

Less common forms of gastritis

Lymphocytic gastritis is so named because of numerous mature lymphocytes in the gastric epithelium.

In eosinophilic gastritis large numbers of eosinophils are found, possibly as a result of an allergic reaction to an antigen in the diet.

Granulomatous gastritis may be seen in granulomatous disease, such as Crohn's and sarcoidosis. Gastric granulomas may also be found in the absence of systemic granulomatous disease, however. Complications include haemorrhage and perforation.

Ulceration

Ulcers arise where damaging factors overwhelm the natural protection of the lining of the gastrointestinal tract It may result from a decrease in protective factors, an increase in damaging factors, or both.

Peptic ulcers are chronic lesions occurring in the upper gastrointestinal tract where gastric acid and pepsin are present and are caused by hyperacidity, *H. pylori* infection, reflux of duodenal contents, NSAIDs, genetic factors (first-degree relatives of people with duodenal ulcers are three times more likely to develop them themselves), and smoking.

Peptic ulcers are most common in:
- The duodenal cap.
- The stomach (especially at the junction of the antrum and body).
- The distal oesophagus, particularly in a Barrett's oesophagus.
- A Meckel's diverticulum (particularly where ectopic gastric mucosa is present).
- Where a gastroenterostomy has been performed.

Like ulcers elsewhere, they may haemorrhage (leading to blood loss and anaemia), perforate, or heal by fibrosis, this causing a stricture.

Duodenal ulcers are commoner amongst blood group O, increase in incidence up to the age of 35 years, and 95% are associated with *H. pylori.*

Gastric ulcers may occur in response to acute gastritis, treatment with NSAIDs, extreme hyperacidity (Zollinger–Ellison syndrome), severe stress and trauma [e.g. following burns (Curling's ulcer)], and ischaemia of the gastric mucosa.

They are commoner in blood group A, increase in incidence with age, and about 70% are associated with *H. pylori* infection.

Zollinger–Ellison syndrome is a rare condition due to gastrin-secreting tumours causing excess acid production. It can lead to acute ulcers in the antrum, duodenum and, in severe cases the jejunum.

Gastric varices

These are uncommon but may occur in submucosal veins below the gastro-oesophageal junction, as a result of portal hypertension.

Like oesophageal varices, they should never be biopsied or they will haemorrhage with potentially fatal consequences.

Hypertrophic gastropathy

Hyperplasia of mucosal epithelial cells causes enlargement of the rugae (which may be mistaken for a neoplasm on radiographs) and an increase in acid secretion. It may be caused by excess gastrin in Zollinger–Ellison syndrome.

Hypertrophy also occurs in Ménétrièr's disease, where gastric glands atrophy while mucosal cells become hyperplastic. Less severe forms are known as Schindler's disease.

Hyperplasia of the parietal and chief cells is known as hypertrophic hypersecretory gastropathy.

Neoplastic disease

As always, neoplasms may be malignant or benign. They are described according to their tissue of origin.

Benign neoplasms
These include:
- Hyperplastic polyps (regenerative polyps)—elongated gastric pits separated by fibrous tissue, usually found in association with *H. pylori* infection in the antrum.
- Simple fundic polyps (glandular cystic dilation in the body of the stomach).
- Hamartomas (most commonly seen in Peutz–Jeghers syndrome).
- Ectopic (heterotopic) pancreatic tissue.
- Leiomyomas, arising from smooth muscle, which may bleed from ulceration.
- Adenomas—these make up 5–10% of polypoid lesions in the stomach and may contain proliferative dysplastic epithelium with the potential for malignant transformation. They are much more common in the colon but, if present in the stomach, are usually in the antrum. They may be pedunculated or sessile, are more common in males and increase in incidence with increasing age.

Malignant neoplasms
Most gastric carcinomas are adenocarcinomas and many arise following gastritis. Lymphomas, carcinoid and malignant spindle-cell tumours also occur but much less frequently.

A number of conditions are premalignant, including chronic peptic ulcers, pernicious anaemia (a three-fold increase in risk), Ménétrièr's disease, and post-gastrectomy (carcinomas often develop 15–20 years

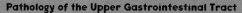
after surgery). The incidence is slightly higher in blood group A.

Genetic factors may be involved but a decrease in gastric acid secretion and corresponding increase in bacteria (which are normally killed by gastric acid), particularly *H. pylori,* are common aetiological factors.

Bacteria reduce nitrates to nitrites and increase the production of carcinogenic nitrosamines, and diets high in nitrates predispose to carcinoma. The incidence is high in Japan but much lower amongst Japanese living in the USA.

Presentation is often late, with a correspondingly poor prognosis.

Four different appearances may be recognized:
- Malignant ulcers with raised, everted edges.
- Polypoid tumours.
- Colloid tumours (which appear gelatinous).
- Linitis plastica (leather bottle stomach—so named because the stomach becomes small, thick and contracted).

Carcinomas may spread through:
- The lymphatic system.
- The blood stream.
- Direct spread locally.
- Transfusion through a body cavity (transcoelomically).

Secondary carcinoma may develop in the ovary from peritoneal seeding (Krukenberg's tumour).

A patient with gastric carcinoma may develop acanthosis nigricans—abnormal pigmentation of the skin of the axilla, a condition also associated with breast carcinoma.

Never ignore it if one of the supraclavicular lymph nodes on the left side of the body is enlarged. Lymph from the cardiac region of the stomach drains to these nodes and they may become enlarged (Virchow's nodes) in gastric carcinoma (Troisier's sign).

- **List the more common congenital abnormalities that may occur in the stomach.**
- **Describe the causes and consequences of acute and chronic gastritis.**
- **Describe the causes and consequences of peptic ulceration.**
- **Why are gastric varices important?**
- **Write short notes on gastric hypertrophy.**
- **What are the more common neoplasms of the stomach?**

10. Pathology of the Liver, Biliary Tract, and Pancreas

Patterns of hepatic injury

The liver is essential to life and has a remarkable capacity to regenerate. Damage from whatever cause (apart from trauma) results in similar pathology, usually an inflammatory reaction, some attempt at regeneration and, if unsuccessful, cell death.

Damage may be acute or chronic, and the same agents may result in either.

The major causes of acute liver failure are:

- Viral infections.
- Excess alcohol.
- Adverse drug reactions.
- Biliary obstruction (often due to gall stones).

These may all produce diffuse injury to the liver. The pattern of injury may help identify the cause (Fig. 10.1).

Bridging necrosis is necrosis of a band stretching from the portal tract to the central vein and is a feature of severe hepatitis. Cirrhosis may develop.

Piecemeal necrosis is less severe and simply means death in a small area around the portal tract from active hepatitis due to a variety of causes.

Apoptotic necrosis (Councilman's bodies) is seen in acute viral hepatitis and means necrosis of individual liver cells. It is even less severe than piecemeal necrosis—complete recovery with no long term sequelae is the norm. Apoptosis comes from the Greek for 'falling away'.

Hydropic necrosis is seen where osmosis causes hepatocytes to swell up and rupture.

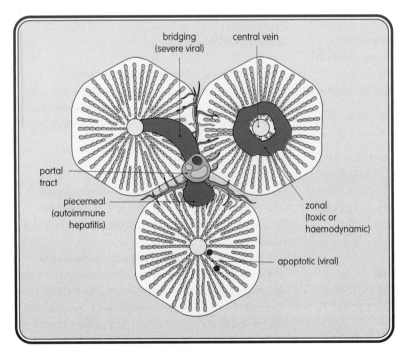

Fig. 10.1 Patterns of hepatic necrosis. (Adapted from: Underwood, JCE. *General and systematic pathology*, 2nd ed. New York:Churchill Livingstone; 1996.)

In toxic or haemodynamic necrosis concentric bands of necrosis are seen around the central veins (an example of zonal necrosis—necrosis confined to a particular region of the lobule). It occurs in cardiac failure, stasis of hepatic venous blood and paracetamol poisoning. Poorly stained, mummified hepatocytes are a feature of ischaemic (coagulative) necrosis. Mid-zonal necrosis is rare, but is seen in yellow fever.

Panacinar necrosis (submassive necrosis) is necrosis affecting the entire acinus—immediate death may result. Massive necrosis affects the entire liver.

Degeneration is less serious than necrosis and is characterized by swollen, oedematous hepatocytes (ballooning degeneration) with irregularly clumped cytoplasm and large clear spaces. Diffuse, foamy, swollen hepatocytes suggest cholestasis.

In inflammation (hepatitis), an influx of acute or chronic inflammatory cells may occur secondary to hepatocellular necrosis.

Regeneration is the norm following injury; hepatocyte proliferation results in a thickening of the cords radiating out from the central vein. The architecture may be disturbed unless the connective tissue framework remained intact.

Fibrosis from inflammation or a direct toxic insult may occur around the portal tracts, the central vein or within the spaces of Disse, disrupting the normal architecture and interfering with liver function. In severe cases cirrhosis results.

Cirrhosis

Cirrhosis is a diffuse and irreversible process resulting in architectural disturbance, characterized by nodules of hepatocytes separated by intervening fibrosis. It may be:
- Micronodular (nodules less than 3 mm in diameter).
- Macronodular (diameters greater than 3 mm),
- Mixed (both forms coexisting).

Architectural disturbance may lead to liver failure (Fig. 10.2), portal hypertension or liver cell carcinoma. The causes of cirrhosis are summarized in Fig. 10.3.

Portal hypertension

Normally the pressure in the hepatic portal vein is about 7 mmHg, but this is increased in portal hypertension. The causes of portal hypertension may be classified as:
- Prehepatic.
- Hepatic.

- Posthepatic.

Prehepatic causes include:
- Portal vein thrombosis.
- Splenomegaly.
- Arteriovenous fistula.

Hepatic causes include:
- Cirrhosis.
- Schistosomiasis.
- Sarcoidosis.
- Miliary tuberculosis.
- Massive fatty change.
- Nodular regenerative hyperplasia.

The main posthepatic causes are constrictive pericarditis, Budd–Chiari syndrome (a rare condition caused by hepatic vein obstruction, sometimes associated with the oral contraceptive) and severe right-sided heart failure.

Cirrhosis results in disruption of the normal liver architecture, which increases hepatic vascular resistance and causes intrahepatic arteriovenous shunting. It is the commonest cause of portal hypertension in the UK; worldwide, most cases are caused by viral hepatitis.

Complications of portal hypertension

Oesophageal varices may form and rupture with fatal consequences. Enlargement of veins at other sites of portosystemic anastomoses may also occur forming caput medusae around the umbilicus, and haemorrhoids.

Ascites (an abnormal collection of fluid in the peritoneal cavity) may form due to hypoproteinaemia and increased intravascular pressure in capillaries. Clinically it may be detected by shifting dullness and a fluid thrill.

It should be managed by reducing sodium intake and increasing renal excretion with diuretics. Fluid may be removed by paracentesis (via a needle through the abdominal wall). However, there is a risk that fluid will reaccumulate in the peritoneal cavity at the expense of the systemic circulation. This leads to shock, so intravenous albumin should also be given.

A peritoneovenous shunt (a catheter from the peritoneal cavity into the internal jugular vein) may be used to return the fluid to the systemic circulation.

Consequences of liver failure	
Feature	Explanation
oedema	decreased synthesis of albumin causing a reduced oncotic pressure gradient across the capillary wall and increased passage of fluid
portal hypertension	disturbed blood flow through the liver
haematemesis	ruptured oesophageal varices
coma	brain oedema and reduced elimination of false neurotransmitters
ascites	hypoalbuminaemia, portal hypertension and secondary hyperaldosteronism
spider naevi and gynaecomastia	reduced metabolism and excretion of oestrogen
purpura and bleeding	reduced synthesis of clotting factors
increased infections	reduced phagocytosis by Kupffer's cells in the liver

Fig. 10.2 Consequences of liver failure.

Portosystemic anastomoses

These occur at four sites in the body:
- The lower end of the oesophagus, between the left gastric and the azygos veins.
- The lower part of the anal canal, between the superior and inferior rectal veins.
- The umbilical region of the anterior abdominal wall, between the epigastric veins and the paraumbilical veins in the falciform ligament of the liver.
- The bare areas of the gastrointestinal tract and its related organs, e.g. veins between the bare area of the liver and the diaphragm.

These anastomoses may enlarge if the portal vein is obstructed by a thrombus or the venous flow through the liver is impeded by cirrhosis.

Enlargement may result in oesophageal varices, haemorrhoids, and caput medusae.

Haemorrhoids are the commonest cause of rectal bleeding and may also cause pruritus ani. If mild, they need no treatment. Diagnosis is by proctoscopy.

Oesophageal varices are diagnosed by endoscopy.

Causes of cirrhosis
unknown (30% of cases)
alcohol (25% of cases)
hepatitis B and C
iron overload (haemochromatosis)
gall stones
autoimmune liver disease
Wilson's disease (leading to deposition of copper in the liver)
α_1-antitrypsin deficiency
type IV glycogenesis
galactosaemia
tyrosinaemia
biliary cholestasis
Budd–Chiari syndrome
drugs

Fig. 10.3 Causes of cirrhosis.

Splenomegaly

Splenomegaly is the term used to describe an enlarged spleen. It may be massive (extending into the right iliac fossa) or moderate and has a large number of causes.

Normally the spleen measures about $2 \times 3 \times 5$ inches, weighs about 7 oz (200 g), and is found between the ninth and eleventh ribs. It plays an important role in immune defence and the removal of effete blood cells.

Portal hypertension may cause moderate congestive

splenomegaly, as may thrombosis of the extrahepatic portion of the portal vein or of the splenic vein.

A raised pressure in the inferior vena cava may be transmitted to the spleen through the portal vein, and is a cause of posthepatic splenomegaly. Ascites and hepatomegaly are also usually present.

More common causes of posthepatic splenomegaly include decompensated right-sided heart failure and pulmonary or tricuspid valve disease.

Splenomegaly may cause abdominal discomfort and an enlarged spleen may rupture following minor trauma. This is easily detected on examination as the spleen is dull to percussion.

Jaundice and cholestasis

Jaundice is present when plasma levels of bilirubin exceed 35 μmol/L and is characterized by yellow skin, sclera and mucosa. The colour of the sclera is the most sensitive indicator but must be examined in a good light!

Jaundice may be:
- Prehepatic (haemolytic).
- Intrahepatic (hepatocellular).
- Posthepatic (obstructive or cholestatic) (Fig. 10.4).

Pre-hepatic jaundice

Bilirubin is formed from the breakdown of haemoglobin and normally it is conjugated by hepatocytes when it reaches the liver. Unconjugated bilirubin only remains in the circulation when the liver is unable to conjugate all the bilirubin that is delivered to it. Unconjugated bilirubin is not soluble and cannot be excreted in the urine.

The liver's capacity to conjugate bilirubin may be exceeded when:
- Too much haemoglobin is being broken down (haemolysis).
- Hepatocytes are unable to take up bilirubin and conjugate it (Gilbert syndrome).
- Hepatocytes are able to take up bilirubin but defective in an enzyme needed to conjugate it (Crigler–Najjar syndrome).

Hepatocellular jaundice

In hepatocellular jaundice, there is damage to the hepatocytes and, usually, the intrahepatic biliary tree. This leads to increased levels of both unconjugated and conjugated bilirubin.

Post-hepatic jaundice

Normally, conjugated bilirubin passes from the liver to the gall bladder where it is stored and then released into the duodenum.

In the gut, intestinal flora convert it first to urobilinogen (some of which is reabsorbed and excreted in the urine) and then to stercobilinogen, which is excreted in the faeces (giving them their brown colour).

Causes of jaundice and diagnostic tests		
Type of jaundice	**Tests**	**Causes**
prehepatic	urine (no bilirubin in it) colour of urine and faeces may be variable in Gilbert syndrome	haemolysis ineffective erythropoiesis Gilbert syndrome Crigler–Najjar syndrome
hepatic	clotting time, ALT and AST all raised because of hepatocellular damage	viral infection (hepatitis A, B, C or E, Epstein–Barr) Weil's disease autoimmune diseases drugs cirrhosis Wilson's disease Dubin–Johnson syndrome Rotor syndrome
posthepatic	urine (dark with bilirubin, but no urobilinogen in it) γ-GT and AP (canalicular enzymes) both raised because of damage to the biliary tree pale stools	primary biliary cirrhosis drugs gall stones carcinoma (of head of pancreas or bile duct) lymphoma (with enlarged nodes in porta hepatis)

Fig. 10.4 Causes of jaundice and diagnostic tests. AST = serum aspartate aminotransferase; ALT = serum alanine aminotransferase.

In post-hepatic jaundice, the passage of conjugated bilirubin through the biliary tree is blocked and it leaks into the circulation instead. It is soluble and excreted in the urine (making it dark). However, the faeces are deprived of their stercobilinogen and are pale (Fig. 10.4).

Further investigations
Ultrasonography, endoscopic retrograde cholangio-pancreatography, liver biopsy, or laparotomy may be necessary.

Hepatic failure
Hepatic encephalopathy
This is a metabolic failure resulting in damage to the central nervous system and neuromuscular system caused by shunting of blood around the liver (as a result of cirrhosis or after portocaval anastomosis) and loss of hepatocyte function.

It may occur in both chronic and acute liver failure. It results in the exposure of the brain to abnormal metabolites, causing oedema and astrocyte reaction.

Normally the liver eliminates the toxic nitrogenous products of gut bacteria. In liver failure, their elimination is reduced and some of them act as false transmitters (mimicking the normal neurotransmitters of the central nervous system). This results in central nervous system disturbances.

Symptoms include disturbances in consciousness ranging from minor changes in behaviour and confusion to coma and death. Asterixis and fluctuating neurological signs (such as rigid limbs and hyperreflexia) may be found on examination.

Hepatorenal syndrome
This is the combination of renal failure in a previously normal kidney and severe liver disease. However, kidney function improves dramatically if the liver failure is reversed.

Renal failure is caused by a drop in renal blood flow, causing a fall in urine output and increased retention of sodium by the kidney. It may be fatal.

Liver transplantation
Liver transplantation is increasingly used in the treatment of:
• Acute and chronic liver disease.
• Alcoholic liver disease (provided the patient has

given up drinking and is well motivated).
• Primary biliary cirrhosis.
• Chronic hepatitis B and C.
• Primary metabolic disease (e.g. Wilson's disease).
• Other conditions including sclerosing cholangitis.

Absolute contraindications are AIDS infection, active sepsis outside the hepatobiliary tree, and metastatic malignancy.

Most organs are taken from cadavers but a relative may donate a single lobe to an infant.

The liver is less aggressively rejected than other organs but early and reversible, or late and irreversible rejection may occur. Cyclosporin has proved useful but

- Summarize the pathological processes that can occur in the liver. What medical conditions result from these processes?
- Describe the patterns of hepatic injury.
- Give the causes, consequences, and classification of cirrhosis.
- Give the causes, consequences, and classification of portal hypertension.
- Describe the causes and management of ascites.
- Describe the causes, classification, and diagnosis of jaundice.
- What are the causes of cholestasis?
- Write short notes on hepatic encephalopathy and the hepatorenal syndrome.
- What are the indications for liver transplantation? What are the risks?

most patients require immunosuppression for life and are therefore susceptible to opportunistic infection.

DISORDERS OF METABOLISM

Haemochromatosis (bronze diabetes)

Primary haemochromatosis is an inherited recessive disorder characterized by the absorption of too much iron which then accumulates in the liver, pancreas, heart, and (to a lesser extent) in other organs, especially those of the endocrine system.

A gene defect on chromosome 6 causes excess absorption of iron from the small intestine even when the iron-binding protein, transferrin, is fully saturated. Iron stores may be 10–15 times greater than normal levels, rising from about 4 g to as much as 60 g.

Heterozygotes show increased absorption but to a lesser degree than homozygotes.

Symptoms are rare in women of child-bearing age as menstrual losses and pregnancy compensate for the excess iron absorption.

The presenting complaint in men is often loss of libido and a decrease in the size of the testes, but diabetes occurs in two-thirds of cases.

Other signs and symptoms include:
- Liver enlargement.
- Fibrosis and cirrhosis.
- Bronze discoloration of the skin.
- Diabetes mellitus resulting from insufficient production of insulin by the pancreas.
- Cardiac arrythmias and other heart disorders.

Untreated, the condition may lead to liver failure and liver cancer as iron is deposited in hepatocytes (as haemosiderin) and then in Kupffer cells, bile duct epithelium, and portal tract connective tissue.

Diagnosis is by blood tests (which characteristically show raised ferritin) and liver biopsy showing heavy deposits of iron (as haemosiderin) in hepatocytes.

Treatment is by phlebotomy, once or twice a week until iron levels return to normal, and then three or four times a year.

Secondary haemochromatosis may result from iron overload (e.g. after repeated blood transfusions) or from excess iron absorption (e.g. in congenital haemolytic anaemias).

Wilson's disease

Wilson's disease is a rare, inherited disorder in which copper accumulates in the liver and the basal ganglia of the brain. It may be released into the general circulation from the liver and cause episodes of haemolysis.

Signs and symptoms may appear in patients at any age from about 5 years to 50 years and include hepatic and neurological abnormalities.

Faint, brown (Kayser–Fleischer) rings may appear in the eye at the limbus (the junction of the cornea and sclera); they are almost diagnostic.

Diagnosis is by measurement of the copper-containing protein caeruloplasmin in the blood (it is low in Wilson's disease) and by liver biopsy showing an excess of copper.

Treatment is with penicillamine, a chelating agent that binds to copper and enables it to be excreted.

Prognosis depends on the stage at which treatment is begun. If started early, before significant amounts of copper have been deposited, prognosis is good.

α_1-antitrypsin deficiency

α_1-antitrypsin is a serum protein that is produced in the liver and has anti-protease effects.

The gene controlling its production is located on chromosome 14 and a number of variants exist.

Homozygous deficiency occurs in about 1 in 5000 births.

Symptoms include emphysema in about 75% of homozygotes and liver cirrhosis in approximately 10%.

Emphysema is a lung disease characterized by enlargement of alveolar walls and destruction of elastin in the walls. Normally, α_1-antitrypsin inhibits neutrophil elastase in the lungs and prevents the elastase destroying the connective tissue of alveolar walls; in α_1-antitrypsin deficiency this protection is lost.

Liver disease only occurs with mutations, such as the Z allele, where α_1-antitrypsin accumulates by polymerization in hepatocytes, shown by PAS (Periodic Acid–Schiff) positive intracellular globules on liver biopsy.

Diagnosis is by measurement of serum α_1-antitrypsin (it is low in deficiency) and by liver biopsy.

Treatment is symptomatic—there is as yet no treatment for the underlying cause. Patients should be advised to stop smoking.

Reye's syndrome

Reye's syndrome is a rare disorder characterized by brain and liver damage following an upper respiratory tract infection, chickenpox or influenza and almost always occurs in children under 15 years of age.

It has been linked to aspirin (in many but not all cases) and children under 12 years of age should not be given this drug (paracetamol is a safer analgesic for this age group).

Symptoms start as the child is recovering from the underlying infection and include vomiting, lethargy, memory loss, disorientation, or delirium. Seizures, deepening coma, disturbed cardiac rhythm, and cessation of breathing may occur because of swelling of the brain; jaundice may result from liver damage.

Microvesicular steatosis occurs in the liver, with inflammation and necrosis, and swelling of the mitochondria. The liver is enlarged and hypoglycaemia may occur.

Treatment is with corticosteroids and mannitol (to reduce brain swelling) and dialysis or transfusion to correct chemical imbalances resulting from liver damage.

Prognosis is worse in those whose symptoms include seizures, coma, or cessation of breathing. Brain damage or death may occur as a result of brain herniation or hypoxia. Overall mortality is about 20%.

Neonatal hepatitis

Neonatal hepatitis is the end-result of a range of injurious processes including:

- Congenital infection with rubella.
- Cytomegalovirus and toxoplasmosis.
- α_1-antitrypsin deficiency.
- Tyrosinosis.
- Cystic fibrosis.
- Storage disorders.
- Galactosaemia.

The histological picture may include giant cells and

○ List the effects of haemochromatosis, Wilson's disease, α_1-antitrypsin deficiency,

Reye's syndrome, and neonatal hepatitis.

cholestasis or hepatocellular necrosis and inflammatory infiltrates in the portal tracts and lobules.

Conjugated hyperbilirubinaemia is present.

The condition is often familial, inheritance being autosomal recessive.

INFECTIOUS AND INFLAMMATORY DISEASE

Viral hepatitis

This is a common cause of liver injury and may be caused by:

- Hepatitis virus A, B, C, D, E, or G.
- Cytomegalovirus (CMV).
- Epstein–Barr virus (EBV).
- Arboviruses (e.g. in yellow fever).

CMV, EBV, and yellow fever may cause general illness, but only subclinical hepatitis. However, liver function tests will be abnormal.

CMV, herpes simplex virus and varicella-zoster virus may cause hepatitis in the immunocompromised.

Rubella and CMV acquired *in utero* may lead to hepatitis. Enteroviruses and herpes simplex virus are causes of perinatal hepatitis. Acute viral hepatitis may be asymptomatic or symptomatic with or without jaundice and itching.

Asymptomatic infection is common particularly in hepatitis A acquired by children and more than 50% of those suffering from hepatitis B and C.

When symptoms occur, they are similar regardless of the virus responsible, typically a prodromal, non-specific flu-like or gastroenteritis-like illness occurs.

Hepatitis B infection may lead to arthritis or arthralgia with a rash (caused by immune complexes). Occasionally, fulminant hepatic failure may occur.

Infection with Hepatitis A and E do not result in chronic infection. Hepatitis A, C, D and E are all RNA viruses; hepatitis B is a DNA virus (Fig. 10.5).

Hepatitis A

This is an RNA virus found worldwide, especially where there is poor sanitation and hygiene, and is spread by the faecal–oral route through contaminated food and water. It may cause outbreaks and is very resistant to heat and disinfectant.

The incubation period is 2–6 weeks and infection

				Viral hepatitis				
Type	Virus	Spread	Incubation period	Carrier state/ chronic infection	Diagnosis of acute infection	Specific prevention	Treatment
A	hepatovirus	faecal–oral	2–6 weeks	no	HAV IgM	vaccine HNIG	n/a
B	hepadnavirus	contaminated blood and body fluids: • percutaneous • sexual • mother to baby	2–6 months	yes adults 5–10% neonates 70–90%	HBsAg HBeAg HBcIgM	vaccine, HBIG	α–interferon
C	pestivirus-like	contaminated blood and body fluids: • percutaneous • sexual • mother to baby	6–8 weeks	yes adults 60–90%	anti-HCV PCR	n/a	α–interferon
D	defective RNA virus coated with HBsAG	contaminated blood and body fluids: • percutaneous • sexual note: requires HBsAg for propagation and hepatotropism	n/a	yes	HD Ag HDV IgM	prevent HBV	n/a
E	calicivirus	faecal–oral	2–9 weeks	no	HEV IgG	n/a	n/a

Fig. 10.5 Viral hepatitis. HAV IgM = hepatitis A immunoglobulin m; HBsAg = hepatitis B surface antigen; HBeAg = hepatitis B e antigen; HBcIgM = hepatitis B core immunoglobulin M; anti-HCV = anti-hepatitis C virus; PCR = polymerase chain reaction; HD Ag = hepatitis D antigen; HDV IgM = hepatitis delta virus immunoglobulin; HEV IgG = hepatitis E virus immunoglobulin G; HBIG = hepatitis B immunoglobulin. (Redrawn with permission from: Dr. Tilzey, St. Thomas's Hospital, London.)

may be asymptomatic (as in most childhood infections) or cause gastroenteritis-like illness. Diagnosis is by virus-specific IgM. Neither carrier states nor chronic infections occur.

Hepatitis B
Infection with Hepatitis B may lead to a chronic carrier state, liver cancer, or cirrhosis.

Transmission is through contaminated blood or blood products, body fluids, sexual contact and vertical transmission from mother to baby.

It is also secreted in breast milk.

It is found worldwide, especially in South East Asia, China, and tropical Africa (areas of high endemicity).

Eastern Europe, Central and South America, and the Mediterranean are areas of intermediate endemicity.

Areas of low endemicity include Northern Europe,

North America, and Australia; infection in these areas is associated with high-risk activity (intravenous drug use, male homosexual contact, or the use of blood products by haemophiliacs).

Incubation is 2–6 months and over 50% of cases are asymptomatic.

Of infected adults, 90–95% recover completely and become immune, the remaining 5–10% become carriers, but infants infected perinatally have a worse prognosis, 70–90% become carriers.

Complications of chronic carriage include chronic, active hepatitis, cirrhosis, and hepatocellular carcinoma.

Carriers may have high, intermediate or low infectivity, depending on their serum antigens (Fig. 10.6). All carriers have surface antigen and anti-core antibody. Immune people have anti-surface and anti-core

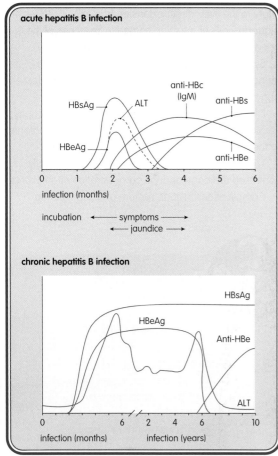

Fig. 10.6 Infectivity of carriers for acute hepatitis B infection and chronic hepatitis B infection. ALT = serum alanine aminotransferase; HBc = hepatitis B core; HBs = hepatitis B surface. (Redrawn with permission from: Kumar PJ, Clarke ML. *Clinical medicine* 3rd ed. London:Bailliere Tindall;1994.)

antibodies. The e-antigen determines infectivity: highly infectious carriers have e-antigen, carriers without e-antigen are intermediately infective, and anti-e antibody means a person has low infectivity. Carriers are defined as people in whom hepatitis B surface antigen has been detected for more than 6 months.

The risk of contracting hepatitis B from a needle contaminated with e-antigen positive (i.e. highly infectious) blood following a needlestick injury is 30%.

Hepatitis C
This is the major cause of post-transfusional non-A, non-B hepatitis.

It may be transmitted parenterally, from mother to baby or through sexual contact.

It is found worldwide, particularly in Japan, parts of South America, the Mediterranean, Africa, and the Middle East.

The UK, Northern Europe, and North America are areas of low seroprevalence and most infection is associated with high-risk activity (intravenous drug abuse and multiple blood transfusions).

The incubation period is 6–8 weeks and infection is asymptomatic in about 90% of cases. However, 60–90% of people become chronic carriers with a risk of developing chronic, active hepatitis, cirrhosis, or hepatocellular carcinoma.

Hepatitis D
This is a defective RNA virus that can only cause infection, and replicate in conjunction with, hepatitis B.

It has a worldwide distribution and is particularly prevalent in the Middle East, parts of Africa, and South America.

Infection in Northern Europe is mainly confined to high-risk behaviour (intravenous drug abuse and multiple blood transfusions). Transmission is mainly parenteral. Hepatitis D may infect at the same time as hepatitis B or infect someone already chronically infected with hepatitis B.

Hepatitis E
This is especially common in Asia, Africa, and the Middle East.

The first documented outbreak was in New Delhi in 1955 when 29 000 people became infected through faecal contamination of water—it is spread by the faecal–oral route. The incubation period is 2–9 weeks (usually 6 weeks).

High-risk age groups include those aged 15–40 and it has a 15–20% mortality rate in pregnant women. It does not lead to chronic infection.

Autoimmune hepatitis
This usually occurs in young and middle-aged women and is associated with other autoimmune diseases and with HLA-B8, HLA-DR3, and HLA-Dw3.

It may be asymptomatic, or present as acute hepatitis (25%).

Chronic autoimmune hepatitis was previously called lupoid hepatitis as a positive lupus erythematosus cell test was found in 50% of cases.

Of those affected, 70% have smooth muscle

antibodies and 80% antinuclear antibodies.

Primary biliary cirrhosis is another form of autoimmune liver disease and mitochondrial antibodies are found in the serum. Patients present with itching and jaundice, and slowly progress to cirrhosis.

Fulminant hepatitis

Fulminant means developing suddenly (from the Latin for 'lightning') and fulminant hepatitis is the development of hepatic encephalopathy within 2–3 weeks of the first symptoms of hepatic insufficiency. Viral infection is the most common cause.

The prognosis depends on the health and age of the patient, as in many other diseases.

Symptoms include those of liver failure, described in Fig. 10.2. However some of these (e.g. spider naevi and loss of body hair) take time to develop and may not be evident.

Hepatic encephalopathy that takes longer to develop is called subfulminant hepatitis.

Liver abscess

Liver abscesses are commoner in developing parts of the world.

In the past, they were relatively common complications of appendicitis or perforation of the gastrointestinal tract but improved management of these conditions has seen a decrease in the formation of abscesses.

They usually result from the spread of infection through the biliary tree (ascending cholangitis) carried from the gut in the portal system, from a penetrating injury to the liver, direct extension from a perinephric or other abscess or infection carried in branches of the hepatic artery.

Symptoms vary from general malaise to febrile jaundice with right upper quadrant pain and tender hepatomegaly.

Diagnosis is by ultrasonography, chest radiography, serological tests, and analysis of the aspirated contents of the abscess.

Treatment of large abscesses is by radiologically controlled drainage and the administration of antibiotics.

Complications include rupture and septicaemia.

- Which viruses may cause hepatitis?
- What are the associations of autoimmune hepatitis?
- Summarize the causes and consequences of cirrhosis and fulminant hepatitis.
- Detail the diagnosis, causes, and treatment of liver abscesses.

Abscesses are collections of pus, caused by an inflammatory reaction, often as a result of bacterial infection.

In general, 'if there is pus about, let it out'—treatment of abscesses in accessible parts of the body is usually by surgical drainage or aspiration.

ALCOHOL, DRUGS, AND TOXINS

Alcoholic liver disease

The pathogenesis of alcoholic liver disease is summarized in Fig. 10.7.

Hepatic steatosis (fatty liver)

Fatty liver is seen in a number of disorders, including alcoholic liver disease.

Normally, lipids from the diet or released from adipose tissue are transported to the liver where they are metabolized.

Alcohol is toxic and when it is drunk in excess, its metabolism becomes a priority and cellular energy is diverted towards this and away from other essential metabolic pathways, including the metabolism of fat in the liver.

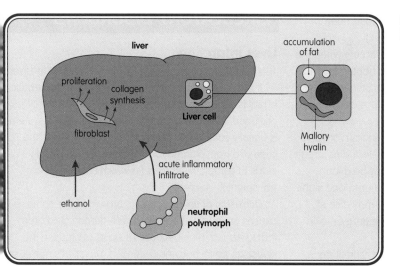

Fig. 10.7 Pathogenesis of alcoholic liver disease.

Fat then accumulates in the cytoplasm of liver cells, particularly in zone 3, the area adjacent to the central vein and furthest from the arterial supply.

In chronic ingestion of alcohol, the liver becomes a large greasy organ weighing as much as 5–6 kg.

If alcohol abuse continues, fibrosis and cirrhosis may occur but fatty change is reversible if alcohol intake is stopped (Fig. 10.8).

Alcoholic hepatitis

This is inflammation of the liver caused by alcohol ingestion.

Alcohol is directly cytotoxic at high concentration and cells swell with granular cytoplasm.

Intracytoplasmic aggregates of intermediate filaments (Mallory bodies) appear in the hepatocytes.

Neutrophils accumulate around damaged liver cells (especially those with Mallory bodies) and lymphocytes and macrophages enter the lobule.

Collagen deposition almost always ensues, especially with repeated bouts of high alcohol intake, and the risk of cirrhosis is greater than in purely fatty change.

Mallory bodies may also be seen in other conditions including primary biliary cirrhosis, Wilson's disease and hepatocellular carcinoma.

Alcoholic cirrhosis

Cirrhosis is the final and irreversible result of alcohol damage.

It usually develops over a number of years but may become apparent in as little as 2–3 years if associated with alcoholic hepatitis.

In the early stages, the liver is usually large and fatty but later it shrinks to become small, brown and almost non-fatty.

The hepatocytes attempt to regenerate but the normal architecture is disturbed and nodules form, separated by fibrous septa.

This disrupts the normal blood flow through the liver and it becomes less efficient at performing its functions.

Cirrhosis may result from a number of causes and is classified into micronodular and macronodular cirrhosis. Both forms may coexist in which case the cirrhosis is described as mixed. Alcohol abuse usually causes micronodular cirrhosis.

The major complications of cirrhosis include liver failure, portal hypertension and liver cell carcinoma.

Drugs and toxins

The liver plays a central role in the metabolism and excretion of drugs and toxins. At least 10% of all adverse reactions to drugs affect the liver.

Drug reactions may be predictable (occur in any individual if a sufficient dose is given) or unpredictable (idiosyncratic). Predictable drug reactions are also known as intrinsic reactions.

Drugs may cause damage to hepatocytes, indistinguishable from viral hepatitis; cholestasis by affecting bile production or excretion, or other liver dysfunction.

The mechanisms of drug-induced damage include direct toxicity to cells, the conversion of the drug to a toxic metabolite and a drug-induced autoimmune reaction.

Drug-induced autoimmunity usually occurs when the drug or one of its metabolites acts as a hapten (a small molecule that is not immunogenic on its own, but which can bind to another molecule and produce an immune response).

A careful drug history should be taken from anyone with signs or symptoms of liver disease, including drugs taken many months before as there may be a long delay between the administration of the drug and signs of any injury becoming apparent. Injury may also of course be immediate, depending on the drug or toxin and the type of damage caused.

Diagnosis is made on the history and clinical signs, the fact that improvement should occur if the patient stops taking the offending drug and by excluding other causes of liver damage.

- **How is alcoholic liver disease classified?**
- **Describe the pathogenesis and clinical course of alcoholic liver disease.**
- **Summarize the mechanisms by which drugs and toxins may cause liver damage.**

Revise the zones of the liver in Fig. 4.4. This should help you understand the causes and effects of circulatory disorders of the liver.

CIRCULATORY DISORDERS

Liver infarction
This is rare, because of the dual blood supply of the liver.

It may occur if an intrahepatic branch of the hepatic artery is occluded. If the main hepatic artery is occluded, blood flow through the portal venous systems is usually sufficient to prevent necrosis, except in the case of a transplanted liver when occlusion usually leads to complete necrosis (in which case another transplant is needed).

Occlusion of an intrahepatic branch of the portal vein causes an infarct of Zahn—a well-demarcated area that looks red–blue because of stasis of blood in the sinusoids which become distended. Despite its name, an infarct of Zahn is not a true infarct (necrosis does not occur), but hepatocellular atrophy may occur secondarily to it.

An infarct is the death of tissue caused by an insufficient blood supply.

Portal vein obstruction and thrombosis
This may occur outside the liver (extrahepatic) or inside (intrahepatic—most commonly caused by cirrhosis).

It may lead to portal hypertension, with abdominal pain, ascites and oesophageal varices.

Passive congestion and centrilobular necrosis and cardiac sclerosis
Passive congestion may be acute or chronic and is usually due to right-sided heart failure. It causes the classic nutmeg liver (a common specimen in oral examinations!). Centrilobular necrosis is usually due to left-sided heart failure or shock causing hypoperfusion of the liver. As might be expected, zone 3 of the acini (being furthest from the portal triad) are most badly affected.

Where both hypoperfusion and congestion occur together, centrilobular haemorrhagic necrosis may occur.

Sclerosis is the hardening of a tissue, usually caused by the production of abnormal amounts of collagen.

Cardiac sclerosis

Fibrosis of the liver is seen in cardiac sclerosis and also in cirrhosis. The fibrosis of cardiac sclerosis is less severe than that in cirrhosis, however, and the fibrosis is principally found in zone 3.

It is caused by chronic congestive heart failure causing hypoperfusion and venous congestion.

Peliosis hepatis

This is a rare, and usually reversible, dilatation of hepatic sinusoids, most commonly caused by anabolic steroids, the contraceptive pill or danazol (an antioestrogenic and antiprogestrogenic drug).

Improvement occurs if the offending drug is stopped.

Hepatic vein thrombosis (Budd–Chiari syndrome)

This may be acute or chronic. Acute presentation is usually with sudden onset of epigastric pain and shock. Chronic thrombosis results in portal hypertension (and its associated signs and symptoms), jaundice and cirrhosis.

It may be caused by any condition that predisposes to the formation of thrombi, most notably:

- Polycythaemia.
- Pregnancy.
- Post partum states.
- Oral contraceptive.
- Hepatocellular carcinoma.
- Other intra-abdominal cancers.

Surgical treatment is often required. Mortality is higher in acute cases but, even in its chronic form, 5-year survival is only about 50%.

Veno-occlusive disease

This is believed to be caused where damage to the endothelium of the sinusoids allows red blood cells into the space of Disse, which activates the coagulation cascade. The products of coagulation are then swept into the central vein, occluding it.

The incidence is higher in those receiving marrow transplants (25% in allogenic recipients), probably because chemotherapy and radiotherapy, given as part of transplant therapy, damage the endothelium.

- List the mechanisms by which hepatic blood flow may be impaired.
- Write short notes on the causes and consequences of liver infarction; portal vein obstruction and thrombosis; passive congestion and centrilobular necrosis; cardiac sclerosis, peliosis hepatis, Budd–Chiari syndrome, and veno-occlusive disease.

HEPATIC DISEASE IN PREGNANCY

Pregnancy-induced hypertension and eclampsia

Pregnancy-induced hypertension (pre-eclamptic toxaemia) is a serious condition affecting about 7% of pregnancies, most commonly in primigravidas (women pregnant for the first time), mothers pregnant by a new partner, and women under 25 or over 35 years of age.

Other risk factors include smoking, diabetes, hypertension, short stature, and kidney disease.

It is characterized by hypertension, oedema, and proteinuria. Symptoms include headache, nausea, vomiting, abdominal pain, and visual disturbances, usually after week 32 of pregnancy.

The cause is a failure of invasion of the trophoblast in the second trimester so that the spinal arteries are obstructed and the abnormal placenta is inadequately perfused.

Vascular endothelial damage leads to platelet and fibrin deposition in sinusoids. The resultant ischaemia leads to hepatocellular necrosis in zone 1.

Untreated, it may lead to eclampsia (seizures) and

maternal death, fetal death, or both.

Caesarean section or induction of labour may be necessary if the pregnancy is close to term, and seizures of eclampsia may be treated with anticonvulsants.

Acute fatty liver of pregnancy

This is a rare condition, usually occurring in late pregnancy. The cause is unknown and there is no treatment apart from early delivery.

Fatty degeneration of centrilobular liver cells occurs and may lead to liver failure, coma, and death of the mother or fetus. Diagnosis is by liver biopsy.

Intrahepatic cholestasis of pregnancy

This is often a benign condition caused by excess oestrogen.

However, malabsorption, gall stones, fetal distress, prematurity, or stillbirth may result.

It may arise from changes in bile acid metabolism and enterohepatic recirculation, decreased inactivation of oestrogens by the liver and an alteration of the secretory function of hepatocytes.

The urine is dark, the stools pale, and there is pruritus. Spontaneous recovery occurs after delivery.

- What are the risk factors for eclampsia?
- What are the changes seen in acute fatty liver of pregnancy?
- List the causes and consequences of intrahepatic cholestasis of pregnancy.

DISORDERS OF THE BILIARY TRACT

Anomalies of the biliary tree

Anomalies of the biliary tree are characterized by changes in the architecture of the biliary tree within the liver.

In normal development, embryonic bile ducts involute (spiral and roll inwards at the edges) and anomalies of the biliary tree are thought to be caused by remnants that have not involuted completely.

Anomalies vary in severity. They may be clinically insignificant or be severe enough to cause hepato-splenomegaly and portal hypertension. They are often inherited.

von Meyenburg's complexes (bile duct microhamartomas)

Microhamartomas are tumour-like malformations but, unlike tumours, are always benign.

They consist of two or more mature tissue elements that are normally present in the tissue in which the hamartoma arises.

Bile duct hamartomas are usually clinically insignificant but may be mistaken for liver metastases on a radiograph!

The complexes are small clusters of slightly dilated bile ducts surrounded by a fibrous stroma and they may communicate with the biliary tree.

They occur sporadically, are slightly more common in females and may present in pregnancy. The kidneys may show medullary sponge change.

Polycystic liver disease

As the word 'polycystic' suggests, the liver contains numerous cysts, lined with flattened or cuboidal biliary epithelium and containing straw-coloured fluid. The condition is inherited as autosomal dominant.

The cysts are not connected to the biliary tree and do not contain pigmented bile.

The number of cysts varies from just a few to several hundred, and the cysts themselves vary in diameter from 0.5 cm to 4.0 cm.

They may cause discomfort or pain if the patient stoops, and rupture of a cyst may cause acute pain.

Asymptomatic cysts do not need treatment; painful ones may require aspiration.

Polycystic liver disease may be associated with polycystic kidney disease, in which case the prognosis is worse.

Congenital hepatic fibrosis

Congenital hepatic fibrosis is inherited as an autosomal recessive disorder which may present with complications of portal hypertension and, perhaps most importantly, with bleeding varices (a medical emergency).

The liver is divided into irregular islands by bands of collagenous tissue that enlarge the portal tracts and form septae.

Abnormally shaped bile ducts are scattered throughout the fibrous tissue and the septal margins contain bile duct remnants.

Associated conditions include polycystic kidneys and medullary sponge kidneys.

Caroli's disease

Caroli's disease is inherited as autosomal recessive and is characterized by segmental dilatations in the larger intrahepatic bile ducts.

The dilated sections may contain inspissated (thickened) bile, and stones, and may become infected.

Caroli's disease rarely occurs on its own—it is usually found in association with congenital hepatic fibrosis.

Diagnosis is by ultrasonography, percutaneous transhepatic cholangiography, or endoscopic retrograde cholangiopancreatography.

Complications include cholangitis, hepatic abscesses, intrahepatic cholelithiasis and portal hypertension.

Disorders associated with biliary cirrhosis

Primary biliary cirrhosis

This is an autoimmune disorder and, in common with most other autoimmune diseases, women are more likely to develop it than men. It may occur in association with other autoimmune diseases.

The epithelium of the bile ducts (especially that of the smaller intrahepatic ducts) is destroyed by an autoimmune reaction and the damaged areas become surrounded by lymphocytes. Granulomas may also be present.

An attempt at regeneration then takes place in the form of a proliferation of small bile ductules, and fibrosis occurs, disturbing the normal architecture of the liver.

Eventually, diffuse and irreversible cirrhosis occurs, and may be complicated by liver failure, portal hypertension and liver cell carcinoma.

Diagnosis is by measurement of serum alkaline phosphatase and IgM (both are raised in the disease), the finding of antimitochondrial antibodies in the serum and pruritus, jaundice, and xanthelasma. Xanthelasma are deposits of lipid-laden macrophages around the eyes and are easily visible to the naked eye.

The course and prognosis of the disease is slow but variable and there is no effective medical treatment although ursodeoxycholate is of benefit in some patients, improving liver function and survival. Cholestyramine lessens pruritus.

Fat-soluble vitamins are given to patients with cholestasis.

Secondary biliary cirrhosis

Secondary biliary cirrhosis is caused by prolonged obstruction of extrahepatic bile ducts, often as a result of gall stones, biliary atresia, strictures caused by previous surgery or carcinoma of the head of the pancreas.

Bile remains in the obstructed ducts and inflammation and periportal fibrosis may result, eventually leading to cirrhosis.

Bile duct proliferation may occur and secondary bacterial infection (ascending cholangitis) may complicate biliary strictures and gall stones.

Diagnosis is by ultrasonography, endoscopic retrograde cholangiopancreatography or percutaneous transhepatic cholangiography.

Primary sclerosing cholangitis

Primary sclerosing cholangitis is a chronic inflammatory disease often associated with inflammatory bowel disease, in 70% of cases with ulcerative colitis.

Male patients outnumber females by 2:1.

Intrahepatic, and sometimes extrahepatic, bile ducts become surrounded by a mantle of chronic inflammatory cells.

Eventually onion skin fibrosis occurs (concentric fibrosis around the ducts) and the lumens become obliterated.

Patients vary from being asymptomatic to suffering from chronic liver disease, with pruritus, jaundice, fatigue and eventually portal hypertension.

Gall stones

Bile contains Ca^{2+} and CO_3^{2-} and calcium carbonate stones may form.

More commonly, stones consist of pure cholesterol (20% of stones), bile pigment (5%), or a mixture of the two (75%).

Gall stones (cholelithiasis) are rare in children, but increase in incidence with age, especially in women (where the incidence is 10% in women in their 40s), the obese, and people with diabetes mellitus. It is often

- Summarize the main anomalies of the biliary tree.
- Describe the disorders associated with biliary cirrhosis.

said they occur in 'fair, fat females in their forties'. The more common complications are shown in Fig. 10.8

DISORDERS OF THE EXOCRINE PANCREAS

Congenital abnormalities
The development of the pancreas is described in Chapter 4.

Agenesis and hypoplasia
As with other organs, the pancreas may fail to develop at all (agenesis) or develop incompletely (hypoplasia).

Annular pancreas and pancreas divisum
In normal development, the ventral duodenal outpouching migrates around the back of the duodenum to fuse with the dorsal duodenal outpouching, allowing fusion of the ventral and dorsal pancreas (Fig. 4.16).

If migration of the ventral pancreas is incomplete, a ring of pancreatic tissue (an annular pancreas) surrounds the duodenum and may cause constriction or, in severe cases, complete obstruction.

In general, autosomal recessive disorders present earlier and have worse consequences than autosomal dominant ones.

Pancreas divisum may occur where fusion of the two pancreatic buds does not take place and is found in 5% of patients undergoing endoscopic retrograde cholangiopancreatography.

Ectopic pancreatic tissue
Heterotopic pancreatic tissue is sometimes found in the mucosa of the stomach and in Meckel's diverticulum. More rarely, it may be found between the distal end of the oesophagus and any point proximal to the remnant of the attachment of the vitelline duct (the position at which Meckel's diverticulum would be found, if present).

The pancreatic tissue is normal (although in an abnormal place) and may produce substances normally made by the pancreas.

Pancreatitis
This may be acute or chronic.

Acute pancreatitis
Acute pancreatitis may lead to rapid death (mortality 5–10%); Ronson's criteria are used to assess the severity. If more than seven of his criteria are present, mortality approaches 100%.

Different agents cause acute pancreatitis by different mechanisms (Fig. 10.9) but all lead to the release of lytic enzymes which are then activated and cause damage.

Pancreatic enzymes digest blood vessel walls causing extravasation of blood, and fat necrosis caused by lipase and phospholipase may be extensive enough to discolour the skin of the flanks (Grey Turner's sign) or around the umbilicus (Cullen's sign).

Calcium ions bind to the released fatty acid, in severe cases causing hypocalcaemia and tetany, to form white precipitates. Proteolytic enzymes may destroy the islets of Langerhans so that insulin (and other hormones) are not produced, leading to hyperglycaemia. The consequences of acute pancreatitis may be divided into early and late.

Diagnosis is by measurement of serum amylase. It is normally greatly elevated in acute pancreatitis (other conditions such as perforated peptic ulcer may cause lesser rises), and characteristic findings on abdominal radiography. The psoas shadow will be absent because of retroperitoneal fluid and an air-filled dilatation of the proximal jejunum will be seen, i.e. a sentinel loop.

The typical presentation is with severe abdominal pain of sudden onset which may radiate into the back,

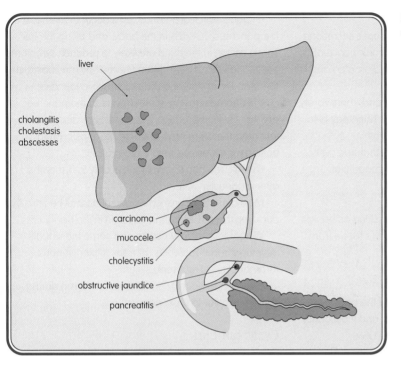

Fig. 10.8 The complications of gall stones.

liver

cholangitis
cholestasis
abscesses

carcinoma

mucocele

cholecystitis

obstructive jaundice

pancreatitis

together with nausea and vomiting. The upper abdomen is usually tender to palpitation.

Chronic pancreatitis

This may or may not be preceded by acute pancreatitis.

It is associated with cystic fibrosis and sometimes with hyperparathyroidism or aminoaciduria. Rarely, it is inherited as an autosomal dominant disorder. However, the commonest cause in developed countries is chronic alcohol consumption.

Other causes include hyperparathyroidism and gall stones.

Patients normally present with a history of:
- Prolonged ill-health.
- Steatorrhoea (lipase deficiency prevents complete breakdown and absorption of fat in the diet).
- Weight loss from malabsorption.
- Recurrent abdominal pain.
- Diabetes mellitus (as a result of destruction of pancreatic islets).

Deficiency of the fat soluble vitamins A, D, E, and K also occurs.

Damage to pancreatic tissue is followed by fibrosis and this may distort the pancreatic ducts.

Diagnosis is by plain abdominal radiography, showing speckled calcification of the pancreas (caused by the binding of calcium ions to necrosed fat), elevated blood glucose (particularly in advanced disease), and endoscopic retrograde cholangiopancreatography (showing distortion of pancreatic ducts caused by fibrosis).

Ultrasonography and CT scans may also be useful.

It is easy to remember the causes of acute pancreatitis—'GET SMASHHH'D': Gall stones, Ethanol, Trauma, Steroids, Mumps, Autoimmune, Scorpion bites, Hyperlipidaemia, Hypothermia, Hyperparathyroidism, Drugs (especially azathioprine and diuretics).

Pseudocysts

These are localized collections of pancreatic secretions and a complication of both acute and chronic pancreatitis.

They are usually solitary, 5–10 cm in diameter, and lie in the lesser sac.

They may produce abdominal pain and, more rarely, haemorrhage, infection and peritonitis. They may also be mistaken for a tumour in the pancreas.

Pseudocysts differ from true cysts in that true cysts have an epithelial lining and are often congenital.

Neoplasms of the pancreas

Tumours, wherever they arrive, are classified as benign or malignant and named according to the tissue from which they arise.

Carcinoma of the pancreas

About 6000 new cases of carcinoma of the pancreas occur in England and Wales every year and it accounts for about 5% of all cancer deaths in the USA.

It is particularly common in black, diabetic males and is most common over the age of 50. It is associated with smoking.

Of pancreatic carcinomas, 60% occur in the head of the pancreas, 15–20% in the body, and 5% in the tail. Those arising in the head are likely to produce symptoms earlier than those arising elsewhere. They may obstruct the ampulla of Vater causing obstructive jaundice.

Carcinomas arising in other parts of the pancreas are less likely to produce symptoms, are discovered late, and therefore have a worse prognosis, often having metastasized before diagnosis.

Overall, median survival time is only 2–3 months after diagnosis.

Most are adenocarcinomas and almost all begin in the ductal epithelium. Less than 1% begin in the acinar cells.

Weight loss usually occurs and some individuals develop thrombophlebitis migrans (flitting venous thromboses)—Trousseau's sign.

The carcinoma may be felt as a firm lump during surgery (similar to a pseudocyst).

Cystic tumours

Cystic tumours may be benign (cystadenoma) or malignant (cystadenocarcinoma).

They comprise only 5% of neoplasms of the pancreas and are usually found in the body or tail.

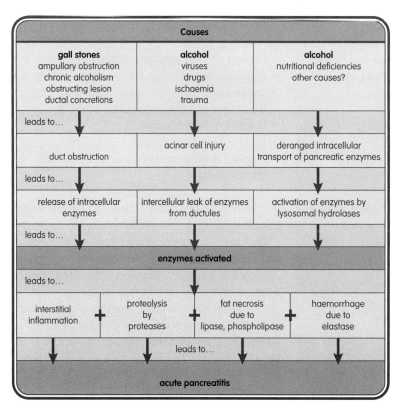

Fig. 10.9 Causes and pathogenesis of acute pancreatitis.

- How do the more common congenital abnormalities of the exocrine pancreas arise?
- What are the causes and complications of acute and chronic pancreatitis?
- Describe the formation and complications of pseudocysts.
- Summarize the classification of pancreatic neoplasms and their most common locations.

11. Pathology of the Small and Large Intestine

Meckel's diverticulum

Meckel's diverticulum is the remnant of the vitelline duct present in embryonic life. It connects the developing embryo with the yolk sac.

Meckel's diverticulum is:

- Present in 2% of the population.
- About 2 inches long.
- Found approximately 2 feet from the caecum (the rule of 2s).
- Twice as common in males compared with females.

In the embryo, the vitelline duct is found at the apex of the primary intestinal loop that forms when the mid gut rapidly elongates (Fig. 5.5). The long sides of the loop are known as the cephalic limb (which forms the duodenum, jejunum, and part of the ileum) and the caudal limb (which forms the remainder of the ileum, the caecum, appendix, ascending colon, and proximal two-thirds of the transverse colon).

Meckel's diverticulum therefore marks the junction of the cranial and caudal limbs of what was the embryonic midgut.

Heterotopic gastric epithelium (normal tissue present in the wrong place) may be found in the diverticulum, including HCl-secreting oxyntic cells, resulting in peptic ulceration. Rarely, ulcers may perforate. Heterotopic pancreatic tissue may also be found there.

Acute inflammation of the diverticulum may occur, mimicking acute appendicitis. The mucosa at the mouth of the diverticulum may become inflamed and lead to intussusception, or the diverticulum may perforate and cause peritonitis. In most cases, however, diverticula are asymptomatic.

If the vitelline duct remains patent throughout its length, a fistula may form onto the umbilicus.

Hirschsprung's disease (congenital aganglionic megacolon)

This is due to an absence of ganglion cells in Auerbach's and Meissner's plexuses in the distal bowel as a result of the failure of neuroblasts to migrate during weeks 5–12 of gestation. It is ten times as likely to occur in children with Down syndrome (trisomy 21) and is often found in association with other congenital abnormalities.

When these parasympathetic plexuses fail to develop, the circular muscle layer of the intestine goes into spasm, resulting in intestinal obstruction and, as in other causes of obstruction, dilatation of the intestine proximal to the area in spasm occurs (Fig. 11.1).

Hirschsprung's disease usually affects the rectum and distal colon but in severe cases may also affect the small intestine. The colon may become distended with faeces resulting in megacolon and death from acute enterocolitis.

It is four times more likely to occur in males and severe cases may become apparent shortly after birth with symptoms of obstruction. Less severe cases may simply result in chronic constipation.

Diagnosis is by barium enema and biopsy showing an absence of ganglion cells. The incidence is 1 in 5000 live births.

Pressure studies show a failure of relaxation of the internal anal sphincter.

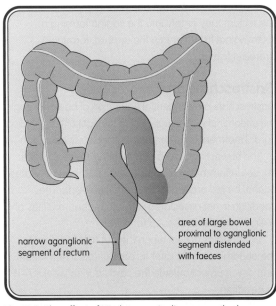

narrow aganglionic segment of rectum

area of large bowel proximal to aganglionic segment distended with faeces

Fig. 11.1 The effect of Hirchsprung's disease on the large bowel.

147

Acquired megacolon

Hirschsprung's disease is a congenital abnormality but megacolon may also be acquired, usually as a result of chronic constipation in childhood. It may also be seen in the elderly.

Causes of acquired megacolon include Chagas' disease, inflammatory bowel disease and bowel obstruction.

Acquired megacolon may be differentiated from Hirschsprung's disease by rectal examination. In patients with Hirschsprung's disease, a narrow empty segment of rectum can be felt above which the colon is dilated and full of faeces. In patients with acquired megacolon, in contrast, no empty segment of rectum is felt and faeces are present in the distal rectum.

The definitive distinguishing test is a rectal biopsy. In acquired megacolon, ganglion cells are present in the rectal wall.

Atresia and stenosis

Atresia is a failure of canalization and results in complete obstruction. Stenosis is a narrowing of the lumen and results in partial obstruction.

Congenital atresia may affect almost any part of the gastrointestinal tract and becomes apparent shortly after birth.

The anus may be imperforate, with the anal canal ending blindly at the anal membrane, or a fistula may form between the rectum and perineum. Alternatively, the rectum may empty into the vagina forming a rectovaginal fistula or into the urethra, forming a urorectal fistula.

Gastroschisis and exomphalos

Gastroschisis is a congenital herniation of bowel through the abdominal wall, usually just to the right of the umbilical cord. Treatment is by surgery, immediately after birth.

The bowel is exposed to fetal urine *in utero* which causes inflammation and paralytic ileus, and neonates cannot be fed orally until the bowel recovers. The condition is not associated with other abnormalities and overall mortality is about 5%.

Exomphalos occurs when the gut fails to return to the abdominal cavity after its physiological herniation and development outside the cavity during weeks 7–11 of gestation.

Affected children are born with gut and sometimes liver protruding through the umbilicus, covered by cord coverings. The gut is not exposed to fetal urine. The condition is associated with other congenital abnormalities, however, most commonly cardiac, renal, or chromosomal. Overall mortality is 25–50%.

- List the embryological origin, site, and frequency of Meckel's diverticulum.
- How does Hirschsprung's disease arise? How does it differ from acquired megacolon?
- Write short notes on atresia and stenosis of the small and large intestines.

INFECTIONS AND ENTEROCOLITIS

Diarrhoea and dysentery

Diarrhoea means different things to different patients and there is no standard definition—the important thing for any individual is a change in bowel habits. Most patients would consider an increase in the volume of stool, decreased viscosity, or increased frequency, to be diarrhoea.

It is generally considered normal for bowels to be opened anything from once every three days to three times a day.

Normally approximately 9 L of fluid pass into the intestine per day, 3–5 L of which are reabsorbed in the jejunum and 2–4 L in the ileum. The colon reabsorbs up to 2 L a day. Failure of reabsorption leads to diarrhoea. Dysentery may be defined as painful, bloody, but low-volume, diarrhoea. The main causes of diarrhoea are summarized in Fig. 11.2.

Infectious enterocolitis

Improved sanitation has led to a decreased prevalence of infectious enterocolitis in the developed world, but infectious enterocolitis accounts for more than 50% of all deaths before the age of 5 years worldwide, and over 12 000 deaths each day amongst children in developing countries.

It may be caused by a variety of agents: in 40–50% no specific agent is isolated and an educated guess must be taken according to the age, circumstances, and degree of immunocompetence of the patient.

Viral gastroenteritis

This may be caused by rotaviruses, enteric adenoviruses, and small round viruses (caliciviruses, astroviruses, and featureless viruses) (Fig. 11.3).

Bacterial enterocolitis

The major causes of bacterial enterocolitis are summarized in Fig. 11.4.

The main categories of diarrhoea
Osmotic diarrhoea disaccharidase deficiencies drug-induced galactose generalized malabsorption
Secretory diarrhoea infectious defects in intraluminal digestion and absorption excess laxative use
Deranged motility increased intestinal transit time decreased motility
Malabsorption
Exudative diseases infectious inflammatory bowel disease

Fig. 11.2 The main categories of diarrhoea.

Common causes of viral gastroenteritis		
Virus	**Host age**	**Transmission method**
rotavirus (group A)	6–24 months	person-to-person, food, water
astroviruses	child	person-to-person, water, raw shellfish
Norwalk-like viruses	school age, adult	person-to-person, water, cold foods, raw shellfish
enteric adenoviruses	child under 2 years	person-to-person
caliciviruses	child	person-to-person, water, cold foods, raw shellfish

Fig. 11.3 Common causes of viral gastroenteritis.

Major causes of bacterial enterocolitis	
Organism	**Source of transmission**
Campylobacter	milk, poultry, animal contact
Clostridium difficile	nosocomial environment
Clostridium perfringens	meat, poultry, fish
Escherichia coli	food, water, undercooked beef products, weaning foods, cheese, person-to-person
Mycobacterium tuberculosis	contaminated milk, swallowing of coughed-up organisms
Salmonella	milk, beef, eggs, poultry
Shigella	person-to-person, low-inoculum
Vibrio cholerae, other vibrios	water, shellfish, person-to-person
Yersinia enterocolitica	milk, pork

Fig. 11.4 Major organisms and causes of bacterial enterocolitis.

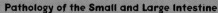

The principal mechanisms by which bacterial infection may lead to gastroenteritis are:

- The ingestion of a bacterial organism which proliferates in the gut lumen and makes an enterotoxin.
- Ingestion of a ready-made (preformed) toxin in contaminated food, e.g. *Staphylococcus aureus*, *Vibrio cholerae* and *Clostridium perfringens*.
- The ingestion of bacterial organisms which proliferate in the gut and destroy the mucosal epithelial cells.

Necrotizing enterocolitis

As the name suggests, this is a necrotizing inflammation of the small and large intestines (primarily the terminal ileum and ascending colon) and is the most common acquired gastrointestinal emergency of neonates.

It is most common within the first few days of life (when infants start oral feeding), but may occur at any time within the first 3 months, especially in premature or low birth weight babies being given formula milk rather than breast milk.

Symptoms vary from mild gastrointestinal upset to perforation of necrosed intestine leading to shock, and if untreated, death.

Surgical resection of affected intestine may be necessary.

Pseudomembranous colitis

This is caused by an overgrowth of *Clostridium difficile* following antibiotic therapy. Any antibiotic may cause it, including penicillin, due to an alteration of intestinal flora.

It is so named because of the appearance of what looks like a membrane (a pseudomembrane) on the surface of the large bowel, formed by an eruption of mucin, polymorphs, and fibrin. Treatment is with vancomycin or metronidazole.

Protozoa and other parasites

A number of different protozoa may be found in the faeces which do not cause disease.

However, the protozoan organisms *Entamoeba histolytica* and *Giardia lamblia* commonly cause diarrhoea and are both transmitted by the faecal–oral route.

Infection may be asymptomatic or cause amoebic dysentery (a notifiable disease) which may not become apparent until many years after infection.

Treatment of acute amoebic dysentery is with metronidazole; diloxanide is given in chronic disease.

Amoebic dysentry is one of a number of diseases which UK law requires doctors to give notification of to the local medical environmental health officer at the Department of Health. Failure to notify is an offence for which a doctor may be fined. Notification is rewarded with a small fee!

Chagas' disease (South American trypanosomiasis)

This is caused by *Trypanosoma cruzi* and may present acutely or chronically after many years, latency.

Hepatosplenomegaly may be present in acute disease and many organs of the body may be invaded by the organism and damaged if the disease becomes chronic. The smooth muscle of the gastrointestinal tract is often involved, leading to megaoesophagus, a dilated stomach and megacolon.

The organism may be isolated in acute disease but diagnosis of chronic disease is by Changas' IgG ELISA (enzyme-linked immunosorbent assay).

Treatment of acute disease is with nifurtimox or benzidazole (the parasite persists in 50% of cases). Treatment of chronic disease is symptomatic.

- **Classify and list the causes of diarrhoea and dysentery.**
- **What are the more common causes of infectious enterocolitis?**

INFLAMMATORY DISORDERS OF THE BOWEL

There are two major non-specific inflammatory bowel diseases: Crohn's disease and ulcerative colitis.

Crohn's disease

Crohn's disease may affect any part of the gastrointestinal tract from the mouth to the anus. It is most common in the lower ileum in young adults, but can affect any age group and the sex distribution is equal. Its aetiology is unknown but the measles virus has been implicated.

Crohn's Disease is more frequent in the Western world, particularly amongst Caucasians, where the incidence is approximately 5–6 per 100 000 and prevalence 50–60 per 100 000.

There is a high rate of concordance in monozygotic twins which suggests both a genetic and environmental cause.

Macroscopically, the bowel appears bright red and swollen. Later small, discrete aphthoid ulcers with a haemorrhagic rim form, so named because they look similar to aphthous ulcers in the mouth.

Later, deeper longitudinal ulcers form which may develop into deep fissures involving the full thickness of the wall of the gastrointestinal tract.

Fibrosis may follow, with stricture formation visible as a narrow string-like area on contrast radiographs: the string sign of Kantor. The mucous membrane of the gastrointestinal tract is often described as cobble-stoned; this occurs where longitudinal fissures are present in oedematous transverse mucosal folds. Aggregations of chronic inflammatory cell infiltrates may be found and the mesenteric lymph nodes may be enlarged due to reactive hyperplasia. Granulomas may be present in the lymph nodes.

Granulomas are collections of epithelioid macrophages and giant cells surrounded by a cuff of lymphocytes.
Granulomas in Crohn's disease are not the same as those found in tuberculosis—tubercular granulomas are characterized by central caseous (cheese-like) necrosis.

Damage to the gastrointestinal tract in Crohn's disease is often patchy (skip lesions) with normal areas of tissue found in between the patches.

Complications of Crohn's Disease

Complications depend on the site and extent of the lesions.

Malabsorption may occur where large areas of small intestine are affected (short bowel syndrome). Fistulae may form because of deep fissuring. These may be internal (between loops of gut or from the gut to the bladder), perianal or, following surgery, open onto the skin.

Acutely, perforation of ulcerated gut may occur and, in the long term, there is an increased risk of adenocarcinoma (most commonly in the terminal ileum).

A variety of lesions may be seen around the anus, most commonly skin tags, fissures, and fistulae in 60% of patients.

Ulcerative colitis

As the name suggests, ulcerative colitis is confined to the large intestine.

The incidence of ulcerative colitis is 5–10 per 100 000 and the prevalence is 80–120 per 100 000.

Ulcerative colitis affects women more than men and is most common between the ages of 20 and 40 although it can occur at any age.

Its aetiology is unknown. It usually starts in the rectum and may extend proximally, although never beyond the colon. Occasionally, inflammation of the terminal ileum is seen (backwash ileitis) but this is due to an incompetent ileocaecal valve rather than ulcerative colitis itself.

Possible causative agents include infection and immunological factors. It has been suggested that ulcerative colitis is the result of an atypical immune response to an enteropathogenic *Escherichia coli*.

Unlike Crohn's, which commonly shows skip lesions, ulcerative colitis is continuous; areas of normal gut are not found between lesions.

The disease is a chronic relapsing inflammatory disorder and diffuse superficial inflammation is seen in the large bowel. Ulcers are typically horizontal and superficial, rarely involving the muscle layer (unlike Crohn's where deep fissure ulcers form) and are often haemorrhagic.

The ulcers often have a wider base than rim (Fig. 11.5) and islands of mucosa may be seen between them.

Both acute and chronic inflammatory cells are found infiltrating the mucosa and aggregates of polymorphs are seen in the crypts (crypt abscesses). Healing of ulcers leads to periods of remission but, in areas of healing, the normal large bowel epithelium may be replaced by a simple layer of mucus-secreting cells without crypts.

Complications of ulcerative colitis

Ulcers may haemorrhage leading to blood loss and anaemia.

Distension and perforation of the colon may occur in acute fulminating cases. Ulcerative colitis is premalignant and carcinoma of the colon develops in about 2% of people with ulcerative colitis.

Extraintestinal complications include:
- skin involvement.
- Liver disease.
- Eye inflammation.
- Association with arthritis.

Comparison of Crohn's disease and ulcerative colitis

It is important to distinguish between a diagnosis of Crohn's and ulcerative colitis as the management of each is different (Fig. 11.6).

Diagnosis and management of Crohn's disease

The main symptoms of Crohn's are diarrhoea, abdominal pain, and weight loss. General feelings of malaise, loss of appetite, nausea, vomiting, and a low-grade fever may also be present.

Presentation may be acute or insidious and can mimic obstruction or appendicitis.

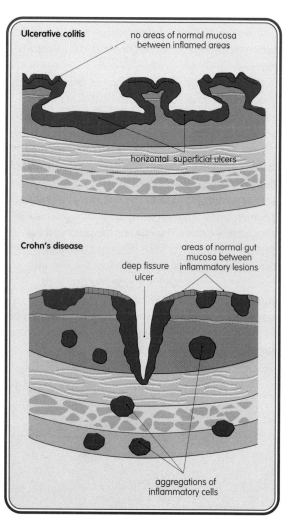

Fig. 11.5 Ulcerative colitis and Crohn's disease. Unlike Crohn's disease, ulcerative colitis is continous; areas of normal gut are not found between lesions.

Comparison of ulcerative colitis and Crohn's disease	
Crohn's disease	**Ulcerative colitis**
affects anywhere from mouth to anus	only affects large bowel (but backwash ileitis occurs in 10%)
deep ulcers and fissures (rose-thorn ulcers) in mucosa	no fissures, horizontal undermining ulcers
malignant change less common than ulcerative colitis	malignant change relatively common
10% have fistulae	fistulae less common
60% have anal involvement	25% have anal involvement
fibrous shortening and early strictures of intestine	muscular shortening of colon but strictures rare and late
skip lesions	no skip lesions
fat and vitamin malabsorption (if small intestine affected)	no fat or vitamin malabsorption
granulomas in 50%	no granulomas
marked lymphoid reaction	mild lymphoid reaction
fibrosis	mild fibrosis
serositis	mild serositis (if any)
no raised ANCA	raised ANCA
increased incidence in smokers	more common in nonsmokers or ex-smokers

Fig. 11.6 Comparison of ulcerative colitis and Crohn's disease.

Bloody diarrhoea may be present in Crohn's and lead to a wrong diagnosis of ulcerative colitis.

Crohn's can affect any part of the gastrointestinal tract from the mouth, to the anus and it is important to examine the mouth where aphthous ulceration may be present. The anus should also be examined as 60% of patients show anal lesions.

An abdominal mass may be palpated, caused by adhesions between affected loops of bowel or abscesses.

Contrast radiography may show fissure ulcers (rose thorn ulcers) and the string sign of Kantor.

Sigmoidoscopy and rectal biopsy should be undertaken.

Treatment is largely symptomatic and includes prednisolone (a steroid), by enema or orally. Other treatment depends on the site and extent of the disease.

Surgery may be needed to resect affected areas of bowel or to relieve strictures but symptoms often recur and repeated operations may be necessary.

Elemental diets sometimes lead to an improvement in Crohn's disease (but have little to offer in colitis).

Almost all patients have a significant relapse and overall mortality is roughly twice as high as normal.

Diagnosis and management of ulcerative colitis

In the developed world this is the most frequent cause of prolonged bloody diarrhoea and should be suspected whenever bloody diarrhoea lasts for more than 7 days.

Acute attacks may lead to severe illness with a fever in excess of 37.5°C. The abdomen may be distended but, unlike Crohn's, the anus is usually normal.

A plain radiograph may show dilatation of the colon. Fine ulceration may be be seen on a barium enema. Sigmoidoscopy and biopsy should be undertaken.

Unlike Crohn's disease, surgery in ulcerative colitis is curative because the disease is limited to the colon. Usually, an ileostomy is performed, with removal of the colon and rectum. Ileal pouches may be fashioned and anastomosed to the rectal stump, thus avoiding an ileostomy.

Prognosis depends on the extent of the disease and is better in proctitis (disease limited to the rectum) than in severe fulminant disease (which carries a 15–25% mortality).

Miscellaneous intestinal inflammatory disorders
Acute manifestation of HIV infection
Diarrhoea, weight loss and malabsorption are common in chronic HIV infection, usually caused by a pathogen, most commonly the coccidian protozoal parasite *Cryptosporidium*. *Microsporidia*, another protozoal parasite, may also cause diarrhoea.

Cytomegalovirus may mimic inflammatory bowel disease and mucocutaneous lesions may be formed at the lower (and upper) end of the GI tract by the herpes simplex virus, particularly in the perianal region.

Mycobacterium tuberculosis infection of the bowel may also occur.

Graft versus host disease
Transplanted bone marrow contains many T lymphocytes and, if the host's immune system is deficient (as it usually is), the grafted bone marrow may reject the host. This leads to skin rashes, hair loss (often sparse anyway because of previous treatment), acute diarrhoea, liver disease and death.

- List the features and complications of Crohn's disease and ulcerative colitis.
- What are the differences between Crohn's disease and ulcerative colitis?
- Summarize the gastrointestinal manifestations of HIV infection.
- Discuss diarrhoea in graft-versus-host disease.

MALABSORPTION SYNDROMES

General aspects of the malabsorption syndromes
Malabsorption is the decreased absorption of nutrients and may be caused by a number of conditions, including biochemical disorders (such as absent or defective digestive enzymes) and disease of the small intestine.

Causes of malabsorption
The causes of decreased nutrient absorption include:
- Reduced surface area of small intestine.
- Infection.
- Defective intraluminal hydrolysis or solubilization.
- Abnormalities of mucosal cells.
- Drug-induced.
- Lymphatic obstruction.
- After surgical resection of gut and/or radiation therapy.

Systemic effects of the malabsorption syndrome
Whatever the cause, the results of malabsorption are essentially the same.

Patients complain of frothy, greasy stools which are difficult to flush away (steatorrhoea), diarrhoea, weight loss and abdominal distension.

Anaemia may be due to deficiency of iron, folate or vitamin B_{12}. Vitamin K deficiency can lead to bleeding disorders, purpura (extravasation of red cells into the skin) characterized by red skin lesions which do not blanch on pressure and petechiae (flat, red, or purple spots about the size of a pinhead in the skin or mucous membranes).

Endocrine disorders may result from generalized malnutrition and deficiencies of vitamin A and B_1 may lead to peripheral neuropathy.

Deficient absorption of protein can result in oedema. Dermatitis and hyperkeratosis may also be evident in the skin. The musculoskeletal system may also be affected with osteopenia and tetany.

Specific malabsorption syndromes
Coeliac disease
Coeliac disease is due to an abnormal reaction to gluten (found in wheat flour) which damages the enterocytes of the small intestine (causing villous atrophy and malabsorption).

It is associated in 90% of cases with human leucocyte antigen-DR3 (HLA-DR3) and, in a smaller percentage, with HLA-B8. It is also associated with dermatitis herpetiformis, an uncommon but extremely itchy skin disease typically found on the forearms and extensor surfaces.

Injury to the enterocytes appears to be due to an abnormal immune response to gliadin (a component of gluten).

Stem cells are unable to keep up with the rate of loss of enterocytes. This results in villous atrophy and the presence of immature cells which are unable to absorb nutrients normally on the flattened surface. This, in turn, causes malabsorption and an intolerance of lactose and other sugars because of a secondary disaccharide deficiency resulting from the loss of surface epithelial cells.

The production of gastrointestinal hormones may also be deficient. This has a knock-on effect on pancreatic secretion and bile flow. Malabsorption of fat therefore predominates.

Typically, the duodenum and proximal jejunum are affected more severely than the ileum, so iron deficiency anaemia is the most frequent form of presentation.

The condition predisposes to T cell lymphomas in the small intestine (an unusual small bowel lymphoma amongst the noncoeliac population in whom most small bowel lymphomas are B cells).

There is also a higher incidence of other gastrointestinal cancers such as cancer of the stomach and oesophagus. Splenic atrophy may occur and all or any of the other features of malabsorption can be present.

Diagnosis is by jejunal biopsy showing evidence of villous atrophy.

Treatment is a permanent gluten-free diet and the vast majority of patients show a marked improvement on dietary change. Gluten is present in wheat, barley, oats and rye and these must all be excluded. It is not, however, present in rice or maize.

Tropical sprue
As the name suggests, this is found in the tropics (but not generally in Africa).

It is similar to coeliac disease in that villous atrophy is present but it does not respond to a gluten-free diet.

Treatment is with broad-spectrum antibiotics as it is believed to be caused by bacteria overgrowth of enterotoxigenic organisms such as *Escherichia coli*,

Klebsiella pneumoniae, and *Enterobacter cloacae* in the upper small bowel. It does not appear to lead to intestinal lymphomas. Megaloblastic anaemia caused by folate deficiency is common.

Whipple's disease
This is a rare bacterial infection usually occurring in men over the age of 50. It is caused by *Tropheryma whippelii* (a Gram-positive actinomycete).

Diagnosis is by jejunal biopsy which shows intact villi where the normal cells of the lamina propria have been replaced by macrophrages containing PAS-positive glycoprotein granules. Similar cells may be found in lymph nodes, the spleen and liver. Treatment is with the antibiotic tetracycline. Whipple's disease is 10 times more common in men. If it is diagnosed in a woman, tetracycline should not be prescribed if the patient is pregnant as tetracycline is teratogenic.

Bacterial overgrowth syndrome
The small intestine normally supports a large number of flora but these are kept in check by peristalsis, the acidity of chyme leaving the stomach, and the secretion of immunoglobulins into the intestinal lumen by the mucosal cells.

Where one or more of these factors is reduced, bacterial overgrowth may result in malabsorption.

Jejunal biopsy may show a normal mucosa. Diagnosis is by aspiration of the contents of the jejunum which show increased numbers of both aerobic and anaerobic organisms.

These organisms may inactivate bile acids in the lumen by dehydroxylation, leading to fat malabsorption. The gut flora may catabolize ingested protein, metabolize sugars and bind vitamin B_{12}, preventing its absorption.

Treatment is with antibiotics, such as tetracycline, clindamycin or lincomycin.

Giardiasis
Giardiasis, prevalent in the Tropics, is an important cause of traveller's diarrhoea. It is caused by the flagellate protozoon, *Giardia lamblia,* which lives in the duodenum and jejunum and is transmitted by the faecal–oral route. It is more common amongst male homosexuals, in the immunosuppressed, and in those with achlorhydria. Cases may occur in Britain among people who have never been abroad.

When prescribing metronidazole advise patients to avoid alcohol. Metronidazole has a disulfiram effect and patients will feel severely ill if they drink alcohol at the same time. Unless they are warned they will understandably think the illness is caused by the metronidazole and stop taking it.

Asymptomatic carriage may occur. Alternatively symptoms may develop within 1 or 2 weeks of ingesting cysts.

Giardia lamblia exists as a trophozoite and a cyst; the cyst being the transmissible form. Intestinal damage varies from slight changes in villous architecture to villous atrophy with severe malabsorption.

Diagnosis is by examination of stool. Cysts and trophozoites may be found but their absence does not exclude the diagnosis: in some cases they are only excreted at intervals. The parasite may also be seen in duodenal aspirates and in jejunal biopsy.

Blood tests may show IgM antibodies to *Giardia* in acute infection and, later, anti-*Giardia* IgG.

Treatment is with metronidazole (but not in pregnant women) or quinacrine.

Abetalipoproteinaemia

This is a rare autosomal recessive disorder in which there is a failure to synthesise apo B-100 in the liver and apo B-48 in interstitial cells.

Normally, lipids (principally triglyceride cholesterol and cholesterol esters) are surrounded by a stabilizing coat of phospholipid because they are insoluble. Apoproteins are embedded in the surface of the complex of lipids and phospholipids to form lipoproteins.

In abetalipoproteinaemia, lipoproteins containing B apoproteins (for example, chylomicrons) cannot be made.

Chylomicrons are principally responsible for transporting the digestion products of fat in the diet to the liver and peripheral tissues after dietary fat has been absorbed from the gut.

An absence of chylomicrons leads to accumulation of triglycerides within the absorptive cells of the gut. Lipid vacuolation can be seen in these cells on biopsy.

Burr cells (spiculed mature red blood cells) are seen in the blood.

The disease is characterized by failure to thrive, diarrhoea and steatorrhoea in infancy.

Disaccharide deficiency

Normally, disaccharides in the diet are hydrolyzed by lactase or sucrase on the luminal surface of mucosal cells. Lactase activity is high at birth but declines during childhood and is low in adults. The decline in lactase activity differs according to race: lactase levels are higher in Caucasians but lower in African, Oriental, and Mediterranean populations.

Disaccharide deficiency leads to diarrhoea, bloating and flatulence, particularly with a high-milk diet.

Diarrhoea in lactase deficiency is due to a failure to digest and absorb lactose. Lactose is broken down by bowel bacteria into its constituents, glucose and galactose, and then to lactic acid. This process causes osmotic diarrhoea.

Increased disaccharide residues in the lower small intestine and colon lead to increased gas production and flatulence.

Congenital lactase deficiency is rare. Acquired deficiency due to decreased activity of lactase is common, however, and seen in about 15% of Caucasians and 70–90% of other races.

Congenital disaccharide deficiency becomes apparent early in life because of milk intolerance which leads to the production of explosive, watery, frothy stools and abdominal distension.

The more common acquired lactase deficiency often becomes apparent during viral and bacterial enteric infection.

- ○ **Summarize the general aspects and classification of malabsorption syndromes.**
- ⊙ **What are the causes and treatment of the more common malabsorption syndromes?**

OBSTRUCTION OF THE BOWEL

Bowel obstruction may have mechanical or non-mechanical causes (pseudo-obstruction).

The signs and symptoms are similar, regardless of the cause, and depend primarily on the level of the obstruction.

Vomiting is a symptom of high obstruction but may be absent (or occur late) in low-level obstruction.

Conversely, distension and colic are early symptoms of obstruction lower in the intestine.

Obstruction causes distension of the gut, with gas and intestinal secretions above the level of the obstruction, progressive depletion of extracellular fluid and the multiplication of bacteria, especially coliforms, *Streptococcus faecalis, Clostridium perfringens,* and *Bacteroides.*

Diagnosis is on the history (as always!) and erect and supine radiography, which shows distended, gas-filled loops of bowel with multiple horizontal fluid levels.

Treatment depends on the cause and level of the obstruction, and whether the bowel is strangulated. Strangulated bowel is an emergency and requires urgent surgery.

Simple obstruction (not due to strangulation) may be treated conservatively initially. Conservative treatment consists of 'drip and suck': intravenous fluids and continuous aspiration by nasogastric tube.

Major causes of bowel obstruction

The major causes of obstruction in the developed world are:

- Adhesions.
- Hernias.
- Intussusception.
- Volvulus.
- Strictures.
- Tumours.
- Gall stones.
- Foreign bodies.
- Faecoliths.
- Atresia.
- Meconium (in cystic fibrosis).
- Imperforate anus.
- Paralytic ileus.
- Myopathies and neuropathies.

Paralytic (adynamic or neurogenic) ileus is atony of the intestine resulting in a lack of peristalsis.

It occurs transiently after almost every laparotomy. Other causes include interruption of the autonomic innervation of the gut, peritonitis (which may cause toxin mediated paralysis of the intrinsic nerve plexuses of the gut), potassium depletion, uraemia and diabetic coma, and drugs (especially anticholinergics).

Meconium ileus occurs in about 10–15% of neonates with cystic fibrosis, a congenital condition characterized by defective mucus secretion. Meconium is unusually sticky and may obstruct the lower ileum.

An enema may resolve the obstruction, if it does not, surgery may be required.

Hernias

Hernias are the protrusion of any viscus or part of a viscus through its coverings into an abnormal position.

They are common, occurring in about 1% of the population, and may be congenital or acquired (Fig. 11.7), reducible, irreducible, or strangulated (Fig. 11.8).

Reducible hernias can be pushed back into the compartment from which they came, irreducible ones

In general, obstruction high in the gastrointestinal tract presents with vomiting. Obstruction lower down causes distension.

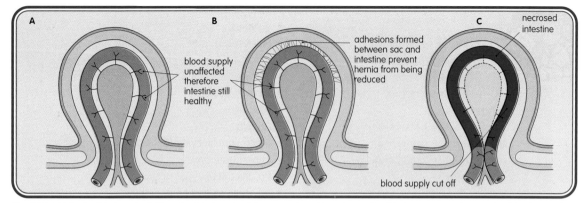

Fig. 11.8 (A) Reducible hernia. (B) Irreducible hernia. (C) Strangulated hernia. Reducible hernias can be pushed back into the compartment from which they came, irreducible ones cannot. Strangulated hernias have had their blood supply cut off.

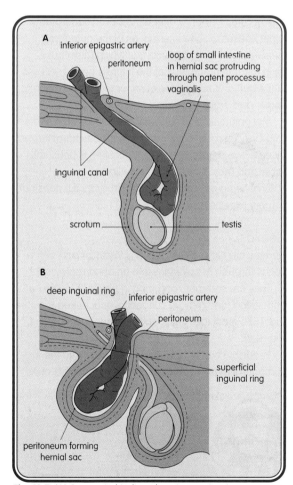

Fig. 11.7 (A) Congenital indirect hernia passing into scrotum through patent processus vaginalis. (B) Acquired direct hernia, passing through a defect in the abdominal wall. (Redrawn with permission from: Hall–Craggs, ECB. *Anatomy as a basis for clinical medicine.* London: Waverly Europe; 1995.)

cannot, and strangulated hernias have had their blood supply cut off by the neck of the sac.

Strangulated hernias present with signs and symptoms of obstruction and, untreated, become gangrenous and necrose.

The most common sites of herniation through the abdominal wall are:

- Inguinal.
- Femoral.
- Umbilical.
- Incisional.
- Ventral.
- Epigastric.

Inguinal hernias may be direct (protruding through the posterior wall of the inguinal canal) or indirect (passing through the inguinal canal).

Direct inguinal hernias lie medial to the internal ring, and the inferior epigastric vessels separate the sites of direct and indirect hernias.

Treatment depends on the type of hernia, reducible ones often require no treatment so long as they remain reducible, but strangulated ones must be treated surgically.

Synthetic meshes are often used to reinforce closure of hernia orifices.

Adhesions

Adhesions occur where two parts of the body that are normally separate are connected by bands of fibrous tissue.

Some are congenital but most occur as a result of postinflammatory scarring (e.g. after peritonitis, endometriosis, or scars that form as a result of surgery).

Examine the patient's abdomen—if there are scars from past abdominal surgery, consider adhesions as a cause of the obstruction.

If the bowel is strangulated, surgery is necessary.

Intussusception

Intussusception occurs when one segment of bowel slides inside the adjacent segment (Fig. 11.9) and is commonest in infants and young children who account for 95% of cases. Males outnumber females by a ratio of 2:1. It most commonly occurs at the ileocaecal valve.

The aetiology is unclear but may be related to an adenovirus causing enlargement of lymphatic tissue in the intestinal wall. This protrudes into the lumen and is pushed into the adjacent section by peristalsis.

In some cases a polyp, Meckel's diverticulum or carcinoma may project into the lumen and be pushed along in a similar way.

Symptoms of all causes of intestinal obstruction are similar. As intussusception usually occurs in infants, however, characteristically it is accompanied by periods of screaming. The child is pale and the tumour may be felt as a sausage-shaped mass on palpation of the abdomen.

Faeculent vomiting, gangrene, and peritonitis may occur within 24 hours if untreated. A barium enema may resolve the intussusception by forcing the invaginated segment back; alternatively, surgery may be required.

Volvulus

Volvulus is relatively rare in Britain (it accounts for about 2% of intestinal obstructions) but is the commonest cause of intestinal obstruction in Africa.

It is a twisting of a loop of bowel about its mesenteric axis and usually occurs in the sigmoid colon but may be found in the caecum, small intestine, the gall bladder and stomach.

Risk factors include chronic constipation, adhesions and abnormally mobile loops of intestine.

Twisting of the bowel causes obstruction and occlusion of the vessels supplying the affected section. Potentially fatal gangrene and peritonitis may occur if the volvulus is not treated. Symptoms include the sudden onset of colicky pain.

Diagnosis is by plain radiography, which shows a dilated section of bowel, full of gas, and forming a characteristic loop, or inverted U. Treatment depends on the site of the volvulus: surgery is often necessary. Sigmoid volvulus is sometimes resolved by sigmoidoscopy and the passing of a flatus tube.

- Give the major causes of bowel obstruction.
- List the more common types of hernia.
- Summarize the causes, prognosis, and management of adhesions.
- How might intussusception occur?
- What is the aetiology of volvulus?

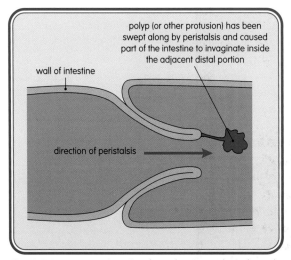

polyp (or other protusion) has been swept along by peristalsis and caused part of the intestine to invaginate inside the adjacent distal portion

wall of intestine

direction of peristalsis

Fig. 11.9 Intussusception. One bowel segment has slipped inside an adjacent one.

COLONIC DIVERTICULOSIS

Definitions
- **Diverticulum** is an outpouching of the wall of the gut.
- **Diverticulosis** means that diverticula are present.
- **Diverticular disease** means that diverticula are causing symptoms.
- **Diverticulitis** means that one or more diverticula are inflamed.

Diverticulosis

Diverticula may be congenital or acquired and occur in any part of the gut.

Congenital diverticula are outpouchings of the full thickness of the bowel wall. They are found most commonly in the duodenum and jejunum.

Congenital diverticula are usually asymptomatic but may lead to bacterial overgrowth, steatorrhoea and vitamin B_{12} malabsorption. They may perforate or haemorrhage.

Acquired colonic diverticula increase in incidence with increasing age and are present in about 50% of people aged over 50 years. There is no difference in distribution between the sexes.

They are more common in the left side of the colon than the right, and are usually found in the sigmoid and descending colon.

They form when the muscle layer of the wall thickens (hypertrophies) and high intraluminal pressures force a pouch of mucosa out through an area of weakness in the muscle layer. Areas of weakness often occur near blood vessels (Fig. 11.10).

Acquired diverticula do not consist of all three layers of the intestinal wall and this differentiates them from congenital ones.

Low-fibre diets are a risk factor. The pouches may become inflamed (diverticulitis) if the neck of the diverticulum becomes obstructed by faeces. Bacterial overgrowth then occurs in the diverticulum, with the risk of abscess formation, perforation (peridiverticulitis) and peritonitis.

Fistulae (abnormal communications between two epithelial surfaces) may also form, usually into the bladder or vagina (causing the patient much distress).

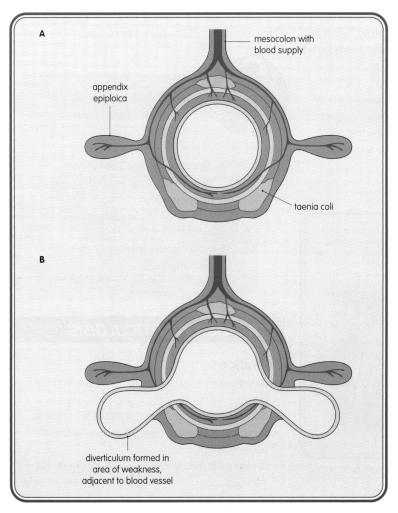

Fig. 11.10 In the diverticulum, high intraluminal pressure has forced pouches of mucosa through weak muscle areas. (Redrawn with permission from: Ellis, H and Sir Roy Calne. *Lecture notes on general surgery*, 8th ed. Oxford:Blackwell Science; 1993.)

Diagnosis of diverticula is often incidental during other investigations and, as 90% of cases are asymptomatic, in many cases no treatment is required.

Patients should, however, be advised to increase the amount of fibre and liquids in their diet (fibre has no beneficial effect unless there is sufficient liquid in the diet).

Patients with acute diverticulitis often present in a similar way to those with appendicitis, except that the pain is usually in the left iliac fossa instead of the right. The most common site of diverticula is the sigmoid colon.

Signs include tenderness and guarding on the left side of the abdomen, pyrexia and tachycardia. Radiographs should be taken to exclude air under the diaphragm (an indication of perforation).

In the absence of complications, acute diverticulitis is treated conservatively with a liquid diet and appropriate antibiotic treatment.

Obstruction or peritonitis is treated in the same way as if caused by other pathology.

Fistulas may heal of their own accord, but not in the presence of inflammation, and surgery is often indicated.

- **Define the terms diverticulum, diverticulosis, diverticulitis, and diverticular disease.**
- **What are the differences between congenital and acquired diverticula?**
- **List the complications of diverticula.**

VASCULAR DISORDERS

Ischaemic bowel disease

Essentially, the causes of ischaemic bowel disease are the same as ischaemia in other parts of the body.

The effect depends on the size of the ischaemic area and the length of time ischaemia has persisted.

It may be classified as mucosal, mural and transmural, the effects of which are summarized in Fig. 11.11.

The blood supply to the wall is 'from outside in' and mucosal or mural infarction often results from underperfusion whereas transmural infarction is usually due to mechanical compromise of the artery.

The splenic flexure and an area of the rectum are particularly prone to ischaemic damage. These are the watershed areas where the arterial supply switches from the superior to the inferior mesenteric artery, and from the inferior mesenteric and hypogastric arteries respectively (Fig. 11.12).

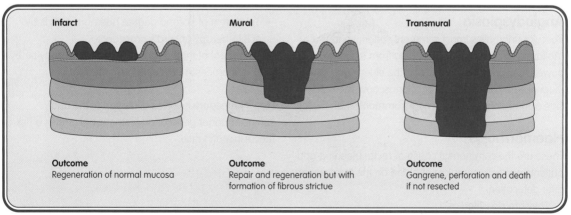

Infarct	Mural	Transmural
Outcome Regeneration of normal mucosa	**Outcome** Repair and regeneration but with formation of fibrous stricture	**Outcome** Gangrene, perforation and death if not resected

Fig. 11.11 The effects of acute intestinal infarction.

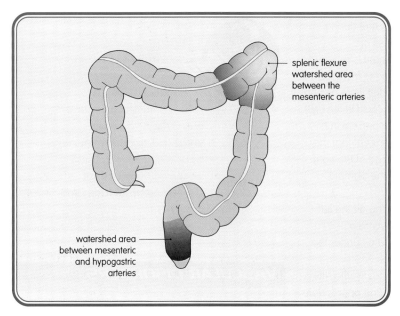

Fig. 11.12 Areas of large bowel particulary prone to ischaemic injury.

splenic flexure watershed area between the mesenteric arteries

watershed area between mesenteric and hypogastric arteries

Reperfusion injury commonly occurs following hypoperfusion and, like reperfusion injury seen in the heart and brain, it is mediated by free-radicals which cause damage to cell membranes.

Damage to the mucosa causes release of proteolytic enzymes which may cause deeper damage to the wall, but complete regeneration is more common.

Ulcers may form after mural infarction, the mucosa looks haemorrhagic, granulation tissue may form and be replaced by fibrotic tissue with the formation of a stricture.

Transmural ischaemia leads to gangrene, perforation and, if untreated, death. Surgical resection of the affected bowel is necessary.

Transmural infarction should be suspected in any elderly patient with atherosclerosis or atrial fibrillation with a tender abdomen and absent bowel sounds.

Angiodysplasia

Vascular anomalies (most commonly arteriovenous malformations) may cause bleeding from the large bowel. They are more common in the elderly and can be diagnosed by angiography or colonoscopy. The right side of the colon is affected more commonly than the left.

Haemorrhoids

These are the commonest cause of rectal bleeding and patients normally complain of blood on the toilet paper after defecation.

They are classified as:

- First degree (confined to the anal canal and which bleed but do not prolapse).
- Second degree (which prolapse on defecation but may be reduced).
- Third degree (which remain outside the anus at all times).

Normally, faecal continence is contributed to by three anal vascular cushions which drain into the superior rectal veins and then into the inferior mesenteric veins. Internal haemorrhoids are varices of the superior rectal veins and can be caused, or made worse, by anything impairing drainage of the superior rectal veins.

The site at which they occur is one of the areas of portosystemic anastomoses.
- Treatment of first degree haemorrhoids is by injection sclerotherapy,
- Treatment of second degree haemorrhoids is by sclerotherapy or Lord's procedure.
- Treatment of third degree haemorrhoids may be by Lord's procedure or haemorrhoidectomy.

Lord's procedure involves dilatation of the anal sphincter under general anaesthetic but carries a risk of faecal incontinence.

- Summarize the causes, classification, complications, and management of bowel ischaemia.
- Write short notes on angiodysplasia.
- Describe the formation of haemorrhoids.

NEOPLASTIC DISEASE OF THE BOWEL

Non-neoplastic polyps

Non-neoplastic polyps make up the vast majority of epithelial polyps found in the large intestine (about 90%) and increase in frequency with age. They are present in about half the population over the age of 60 years.

Most epithelial polyps are found in the large bowel; they are relatively rare in the small intestine. Mesenchymal polyps may also be found but these are rarer than epithelial ones.

Hyperplastic polyps

Hyperplastic (metaplastic) polyps are relatively common in the rectum, especially in the elderly. They are sessile and have well formed crypts containing mature goblet or absorptive cells.

They are usually small (less than 5 mm in diameter) and have no malignant potential.

A hamartoma is a malformation containing two or more mature cell types that are normally present in the organ in which they arise. They are always benign.

Hamartomatous polyps

These include juvenile polyps and polyps of the Peutz–Jeghers syndrome.

Juvenile polyps

Juvenile polyps are usually solitary focal hamartomatous malformations of mucosal tissue.

They are most common below the age of 5 years and about 80% of them occur in the rectum.

They are often large (up to 3 cm in diameter) with long stalks (up to 2 cm in length) but have no malignant potential.

Peutz–Jeghers polyps

Peutz–Jeghers syndrome is a rare autosomal dominant syndrome characterized by multiple polyps scattered throughout the gastrointestinal tract. Abnormal pigmentation also occurs in the skin and oral mucosa. Although the polyps themselves are not premalignant, being hamartoma, people with Peutz–Jeghers syndrome do have an increased risk of developing certain carcinomas, notably in the pancreas, breast, lung, ovary, and uterus.

Neoplastic epithelial lesions
Adenomas

These are derived from secretory epithelium and are the most important of the epithelial polyps. They are relatively common, especially in the elderly.

Of all adenomas, 75% are tubular, 10% villous, and the remainder a mixture of the two (tubulovillous).

Tubular adenomas are smaller than villous adenomas (up to 1 cm in diameter) and are usually pedunculated. They look a little like a blackberry on a stalk.

Villous adenomas, on the other hand, are usually sessile and larger (up to several centimetres in diameter) and, as the name suggests, have villi lined by dysplastic columnar epithelium protruding from their surface.

Villous adenomas have a greater tendency to malignant change and carry the additional risk of electrolyte imbalance and, more rarely, acute renal failure resulting from their secretion of electrolyte-rich mucus.

People with familial adenomatous polyposis, a rare autosomal dominant disorder, almost always develop cancer of the intestine by the age of 35 years. Familial adenomatous polyposis is characterized by the development of numerous adenomas in the large and, to a lesser extent, the small intestine during the teens and twenties.

Colorectal cancer

Colorectal cancer is common in the developed world and is the second biggest cause of cancer death in the UK (coming second to lung cancer).

It is closely related to diet. Its incidence is low in Japan but amongst second generation Japanese living in the United States, the incidence is the same as that of the indigenous American population. Dietary factors carrying a greater risk of colorectal cancer are low fibre, high carbohydrate and fat. Fibre increases the bulk of faeces, as long as fluid intake is adequate, and reduces the time taken for the contents of the intestine to pass through and out of the rectum. In a low fibre diet, faeces remain in the intestine for longer, altering the normal flora and this is thought to predispose to cancer.

Inadequate intake of the free radical scavengers, vitamins A, C, and E also leads to an increased risk of colorectal and some other cancers.

Survival after diagnosis of colorectal cancer depends on the stage. Dukes' classification is most widely used (Fig. 11.13). Some clinicians add an additional stage D to Dukes' classification: the presence of distant visceral metastases.

Other neoplasms

Carcinoid tumours

The normal intestine secretes a number of gastrointestinal hormones from endocrine cells. These cells are known as APUD (amine precursor uptake and decarboxylation) cells and comprise enterochromaffin and enteroendocrine cells.

Neuroendocrine cells are also found in other organs, for example the lung, pancreas and biliary tract and tumours may arise in neuroendocrine cells in the gut and elsewhere. These tumours are slow growing and are called carcinoid.

Carcinoid tumours are potentially malignant but their malignant potential depends on the site. Larger tumours in the appendix and ileum tend to spread to regional lymph nodes and the liver. Small tumours (less than 2 cm diameter) near the tip of the appendix rarely do so.

Because of the cells in which they arise, tumours produce hormones which may have local or systemic effects:

- 5-HT (5-hydroxytryptamine) produced by midgut carcinoid tumours cause diarrhoea and borborygmi as a result of local stimulation of the contractility of the intestine.
- 5-HT may also be produced from metastases in the liver and give rise to the carcinoid syndrome with facial flushing, cyanosis and pulmonary and tricuspid valve stenosis or incompetence.

Gastrointestinal lymphoma

Lymphomas are common in the small intestine (less so in the large) and may be of B cell or T cell lineage.

T cell lymphomas are associated with coeliac disease, B cell lymphomas are not and most occur sporadically.

Alpha-chain disease most commonly found in the Mediterranean (but also in South America and the Far East) is characterized by a proliferation of plasma cells in the lamina propria of the upper small bowel; a B-lymphocyte disorder may lead to lymphoma of the small intestine.

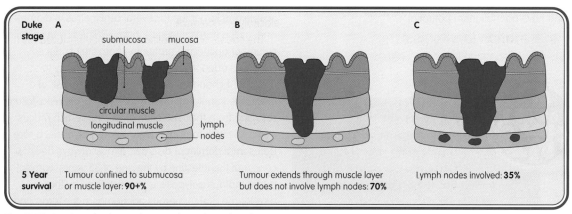

Fig. 11.13 Staging of colorectal cancer by Dukes' classification.

Mesenchymal tumours

These may occur in any part of the alimentary tract and include leiomyomas (arising from smooth muscle), lipomas and Kaposi's sarcoma (a malignant neoplasm of vascular endothelium, commonly associated with AIDS).

Neoplasms of the appendix

Carcinoid tumours, adenocarcinomas and lymphomas may all occur in the appendix but are rare. Proliferation of the epithelium may also occur causing an increase in secretion of mucus and dilating the lumen of the appendix (mucocele).

The most common cause of a mucocele is mucinous cystadenoma.

A less common cause is mucinous cystadeno-carcinoma, from which neoplastic cells may implant into the peritoneum causing pseudomyoxoma peritonei (a distended peritoneal cavity containing semisolid mucin) which may be fatal.

Mucoceles may also be caused by simple epithelial hyperplasia.

- **List the types of tumours that may be found in the intestine.**
- **Summarize the classification and complications of intestinal polyps.**

THE PERITONEUM

Inflammation (peritonitis)

Peritonitis is inflammation of the peritoneum.

It may be limited to a small area, for example where an abscess has formed, but is usually generalized, extending to both the visceral and parietal peritoneum. Untreated, it is usually fatal.

Whatever the cause, the onset is usually sudden, with severe pain which is localized at first but becomes generalized, with guarding, tenderness to palpation and the eventual disappearance of bowel sounds (due to ileus).

The patient will look shocked, with tachycardia, and lie still, sometimes with his or her knees drawn up.

He or she will take very shallow breaths as any movement of the peritoneum (e.g. movement of the diaphragm in inspiration) is extremely painful.

Peritoneal infection

This is caused by organisms which spread from the intestinal lumen or from outside as a result of surgery or penetrating injury, an ulcer that has eroded through the wall of the gut, acute salpingitis, strangulated bowel, peritoneal dialysis, cholecystitis, diverticulitis, or appendicitis. In short, anything that disrupts the integrity of the intestinal wall and allows organisms out of the lumen into the peritoneal cavity, or disrupts the integrity of the abdominal wall and allows organisms in from the outside world can cause peritoneal infection.

The organism responsible varies depending on the site of the offending lesion.

Infection from the bowel is most common and organisms include *Bacteroides, Escherichia coli, Clostridium perfringens, Pseudomonas* and *Klebsiella*.

The most common organisms introduced from outside the body are *Staphylococcus aureus* and streptococci.

Diagnosis

As always, diagnosis is on the history and clinical findings. In addition, erect radiographs should be taken to look for air under the diaphragm (a sign of perforation) and blood tests performed to exclude pancreatitis.

Exploratory laparotomy may be necessary.

Treatment

The patient will be shocked and resuscitation is essential, with intravenous fluids and correction of electrolyte imbalance.

The cause, once identified, should be removed and the infection treated with appropriate antibiotics.

As with any patient in pain, adequate analgesia should be given.

Sclerosing peritonitis (retroperitoneal fibromatosis)

This is a rare condition characterized by marked fibrosis behind the peritoneum and an infiltrate of inflammatory cells (lymphocytes, plasma cells and neutrophils).

The fibrous tissue may encroach on adjacent structures (most commonly the ureters), producing

165

symptoms which vary according to the structures involved.

Patients often present in middle age with malaise, fever, weight loss and renal failure.

Blood tests may show a raised ESR (a very non specific sign) and anaemia. The diagnosis may be made with certainty on a CT scan. Surgery may be required. The cause is unclear but may be autoimmune. It is sometimes associated with the carcinoid syndrome.

Mesenteric cysts

Cysts may form in the mesenteries of the abdomen and present as abdominal masses.

They may originate from:
- Walled off infections following pancreatitis (pseudocysts).
- Diverticula of the developing foregut and hindgut.
- The urogenital ridge (the embryological origin of part of the urinary and genital systems).
- Sequestered lymphatic channels.

They may also be of malignant origin.

Neoplasms

As with all tumours, those of the peritoneum can be divided into primary or secondary, and malignant or benign.

Benign tumours of the peritoneum are very rare.

Tumours may arise from any organ or structure in the abdomen, or seed from elsewhere, and arise from any tissue.

Tumours arising from the mesothelium of the peritoneum are called mesotheliomas and (although more rare) are similar to mesotheliomas arising in the pleura and pericardium.

Primary mesothelioma

Primary mesothelioma of the peritoneum is very rare but when it does occur it is usually associated with heavy asbestos exposure (80% of cases). Asbestos is also associated with pleural mesotheliomas and the risk of developing one is increased up to several hundredfold if the person who was exposed also smokes.

Of patients with primary mesothelioma, 50% also have pulmonary fibrosis. Fifty per cent of cases of primary mesothelioma stay confined to the abdominal cavity, but the intestines may become involved in the remainder and lead to intestinal obstruction.

Secondary mesothelioma

The peritoneum is a common site of transcoelomic metastasis, especially from the ovaries and pancreas. Less commonly, seeding may occur from extra-peritoneal tumours.

This results in ascites (an effusion of fluid into the peritoneal cavity) with a fluid rich in protein (an exudate).

The fluid also contains the neoplastic cells that have seeded from the primary and are visible on appropriate staining of a sample of fluid aspirated from the peritoneal cavity.

The presence of neoplastic cells is important in distinguishing this from other causes of ascites.

- **What are the more common disorders of the peritoneum, including peritonitis and neoplasms?**
- **Describe the treatment of peritonitis.**

Exudates and transudates are both abnormal collections of fluid outside the vascular system:
- **An exudate results from an increase in vascular permeability and is rich in protein (> 2 g per 100 mL).**
- **A transudate is due to increased intravascular pressure or hypoproteinaemia and is low in protein (< 2 g per 100 mL).**

SELF-ASSESSMENT

Multiple-choice Questions

Indicate whether each answer is true or false.

1. Regarding the GI tract:

(a) The tract develops from the endodermal germ layer. T ✓
(b) Most bacteria are able to survive in the stomach. F ✓
(c) The cardiac orifice of the stomach lies behind the 7th costal cartilage, about 2.5 cm to the left of the median plane. ? T
(d) The caecum is part of the small intestine. F ✓
(e) The gall bladder is essential to life. T × F

2. In the diet:

(a) Carbohydrates with β-glycosidic linkages cannot be absorbed. T
(b) Fat should comprise about 40% of the total food intake. F ✓
(c) We need about 0.75 g/kg/day of protein. T ✓
(d) Excess protein has no harmful effects. F
(e) Vitamins A, B, E, and K are fat soluble. T × F
    D

3. In the oropharynx:

(a) The vestibule lies posterior to the teeth.
(b) The blood supply of the oral cavity proper is principally from the internal carotid artery.
(c) The intrinsic muscles of the tongue have no point of attachment outside it.
(d) The external muscles of the tongue are genioglossus, hyoglossus, styloglossus and palatoglossus.
(e) Styloglossus is innervated by the accessory nerve (XI) via the pharyngeal branch of the vagus.

4. In the oropharynx:

(a) All of the muscles of the soft palate are supplied by branchial motor fibres carried to the pharyngeal plexus by the vagus (X).
(b) The pharynx extends from the base of the skull to the level of C7.
(c) The gingiva and hard palate are covered by stratified squamous epithelium.
(d) The muscles of mastication develop from the first branchial arch.
(e) The medial pterygoid muscle has two heads.

5. Regarding the salivary glands:

(a) The parotid gland produces serous saliva.
(b) The parotid gland is innervated by both the parasympathetic and sympathetic system.
(c) The submandibular gland produces mixed secretions.
(d) Salivary secretions are modified as they pass through the salivary ducts.
(e) The opening of the parotid gland lies opposite the second lower molar tooth.

6. The oesophagus:

(a) Passes into the thorax just to the right of the midline. F ×
(b) Is supplied by the inferior thyroid artery, branches of the thoracic aorta and branches of the left gastric artery. T ✓
(c) Develops from the tracheobronchial diverticulum which appears in week 7 of gestation. F ✓
(d) Has a venous drainage which forms a portosystemic anastomosis. T ✓
(e) Has a muscular lower sphincter. T × F

169

7. Regarding the intake of food:

(a) The ability to burn off excess calories in the form of heat increases with age.   F ✓
(b) CCK is a satiety hormone.   T
(c) Carbohydrates are primarily metabolized during the day and fats are metabolized at night.   F × T
(d) Lesions of the ventromedial hypothalamus cause hyperphagia.   T
(e) Lesions of the lateral hypothalamus cause aphagia.   T

8. Regarding salivation:

(a) The components of saliva vary according to the rate and site of production.
(b) Saliva has an acid pH.
(c) The normal rate of secretion is 1–2 L in 24 hours.
(d) Excess salivation may cause death from potassium loss.
(e) Denervation of the salivary glands results in a dry mouth.

9. Regarding swallowing:

(a) The swallowing reflex is triggered by afferent impulses in the trigeminal, facial and hypoglossal nerves.
(b) It is controlled by centres in the medulla.
(c) Peristaltic tertiary waves propel food towards the stomach.
(d) Food cannot pass down the oesophagus in the absence of peristalsis.
(e) The swallowing reflex inhibits respiration.

10. Regarding vomiting:

(a) Salivation is inhibited prior to vomiting.
(b) Antiemetic drugs should be prescribed as soon as possible.
(c) It is a common side effect of drugs.
(d) The presence or absence of bile is helpful in determining the cause.
(e) The vomiting centre is located in the lateral reticular formation of the medulla.

11. Regarding the stomach:

(a) The fundus lies below the pyloric sphincter.   F ✓
(b) The greater omentum is formed by a reflection of the peritoneum at the greater curvature.   T
(c) The stomach is supplied by branches of the superior mesenteric artery.   F ✓
(d) It develops from a fusiform dilatation of the foregut that appears at about week 4 of development.   T ✓
(e) It has an outer oblique muscle layer.   T × F

12. In the stomach:

(a) The fundic (gastric) glands are the most numerous.   F ×
(b) The appearance of the parietal (oxyntic) glands changes with the presence of food in the stomach.   T ✓
(c) Chief cells secrete pepsin.   T × F   pepsinogen
(d) HCl and intrinsic factor are secreted by parietal cells.   T ✓
(e) Venous drainage is to the hepatic portal system.   F ✓

13. In the stomach:

(a) A thick, mucopolysaccharide gel protects the stomach wall from enzymatic digestion.   T ✓
(b) Lipase activity is of great physiological significance in the digestion of lipids.   T × F
(c) An acidic resting juice is secreted between meals.   F
(d) The cephalic phase of gastric secretion is unaffected by ligation of the vagal innervation of the stomach.   F ✓
(e) H$_2$ receptor agonists reduce acid secretion.   T × F

14. The liver:

(a) Weighs approximately 2.5 kg.   F
(b) Has a bare area related to the superior vena cava.   IVC   F ✓
(c) Is innervated by both vagi and the coeliac plexus.   T
(d) Has a substantial capacity to regenerate after injury.   T
(e) Forms ketone bodies in poorly controlled diabetes.   T ✓

15. Regarding the metabolism of drugs:

(a) Phase I metabolism by the liver almost always produces less reactive products than the parent drug. F ✓
(b) Oxidative phase I reactions are carried out by the mixed function oxygenase system of the smooth endoplasmic reticulum. T ✓
(c) Phase II reactions include conjugation with glucuronic acid. T ✓
(d) Phenobarbitone and phenylbutazone are enzyme-inducing drugs. T
(e) Hydrolytic reactions occur in many tissues. T

16. Regarding bile:

(a) The majority of bile acids in the body are synthesized *de novo* every day. T × F
(b) The critical micelle concentration is the maximum concentration found in health. F ✓
(c) The principal bile pigment is bilirubin. T ✓
(d) An aqueous isotonic secretion of the epithelial cells lining the bile ducts accounts for about 80% of the total volume of bile. F
(e) Low levels of bile acids in the portal blood stimulate the secretion of bile acids. F

17. The gall bladder:

(a) Concentrates and stores bile. T ✓
(b) Only contracts during the gastric and intestinal phases of gastric secretion. T × F
(c) Is more likely to contain pigment stones than cholesterol stones. F ✓
(d) Is often removed in childhood due to the presence of stones. F
(e) Has a capacity of about 150 mL. T × F

18. The pancreas:

(a) Has a poor blood supply. F ✓
(b) Is innervated by the splanchnic and vagus nerves. T ✓
(c) Produces insulin from month 3 after conception. T × F
(d) Contains cell types A, B, D, and F. T
(e) Has islet cells which are most abundant in the body. F ✓

19. The exocrine pancreas:

(a) Secretes about 10 times its own weight in fluid every day. T
(b) Secretes a fluid richer in bicarbonate when the rate of secretion is higher. T ✓
(c) Secretes most of its enzymes in an active form. F ✓
(d) Has an increased rate of secretion following sympathetic stimulation. F ✓
(e) Has an increased rate of secretion in response to insulin. T

20. The small intestine:

(a) On X-ray in the adult is difficult to distinguish from the large intestine. F ✓
(b) Develops entirely from the embryological foregut. F ✓
(c) Herniates outside the abdominal cavity at about week 6 from conception. T
(d) Rotates about the inferior mesenteric artery during its development. F ✓
(e) Is supplied by branches of the coeliac and superior mesenteric arteries. T ✓

21. The mucosa of the small intestine:

(a) Contains tall columnar enterocytes. T
(b) Contains mucus-secreting goblet cells. T ✓
(c) Contains protein-secreting Paneth cells in the most superficial parts of the glands. T × F
(d) Loses about 17 billion enterocytes a day. T
(e) May become flattened, leading to malabsorption. T ✓

22. Regarding flora of the GI tract:

(a) *Bacteroides fragilis* is commonly found in the mouth.
(b) Bacteria of the *Neisseria* species are often found in the small intestine.
(c) Anaerobes cannot survive in the mouth. F ✓
(d) Anaerobes in the large intestine produce vitamin K.
(e) *E. coli* makes up about 90% of the bacteria in the bowel.

23. Regarding haematological tests:

(a) The MCV (mean corpuscular volume) is raised in chronic alcohol abuse.
(b) The MCV is lowered in thalassaemia.
(c) Lymphocytes make up about 75% of the total white cell count.
(d) Eosinophils are raised in atopic conditions.
(e) Prothrombin time is decreased in liver disease. F ✓

24. In the large intestine:

(a) Mass movements occur about every 15 minutes in the fed state. F ✓
(b) Intestinal contents move more quickly than through the small intestine. F ✓
(c) Gastric distension inhibits peristalsis. F
(d) In Hirschsprung's disease the internal anal sphincter is hypotonic. F
(e) The anal canal can sense the difference between air, liquid and solid. T

25. The following statements are correct:

(a) Progressive dysphagia may be due to malignancy. T
(b) Jaundice is usually apparent once plasma bilirubin levels exceed 17 µmol/L. F ✓
(c) Diarrhoea is rarely life-threatening. T ✗
(d) Flatulence occuring more than five times a day should always be investigated. T ✗
(e) Anal masses may present with tenesmus. T ✓

26. Regarding signs and symptoms:

(a) Areas of baldness on the scalp may be due to internal malignancy.
(b) Seborrhoeic warts are never a cause for concern.
(c) Itchy tissue-paper skin may be present in malabsorption.
(d) Palmar erythema is almost always due to malignancy.
(e) Long spidery fingers may be an indication of Marfan's syndrome.

27. The following statements are correct:

(a) Reiter's syndrome may follow dysentery.
(b) Clubbing may occur in inflammatory bowel disease.
(c) Small pigmented macules may be seen in the mouth in Peutz–Jeghers syndrome.
(d) A high arched palate is common in Down syndrome.
(e) White patches which can be brushed off are known as leucoplakia.

28. On inspection of the abdomen:

(a) Sister Joseph's nodule is a sign of carcinoma.
(b) Up to 10 spider naevi are considered normal.
(c) Visible peristalsis from right to left indicates pyloric stenosis.
(d) Grey Turner's sign is discolouration around the umbilicus.
(e) Purple striae may be seen in pregnancy.

29. Regarding hernias:

(a) Congenital hernias are almost always direct.
(b) Strangulated hernias are a surgical emergency.
(c) Indirect inguinal hernias lie medial to the internal ring.
(d) Surgical repair of hernias may lead to adhesions.
(e) Reducible hernias should be treated surgically.

30. Regarding liver function tests:

(a) Alanine aminotransferase is present in canaliculi and sinusoidal membranes. T ✗ F
(b) Bililrubin levels normally increase in liver disease. T ✓
(c) The pattern of changes is more important than a single rise or fall. T
(d) Prothrombin time is increased in vitamin K deficiency. T
(e) High levels of both γ-GT and alkaline phosphatase indicate cholestasis. T ✓

31. In the small intestine:

(a) Chronic radiation enteritis is present where symptoms persist for more than one month.
(b) Secretory diarrhoea occurs when enterocytes secrete more fluid than they absorb.
(c) Most of the immunoglobulins produced are IgG. F ✓
(d) Chyme is propelled forward at about 50 cm an hour.
(e) Peristaltic rushes are normally experienced about three times a day.

32. In the mouth:

(a) Simple cleft palate is more common in the male.
(b) Cleft palate does not affect breast-feeding.
(c) Painless apthous ulcers may occur in the mouth in association with inflammatory bowel disease or coeliac disease.
(d) Infection with herpes simplex II is more common than herpes simplex I.
(e) Leukoplakia is a premalignant condition.

33. Regarding the oesophagus:

(a) Oesophageal atresia and fistula rarely occur together.
(b) Diagnosis of oesophageal varices is by biopsy.
(c) Basal cell hyperplasia is seen in reflux oesophagitis.
(d) Killian's dehiscence is more common in middle-aged women.
(e) Chagas' disease may lead to denervation of the oesophagus and dysphagia.

34. The following statements are correct:

(a) Diaphragmatic hernia occurs in about 1/10 000 live births.
(b) Pyloric stenosis is more common among first-born males.
(c) Acute and chronic gastritis may be caused by *Helicobacter pylori* infection.
(d) Body stores of vitamin B_{12} are sufficient for 2 or 3 years.
(e) Vitamin B_{12} is absorbed from the duodenum in the presence of intrinsic factor.

35. The following statements are correct:

(a) A portosystemic anastomosis exists between the epigastric and paraumbilical veins.
(b) Oesophageal varices are a benign condition.
(c) Councilman bodies are seen in the liver in acute viral hepatitis.
(d) Yellow fever causes mid-zonal necrosis.
(e) Cirrhosis is a common cause of portal hypertension.

36. The following statements are correct:

(a) Primary haemochromatosis is characterized by the absorption of too much copper.
(b) Kayser-Fleisher rings are seen in Wilson's disease.
(c) α_1-antitrypsin causes lung disease.
(d) Microvesicular steatosis occurs in the liver in Reye's syndrome.
(e) Rubella infection in pregnancy may cause hepatitis in the infant.

37. Regarding viruses:

(a) Diagnosis of hepatitis A is by detection of virus-specific IgM. F × T
(b) Infection with hepatitis A leads to carrier status in 90% of cases. F
(c) Hepatitis B is spread by the faecal–oral route. F ✓
(d) Hepatitis C has an incubation period of 6–8 weeks. T
(e) Hepatitis D is a defective RNA virus. T ✓

38. The following statements concern the effects of toxins on the liver:

(a) Zone 1 of the liver is most susceptible to alcoholic liver damage. 3   F × T
(b) Mallory bodies are seen in hepatocytes following alcoholic damage. T
(c) Cirrhosis is reversible. T × F
(d) Irreversible steatosis may result from alcohol ingestion. F
(e) Unpredictable drug reactions will occur in any individual if the dose is sufficient. F

39. The following statements regarding the liver are correct:

(a) Severe ischaemic damage is common.
(b) Zone 1 is closest to the central vein. F ✓
(c) The Budd–Chiari syndrome is caused by thrombosis of the hepatic artery.
(d) 5-year survival in chronic Budd–Chiari syndrome is about 70%.
(e) Passive congestion results in a 'nutmeg liver'. T ✓

40. Regarding pregnancy:

(a) Pregnancy-induced hypertension is more common among primigravidas.
(b) Pregnancy-induced hypertension is a benign condition.
(c) Acute fatty liver is common in early pregnancy.
(d) Intrahepatic cholestasis may ocur in the third trimester.
(e) Intrahepatic cholestasis is often benign.

41. The following statements regarding the biliary tract are correct:

(a) Secondary biliary cirrhosis is more common in males.
(b) Congenital hepatic fibrosis is inherited as an autosomal-dominant condition.
(c) Caroli's disease is inherited as an autosomal-recessive condition.
(d) Primary biliary cirrhosis is an autoimmune disorder.
(e) 70% of cases of primary sclerosing cholangitis are associated with ulcerative colitis.

42. Regarding the pancreas:

(a) Ectopic pancreatic tissue may be found in the distal end of the oesophagus.
(b) Ronson's criteria are used to stage chronic pancreatitis.
(c) Speckled calcification of the pancreas may occur in chronic pancreatitis.
(d) Pseudocysts are usually multiple.
(e) Diabetic smokers have an increased risk of developing carcinoma of the pancreas.

43. The following statements about congenital abnormalities are correct:

(a) Meckel's diverticulum occurs about 2 in from the ileocaecal valve.
(b) A Meckel's diverticulum may contain ectopic gastric tissue.
(c) Hirschprung's disease usually presents with projectile vomiting.
(d) Faeces can be felt in the distal rectum in Hirschprung's disease.
(e) The incidence of Hirschprung's disease is higher in children with Down syndrome.

44. Regarding infections and enterocolitis:

(a) Diarrhoea means the passage of more than two stools a day.
(b) Infectious enterocolitis accounts for 50% of deaths before the age of five in developing countries.
(c) Rotavirus infection is commoner in the summer months in temperate climates.
(d) *S. aureus enterocolitis* is caused by ingestion of a preformed toxin.
(e) Necrotising enterocolitis is uncommon before the age of three.

45. Regarding inflammatory bowel disease:

(a) Crohn's disease may occur anywhere from the mouth to the anus. T ✓
(b) Crohn's disease is four times commoner in males. F ✓
(c) Ulcerative colitis is characterized by skip lesions. F ✓
(d) Ulcerative colitis is commoner amongst smokers. F ✓
(e) Cryptosporidium is a common cause of diarrhoea in people with HIV infection. T

46. Regarding malabsorption syndromes:

(a) Malabsorption from different causes presents with different signs and symptoms. T
(b) Tropical sprue is common in Africa.
(c) Whipple's disease is more common in women.
(d) Treatment of coeliac disease is with tetracycline.
(e) The absence of cysts and trophozoites in stools excludes a diagnosis of giardiasis.

47. Obstruction:

(a) Due to non-mechanical causes is called pseudo-obstruction.
(b) High in the GI tract presents with distension.
(c) May be due to a strangulated hernia.
(d) Should always be treated surgically.
(e) Due to volvulus is more common in developed countries than in developing ones.

48. Regarding colonic diverticula:

(a) Diverticulosis means that diverticula are causing symptoms.
(b) Congenital diverticula are outpouchings of the full thickness of the bowel wall.
(c) Congenital diverticula are usually symptomatic.
(d) Acquired diverticula are more common on the left side of the colon.
(e) Patients with diverticulitis should be advised to decrease the amount of fibre in their diet.

49. Regarding neoplasms of the bowel:

(a) Adenomas may cause electrolyte imbalances.
(b) Colorectal cancer is the second biggest cause of cancer death in the UK.
(c) Diet has no effect on the risk of developing colorectal cancer.
(d) Dukes' classification is used to assess the stage of carcinoid tumours.
(e) B cell lymphomas are associated with coeliac disease.

50. Peritonitis:

(a) Is usually limited to a small area.
(b) Is often due to *E. coli*.
(c) Should be treated by resuscitation and removal of the cause.
(d) May lead to air under the diaphragm being visible on an erect X-ray.
(e) May be due to retroperitoneal fibromatosis.

Short-answer Questions

1. List the signals for the release of gastrin. What are its actions?

2. List the main functions of hepatocytes.

3. Describe the main congenital abnormalities of the oesophagus.

4. Describe the nerve supply to the tongue.

5. Why is iron deficiency relatively common among women of reproductive age?

6. Describe how the composition of saliva varies with the rate of flow.

7. Describe the arterial blood supply to the stomach.

8. What are lipoproteins?

9. What quantity of water passes into the GI tract and how much is reabsorbed from it each day?

10. Describe the layers of the GI tract.

11. How should one perform a rectal examination on an adult male?

12. What signs, symptoms and results of investigations would lead you to suspect posthepatic jaundice? What are the principal causes of this type of jaundice?

13. Write brief notes on hepatitis B.

14. What are the effects of a carcinoid tumour of the small intestine?

15. What are the main causes and consequences of acute pancreatitis?

16. What are the main effects of gall stones?

17. Give a brief comparison of the main features of Crohn's disease and ulcerative colitis.

18. How is the gastric proton pump stimulated?

19. What is Hirschprung's disease?

20. List the systemic effects of malabsorption.

Essay Questions

1. What is malrotation of the gut? How may it arise and what are its effects?

2. Describe the effect of alcohol, drugs, and toxins on the liver.

3. What are the main causes of obstruction of the bowel?

4. What is bile? How is it produced and released into the duodenum?

5. Describe the aetiology, pathogenesis and pathology of circulatory disorders of the liver. What complications may arise, how do they develop and how are they treated?

6. Give an account of neoplasms of the GI tract.

7. Do X-ray investigations still have a place in the diagnosis of GI disorders?

8. Discuss the causes of and biochemical findings in jaundice.

9. What are the main causes of epigastric pain? Briefly discuss how it may be evaluated.

10. What diagnostic inferences may be made from an inspection of the abdomen?

1. (a) T, (b) F, (c) T, (d) F, (e) F
2. (a) T, (b) F, (c) T, (d) F, (e) F
3. (a) F, (b) F, (c) T, (d) T, (e) F
4. (a) F, (b) F, (c) T, (d) T, (e) F
5. (a) T, (b) T, (c) T, (d) T, (e) F
6. (a) T, (b) T, (c) F, (d) T, (e) F
7. (a) F, (b) T, (c) T, (d) T, (e) T
8. (a) T, (b) F, (c) T, (d) T, (e) F
9. (a) F, (b) T, (c) F, (d) F, (e) T
10. (a) F, (b) F, (c) T, (d) T (e) T
11. (a) F, (b) T, (c) F, (d) T, (e) F
12. (a) T, (b) T, (c) F, (d) T, (e) T
13. (a) T, (b) F, (c) F, (d) F, (e) F
14. (a) F, (b) F, (c) T, (d) T, (e) T
15. (a) F, (b) T, (c) T, (d) T, (e) T
16. (a) F, (b) F, (c) T, (d) F, (e) F
17. (a) T, (b) F, (c) F, (d) F, (e) F
18. (a) F, (b) T, (c) F, (d) T, (e) F
19. (a) T, (b) T, (c) F, (d) F, (e) T
20. (a) F, (b) F, (c) T, (d) F, (e) T
21. (a) T, (b) T, (c) F, (d) T, (e) T
22. (a) F, (b) F, (c) F, (d) T, (e) F
23. (a) T, (b) T, (c) F, (d) T, (e) F
24. (a) F, (b) F, (c) F, (d) F, (e) T
25. (a) T, (b) F, (c) F, (d) F, (e) T

26. (a) T, (b) F, (c) T, (d) F, (e) T
27. (a) T, (b) T, (c) T, (d) F, (e) F
28. (a) T, (b) F, (c) F, (d) F, (e) T
29. (a) F, (b) T, (c) F, (d) T, (e) F
30. (a) F, (b) T, (c) T, (d) T, (e) T
31. (a) F, (b) T, (c) F, (d) F, (e) F
32. (a) F, (b) F, (c) F, (d) F, (e) T
33. (a) F, (b) F, (c) T, (d) F, (e) T
34. (a) F, (b) T, (c) T, (d) T, (e) F
35. (a) T, (b) F, (c) T, (d) T, (e) T
36. (a) F, (b) T, (c) F, (d) T, (e) T
37. (a) T, (b) F, (c) F, (d) T, (e) T
38. (a) T, (b) T, (c) F, (d) F, (e) F
39. (a) F, (b) F, (c) F, (d) F, (e) F
40. (a) T, (b) F, (c) F, (d) T, (e) T
41. (a) F, (b) F, (c) T, (d) T, (e) T
42. (a) T, (b) F, (c) T, (d) F, (e) T
43. (a) F, (b) T, (c) F, (d) F, (e) T
44. (a) F, (b) T, (c) F, (d) T, (e) F
45. (a) T, (b) F, (c) F, (d) F, (e) T
46. (a) F, (b) F, (c) F, (d) F, (e) F
47. (a) T, (b) F, (c) T, (d) F, (e) F
48. (a) F, (b) T, (c) F, (d) T, (e) F
49. (a) T, (b) T, (c) F, (d) F, (e) F
50. (a) F, (b) T, (c) T, (d) T, (e) T

1. Gastrin is released from the G cells in the gastric antrum in response to the presence of peptides and amino acids, distension, vagal stimulation, blood-borne calcium and adrenaline.
   Gastrin:
   (i) Increases the secretion of acid from parietal cells and pepsinogen from chief cells.
   (ii) Is trophic to the mucosa of the stomach and small and large intestines.
   (iii) Increases gastric motility.
   (iv) May increase the tone of the lower oesophageal sphincter.
   (v) Stimulates the secretion of glucagon from pancreatic B cells and glucagon from pancreatic A cells after a protein meal.

2. The main functions of hepatocytes are:
   (i) The synthesis and secretion of the main plasma protein albumin, prothrombin (coagulation factor II), fibrinogen and lipoprotein.
   (ii) The formation, secretion and recycling of bile.
   (iii) The metabolism of carbohydrate.
   (iv) The metabolism and synthesis of cholesterol and steroids.
   (v) The metabolism and detoxification of lipid soluble drugs.
   (vi) The removal of ammonium ions by making them into urea.

3. The main congenital abnormalities of the oesophagus are:
   (i) Atresia (failure of canalization)—presents with regurgitation and may be suspected antenatally in hydramnios (abnormally large amounts of amniotic fluid).
   (ii) Fistula (abnormal connection between two epithelial surfaces)—in 90% of cases, atresia and fistula occur together (see Fig. 9.1).
   (iii) Agenesis (complete failure of development).
   (iv) Stenosis (narrowing).

4. The tongue has a motor supply to the muscles as follows:
   (i) The hypoglossal nerve (cranial nerve XII) to the external muscles genioglossus, hyoglossus and styloglossus.
   (ii) The accessory nerve (XI) via the pharyngeal branch of the vagus (X) to the remaining external muscle, palatoglossus.
   It also has innervation for common (general) sensation and for taste:
   (i) Posterior third—both common sensation and taste are supplied by cranial nerve IX.
   (ii) Anterior two-thirds:
      (a) The lingual nerve (from the mandibular division of the trigeminal nerve) is the innervation for common sensation.
      (b) The chorda tympani, which joins the lingual nerve to be distributed, provides the innervation for taste.

5. Body stores of iron are about 3 or 4 g, of which two-thirds are contained in haemoglobin.
   An average diet contains roughly 20 mg of iron a day, only about 10% of which (2 mg) can be absorbed (although pregnant women and growing children are able to absorb a slightly higher proportion, and absorption is increased in acidic conditions, for example if iron is taken with vitamin C).
   Daily losses are approximately 1 mg (in urine and desquamated cells) and monthly menstrual losses of about 50 mg.
   Average daily losses in non-pregnant women of child-bearing age are therefore slightly in excess of 2 mg a day (the amount of iron absorbed on an average diet) and deficiency is relatively common.

6. The main components of saliva are water, proteins (amylase, ribonuclease, lysozyme, lipase, R-protein for the protection of vitamin B_{12}, SIgA, IgM, and IgG) and electrolytes (principally Na^+, Cl^-, HCO_3^-, and K^+).

   Primary secretion in the acini of the salivons produces isotonic saliva which is modified as it passes through the ducts where Na^+ is actively reabsorbed in exchange for K^+, and Cl^- is reabsorbed by passive uptake. See Fig. 2.8.

7. The stomach develops from the embryological foregut and, in common with other derivatives of the foregut, is supplied by branches of the coeliac artery, see Fig. 3.2.

8. Lipoproteins are complexes of lipids and proteins, with polar coats consisting of phospholipid and apoprotein (made in the liver and intestine). Cholesterol esters and some unesterified cholesterol are present in the centre.

   They are assembled in the liver, transport water-insoluble lipids around the blood and are classified as: chylomicrons (the lowest density), very low, intermediate, low and high density according to their composition.

   High-density lipoproteins are protective against heart disease and, ideally, levels should be high. Levels of low density chylomicrons should be kept low as they have been implicated in atheroma.

9. About 9 L of fluid passes into the GI tract each day, of which about 2 L has been ingested. The remaining 7 L is made up of various secretions (e.g. from the pancreas).

   The quantity of fluid reabsorbed and the sites at which this occurs are shown in Fig. 5.16.

10. The layers of the GI tract are essentially the same throughout, consisting of a mucosa, submucosa, muscularis externa (an internal circular layer, outer longitudinal layer and, in the stomach, an incomplete innermost oblique layer) and serosa or adventitia. See Fig. 1.2.

11. If meeting a patient for the first time, shake hands, introduce oneself and establish a rapport, explain what one is about to do, and tell the patient why.

    Then ask the patient to remove the appropriate clothing and lie on his or her left side with his or her knees drawn up. Put on gloves, inspect the external anal area under a good light, lubricate one's index finger with KY jelly (or other suitable, water-soluble lubricant) gently spread the buttocks with one hand and lay the lubricated index finger at the entrance to the anus, gently insert it as far as comfortably possible and carefully sweep it around, feeling the walls of the rectum and anus.

    In particular, feel for the size, uniformity of texture, and any tenderness of the prostate through the anterior wall of the rectum.

    Withdraw the examining finger and inspect glove for colour of faecal material on it and the presence of blood and/or mucus.

    Remove glove and dispose of it in a clinical waste bag. Wash your hands. Ask the patient to get dressed again, explain what you found on examination, whether you wish to carry out any further investigations or tests and, if so, why.

12. Jaundice from any cause is apparent when bilirubin levels reach about 35 μmol/L—the skin and sclera appear yellow (in a good light).

    Symptoms of pale stools and dark urine suggest the cause is post-hepatic.

    Investigation of urine in post-hepatic jaundice shows bilirubin (responsible for the colour) but no urobilinogen, and raised plasma levels of the canalicular enzymes γ-GT (γ-glutamyl transferase) and AP (alkaline phosphatase) as a result of damage to the biliary tree.

    Causes include primary biliary cirrhosis, drugs, gall stones, carcinoma of the head of the pancreas or the bile duct and, more rarely, enlarged lymph nodes in the porta hepatis as a result of lymphoma.

13. Hepatitis B is a hepadnavirus (DNA), 4 nm diameter, spread in contaminated blood and body fluids sexually, percutaneously or vertically (mother to baby) with an incubation period of 2–6 months. Diagnosis of acute infection is by detection of surface antigen, e-antigen and IgM antibodies to the C-protein. Over 50% of infections are asymptomatic.

    5–10% of adults infected and 70–90% of neonates become carriers (i.e. surface antigen has been detected for at least 6 months), complications of which include chronic, active hepatitis, cirrhosis and hepatocellular carcinoma. Those who survive but do not become carriers become immune.

All carriers have surface antigen. Highly infectious carriers also have e-antigen, carriers of intermediate infectivity do not have e-antigen and carriers with low infectivity have anti-e antibody.

Those who are immune have anti-surface and anti-core antibodies.

It is found worldwide although countries may be of high endemicity (e.g. South-East Asia), intermediate (e.g. the Mediterranean) or low endemicity (e.g. Northern Europe).

Infection with hepatitis B is required for infection with, and replication of, the defective RNA virus hepatitis D.

14. Local effects are episodic diarrhoea and borborygmi (increased bowel sounds), appendicitis, GI obstruction and intussusception.

Systemic effects become apparent once the tumour has metastasised to the liver (the carcinoid syndrome, occurring in about 5% of carcinoid tumours) and are due to an increase of 5-hydroxytryptamine (5-HT), prostaglandins, polypeptides and kinins in the systemic circulation.

The main symptoms are flushing, especially after coffee, alcohol, certain other foods and drugs; cyanosis; pulmonary and tricuspid stenosis; asthma-like attacks; oedema and thickening of the endocardium in the right heart.

Rare symptoms are pellagra and Cushing's syndrome.

15. Gall stones (cholelithiasis), ethanol, nutritional deficiency, trauma, steroids, viruses (e.g. mumps), autoimmune disease, hyperlipidaemia, hypothermia, hyperparathyroidism, ischaemia, drugs (e.g. azathioprine and diuretics) and, more rarely, scorpion bites.

All causes lead to a release of pancreatic enzymes (by different mechanisms) resulting in interstitial inflammation, proteolysis (the breakdown of proteins by proteases), fat necrosis (by lipase and phospholipase) and haemorrhage (as a result of elastase).

Ronson's criteria are used to assess the severity (if more than 7 are present mortality approaches 100%). Overall, mortality is 5–10%.

16. Gall stones increase in incidence with age and may be cholesterol stones (about 20% of all stones, formed as a result of high levels of biliary cholesterol), pigment stones (about 5% of all stones, formed as a result of excess haemolysis) or mixed (75%, formed as a result of an alteration in the composition of bile).

Whatever the type, the effects are similar (see Fig. 10.8).

17. See Figs 11.5 and 11.6.

18. It pumps hydrogen ions into the lumen of the stomach in exchange for potassium, in response to gastrin (from G cells in the antrum), acetylcholine or histamine. See Fig. 3.6.

19. A congenital abnormality due to failure of migration of ganglion cells during weeks 5–12 of gestation, resulting in an absence of ganglion cells in the most distal part of the GI tract, sometimes extending proximally as far as the terminal ileum.

The affected segment is narrow and fails to relax, disrupting peristalsis and causing a functional obstruction with distension due to air and faeces above it.

It is four times more common in male children, with an overall incidence of 1/5000, and usually presents shortly after birth with distension and failure to pass meconium, although milder cases may not be diagnosed for a few years.

It may be suspected clinically on the history and rectal examination (classically a narrow empty rectum and a gush of air and faeces on withdrawing the examining finger) but diagnosis is by histological examination of a rectal biopsy showing an absence of ganglion cells.

Complications include megacolon and death from acute enterocolitis.

20. (i) Steatorrhoea (fatty stools that are difficult to flush away), diarrhoea, weight loss and abdominal distension.
  (ii) Iron, folate or B_{12} deficiency leading to anaemia.
  (iii) Vitamin K deficiency resulting in reduced activity of vitamin K-dependent clotting factors and bleeding disorders, e.g petechiae and purpura.
  (iv) Peripheral neuropathy as a result of vitamin B_1, B_6, and B_{12} deficiency.
  (v) Oedema from protein deficiency.
  (vi) Dermatitis and hyperkeratosis.
  (vii) Osteopenia and tetany.

Index

Index